Mining of Massive Datasets

The popularity of the Web and Internet commerce provides many extremely large datasets from which information can be gleaned by data mining. This book focuses on practical algorithms that have been used to solve key problems in data mining and can be used on even the largest datasets.

It begins with a discussion of the map-reduce framework, an important tool for parallelizing algorithms automatically. The tricks of locality-sensitive hashing are explained. This body of knowledge, which deserves to be more widely known, is essential when seeking similar objects in a very large collection without having to compare each pair of objects. Stream processing algorithms for mining data that arrives too fast for exhaustive processing are also explained. The PageRank idea and related tricks for organizing the Web are covered next. Other chapters cover the problems of finding frequent itemsets and clustering, each from the point of view that the data is too large to fit in main memory. The final chapters cover two applications: recommendation systems and Web advertising, each vital in e-commerce.

Written by two authorities in database and web technologies, this book will be essential for students and practitioners alike.

Mining of Massive Datasets

ANAND RAJARAMAN
@WalmartLabs

JEFFREY DAVID ULLMAN
Stanford University

CAMBRIDGE UNIVERSITY PRESS
Cambridge, New York, Melbourne, Madrid, Cape Town,
Singapore, São Paulo, Delhi, Tokyo, Mexico City

Cambridge University Press
The Edinburgh Building, Cambridge CB2 8RU, UK

Published in the United States of America by Cambridge University Press, New York

www.cambridge.org
Information on this title: www.cambridge.org/9781107015357

First published 2012

Printed in the United Kingdom at the University Press, Cambridge

A catalogue record for this publication is available from the British Library

ISBN 978-1-107-01535-7 Hardback

Contents

Preface

This book evolved from material developed over several years by Anand Rajaraman and Jeff Ullman for a one-quarter course at Stanford. The course CS345A,
titled "Web Mining," was designed as an advanced graduate course, although it
has become accessible and interesting to advanced undergraduates.

What the Book Is About

At the highest level of description, this book is about data mining. However,
it focuses on data mining of very large amounts of data, that is, data so large
it does not fit in main memory. Because of the emphasis on size, many of our
examples are about the Web or data derived from the Web. Further, the book
takes an algorithmic point of view: data mining is about applying algorithms to
data, rather than using data to "train" a machine-learning engine of some sort.
The principal topics covered are:

(1) Distributed file systems and map-reduce as a tool for creating parallel algorithms that succeed on very large amounts of data.

(2) Similarity search, including the key techniques of minhashing and locality-
sensitive hashing.

(3) Data-stream processing and specialized algorithms for dealing with data that
arrives so fast it must be processed immediately or lost.

(4) The technology of search engines, including Google's PageRank, link-spam
detection, and the hubs-and-authorities approach.

(5) Frequent-itemset mining, including association rules, market-baskets, the A-
Priori Algorithm and its improvements.

(6) Algorithms for clustering very large, high-dimensional datasets.

(7) Two key problems for Web applications: managing advertising and recommendation systems.

Prerequisites

CS345A, although its number indicates an advanced graduate course, has been found accessible by advanced undergraduates and beginning masters students. In the future, it is likely that the course will be given a mezzanine-level number. The prerequisites for CS345A are:

(1) The first course in database systems, covering application programming in SQL and other database-related languages such as XQuery.
(2) A sophomore-level course in data structures, algorithms, and discrete math.
(3) A sophomore-level course in software systems, software engineering, and programming languages.

Exercises

The book contains extensive exercises, with some for almost every section. We indicate harder exercises or parts of exercises with an exclamation point. The hardest exercises have a double exclamation point.

Support on the Web

You can find materials from past offerings of CS345A at:

> http://infolab.stanford.edu/~ullman/mining/mining.html

There, you will find slides, homework assignments, project requirements, and in some cases, exams.

Acknowledgements

Cover art is by Scott Ullman. We would like to thank Foto Afrati and Arun Marathe for critical readings of the draft of this manuscript. Errors were also reported by Leland Chen, Shrey Gupta, Xie Ke, Haewoon Kwak, Brad Penoff, Philips Kokoh Prasetyo, Mark Storus, Tim Triche Jr., and Roshan Sumbaly. The remaining errors are ours, of course.

A. R.
J. D. U.
Palo Alto, CA
June, 2011

1   Data Mining

In this intoductory chapter we begin with the essence of data mining and a discussion of how data mining is treated by the various disciplines that contribute to this field. We cover "Bonferroni's Principle," which is really a warning about overusing the ability to mine data. This chapter is also the place where we summarize a few useful ideas that are not data mining but are useful in understanding some important data-mining concepts. These include the TF.IDF measure of word importance, behavior of hash functions and indexes, and identities involving e, the base of natural logarithms. Finally, we give an outline of the topics covered in the balance of the book.

1.1   What is Data Mining?

The most commonly accepted definition of "data mining" is the discovery of "models" for data. A "model," however, can be one of several things. We mention below the most important directions in modeling.

1.1.1   Statistical Modeling

Statisticians were the first to use the term "data mining." Originally, "data mining" or "data dredging" was a derogatory term referring to attempts to extract information that was not supported by the data. Section 1.2 illustrates the sort of errors one can make by trying to extract what really isn't in the data. Today, "data mining" has taken on a positive meaning. Now, statisticians view data mining as the construction of a *statistical model*, that is, an underlying distribution from which the visible data is drawn.

EXAMPLE 1.1 Suppose our data is a set of numbers. This data is much simpler than data that would be data-mined, but it will serve as an example. A statistician might decide that the data comes from a Gaussian distribution and use a formula to compute the most likely parameters of this Gaussian. The mean and standard deviation of this Gaussian distribution completely characterize the distribution and would become the model of the data.

1.1.2   Machine Learning

There are some who regard data mining as synonymous with machine learning. There is no question that some data mining appropriately uses algorithms from machine learning. Machine-learning practitioners use the data as a training set, to train an algorithm of one of the many types used by machine-learning practitioners, such as Bayes nets, support-vector machines, decision trees, hidden Markov models, and many others.

There are situations where using data in this way makes sense. The typical case where machine learning is a good approach is when we have little idea of what we are looking for in the data. For example, it is rather unclear what it is about movies that makes certain movie-goers like or dislike it. Thus, in answering the "Netflix challenge" to devise an algorithm that predicts the ratings of movies by users, based on a sample of their responses, machine-learning algorithms have proved quite successful. We shall discuss a simple form of this type of algorithm in Section 9.4.

On the other hand, machine learning has not proved successful in situations where we can describe the goals of the mining more directly. An interesting case in point is the attempt by WhizBang! Labs[1] to use machine learning to locate people's resumes on the Web. It was not able to do better than algorithms designed by hand to look for some of the obvious words and phrases that appear in the typical resume. Since everyone who has looked at or written a resume has a pretty good idea of what resumes contain, there was no mystery about what makes a Web page a resume. Thus, there was no advantage to machine-learning over the direct design of an algorithm to discover resumes.

1.1.3   Computational Approaches to Modeling

More recently, computer scientists have looked at data mining as an algorithmic problem. In this case, the model of the data is simply the answer to a complex query about it. For instance, given the set of numbers of Example 1.1, we might compute their average and standard deviation. Note that these values might not be the parameters of the Gaussian that best fits the data, although they will almost certainly be very close if the size of the data is large.

There are many different approaches to modeling data. We have already mentioned the possibility of constructing a statistical process whereby the data could have been generated. Most other approaches to modeling can be described as either

(1) Summarizing the data succinctly and approximately, or
(2) Extracting the most prominent features of the data and ignoring the rest.

We shall explore these two approaches in the following sections.

---

[1] This startup attempted to use machine learning to mine large-scale data, and hired many of the top machine-learning people to do so. Unfortunately, it was not able to survive.

1.1.4 Summarization

One of the most interesting forms of summarization is the PageRank idea, which made Google successful and which we shall cover in Chapter 5. In this form of Web mining, the entire complex structure of the Web is summarized by a single number for each page. This number, the "PageRank" of the page, is (oversimplifying somewhat) the probability that a random walker on the graph would be at that page at any given time. The remarkable property this ranking has is that it reflects very well the "importance" of the page – the degree to which typical searchers would like that page returned as an answer to their search query.

Another important form of summary – clustering – will be covered in Chapter 7. Here, data is viewed as points in a multidimensional space. Points that are "close" in this space are assigned to the same cluster. The clusters themselves are summarized, perhaps by giving the centroid of the cluster and the average distance from the centroid of points in the cluster. These cluster summaries become the summary of the entire data set.

EXAMPLE 1.2   A famous instance of clustering to solve a problem took place long ago in London, and it was done entirely without computers.[2] The physician John Snow, dealing with a Cholera outbreak plotted the cases on a map of the city. A small illustration suggesting the process is shown in Fig. 1.1.

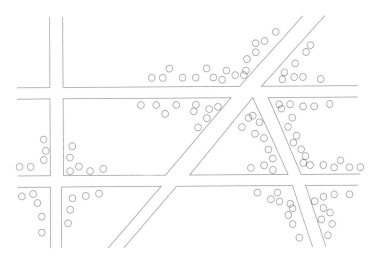

Figure 1.1 Plotting cholera cases on a map of London

The cases clustered around some of the intersections of roads. These intersections were the locations of wells that had become contaminated; people who lived nearest these wells got sick, while people who lived nearer to wells that had not been contaminated did not get sick. Without the ability to cluster the data, the cause of Cholera would not have been discovered.

[2] See http://en.wikipedia.org/wiki/1854_Broad_Street_cholera_outbreak.

1.1.5   Feature Extraction

The typical feature-based model looks for the most extreme examples of a phenomenon and represents the data by these examples. If you are familiar with Bayes nets, a branch of machine learning and a topic we do not cover in this book, you know how a complex relationship between objects is represented by finding the strongest statistical dependencies among these objects and using only those in representing all statistical connections. Some of the important kinds of feature extraction from large-scale data that we shall study are:

(1) *Frequent Itemsets.* This model makes sense for data that consists of "baskets" of small sets of items, as in the market-basket problem that we shall discuss in Chapter 6. We look for small sets of items that appear together in many baskets, and these "frequent itemsets" are the characterization of the data that we seek. The orignal application of this sort of mining was true market baskets: the sets of items, such as hamburger and ketchup, that people tend to buy together when checking out at the cash register of a store or super market.

(2) *Similar Items.* Often, your data looks like a collection of sets, and the objective is to find pairs of sets that have a relatively large fraction of their elements in common. An example is treating customers at an on-line store like Amazon as the set of items they have bought. In order for Amazon to recommend something else they might like, Amazon can look for "similar" customers and recommend something many of these customers have bought. This process is called "collaborative filtering." If customers were single-minded, that is, they bought only one kind of thing, then clustering customers might work. However, since customers tend to have interests in many different things, it is more useful to find, for each customer, a small number of other customers who are similar in their tastes, and represent the data by these connections. We discuss similarity in Chapter 3.

1.2   Statistical Limits on Data Mining

A common sort of data-mining problem involves discovering unusual events hidden within massive amounts of data. This section is a discussion of the problem, including "Bonferroni's Principle," a warning against overzealous use of data mining.

1.2.1   Total Information Awareness

In 2002, the Bush administration put forward a plan to mine all the data it could find, including credit-card receipts, hotel records, travel data, and many other kinds of information in order to track terrorist activity. This idea naturally caused great concern among privacy advocates, and the project, called TIA, or

Total Information Awareness, was eventually killed by Congress, although it is unclear whether the project in fact exists under another name. It is not the purpose of this book to discuss the difficult issue of the privacy-security tradeoff. However, the prospect of TIA or a system like it does raise technical questions about its feasibility and the realism of its assumptions.

The concern raised by many is that if you look at so much data, and you try to find within it activities that look like terrorist behavior, are you not going to find many innocent activities – or even illicit activities that are not terrorism – that will result in visits from the police and maybe worse than just a visit? The answer is that it all depends on how narrowly you define the activities that you look for. Statisticians have seen this problem in many guises and have a theory, which we introduce in the next section.

1.2.2 Bonferroni's Principle

Suppose you have a certain amount of data, and you look for events of a certain type within that data. You can expect events of this type to occur, even if the data is completely random, and the number of occurrences of these events will grow as the size of the data grows. These occurrences are "bogus," in the sense that they have no cause other than that random data will always have some number of unusual features that look significant but aren't. A theorem of statistics, known as the *Bonferroni correction* gives a statistically sound way to avoid most of these bogus positive responses to a search through the data. Without going into the statistical details, we offer an informal version, *Bonferroni's principle*, that helps us avoid treating random occurrences as if they were real. Calculate the expected number of occurrences of the events you are looking for, on the assumption that data is random. If this number is significantly larger than the number of real instances you hope to find, then you must expect almost anything you find to be bogus, i.e., a statistical artifact rather than evidence of what you are looking for. This observation is the informal statement of Bonferroni's principle.

In a situation like searching for terrorists, where we expect that there are few terrorists operating at any one time, Bonferroni's principle says that we may only detect terrorists by looking for events that are so rare that they are unlikely to occur in random data. We shall give an extended example in the next section.

1.2.3 An Example of Bonferroni's Principle

Suppose there are believed to be some "evil-doers" out there, and we want to detect them. Suppose further that we have reason to believe that periodically, evil-doers gather at a hotel to plot their evil. Let us make the following assumptions about the size of the problem:

(1) There are one billion people who might be evil-doers.
(2) Everyone goes to a hotel one day in 100.

(3) A hotel holds 100 people. Hence, there are 100,000 hotels – enough to hold the 1% of a billion people who visit a hotel on any given day.

(4) We shall examine hotel records for 1000 days.

To find evil-doers in this data, we shall look for people who, on two different days, were both at the same hotel. Suppose, however, that there really are no evil-doers. That is, everyone behaves at random, deciding with probability 0.01 to visit a hotel on any given day, and if so, choosing one of the 10^5 hotels at random. Would we find any pairs of people who appear to be evil-doers?

We can do a simple approximate calculation as follows. The probability of any two people both deciding to visit a hotel on any given day is .0001. The chance that they will visit the same hotel is this probability divided by 10^5, the number of hotels. Thus, the chance that they will visit the same hotel on one given day is 10^{-9}. The chance that they will visit the same hotel on two different given days is the square of this number, 10^{-18}. Note that the hotels can be different on the two days.

Now, we must consider how many events will indicate evil-doing. An "event" in this sense is a pair of people and a pair of days, such that the two people were at the same hotel on each of the two days. To simplify the arithmetic, note that for large n, $\binom{n}{2}$ is about $n^2/2$. We shall use this approximation in what follows. Thus, the number of pairs of people is $\binom{10^9}{2} = 5 \times 10^{17}$. The number of pairs of days is $\binom{1000}{2} = 5 \times 10^5$. The expected number of events that look like evil-doing is the product of the number of pairs of people, the number of pairs of days, and the probability that any one pair of people and pair of days is an instance of the behavior we are looking for. That number is

$$5 \times 10^{17} \times 5 \times 10^5 \times 10^{-18} = 250,000$$

That is, there will be a quarter of a million pairs of people who look like evil-doers, even though they are not.

Now, suppose there really are 10 pairs of evil-doers out there. The police will need to investigate a quarter of a million other pairs in order to find the real evil-doers. In addition to the intrusion on the lives of half a million innocent people, the work involved is sufficiently great that this approach to finding evil-doers is probably not feasible.

1.2.4   Exercises for Section 1.2

EXERCISE 1.2.1   Using the information from Section 1.2.3, what would be the number of suspected pairs if the following changes were made to the data (and all other numbers remained as they were in that section)?

(a) The number of days of observation was raised to 2000.

(b) The number of people observed was raised to 2 billion (and there were therefore 200,000 hotels).

(c) We only reported a pair as suspect if they were at the same hotel at the same time on three different days.

! EXERCISE 1.2.2   Suppose we have information about the supermarket purchases of 100 million people. Each person goes to the supermarket 100 times in a year and buys 10 of the 1000 items that the supermarket sells. We believe that a pair of terrorists will buy exactly the same set of 10 items (perhaps the ingredients for a bomb?) at some time during the year. If we search for pairs of people who have bought the same set of items, would we expect that any such people found were truly terrorists?[3]

1.3   Things Useful to Know

In this section, we offer brief introductions to subjects that you may or may not have seen in your study of other courses. Each will be useful in the study of data mining. They include:

(1) The TF.IDF measure of word importance.
(2) Hash functions and their use.
(3) Secondary storage (disk) and its effect on running time of algorithms.
(4) The base e of natural logarithms and identities involving that constant.
(5) Power laws.

1.3.1   Importance of Words in Documents

In several applications of data mining, we shall be faced with the problem of categorizing documents (sequences of words) by their topic. Typically, topics are identified by finding the special words that characterize documents about that topic. For instance, articles about baseball would tend to have many occurrences of words like "ball," "bat," "pitch,", "run," and so on. Once we have classified documents to determine they are about baseball, it is not hard to notice that words such as these appear unusually frequently. However, until we have made the classification, it is not possible to identify these words as characteristic.

Thus, classification often starts by looking at documents, and finding the significant words in those documents. Our first guess might be that the words appearing most frequently in a document are the most significant. However, that intuition is exactly opposite of the truth. The most frequent words will most surely be the common words such as "the" or "and," which help build ideas but do not carry any significance themselves. In fact, the several hundred most common words in English (called *stop words*) are often removed from documents before any attempt to classify them.

---

[3] That is, assume our hypothesis that terrorists will surely buy a set of 10 items in common at some time during the year. We don't want to address the matter of whether or not terrorists would necessarily do so.

In fact, the indicators of the topic are relatively rare words. However, not all rare words are equally useful as indicators. There are certain words, for example "notwithstanding" or "albeit," that appear rarely in a collection of documents, yet do not tell us anything useful. On the other hand, a word like "chukker" is probably equally rare, but tips us off that the document is about the sport of polo. The difference between rare words that tell us something and those that do not has to do with the concentration of the useful words in just a few documents. That is, the presence of a word like "albeit" in a document does not make it terribly more likely that it will appear multiple times. However, if an article mentions "chukker" once, it is likely to tell us what happened in the "first chukker," then the "second chukker," and so on. That is, the word is likely to be repeated if it appears at all.

The formal measure of how concentrated into relatively few documents are the occurrences of a given word is called TF.IDF (*Term Frequency times Inverse Document Frequency*). It is normally computed as follows. Suppose we have a collection of N documents. Define f_{ij} to be the *frequency* (number of occurrences) of term (word) i in document j. Then, define the *term frequency* TF_{ij} to be:

$$TF_{ij} = \frac{f_{ij}}{\max_k f_{kj}}$$

That is, the term frequency of term i in document j is f_{ij} normalized by dividing it by the maximum number of occurrences of any term (perhaps excluding stop words) in the same document. Thus, the most frequent term in document j gets a TF of 1, and other terms get fractions as their term frequency for this document.

The IDF for a term is defined as follows. Suppose term i appears in n_i of the N documents in the collection. Then $IDF_i = \log_2(N/n_i)$. The TF.IDF score for term i in document j is then defined to be $TF_{ij} \times IDF_i$. The terms with the highest TF.IDF score are often the terms that best characterize the topic of the document.

EXAMPLE 1.3   Suppose our repository consists of $2^{20} = 1,048,576$ documents. Suppose word w appears in $2^{10} = 1024$ of these documents. Then $IDF_w = \log_2(2^{20}/2^{10}) = \log 2(2^{10}) = 10$. Consider a document j in which w appears 20 times, and that is the maximum number of times in which any word appears (perhaps after eliminating stop words). Then $TF_{wj} = 1$, and the TF.IDF score for w in document j is 10.

Suppose that in document k, word w appears once, while the maximum number of occurrences of any word in this document is 20. Then $TF_{wk} = 1/20$, and the TF.IDF score for w in document k is $1/2$.

1.3.2   Hash Functions

The reader has probably heard of hash tables, and perhaps used them in Java classes or similar packages. The hash functions that make hash tables feasible are also essential components in a number of data-mining algorithms, where the hash table takes an unfamiliar form. We shall review the basics here.

First, a hash function h takes a *hash-key* value as an argument and produces a *bucket number* as a result. The bucket number is an integer, normally in the range 0 to $B-1$, where B is the number of buckets. Hash-keys can be of any type. There is an intuitive property of hash functions that they "randomize" hash-keys. To be precise, if hash-keys are drawn randomly from a reasonable population of possible hash-keys, then h will send approximately equal numbers of hash-keys to each of the B buckets. It would be impossible to do so if, for example, the population of possible hash-keys were smaller than B. Such a population would not be "reasonable." However, there can be more subtle reasons why a hash function fails to achieve an approximately uniform distribution into buckets.

EXAMPLE 1.4   Suppose hash-keys are positive integers. A common and simple hash function is to pick $h(x) = x \mod B$, that is, the remainder when x is divided by B. That choice works fine if our population of hash-keys is all positive integers. $1/B$th of the integers will be assigned to each of the buckets. However, suppose our population is the even integers, and $B = 10$. Then only buckets 0, 2, 4, 6, and 8 can be the value of $h(x)$, and the hash function is distinctly nonrandom in its behavior. On the other hand, if we picked $B = 11$, then we would find that $1/11$th of the even integers get sent to each of the 11 buckets, so the hash function would work very well.

The generalization of Example 1.4 is that when hash-keys are integers, chosing B so it has any common factor with all (or even most of) the possible hash-keys will result in nonrandom distribution into buckets. Thus, it is normally preferred that we choose B to be a prime. That choice reduces the chance of nonrandom behavior, although we still have to consider the possibility that all hash-keys have B as a factor. Of course there are many other types of hash functions not based on modular arithmetic. We shall not try to summarize the options here, but some sources of information will be mentioned in the bibliographic notes.

What if hash-keys are not integers? In a sense, all data types have values that are composed of bits, and sequences of bits can always be interpreted as integers. However, there are some simple rules that enable us to convert common types to integers. For example, if hash-keys are strings, convert each character to its ASCII or Unicode equivalent, which can be interpreted as a small integer. Sum the integers before dividing by B. As long as B is smaller than the typical sum of character codes for the population of strings, the distribution into buckets will be relatively uniform. If B is larger, then we can partition the characters of a string into groups of several characters each. Treat the concatenation of the codes for the characters of a group as a single integer. Sum the integers associated with all the groups of a string, and divide by B as before. For instance, if B is around a billion, or 2^{30}, then grouping characters four at a time will give us 32-bit integers. The sum of several of these will distribute fairly evenly into a billion buckets.

For more complex data types, we can extend the idea used for converting strings to integers, recursively.

- For a type that is a record, each of whose components has its own type, recursively convert the value of each component to an integer, using the algorithm appropriate for the type of that component. Sum the integers for the components, and convert the integer sum to buckets by dividing by B.

- For a type that is an array, set, or bag of elements of some one type, convert the values of the elements' type to integers, sum the integers, and divide by B.

1.3.3   Indexes

An *index* is a data structure that makes it efficient to retrieve objects given the value of one or more elements of those objects. The most common situation is one where the objects are records, and the index is on one of the fields of that record. Given a value v for that field, the index lets us retrieve all the records with value v in that field. For example, we could have a file of (name, address, phone) triples, and an index on the phone field. Given a phone number, the index allows us to find quickly the record or records with that phone number.

There are many ways to implement indexes, and we shall not attempt to survey the matter here. The bibliographic notes give suggestions for further reading. However, a hash table is one simple way to build an index. The field or fields on which the index is based form the hash-key for a hash function. Records have the hash function applied to value of the hash-key, and the record itself is placed in the bucket whose number is determined by the hash function. The bucket could be a list of records in main-memory, or a disk block, for example.

Then, given a hash-key value, we can hash it, find the bucket, and need to search only that bucket to find the records with that value for the hash-key. If we choose the number of buckets B to be comparable to the number of records in the file, then there will be relatively few records in any bucket, and the search of a bucket takes little time.

EXAMPLE 1.5   Figure 1.2 suggests what a main-memory index of records with name, address, and phone fields might look like. Here, the index is on the phone field, and buckets are linked lists. We show the phone 800-555-1212 hashed to bucket number 17. There is an array of *bucket headers*, whose ith element is the head of a linked list for the bucket numbered i. We show expanded one of the elements of the linked list. It contains a record with name, address, and phone fields. This record is in fact one with the phone number 800-555-1212. Other records in that bucket may or may not have this phone number. We only know that whatever phone number they have is a phone that hashes to 17.

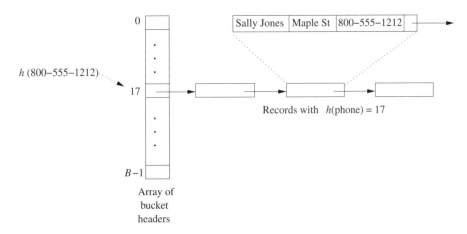

Figure 1.2 A hash table used as an index; phone numbers are hashed to buckets, and the entire record is placed in the bucket whose number is the hash value of the phone

1.3.4   Secondary Storage

It is important, when dealing with large-scale data, that we have a good understanding of the difference in time taken to perform computations when the data is initially on disk, as opposed to the time needed if the data is initially in main memory. The physical characteristics of disks is another subject on which we could say much, but shall say only a little and leave the interested reader to follow the bibliographic notes.

Disks are organized into *blocks*, which are the minimum units that the operating system uses to move data between main memory and disk. For example, the Windows operating system uses blocks of 64K bytes (i.e., $2^{16} = 65{,}536$ bytes to be exact). It takes approximately ten milliseconds to *access* (move the disk head to the track of the block and wait for the block to rotate under the head) and read a disk block. That delay is at least five orders of magnitude (a factor of 10^5) slower than the time taken to read a word from main memory, so if all we want to do is access a few bytes, there is an overwhelming benefit to having data in main memory. In fact, if we want to do something simple to every byte of a disk block, e.g., treat the block as a bucket of a hash table and search for a particular value of the hash-key among all the records in that bucket, then the time taken to move the block from disk to main memory will be far larger than the time taken to do the computation.

By organizing our data so that related data is on a single *cylinder* (the collection of blocks reachable at a fixed radius from the center of the disk, and therefore accessible without moving the disk head), we can read all the blocks on the cylinder into main memory in considerably less than 10 milliseconds per block. You can assume that a disk cannot transfer data to main memory at more than a hundred million bytes per second, no matter how that data is organized. That is not a problem when your dataset is a megabyte. But a dataset of a hundred gigabytes or a terabyte presents problems just accessing it, let alone doing anything useful with it.

1.3.5 The Base of Natural Logarithms

The constant $e = 2.7182818\cdots$ has a number of useful special properties. In particular, e is the limit of $(1 + \frac{1}{x})^x$ as x goes to infinity. The values of this expression for $x = 1, 2, 3, 4$ are approximately $2, 2.25, 2.37, 2.44$, so you should find it easy to believe that the limit of this series is around 2.72.

Some algebra lets us obtain approximations to many seemingly complex expressions. Consider $(1 + a)^b$, where a is small. We can rewrite the expression as $(1 + a)^{(1/a)(ab)}$. Then substitute $a = 1/x$ and $1/a = x$, so we have $(1 + \frac{1}{x})^{x(ab)}$, which is

$$\left(\left(1 + \frac{1}{x} \right)^x \right)^{ab}$$

Since a is assumed small, x is large, so the subexpression $(1 + \frac{1}{x})^x$ will be close to the limiting value of e. We can thus approximate $(1 + a)^b$ as e^{ab}.

Similar identities hold when a is negative. That is, the limit as x goes to infinity of $(1 - \frac{1}{x})^x$ is $1/e$. It follows that the approximation $(1 + a)^b = e^{ab}$ holds even when a is a small negative number. Put another way, $(1 - a)^b$ is approximately e^{-ab} when a is small and b is large.

Some other useful approximations follow from the Taylor expansion of e^x. That is, $e^x = \sum_{i=0}^{\infty} x^i/i!$, or $e^x = 1 + x + x^2/2 + x^3/6 + x^4/24 + \cdots$. When x is large, the above series converges slowly, although it does converge because $n!$ grows faster than x^n for any constant x. However, when x is small, either positive or negative, the series converges rapidly, and only a few terms are necessary to get a good approximation.

EXAMPLE 1.6 Let $x = 1/2$. Then

$$e^{1/2} = 1 + \frac{1}{2} + \frac{1}{8} + \frac{1}{48} + \frac{1}{384} + \cdots$$

or approximately $e^{1/2} = 1.64844$.

Let $x = -1$. Then

$$e^{-1} = 1 - 1 + \frac{1}{2} - \frac{1}{6} + \frac{1}{24} - \frac{1}{120} + \frac{1}{720} - \frac{1}{5040} + \cdots$$

or approximately $e^{-1} = 0.36786$.

1.3.6 Power Laws

There are many phenomena that relate two variables by a *power law*, that is, a linear relationship between the logarithms of the variables. Figure 1.3 suggests such a relationship. If x is the horizontal axis and y is the vertical axis, then the relationship is $\log_{10} y = 6 - 2 \log_{10} x$.

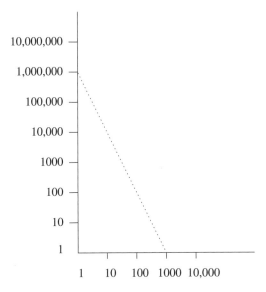

Figure 1.3 A power law with a slope of -2

EXAMPLE 1.7 We might examine book sales at Amazon.com, and let x represent the rank of books by sales. Then y is the number of sales of the xth best-selling book over some period. The implication of the graph of Fig. 1.3 would be that the best-selling book sold 1,000,000 copies, the 10th best-selling book sold 10,000 copies, the 100th best-selling book sold 100 copies, and so on for all ranks between these numbers and beyond. The implication that above rank 1000 the sales are a fraction of a book is too extreme, and we would in fact expect the line to flatten out for ranks much higher than 1000.

The general form of a power law relating x and y is $\log y = b + a \log x$. If we raise the base of the logarithm (which doesn't actually matter), say e, to the values on both sides of this equation, we get $y = e^b e^{a \log x} = e^b x^a$. Since e^b is just "some constant," let us replace it by constant c. Thus, a power law can be written as $y = c x^a$ for some constants a and c.

EXAMPLE 1.8 In Fig. 1.3 we see that when $x = 1$, $y = 10^6$, and when $x = 1000$, $y = 1$. Making the first substitution, we see $10^6 = c$. The second substitution gives us $1 = c(1000)^a$. Since we now know $c = 10^6$, the second equation gives us $1 = 10^6 (1000)^a$, from which we see $a = -2$. That is, the law expressed by Fig. 1.3 is $y = 10^6 x^{-2}$, or $y = 10^6 / x^2$.

We shall meet in this book many ways that power laws govern phenomena. Here are some examples:

(1) *Node Degrees in the Web Graph*: Order all pages by the number of in-links to that page. Let x be the position of a page in this ordering, and let y be the number of in-links to the xth page. Then y as a function of x looks

---

> **The Matthew Effect**
>
> Often, the existence of power laws with values of the exponent higher than 1 are explained by the *Matthew effect*. In the biblical *Book of Matthew*, there is a verse about "the rich get richer." Many phenomena exhibit this behavior, where getting a high value of some property causes that very property to increase. For example, if a Web page has many links in, then people are more likely to find the page and may choose to link to it from one of their pages as well. As another example, if a book is selling well on Amazon, then it is likely to be advertised when customers go to the Amazon site. Some of these people will choose to buy the book as well, thus increasing the sales of this book.

very much like Fig. 1.3. The exponent a is slightly larger than the -2 shown there; it has been found closer to 2.1.

(2) *Sales of Products*: Order products, say books at Amazon.com, by their sales over the past year. Let y be the number of sales of the xth most popular book. Again, the function $y(x)$ will look something like Fig. 1.3. we shall discuss the consequences of this distribution of sales in Section 9.1.2, where we take up the matter of the "long tail."

(3) *Sizes of Web Sites*: Count the number of pages at Web sites, and order sites by the number of their pages. Let y be the number of pages at the xth site. Again, the function $y(x)$ follows a power law.

(4) *Zipf's Law*: This power law originally referred to the frequency of words in a collection of documents. If you order words by frequency, and let y be the number of times the xth word in the order appears, then you get a power law, although with a much shallower slope than that of Fig. 1.3. Zipf's observation was that $y = cx^{-1/2}$. Interestingly, a number of other kinds of data follow this particular power law. For example, if we order states in the US by population and let y be the population of the xth most populous state, then x and y obey Zipf's law approximately.

1.3.7   Exercises for Section 1.3

EXERCISE 1.3.1   Suppose there is a repository of ten million documents. What (to the nearest integer) is the IDF for a word that appears in (a) 40 documents (b) 10,000 documents?

EXERCISE 1.3.2   Suppose there is a repository of ten million documents, and word w appears in 320 of them. In a particular document d, the maximum number of occurrences of a word is 15. Approximately what is the TF.IDF score for w if that word appears (a) once (b) five times?

! EXERCISE 1.3.3   Suppose hash-keys are drawn from the population of all non-negative integers that are multiples of some constant c, and hash function $h(x)$

is x mod 15. For what values of c will h be a suitable hash function, i.e., a large random choice of hash-keys will be divided roughly equally into buckets?

EXERCISE 1.3.4 In terms of e, give approximations to

$$\text{(a) } (1.01)^{500} \text{ (b) } (1.05)^{1000} \text{ (c) } (0.9)^{40}$$

EXERCISE 1.3.5 Use the Taylor expansion of e^x to compute, to three decimal places: (a) $e^{1/10}$ (b) $e^{-1/10}$ (c) e^2.

1.4 Outline of the Book

This section gives brief summaries of the remaining chapters of the book.

Chapter 2 is not about data mining per se. Rather, it introduces us to the map-reduce methodology for exploiting parallelism in computing clouds (racks of interconnected processors). There is reason to believe that cloud computing, and map-reduce in particular, will become the normal way to compute when analysis of very large amounts of data is involved. A pervasive issue in later chapters will be the exploitation of the map-reduce methodology to implement the algorithms we cover.

Chapter 3 is about finding similar items. Our starting point is that items can be represented by sets of elements, and similar sets are those that have a large fraction of their elements in common. The key techniques of minhashing and locality-sensitive hashing are explained. These techniques have numerous applications and often give surprisingly efficient solutions to problems that appear impossible for massive data sets.

In Chapter 4, we consider data in the form of a stream. The difference between a stream and a database is that the data in a stream is lost if you do not do something about it immediately. Important examples of streams are the streams of search queries at a search engine or clicks at a popular Web site. In this chapter, we see several of the surprising applications of hashing that make management of stream data feasible.

Chapter 5 is devoted to a single application: the computation of PageRank. This computation is the idea that made Google stand out from other search engines, and it is still an essential part of how search engines know what pages the user is likely to want to see. Extensions of PageRank are also essential in the fight against spam (euphemistically called "search engine optimization"), and we shall examine the latest extensions of the idea for the purpose of combating spam.

Then, Chapter 6 introduces the market-basket model of data, and its canonical problems of association rules and finding frequent itemsets. In the market-basket model, data consists of a large collection of baskets, each of which contains a small set of items. We give a sequence of algorithms capable of finding all frequent pairs of items, that is pairs of items that appear together in many baskets. Another sequence of algorithms are useful for finding most of the frequent itemsets larger than pairs, with high efficiency.

Chapter 7 examines the problem of clustering. We assume a set of items with a distance measure defining how close or far one item is from another. The goal is to examine a large amount of data and partition it into subsets (clusters), each cluster consisting of items that are all close to one another, yet far from items in the other clusters.

Chapter 8 is devoted to on-line advertising and the computational problems it engenders. We introduce the notion of an on-line algorithm – one where a good response must be given immediately, rather than waiting until we have seen the entire dataset. The idea of competitive ratio is another important concept covered in this chapter; it is the ratio of the guaranteed performance of an on-line algorithm compared with the performance of the optimal algorithm that is allowed to see all the data before making any decisions. These ideas are used to give good algorithms that match bids by advertisers for the right to display their ad in response to a query against the search queries arriving at a search engine.

Finally, Chapter 9 is devoted to recommendation systems. Many Web applications involve advising users on what they might like. The Netflix challenge is one example, where it is desired to predict what movies a user would like, or Amazon's problem of pitching a product to a customer based on information about what they might be interested in buying. There are two basic approaches to recommendation. We can characterize items by features, e.g., the stars of a movie, and recommend items with the same features as those the user is known to like. Or, we can look at what other users with preferences similar to that of the user in question, and see what they liked (a technique known as collaborative filtering).

1.5   Summary of Chapter 1

✦ *Data Mining*: This term refers to the process of extracting useful models of data. Sometimes, a model can be a summary of the data, or it can be the set of most extreme features of the data.

✦ *Bonferroni's Principle*: If we are willing to view as an interesting feature of data something of which many can be expected to exist in random data, then we cannot rely on such features being significant. This observation limits our ability to mine data for features that are not sufficiently rare in practice.

✦ *TF.IDF*: The measure called TF.IDF lets us identify words in a collection of documents that are useful for determining the topic of each document. A word has high TF.IDF score in a document if it appears in relatively few documents, but appears in this one, and when it appears in a document it tends to appear many times.

✦ *Hash Functions*: A hash function maps hash-keys of some data type to integer bucket numbers. A good hash function distributes the possible hash-key values approximately evenly among buckets. Any data type can be the domain of a hash function.

✦ *Indexes*: An index is a data structure that allows us to store and retrieve data records efficiently, given the value in one or more of the fields of the record. Hashing is one way to build an index.

✦ *Storage on Disk*: When data must be stored on disk (secondary memory), it takes very much more time to access a desired data item than if the same data were stored in main memory. When data is large, it is important that algorithms strive to keep needed data in main memory.

✦ *Power Laws*: Many phenomena obey a law that can be expressed as $y = cx^a$ for some power a, often around -2. Such phenomena include the sales of the xth most popular book, or the number of in-links to the xth most popular page.

1.6   References for Chapter 1

[(7)] is a clear introduction to the basics of data mining. [(2)] covers data mining principally from the point of view of machine learning and statistics.

For construction of hash functions and hash tables, see [(4)]. Details of the TF.IDF measure and other matters regarding document processing can be found in [(5)]. See [(3)] for more on managing indexes, hash tables, and data on disk.

Power laws pertaining to the Web were explored by [(1)]. The Matthew effect was first observed in [(6)].

(1) A. Broder, R. Kumar, F. Maghoul, P. Raghavan, S. Rajagopalan, R. Stata, A. Tomkins, and J. Weiner, "Graph structure in the web," *Computer Networks* **33**:1–6, pp. 309–320, 2000.

(2) M.M. Gaber, *Scientific Data Mining and Knowledge Discovery — Principles and Foundations*, Springer, New York, 2010.

(3) H. Garcia-Molina, J.D. Ullman, and J. Widom, *Database Systems: The Complete Book* Second Edition, Prentice-Hall, Upper Saddle River, NJ, 2009.

(4) D.E. Knuth, *The Art of Computer Programming* Vol. 3 (*Sorting and Searching*), Second Edition, Addison-Wesley, Upper Saddle River, NJ, 1998.

(5) C.P. Manning, P. Raghavan, and H. Schütze, *Introduction to Information Retrieval*, Cambridge Univ. Press, 2008.

(6) R.K. Merton, "The Matthew effect in science," *Science* **159**:3810, pp. 56–63, Jan. 5, 1968.

(7) P.-N. Tan, M. Steinbach, and V. Kumar, *Introduction to Data Mining*, Addison-Wesley, Upper Saddle River, NJ, 2005.

2 Large-Scale File Systems and Map-Reduce

Modern Internet applications have created a need to manage immense amounts of data quickly. In many of these applications, the data is extremely regular, and there is ample opportunity to exploit parallelism. Important examples are:

(1) The ranking of Web pages by importance, which involves an iterated matrix-vector multiplication where the dimension is in the tens of billions, and

(2) Searches in "friends" networks at social-networking sites, which involve graphs with hundreds of millions of nodes and many billions of edges.

To deal with applications such as these, a new software stack has developed. It begins with a new form of file system, which features much larger units than the disk blocks in a conventional operating system and also provides replication of data to protect against the frequent media failures that occur when data is distributed over thousands of disks.

On top of these file systems, we find higher-level programming systems developing. Central to many of these is a programming system called *map-reduce*. Implementations of map-reduce enable many of the most common calculations on large-scale data to be performed on large collections of computers, efficiently and in a way that is tolerant of hardware failures during the computation.

Map-reduce systems are evolving and extending rapidly. We include in this chapter a discussion of generalizations of map-reduce, first to acyclic workflows and then to recursive algorithms. We conclude with a discussion of communication cost and what it tells us about the most efficient algorithms in this modern computing environment.

2.1 Distributed File Systems

Most computing is done on a single processor, with its main memory, cache, and local disk (a *compute node*). In the past, applications that called for parallel processing, such as large scientific calculations, were done on special-purpose parallel computers with many processors and specialized hardware. However, the prevalence of large-scale Web services has caused more and more computing to be done on installations with thousands of compute nodes operating more or less independently. In these installations, the compute nodes are commodity hardware, which greatly reduces the cost compared with special-purpose parallel machines.

These new computing facilities have given rise to a new generation of programming systems. These systems take advantage of the power of parallelism and at the same time avoid the reliability problems that arise when the computing hardware consists of thousands of independent components, any of which could fail at any time. In this section, we discuss both the characteristics of these computing installations and the specialized file systems that have been developed to take advantage of them.

2.1.1   Physical Organization of Compute Nodes

The new parallel-computing architecture, sometimes called *cluster computing*, is organized as follows. Compute nodes are stored on *racks*, perhaps 8–64 on a rack. The nodes on a single rack are connected by a network, typically gigabit Ethernet. There can be many racks of compute nodes, and racks are connected by another level of network or a switch. The bandwidth of inter-rack communication is somewhat greater than the intrarack Ethernet, but given the number of pairs of nodes that might need to communicate between racks, this bandwidth may be essential. Figure 2.1 suggests the architecture of a large-scale computing system. However, there may be many more racks and many more compute nodes per rack.

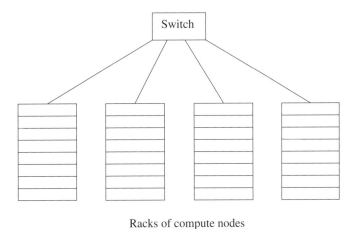

Racks of compute nodes

Figure 2.1 Compute nodes are organized into racks, and racks are interconnected by a switch

It is a fact of life that components fail, and the more components, such as compute nodes and interconnection networks, a system has, the more frequently something in the system will not be working at any given time. For systems such as Fig. 2.1, the principal failure modes are the loss of a single node (e.g., the disk

at that node crashes) and the loss of an entire rack (e.g., the network connecting
its nodes to each other and to the outside world fails).

Some important calculations take minutes or even hours on thousands of compute nodes. If we had to abort and restart the computation every time one
component failed, then the computation might never complete successfully. The
solution to this problem takes two forms:

(1) Files must be stored redundantly. If we did not duplicate the file at several
compute nodes, then if one node failed, all its files would be unavailable
until the node is replaced. If we did not back up the files at all, and the
disk crashes, the files would be lost forever. We discuss file management in
Section 2.1.2.

(2) Computations must be divided into tasks, such that if any one task fails
to execute to completion, it can be restarted without affecting other tasks.
This strategy is followed by the map-reduce programming system that we
introduce in Section 2.2.

2.1.2   Large-Scale File-System Organization

To exploit cluster computing, files must look and behave somewhat differently
from the conventional file systems found on single computers. This new file system, often called a *distributed file system* or *DFS* (although this term has had
other meanings in the past), is typically used as follows.

- Files can be enormous, possibly a terabyte in size. If you have only small
files, there is no point using a DFS for them.

- Files are rarely updated. Rather, they are read as data for some calculation,
and possibly additional data is appended to files from time to time. For
example, an airline reservation system would not be suitable for a DFS,
even if the data were very large, because the data is changed so frequently.

Files are divided into *chunks*, which are typically 64 megabytes in size. Chunks
are replicated, perhaps three times, at three different compute nodes. Moreover,
the nodes holding copies of one chunk should be located on different racks, so
we don't lose all copies due to a rack failure. Normally, both the chunk size and
the degree of replication can be decided by the user.

To find the chunks of a file, there is another small file called the *master node*
or *name node* for that file. The master node is itself replicated, and a directory
for the file system as a whole knows where to find its copies. The directory itself
can be replicated, and all participants using the DFS know where the directory
copies are.

> ### DFS Implementations
>
> There are several distributed file systems of the type we have described that are used in practice. Among these:
>
> (1) The *Google File System* (GFS), the original of the class.
> (2) *Hadoop Distributed File System* (HDFS), an open-source DFS used with Hadoop, an implementation of map-reduce (see Section 2.2) and distributed by the Apache Software Foundation.
> (3) *CloudStore*, an open-source DFS originally developed by Kosmix.

2.2   Map-Reduce

Map-reduce is a style of computing that has been implemented several times. You can use an implementation of map-reduce to manage many large-scale computations in a way that is tolerant of hardware faults. All you need to write are two functions, called *Map* and *Reduce*, while the system manages the parallel execution, coordination of tasks that execute Map or Reduce, and also deals with the possibility that one of these tasks will fail to execute. In brief, a map-reduce computation executes as follows:

(1) Some number of Map tasks each are given one or more chunks from a distributed file system. These Map tasks turn the chunk into a sequence of *key-value* pairs. The way key-value pairs are produced from the input data is determined by the code written by the user for the Map function.
(2) The key-value pairs from each Map task are collected by a *master controller* and sorted by key. The keys are divided among all the Reduce tasks, so all key-value pairs with the same key wind up at the same Reduce task.
(3) The Reduce tasks work on one key at a time, and combine all the values associated with that key in some way. The manner of combination of values is determined by the code written by the user for the Reduce function.

Figure 2.2 suggests this computation.

2.2.1   The Map Tasks

We view input files for a Map task as consisting of *elements*, which can be any type: a tuple or a document, for example. A chunk is a collection of elements, and no element is stored across two chunks. Technically, all inputs to Map tasks and outputs from Reduce tasks are of the key-value-pair form, but normally the keys of input elements are not relevant and we shall tend to ignore them. Insisting on this form for inputs and outputs is motivated by the desire to allow composition of several map-reduce processes.

A Map function is written to convert input elements to key-value pairs. The

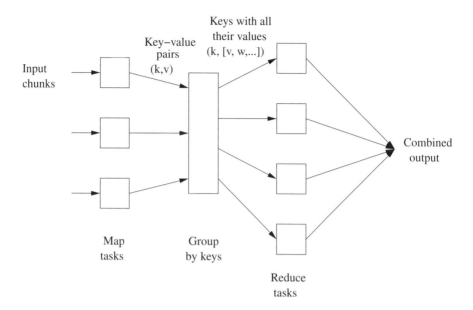

Figure 2.2 Schematic of a map-reduce computation

types of keys and values are each arbitrary. Further, keys are not "keys" in the usual sense; they do not have to be unique. Rather a Map task can produce several key-value pairs with the same key, even from the same element.

EXAMPLE 2.1   We shall illustrate a map-reduce computation with what has become the standard example application: counting the number of occurrences for each word in a collection of documents. In this example, the input file is a repository of documents, and each document is an element. The Map function for this example uses keys that are of type String (the words) and values that are integers. The Map task reads a document and breaks it into its sequence of words $w_1, w_2, \ldots, w_n$. It then emits a sequence of key-value pairs where the value is always 1. That is, the output of the Map task for this document is the sequence of key-value pairs:

$$(w_1, 1), \ (w_2, 1), \ldots, (w_n, 1)$$

Note that a single Map task will typically process many documents – all the documents in one or more chunks. Thus, its output will be more than the sequence for the one document suggested above. Note also that if a word w appears m times among all the documents assigned to that process, then there will be m key-value pairs $(w, 1)$ among its output. An option, which we discuss in Section 2.2.4, is to combine these m pairs into a single pair (w, m), but we can only do that because, as we shall see, the Reduce tasks apply an associative and commutative operation, addition, to the values.

2.2.2   Grouping and Aggregation

Grouping and aggregation is done the same way, regardless of what Map and Reduce tasks do. The master controller process knows how many Reduce tasks there will be, say r such tasks. The user typically tells the map-reduce system what r should be. Then the master controller normally picks a hash function that applies to keys and produces a bucket number from 0 to $r - 1$. Each key that is output by a Map task is hashed and its key-value pair is put in one of r local files. Each file is destined for one of the Reduce tasks.[1]

After all the Map tasks have completed successfully, the master controller merges the file from each Map task that are destined for a particular Reduce task and feeds the merged file to that process as a sequence of key-list-of-value pairs. That is, for each key k, the input to the Reduce task that handles key k is a pair of the form $(k, [v_1, v_2, \ldots, v_n])$, where (k, v_1), $(k, v_2), \ldots, (k, v_n)$ are all the key-value pairs with key k coming from all the Map tasks.

2.2.3   The Reduce Tasks

The Reduce function is written to take pairs consisting of a key and its list of associated values and combine those values in some way. The output of a Reduce task is a sequence of key-value pairs consisting of each input key k that the Reduce task received, paired with the combined value constructed from the list of values that the Reduce task received along with key k. The outputs from all the Reduce tasks are merged into a single file.

EXAMPLE 2.2   Let us continue with the word-count example of Example 2.1. The Reduce function simply adds up all the values. Thus, the output of the Reduce tasks is a sequence of (w, m) pairs, where w is a word that appears at least once among all the input documents and m is the total number of occurrences of w among all those documents.

2.2.4   Combiners

It is common for the Reduce function to be associative and commutative. That is, the values to be combined can be combined in any order, with the same result. The addition performed in Example 2.2 is an example of an associative and commutative operation. It doesn't matter how we group a list of numbers $v_1, v_2, \ldots, v_n$; the sum will be the same.

When the Reduce function is associative and commutative, it is possible to push some of what Reduce does to the Map tasks. For example, instead of the Map tasks in Example 2.1 producing many pairs $(w, 1)$, $(w, 1), \ldots$, we could apply the Reduce function within the Map task, before the output of the Map

---

[1] Optionally, users can specify their own hash function or other method for assigning keys to Reduce tasks. However, whatever algorithm is used, each key is assigned to one and only one Reduce task.

> ### Implementations of Map-Reduce
>
> The original implementation of map-reduce was as an internal and proprietary system at Google. It was called simply "Map-Reduce." There is an open-source implementation called Hadoop. It can be downloaded, along with the HDFS distributed file system, from the Apache Foundation.

tasks is subject to grouping and aggregation. These key-value pairs would thus be replaced by one pair with key w and value equal to the sum of all the 1's in all those pairs. That is, the pairs with key w generated by a single Map task would be combined into a pair (w, m), where m is the number of times that w appears among the documents handled by this Map task. Note that it is still necessary to do grouping and aggregation and to pass the result to the Reduce tasks, since there will typically be one key-value pair with key w coming from each of the Map tasks.

2.2.5   Details of Map-Reduce Execution

Let us now consider in more detail how a program using map-reduce is executed. Figure 2.3 offers an outline of how processes, tasks, and files interact. Taking advantage of a library provided by a map-reduce system such as Hadoop, the user program forks a Master controller process and some number of Worker processes at different compute nodes. Normally, a Worker handles either Map tasks (a *Map worker*) or Reduce tasks (a *Reduce worker*), but not both.

The Master has many responsibilities. One is to create some number of Map tasks and some number of Reduce tasks, these numbers being selected by the user program. These tasks will be assigned to Worker processes by the Master. It is reasonable to create one Map task for every chunk of the input file(s), but we may wish to create fewer Reduce tasks. The reason for limiting the number of Reduce tasks is that it is necessary for each Map task to create an intermediate file for each Reduce task, and if there are too many Reduce tasks the number of intermediate files explodes.

The Master keeps track of the status of each Map and Reduce task (idle, executing at a particular Worker, or completed). A Worker process reports to the Master when it finishes a task, and a new task is scheduled by the Master for that Worker process.

Each Map task is assigned one or more chunks of the input file(s) and executes on it the code written by the user. The Map task creates a file for each Reduce task on the local disk of the Worker that executes the Map task. The Master is informed of the location and sizes of each of these files, and the Reduce task for which each is destined. When a Reduce task is assigned by the Master to a Worker process, that task is given all the files that form its input. The Reduce

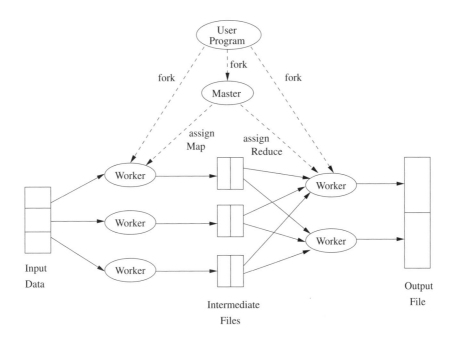

Figure 2.3 Overview of the execution of a map-reduce program

task executes code written by the user and writes its output to a file that is part of the surrounding distributed file system.

2.2.6 Coping With Node Failures

The worst thing that can happen is that the compute node at which the Master is executing fails. In this case, the entire map-reduce job must be restarted. But only this one node can bring the entire process down; other failures will be managed by the Master, and the map-reduce job will complete eventually.

Suppose the compute node at which a Map worker resides fails. This failure will be detected by the Master, because it periodically pings the Worker processes. All the Map tasks that were assigned to this Worker will have to be redone, even if they had completed. The reason for redoing completed Map tasks is that their output destined for the Reduce tasks resides at that compute node, and is now unavailable to the Reduce tasks. The Master sets the status of each of these Map tasks to idle and will schedule them on a Worker when one becomes available. The Master must also inform each Reduce task that the location of its input from that Map task has changed.

Dealing with a failure at the node of a Reduce worker is simpler. The Master simply sets the status of its currently executing Reduce tasks to idle. These will be rescheduled on another reduce worker later.

2.3   Algorithms Using Map-Reduce

Map-reduce is not a solution to every problem, not even every problem that profitably can use many compute nodes operating in parallel. As we mentioned in Section 2.1.2, the entire distributed-file-system milieu makes sense only when files are very large and are rarely updated in place. Thus, we would not expect to use either a DFS or an implementation of map-reduce for managing on-line retail sales, even though a large on-line retailer such as Amazon.com uses thousands of compute nodes when processing requests over the Web. The reason is that the principal operations on Amazon data involve responding to searches for products, recording sales, and so on, processes that involve relatively little calculation and that change the database.[2] On the other hand, Amazon might use map-reduce to perform certain analytic queries on large amounts of data, such as finding for each user those users whose buying patterns were most similar.

The original purpose for which the Google implementation of map-reduce was created was to execute very large matrix-vector multiplications as are needed in the calculation of PageRank (See Chapter 5). We shall see that matrix-vector and matrix-matrix calculations fit nicely into the map-reduce style of computing. Another important class of operations that can use map-reduce effectively are the relational-algebra operations. We shall examine the map-reduce execution of these operations as well.

2.3.1   Matrix-Vector Multiplication by Map-Reduce

Suppose we have an $n \times n$ matrix M, whose element in row i and column j will be denoted m_{ij}. Suppose we also have a vector $\mathbf{v}$ of length n, whose jth element is v_j. Then the matrix-vector product is the vector $\mathbf{x}$ of length n, whose ith element x_i is given by

$$x_i = \sum_{j=1}^{n} m_{ij} v_j$$

If $n = 100$, we do not want to use a DFS or map-reduce for this calculation. But this sort of calculation is at the heart of the ranking of Web pages that goes on at search engines, and there, n is in the tens of billions.[3] Let us first assume that n is large, but not so large that vector $\mathbf{v}$ cannot fit in main memory, and be part of the input to every Map task. It is useful to observe at this time that there is nothing in the definition of map-reduce that forbids providing the same input to more than one Map task.

The matrix M and the vector $\mathbf{v}$ each will be stored in a file of the DFS.

---

[2] Remember that even looking at a product you don't buy causes Amazon to remember that you looked at it.

[3] The matrix is sparse, with on the average of 10 to 15 nonzero elements per row, since the matrix represents the links in the Web, with m_{ij} nonzero if and only if there is a link from page j to page i. Note that there is no way we could store a dense matrix whose side was 10^{10}, since it would have 10^{20} elements.

We assume that the row-column coordinates of each matrix element will be discoverable, either from its position in the file, or because it is stored with explicit coordinates, as a triple (i, j, m_{ij}). We also assume the position of element v_j in the vector $\mathbf{v}$ will be discoverable in the analogous way.

The Map Function Each Map task will take the entire vector $\mathbf{v}$ and a chunk of the matrix M. From each matrix element m_{ij} it produces the key-value pair $(i, m_{ij}v_j)$. Thus, all terms of the sum that make up the component x_i of the matrix-vector product will get the same key.

The Reduce Function A Reduce task has simply to sum all the values associated with a given key i. The result will be a pair (i, x_i).

2.3.2 If the Vector $\mathbf{v}$ Cannot Fit in Main Memory

However, it is possible that the vector $\mathbf{v}$ is so large that it will not fit in its entirety in main memory. We don't have to fit it in main memory at a compute node, but if we do not then there will be a very large number of disk accesses as we move pieces of the vector into main memory to multiply components by elements of the matrix. Thus, as an alternative, we can divide the matrix into vertical *stripes* of equal width and divide the vector into an equal number of horizontal stripes, of the same height. Our goal is to use enough stripes so that the portion of the vector in one stripe can fit conveniently into main memory at a compute node. Figure 2.4 suggests what the partition looks like if the matrix and vector are each divided into five stripes.

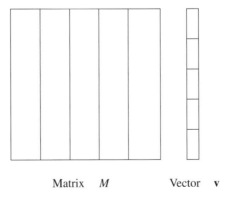

Matrix M Vector $\mathbf{v}$

Figure 2.4 Division of a matrix and vector into fives stripes

The ith stripe of the matrix multiplies only components from the ith stripe of the vector. Thus, we can divide the matrix into one file for each stripe, and do the same for the vector. Each Map task is assigned a chunk from one of the stripes of the matrix and gets the entire corresponding stripe of the vector. The

Map and Reduce tasks can then act exactly as was described above for the case where Map tasks get the entire vector.

We shall take up matrix-vector multiplication using map-reduce again in Section 5.2. There, because of the particular application (PageRank calculation), we have an additional constraint that the result vector should be partitioned in the same way as the input vector, so the output may become the input for another iteration of the matrix-vector multiplication. We shall see there that the best strategy involves partitioning the matrix M into square blocks, rather than stripes.

2.3.3   Relational-Algebra Operations

There are a number of operations on large-scale data that are used in database queries. In many traditional database applications, these queries involve retrieval of small amounts of data, even though the database itself may be large. For example, a query may ask for the bank balance of one particular account. Such queries are not useful applications of map-reduce.

However, there are many operations on data that can be described easily in terms of the common database-query primitives, even if the queries themselves are not executed within a database management system. Thus, a good starting point for seeing applications of map-reduce is by considering the standard operations on relations. We assume you are familiar with database systems, the query language SQL, and the relational model, but to review, a *relation* is a table with column headers called *attributes*. Rows of the relation are called *tuples*. The set of attributes of a relation is called its *schema*. We often write an expression like $R(A_1, A_2, \ldots, A_n)$ to say that the relation name is R and its attributes are A_1, $A_2, \ldots, A_n$.

From	To
url1	url2
url1	url3
url2	url3
url2	url4
...	...

Figure 2.5 Relation *Links* consists of the set of pairs of URL's, such that the first has one or more links to the second

EXAMPLE 2.3   In Fig. 2.5 we see part of the relation *Links* that describes the structure of the Web. There are two attributes, *From* and *To*. A row, or tuple, of the relation is a pair of URL's, such that there is at least one link from the first URL to the second. For instance, the first row of Fig. 2.5 is the pair $(url1, url2)$ that says the Web page $url1$ has a link to page $url2$. While we have shown only four tuples, the real relation of the Web, or the portion of it that would be stored by a typical search engine, has billions of tuples.

A relation, however large, can be stored as a file in a distributed file system. The elements of this file are the tuples of the relation.

There are several standard operations on relations, often referred to as *relational algebra*, that are used to implement queries. The queries themselves usually are written in SQL. The relational-algebra operations we shall discuss are:

(1) *Selection*: Apply a condition C to each tuple in the relation and produce as output only those tuples that satisfy C. The result of this selection is denoted $\sigma_C(R)$.

(2) *Projection*: For some subset S of the attributes of the relation, produce from each tuple only the components for the attributes in S. The result of this projection is denoted $\pi_S(R)$.

(3) *Union, Intersection*, and *Difference*: These well-known set operations apply to the sets of tuples in two relations that have the same schema. There are also bag (multiset) versions of the operations in SQL, with somewhat unintuitive definitions, but we shall not go into the bag versions of these operations here.

(4) *Natural Join*: Given two relations, compare each pair of tuples, one from each relation. If the tuples agree on all the attributes that are common to the two schemas, then produce a tuple that has components for each of the attributes in either schema and agrees with the two tuples on each attribute. If the tuples disagree on one or more shared attributes, then produce nothing from this pair of tuples. The natural join of relations R and S is denoted $R \bowtie S$. While we shall discuss executing only the natural join with map-reduce, all *equijoins* (joins where the tuple-agreement condition involves equality of attributes from the two relations that do not necessarily have the same name) can be executed in the same manner. We shall give an illustration in Example 2.4.

(5) *Grouping* and *Aggregation*:[4] Given a relation R, partition its tuples according to their values in one set of attributes G, called the *grouping attributes*. Then, for each group, aggregate the values in certain other attributes. The normally permitted aggregations are SUM, COUNT, AVG, MIN, and MAX, with the obvious meanings. Note that MIN and MAX require that the aggregated attributes have a type that can be compared, e.g., numbers or strings, while SUM and AVG require that the type be arithmetic. We denote a grouping-and-aggregation operation on a relation R by $\gamma_X(R)$, where X is a list of elements that are either

(a) A grouping attribute, or

---

[4] Some descriptions of relational algebra do not include these operations, and indeed they were not part of the original definition of this algebra. However, these operations are so important in SQL, that modern treatments of relational algebra include them.

(b) An expression $\theta(A)$, where θ is one of the five aggregation operations such as SUM, and A is an attribute not among the grouping attributes.

The result of this operation is one tuple for each group. That tuple has a component for each of the grouping attributes, with the value common to tuples of that group, and a component for each aggregation, with the aggregated value for that group. We shall see an illustration in Example 2.5.

EXAMPLE 2.4   Let us try to find the paths of length two in the Web, using the relation *Links* of Fig. 2.5. That is, we want to find the triples of URL's (u, v, w) such that there is a link from u to v and a link from v to w. We essentially want to take the natural join of *Links* with itself, but we first need to imagine that it is two relations, with different schemas, so we can describe the desired connection as a natural join. Thus, imagine that there are two copies of *Links*, namely $L1(U1, U2)$ and $L2(U2, U3)$. Now, if we compute $L1 \bowtie L2$, we shall have exactly what we want. That is, for each tuple $t1$ of $L1$ (i.e., each tuple of *Links*) and each tuple $t2$ of $L2$ (another tuple of *Links*, possibly even the same tuple), see if their $U2$ components are the same. Note that these components are the second component of $t1$ and the first component of $t2$. If these two components agree, then produce a tuple for the result, with schema $(U1, U2, U3)$. This tuple consists of the first component of $t1$, the second component of $t1$ (which must equal the first component of $t2$), and the second component of $t2$.

We may not want the entire path of length two, but only want the pairs (u, w) of URL's such that there is at least one path from u to w of length two. If so, we can project out the middle components by computing $\pi_{U1,U3}(L1 \bowtie L2)$.

EXAMPLE 2.5   Imagine that a social-networking site has a relation

$$\text{Friends(User, Friend)}$$

This relation has tuples that are pairs (a, b) such that b is a friend of a. The site might want to develop statistics about the number of friends members have. Their first step would be to compute a count of the number of friends of each user. This operation can be done by grouping and aggregation, specifically

$$\gamma_{\text{User,COUNT(Friend)}}(\text{Friends})$$

This operation groups all the tuples by the value in their first component, so there is one group for each user. Then, for each group the count of the number of friends of that user is made.[5] The result will be one tuple for each group, and a typical tuple would look like (Sally, 300), if user "Sally" has 300 friends.

---

[5] The COUNT operation applied to an attribute does not consider the values of that attribute, so it is really counting the number of tuples in the group. In SQL, there is a count-distinct operator that counts the number of different values, but we do not discuss this operator here.

2.3.4   Computing Selections by Map-Reduce

Selections really do not need the full power of map-reduce. They can be done most conveniently in the map portion alone, although they could also be done in the reduce portion alone. Here is a map-reduce implementation of selection $\sigma_C(R)$.

The Map Function For each tuple t in R, test if it satisfies C. If so, produce the key-value pair (t, t). That is, both the key and value are t.

The Reduce Function The Reduce function is the identity. It simply passes each key-value pair to the output.

Note that the output is not exactly a relation, because it has key-value pairs. However, a relation can be obtained by using only the value components (or only the key components) of the output.

2.3.5   Computing Projections by Map-Reduce

Projection is performed similarly to selection, because projection may cause the same tuple to appear several times, the Reduce function must eliminate duplicates. We may compute $\pi_S(R)$ as follows.

The Map Function For each tuple t in R, construct a tuple t' by eliminating from t those components whose attributes are not in S. Output the key-value pair (t', t').

The Reduce Function For each key t' produced by any of the Map tasks, there will be one or more key-value pairs (t', t'). The Reduce function turns $(t', [t', t', \ldots, t'])$ into (t', t'), so it produces exactly one pair (t', t') for this key t'.

Observe that the Reduce operation is duplicate elimination. This operation is associative and commutative, so a combiner associated with each Map task can eliminate whatever duplicates are produced locally. However, the Reduce tasks are still needed to eliminate two identical tuples coming from different Map tasks.

2.3.6   Union, Intersection, and Difference by Map-Reduce

First, consider the union of two relations. Suppose relations R and S have the same schema. Map tasks will be assigned chunks from either R or S; it doesn't matter which. The Map tasks don't really do anything except pass their input tuples as key-value pairs to the Reduce tasks. The latter need only eliminate duplicates as for projection.

The Map Function Turn each input tuple t into a key-value pair (t, t).

The Reduce Function Associated with each key t there will be either one or two values. Produce output (t, t) in either case.

To compute the intersection, we can use the same Map function. However, the Reduce function must produce a tuple only if both relations have the tuple. If the key t has two values $[t, t]$ associated with it, then the Reduce task for t should produce (t, t). However, if the value associated with key t is just $[t]$, then one of R and S is missing t, so we don't want to produce a tuple for the intersection. We need to produce a value that indicates "no tuple," such as the SQL value NULL. When the result relation is constructed from the output, such a tuple will be ignored.

The Map Function Turn each tuple t into a key-value pair (t, t).

The Reduce Function If key t has value list $[t, t]$, then produce (t, t). Otherwise, produce (t, NULL).

The Difference $R - S$ requires a bit more thought. The only way a tuple t can appear in the output is if it is in R but not in S. The Map function can pass tuples from R and S through, but must inform the Reduce function whether the tuple came from R or S. We shall thus use the relation as the value associated with the key t. Here is a specification for the two functions.

The Map Function For a tuple t in R, produce key-value pair (t, R), and for a tuple t in S, produce key-value pair (t, S). Note that the intent is that the value is the name of R or S, not the entire relation.

The Reduce Function For each key t, do the following.

(1) If the associated value list is $[R]$, then produce (t, t).
(2) If the associated value list is anything else, which could only be $[R, S]$, $[S, R]$, or $[S]$, produce (t, NULL).

2.3.7   Computing Natural Join by Map-Reduce

The idea behind implementing natural join via map-reduce can be seen if we look at the specific case of joining $R(A, B)$ with $S(B, C)$. We must find tuples that agree on their B components, that is the second component from tuples of R and the first component of tuples of S. We shall use the B-value of tuples from either relation as the key. The value will be the other component and the name of the relation, so the Reduce function can know where each tuple came from.

The Map Function For each tuple (a, b) of R, produce the key-value pair $\big(b, (R, a)\big)$. For each tuple (b, c) of S, produce the key-value pair $\big(b, (S, c)\big)$.

The Reduce Function Each key value b will be associated with a list of pairs that are either of the form (R, a) or (S, c). Construct all pairs consisting of one with first component R and the other with first component S, say (R, a) and (S, c). The output for key b is $(b, [(a_1, b, c_1), (a_2, b, c_2), \ldots])$, that is, b associated with the list of tuples that can be formed from an R-tuple and an S-tuple with a common b value.

There are a few observations we should make about this join algorithm. First, the relation that is the result of the join is recovered by taking all the tuples that appear on the lists for any key. Second, map-reduce implementations such as Hadoop pass values to the Reduce tasks sorted by key. If so, then identifying all the tuples from both relations that have key b is easy. If another implementation were not to provide key-value pairs sorted by key, then the Reduce function could still manage its task efficiently by hashing key-value pairs locally by key. If enough buckets were used, most buckets would have only one key. Finally, if there are n tuples of R with B-value b and m tuples from S with B-value b, then there are mn tuples with middle component b in the result. In the extreme case, all tuples from R and S have the same b-value, and we are really taking a Cartesian product. However, it is quite common for the number of tuples with shared B-values to be small, and in that case, the time complexity of the Reduce function is closer to linear in the relation sizes than to quadratic.

2.3.8 Generalizing the Join Algorithm

The same algorithm works if the relations have more than two attributes. You can think of A as representing all those attributes in the schema of R but not S. B represents the attributes in both schemas, and C represents attributes only in the schema of S. The key for a tuple of R or S is the list of values in all the attributes that are in the schemas of both R and S. The value for a tuple of R is the name R and the values of all the attributes of R but not S, and the value for a tuple of S is the name S and the values of the attributes of S but not R.

The Reduce function looks at all the key-value pairs with a given key and combines those values from R with those values of S in all possible ways. From each pairing, the tuple produced has the values from R, the key values, and the values from S.

2.3.9 Grouping and Aggregation by Map-Reduce

As with the join, we shall discuss the minimal example of grouping and aggregation, where there is one grouping attribute and one aggregation. Let $R(A, B, C)$ be a relation to which we apply the operator $\gamma_{A, \theta(B)}(R)$. Map will perform the grouping, while Reduce does the aggregation.

The Map Function For each tuple (a, b, c) produce the key-value pair (a, b).

The Reduce Function Each key a represents a group. Apply the aggregation operator θ to the list $[b_1, b_2, \ldots, b_n]$ of B-values associated with key a. The output is the pair (a, x), where x is the result of applying θ to the list. For example, if θ is SUM, then $x = b_1 + b_2 + \cdots + b_n$, and if θ is MAX, then x is the largest of $b_1, b_2, \ldots, b_n$.

If there are several grouping attributes, then the key is the list of the values of a tuple for all these attributes. If there is more than one aggregation, then the Reduce function applies each of them to the list of values associated with a given key and produces a tuple consisting of the key, including components for all grouping attributes if there is more than one, followed by the results of each of the aggregations.

2.3.10   Matrix Multiplication

If M is a matrix with element m_{ij} in row i and column j, and N is a matrix with element n_{jk} in row j and column k, then the product $P = MN$ is the matrix P with element p_{ik} in row i and column k, where

$$p_{ik} = \sum_j m_{ij} n_{jk}$$

It is required that the number of columns of M equals the number of rows of N, so the sum over j makes sense.

We can think of a matrix as a relation with three attributes: the row number, the column number, and the value in that row and column. Thus, we could view matrix M as a relation $M(I, J, V)$, with tuples (i, j, m_{ij}) and we could view matrix N as a relation $N(J, K, W)$, with tuples (j, k, n_{jk}). As large matrices are often sparse (mostly 0's), and since we can omit the tuples for matrix elements that are 0, this relational representation is often a very good one for a large matrix. However, it is possible that i, j, and k are implicit in the position of a matrix element in the file that represents it, rather than written explicitly with the element itself. In that case, the Map function will have to be designed to construct the I, J, and K components of tuples from the position of the data.

The product MN is almost a natural join followed by grouping and aggregation. That is, the natural join of $M(I, J, V)$ and $N(J, K, W)$, having only attribute J in common, would produce tuples (i, j, k, v, w) from each tuple (i, j, v) in M and tuple (j, k, w) in N. This five-component tuple represents the pair of matrix elements (m_{ij}, n_{jk}). What we want instead is the product of these elements, that is, the four-component tuple $(i, j, k, v \times w)$, because that represents the product $m_{ij} n_{jk}$. Once we have this relation as the result of one map-reduce operation, we can perform grouping and aggregation, with I and K as the grouping attributes and the sum of $V \times W$ as the aggregation. That is, we can implement matrix multiplication as the cascade of two map-reduce operations, as follows. First:

The Map Function Send each matrix element m_{ij} to the key value pair

$$\big(j, (M, i, m_{ij})\big)$$

Send each matrix element n_{jk} to the key value pair $\big(j, (N, k, n_{jk})\big)$.

The Reduce Function For each key j, examine its list of associated values. For each value that comes from M, say (M, i, m_{ij}), and each value that comes from N, say (N, k, n_{jk}), produce the tuple $(i, k, m_{ij}n_{jk})$. Note that the output of the Reduce function is a key j paired with the list of all the tuples of this form that we get from j.

Now, we perform a grouping and aggregation by another map-reduce operation.

The Map Function The elements to which this Map function is applied are the pairs that are output from the previous Reduce function. These pairs are of the form

$$\big(j, [(i_1, k_1, v_1),\ (i_2, k_2, v_2), \dots, (i_p, k_p, v_p)]\big)$$

where each v_q is the product of elements $m_{i_q j}$ and $n_{j k_q}$. From this element we produce p key-value pairs:

$$\big((i_1, k_1), v_1\big),\ \big((i_2, k_2), v_2\big), \dots, \big((i_p, k_p), v_p\big)$$

The Reduce Function For each key (i, k), produce the sum of the list of values associated with this key. The result is a pair $\big((i, k), v\big)$, where v is the value of the element in row i and column k of the matrix $P = MN$.

2.3.11 Matrix Multiplication with One Map-Reduce Step

There often is more than one way to use map-reduce to solve a problem. You may wish to use only a single map-reduce pass to perform matrix multiplication $P = MN$. It is possible to do so if we put more work into the two functions. Start by using the Map function to create the sets of matrix elements that are needed to compute each element of the answer P. Notice that an element of M or N contributes to many elements of the result, so one input element will be turned into many key-value pairs. The keys will be pairs (i, k), where i is a row of M and k is a column of N. Here is a synopsis of the Map and Reduce functions.

The Map Function For each element m_{ij} of M, produce a key-value pair $\big((i, k),\ (M, j, m_{ij})\big)$ for $k = 1, 2, \dots$, up to the number of columns of N. Also, for each element n_{jk} of N, produce a key-value pair $\big((i, k),\ (N, j, n_{jk})\big)$ for $i = 1, 2, \dots$, up to the number of rows of M.

The Reduce Function Each key (i, k) will have an associated list with all the values (M, j, m_{ij}) and (N, j, n_{jk}), for all possible values of j. The Reduce function needs to connect the two values on the list that have the same value of j, for each j. An easy way to do this step is to sort by j the values that begin with M and sort by j the values that begin with N, in separate lists. The jth values on each list must have their third components, m_{ij} and n_{jk} extracted and multiplied. Then, these products are summed and the result is paired with (i, k) in the output of the Reduce function.

You may notice that if a row of the matrix M or a column of the matrix N is so large that it will not fit in main memory, then the Reduce tasks will be forced to use an external sort to order the values associated with a given key (i, k). However, it that case, the matrices themselves are so large, perhaps 10^{20} elements, that it is unlikely we would attempt this calculation if the matrices were dense. If they are sparse, then we would expect many fewer values to be associated with any one key, and it would be feasible to do the sum of products in main memory.

2.3.12   Exercises for Section 2.3

EXERCISE 2.3.1   Design map-reduce algorithms to take a very large file of integers and produce as output:

(a) The largest integer.
(b) The average of all the integers.
(c) The same set of integers, but with each integer appearing only once.
(d) The count of the number of distinct integers in the input.

EXERCISE 2.3.2   Our formulation of matrix-vector multiplication assumed that the matrix M was square. Generalize the algorithm to the case where M is an r-by-c matrix for some number of rows r and columns c.

! EXERCISE 2.3.3   In the form of relational algebra implemented in SQL, relations are not sets, but bags; that is, tuples are allowed to appear more than once. There are extended definitions of union, intersection, and difference for bags, which we shall define below. Write map-reduce algorithms for computing the following operations on bags R and S:

(a) *Bag Union*, defined to be the bag of tuples in which tuple t appears the sum of the numbers of times it appears in R and S.
(b) *Bag Intersection*, defined to be the bag of tuples in which tuple t appears the minimum of the numbers of times it appears in R and S.
(c) *Bag Difference*, defined to be the bag of tuples in which the number of times a tuple t appears is equal to the number of times it appears in R minus the number of times it appears in S. A tuple that appears more times in S than in R does not appear in the difference.

! EXERCISE 2.3.4   Selection can also be performed on bags. Give a map-reduce implementation that produces the proper number of copies of each tuple t that passes the selection condition. That is, produce key-value pairs from which the correct result of the selection can be obtained easily from the values.

EXERCISE 2.3.5   The relational-algebra operation $R(A, B) \bowtie_{B < C} S(C, D)$ produces all tuples (a, b, c, d) such that tuple (a, b) is in relation R, tuple (c, d) is in S, and $b < c$. Give a map-reduce implementation of this operation, assuming R and S are sets.

2.4   Extensions to Map-Reduce

Map-reduce has proved so influential that it has spawned a number of extensions and modifications. These systems typically share a number of characteristics with map-reduce systems:

(1) They are built on a distributed file system.
(2) They manage very large numbers of tasks that are instantiations of a small number of user-written functions.
(3) They incorporate a method for dealing with most of the failures that occur during the execution of a large job, without having to restart that job from the beginning.

In this section, we shall mention some of the interesting directions being explored. References to the details of the systems mentioned can be found in the bibliographic notes for this chapter.

2.4.1   Workflow Systems

Two experimental systems called Clustera from the University of Wisconsin and Hyracks from the University of California at Irvine extend map-reduce from the simple two-step workflow (the Map function feeds the Reduce function) to any collection of functions, with an acyclic graph representing workflow among the functions. That is, there is an acyclic *flow graph* whose arcs $a \rightarrow b$ represent the fact that function a's output is input to function b. A suggestion of what a workflow might look like is in Fig. 2.6. There, five functions, f through j, pass data from left to right in specific ways, so the flow of data is acyclic and no task needs to provide data out before its input is available. For instance, function h takes ts input from a preexisting file of the distributed file system. Each of h's output elements is passed to at least one of the functions i and j.

In analogy to Map and Reduce functions, each function of a workflow can be executed by many tasks, each of which is assigned a portion of the input to the function. A master controller is responsible for dividing the work among the tasks that implement a function, usually by hashing the input elements to decide on the proper task to receive an element. Thus, like Map tasks, each task

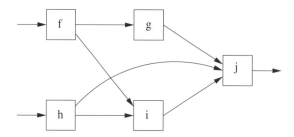

Figure 2.6 An example of a workflow that is more complex than Map feeding Reduce

implementing a function f has an output file of data destined for each of the tasks that implement the successor function(s) of f. These files are delivered by the Master at the appropriate time – after the task has completed its work.

The functions of a workflow, and therefore the tasks, share with map-reduce tasks the important property that they only deliver output after they complete. As a result, if a task fails, it has not delivered output to any of its successors in the flow graph. A master controller can therefore restart the failed task at another compute node, without worrying that the output of the restarted task will duplicate output that previously was passed to some other task.

Many applications of workflow systems such as Clustera or Hyracks are cascades of map-reduce jobs. An example would be the join of three relations, where one map-reduce job joins the first two relations, and a second map-reduce job joins the third relation with the result of joining the first two relations. Both jobs would use an algorithm like that of Section 2.3.7.

There is an advantage to implementing such cascades as a single workflow. For example, the flow of data among tasks, and its replication, can be managed by the master controller, without need to store the temporary file that is output of one map-reduce job in the distributed file system. By locating tasks at compute nodes that have a copy of their input, we can avoid much of the communication that would be necessary if we stored the result of one map-reduce job and then initiated a second map-reduce job (although Hadoop and other map-reduce systems also try to locate Map tasks where a copy of their input is already present).

2.4.2 Recursive Extensions to Map-Reduce

Many large-scale computations are really recursions. An important example is PageRank, which is the subject of Chapter 5. That computation is, in simple terms, the computation of the fixedpoint of a matrix-vector multiplication. It is computed under map-reduce systems by the iterated application of the matrix-vector multiplication algorithm described in Section 2.3.1, or by a more complex strategy that we shall introduce in Section 5.2. The iteration typically continues for an unknown number of steps, each step being a map-reduce job, until the results of two consecutive iterations are sufficiently close that we believe convergence has occurred.

The reason recursions are normally implemented by iterated map-reduce jobs is that a true recursive task does not have the property necessary for independent restart of failed tasks. It is impossible for a collection of mutually recursive tasks, each of which has an output that is input to at least some of the other tasks, to produce output only at the end of the task. If they all followed that policy, no task would ever receive any input, and nothing could be accomplished. As a result, some mechanism other than simple restart of failed tasks must be implemented in a system that handles recursive workflows (flow graphs that are not acyclic). We shall start by studying an example of a recursion implemented as a workflow, and then discuss approaches to dealing with task failures.

EXAMPLE 2.6   Suppose we have a directed graph whose arcs are represented by the relation $E(X, Y)$, meaning that there is an arc from node X to node Y. We wish to compute the paths relation $P(X, Y)$, meaning that there is a path of length 1 or more from node X to node Y. A simple recursive algorithm to do so is:

(1) Start with $P(X, Y) = E(X, Y)$.
(2) While changes to the relation P occur, add to P all tuples in

$$\pi_{X,Y}\bigl(R(X, Z) \bowtie R(Z, Y)\bigr)$$

That is, find pairs of nodes X and Y such that for some node Z there is known to be a path from X to Z and also a path from Z to Y.

Figure 2.7 suggests how we could organize recursive tasks to perform this computation. There are two kinds of tasks: *Join tasks* and *Dup-elim tasks*. There are n Join tasks, for some n, and each corresponds to a bucket of a hash function h. A path tuple $P(a, b)$, when it is discovered, becomes input to two Join tasks: those numbered $h(a)$ and $h(b)$. The job of the ith Join task, when it receives input tuple $P(a, b)$, is to find certain other tuples seen previously (and stored locally by that task).

(1) Store $P(a, b)$ locally.
(2) If $h(a) = i$ then look for tuples $P(x, a)$ and produce output tuple $P(x, b)$.
(3) If $h(b) = i$ then look for tuples $P(b, y)$ and produce output tuple $P(a, y)$.

Note that in rare cases, we have $h(a) = h(b)$, so both (2) and (3) are executed. But generally, only one of these needs to be executed for a given tuple.

There are also m Dup-elim tasks, and each corresponds to a bucket of a hash function g that takes two arguments. If $P(c, d)$ is an output of some Join task, then it is sent to Dup-elim task $j = g(c, d)$. On receiving this tuple, the jth Dup-elim task checks that it had not received it before, since its job is duplicate elimination. If previously received, the tuple is ignored. But if this tuple is new, it is stored locally and sent to two Join tasks, those numbered $h(c)$ and $h(d)$.

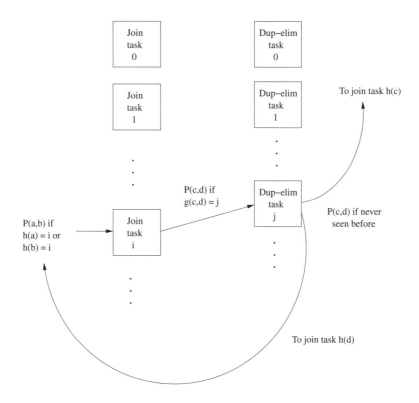

Figure 2.7 Implementation of transitive closure by a collection of recursive tasks

Every Join task has m output files – one for each Dup-elim task – and every Dup-elim task has n output files – one for each Join task. These files may be distributed according to any of several strategies. Initially, the $E(a,b)$ tuples representing the arcs of the graph are distributed to the Dup-elim tasks, with $E(a,b)$ being sent as $P(a,b)$ to Dup-elim task $g(a,b)$. The Master can wait until each Join task has processed its entire input for a round. Then, all output files are distributed to the Dup-elim tasks, which create their own output. That output is distributed to the Join tasks and becomes their input for the next round. Alternatively, each task can wait until it has produced enough output to justify transmitting its output files to their destination, even if the task has not consumed all its input.

In Example 2.6 it is not essential to have two kinds of tasks. Rather, Join tasks could eliminate duplicates as they are received, since they must store their previously received inputs anyway. However, this arrangement has an advantage when we must recover from a task failure. If each task stores all the output files it has ever created, and we place Join tasks on different racks from the Dup-elim tasks, then we can deal with any single compute node or single rack failure. That is, a Join task needing to be restarted can get all the previously generated inputs that it needs from the Dup-elim tasks, and vice-versa.

In the particular case of computing transitive closure, it is not necessary to prevent a restarted task from generating outputs that the original task generated previously. In the computation of the transitive closure, the rediscovery of a path does not influence the eventual answer. However, many computations cannot tolerate a situation where both the original and restarted versions of a task pass the same output to another task. For example, if the final step of the computation were an aggregation, say a count of the number of nodes reached by each node in the graph, then we would get the wrong answer if we counted a path twice. In such a case, the master controller can record what files each task generated and passed to other tasks. It can then restart a failed task and ignore those files when the restarted version produces them a second time.

2.4.3   Pregel

Another approach to managing failures when implementing recursive algorithms on a computing cluster is represented by the Pregel system. This system views its data as a graph. Each node of the graph corresponds roughly to a task (although in practice many nodes of a large graph would be bundled into a single task, as in the Join tasks of Example 2.6). Each graph node generates output messages that are destined for other nodes of the graph, and each graph node processes the inputs it receives from other nodes.

EXAMPLE 2.7   Suppose our data is a collection of weighted arcs of a graph, and we want to find, for each node of the graph, the length of the shortest path to each of the other nodes. Initially, each graph node a stores the set of pairs (b, w) such that there is an arc from a to b of weight w. These facts are initially sent to all other nodes, as triples (a, b, w).[6] When the node a receives a triple (c, d, w), it looks up its current distance to c; that is, it finds the pair (c, v) stored locally, if there is one. It also finds the pair (d, u) if there is one. If $w + v < u$, then the pair (d, u) is replaced by $(d, w + v)$, and if there was no pair (d, u), then the pair $(d, w + v)$ is stored at the node a. Also, the other nodes are sent the message $(a, d, w + v)$ in either of these two cases.

Computations in Pregel are organized into *supersteps*. In one superstep, all the messages that were received by any of the nodes at the previous superstep (or initially, if it is the first superstep) are processed, and then all the messages generated by those nodes are sent to their destination.

In case of a compute-node failure, there is no attempt to restart the failed tasks at that compute node. Rather, Pregel *checkpoints* its entire computation after some of the supersteps. A checkpoint consists of making a copy of the entire state

---

[6] This algorithm uses much too much communication, but it will serve as a simple example of the Pregel computation model.

of each task, so it can be restarted from that point if necessary. If any compute node fails, the entire job is restarted from the most recent checkpoint.

Although this recovery strategy causes many tasks that have not failed to redo their work, it is satisfactory in many situations. Recall that the reason map-reduce systems support restart of only the failed tasks is that we want assurance that the expected time to complete the entire job in the face of failures is not too much greater than the time to run the job with no failures. Any failure-management system will have that property as long as the time to recover from a failure is much less than the average time between failures. Thus, it is only necessary that Pregel checkpoints its computation after a number of supersteps such that the probability of a failure during that number of supersteps is low.

2.4.4   Exercises for Section 2.4

! EXERCISE 2.4.1   Suppose a job consists of n tasks, each of which takes time t seconds. Thus, if there are no failures, the sum over all compute nodes of the time taken to execute tasks at that node is nt. Suppose also that the probability of a task failing is p per job per second, and when a task fails, the overhead of management of the restart is such that it adds $10t$ seconds to the total execution time of the job. What is the total expected execution time of the job?

! EXERCISE 2.4.2   Suppose a Pregel job has a probability p of a failure during any superstep. Suppose also that the execution time (summed over all compute nodes) of taking a checkpoint is c times the time it takes to execute a superstep. To minimize the expected execution time of the job, how many supersteps should elapse between checkpoints?

2.5   Efficiency of Cluster-Computing Algorithms

In this section we shall introduce a model for measuring the quality of algorithms implemented on a computing cluster of the type so far discussed in this chapter. We assume the computation is described by an acyclic workflow, as discussed in Section 2.4.1. We then argue that for many applications, the bottleneck is moving data among tasks, such as transporting the outputs of Map tasks to their proper Reduce tasks. As an example, we explore the computation of multiway joins as single map-reduce jobs, and we see that in some situations, this approach is more efficient than the straightforward cascade of 2-way joins.

2.5.1   The Communication-Cost Model for Cluster Computing

Imagine that an algorithm is implemented by an acyclic network of tasks. These could be Map tasks feeding Reduce tasks, as in a standard map-reduce algorithm, or they could be several map-reduce jobs cascaded, or a more general workflow structure, such as a collection of tasks each of which implements the workflow of Fig. 2.6.[7] The *communication cost* of a task is the size of the input to the task. This size can be measured in bytes. However, since we shall be using relational database operations as examples, we shall often use the number of tuples as a measure of size.

The *communication cost of an algorithm* is the sum of the communication cost of all the tasks implementing that algorithm. We shall focus on the communication cost as the way to measure the efficiency of an algorithm. In particular, we do not consider the amount of time it takes each task to execute when estimating the running time of an algorithm. While there are exceptions, where execution time of tasks dominates, we justify the focus on communication cost as follows.

- The algorithm executed by each task tends to be very simple, at most linear in the size of its input.
- The typical interconnect speed for a computing cluster is gigabit. That may seem like a lot, but it is slow compared with the speed at which a processor executes instructions. As a result, the compute node can do a lot of work on a received input element in the time it takes to deliver that element.
- Even if a task executes at a compute node that has a copy of the chunk(s) on which the task operates, that chunk normally will be stored on disk, and the time taken to move the data into main memory may exceed the time needed to operate on the data once it is available in memory.

Assuming that communication cost is the dominant cost, we might still ask why we count only input size, and not output size. The answer to this question involves two points:

(1) If the output of one task τ is input to another task, then the size of τ's output will be accounted for when measuring the input size for the receiving task. Thus, there is no reason to count the size of any output except for those tasks whose output forms the result of the entire algorithm.

(2) In practice, the output of a job is rarely large compared with the input or the intermediate data produced by the job. The reason is that massive outputs cannot be used unless they are summarized or aggregated in some way. For example, although we talked in Example 2.6 of computing the entire transitive closure of a graph, in practice we would want something much simpler, such as the count of the number of nodes reachable from each node, or the set of nodes reachable from a single node.

EXAMPLE 2.8 Let us evaluate the communication cost for the join algorithm from Section 2.3.7. Suppose we are joining $R(A, B) \bowtie S(B, C)$, and the sizes of relations R and S are r and s, respectively. Each chunk of the files holding R and S is fed to one Map task, so the sum of the communication costs for

---

[7] Note that this figure represented functions, not tasks. As a network of tasks, there would be, for example, many tasks implementing function f, each of which feeds data to each of the tasks for function g and each of the tasks for function i.

all the Map tasks is $r + s$. Note that in a typical execution, the Map tasks will each be executed at a compute node holding a copy of the chunk to which it applies. Thus, no internode communication is needed for the Map tasks, but they still must read their data from disk. Since all the Map tasks do is make a simple transformation of each input tuple into a key-value pair, we expect that the computation cost will be small compared with the communication cost, regardless of whether the input is local to the task or must be transported to its compute node.

The sum of the outputs of the Map tasks is roughly as large as their inputs. Each output key-value pair is sent to exactly one Reduce task, and it is unlikely that this Reduce task will execute at the same compute node. Therefore, communication from Map tasks to Reduce tasks is likely to be across the interconnect of the cluster, rather than memory-to-disk. This communication is $O(r + s)$, so the communication cost of the join algorithm is $O(r + s)$.

Observe that the Reduce tasks can use a hash join of the tuples received. This process involves hashing each of the tuples received on their B-values, using a different hash function from the one that divided the tuples among Reduce tasks. The local hash join takes time that is linear in the number of tuples received, and thus is also $O(r + s)$. We do not count this execution time in the communication-cost model, but it is comforting to know that the computation cost is surely not the dominant factor for this algorithm.

The output size for the join can be either larger or smaller than $r + s$, depending on how likely it is that a given R-tuple joins with a given S-tuple. For example, if there are many different B-values, we would expect the output to be small, while if there are few B-values, a large output is likely. However, we shall rely on our supposition that if the output of the join is large, then there is probably some aggregation being done to reduce the size of the output. This aggregation typically can be executed by the Reduce tasks as they produce their output.

2.5.2   Elapsed Communication Cost

There is another measure of cost based on communication that is worth mentioning, although we shall not use in the developments of this section. The *elapsed communication cost* is the maximum, over all paths through the acyclic network, of the sum of the communication costs of the tasks along that path. For example, in a map-reduce job, the elapsed communication cost is the sum of the maximum input size for any Map task, plus the maximum input size for any Reduce task.

Elapsed communication cost corresponds to the minimum wall-clock time for the execution of a parallel algorithm. Using careless reasoning, one could minimize total communication cost by assigning all the work to one task, and thereby minimize total communication. However, the elapsed time of such an algorithm would be quite high. The algorithms we suggest, or have suggested so far, have the property that the work is divided fairly among the tasks, so the elapsed communication cost would be approximately as small as it could be.

2.5.3   Multiway Joins

To see how analyzing the communication cost can help us choose an algorithm in the cluster-computing environment, we shall examine carefully the case of a multiway join. There is a general theory in which we:

(1) Select certain attributes of the relations involved in a natural join to have their values hashed to some number of buckets.

(2) Select the number of buckets for each of these attributes, subject to the constraint that the product of the numbers of buckets for each attribute is k, the number of Reduce tasks that will be used.

(3) Identify each of the k Reduce tasks with a vector of bucket numbers, one for each of the hashed attributes.

(4) Send tuples of each relation to all those Reduce tasks where it might find tuples to join with. That is, the given tuple t will have values for some of the hashed attributes, so we can apply the hash function(s) to those values to determine certain components of the vector identifying the Reduce tasks. Other components of the vector are unknown, so t must be sent to all the Reduce tasks having any value in these unknown components.

Some examples of this general technique appear in the exercises.

Here, we shall look only at the join $R(A, B) \bowtie S(B, C) \bowtie T(C, D)$. Suppose that the relations R, S, and T have sizes r, s, and t, respectively, and for simplicity, suppose that the probability is p that

(1) An R-tuple and and S-tuple agree on B, and also the probability that

(2) An S-tuple and a T-tuple agree on C.

If we join R and S first, using the map-reduce algorithm of Section 2.3.7, then the communication cost is $O(r + s)$, and the size of the intermediate join $R \bowtie S$ is prs. When we join this result with T, the communication of this second map-reduce job is $O(t + prs)$. Thus, the entire communication cost of the algorithm consisting of two 2-way joins is $O(r+s+t+prs)$. If we instead join S and T first, and then join R with the result, we get another algorithm whose communication cost is $O(r + s + t + pst)$.

A third way to take this join is to use a single map-reduce job that joins the three relations at once. Suppose that we plan to use k Reduce tasks for this job. Pick numbers b and c representing the number of buckets into which we shall hash B- and C-values, respectively. Let h be a hash function that sends B-values into b buckets, and let g be another hash function that sends C-values into c buckets. We require that $bc = k$; that is, each Reduce task corresponds to a pair of buckets, one for the B-value and one for the C-value. The Reduce task corresponding to bucket pair (i, j) is responsible for joining the tuples $R(u, v)$, $S(v, w)$, and $T(w, x)$ whenever $h(v) = i$ and $g(w) = j$.

As a result, the Map tasks that send tuples of R, S, and T to the Reduce tasks that need them must send R- and T-tuples to more than one Reduce task. For an S-tuple $S(v, w)$, we know the B- and C-values, so we can send this tuple only to the Reduce task $(h(v), g(w))$. However, consider an R-tuple $R(u, v)$. We know it only needs to go to Reduce tasks $(h(v), y)$, but we don't know the value of y. The value of C could be anything as far as we know. Thus, we must send $R(u, v)$ to c reduce tasks, since y could be any of the c buckets for C-values. Similarly, we must send the T-tuple $T(w, x)$ to each of the Reduce tasks $(z, g(w))$ for any z. There are b such tasks.

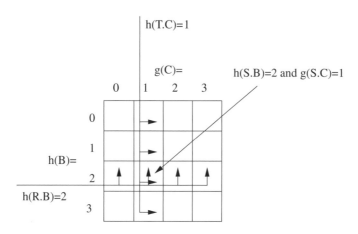

Figure 2.8 Sixteen Reduce tasks together perform a 3-way join

EXAMPLE 2.9   Suppose that $b = c = 4$, so $k = 16$. The sixteen Reduce tasks can be thought of as arranged in a rectangle, as suggested by Fig. 2.8. There, we see a hypothetical S-tuple $S(v, w)$ for which $h(v) = 2$ and $g(w) = 1$. This tuple is sent by its Map task only to the Reduce task $(2, 1)$. We also see an R-tuple $R(u, v)$. Since $h(v) = 2$, this tuple is sent to all Reduce tasks $(2, y)$, for $y = 1, 2, 3, 4$. Finally, we see a T-tuple $T(w, x)$. Since $g(w) = 1$, this tuple is sent to all Reduce tasks $(z, 1)$ for $z = 1, 2, 3, 4$. Notice that these three tuples join, and they meet at exactly one Reduce task, the task numbered $(2, 1)$.

Now, suppose that the sizes of R, S, and T are different; recall we use r, s, and t, respectively, for those sizes. If we hash B-values to b buckets and C-values to c buckets, where $bc = k$, then the total communication cost for moving the tuples to the proper Reduce task is the sum of:

(1) s to move each tuple $S(v, w)$ once to the Reduce task $(h(v), g(w))$.
(2) cr to move each tuple $R(u, v)$ to the c Reduce tasks $(h(v), y)$ for each of the c possible values of y.
(3) bt to move each tuple $T(w, x)$ to the b Reduce tasks $(z, g(w))$ for each of the b possible values of z.

There is also a cost $r + s + t$ to make each tuple of each relation be input to one of the Map tasks. This cost is fixed, independent of b, c, and k.

Computation Cost of the 3-Way Join

Each of the Reduce tasks must join of parts of the three relations, and it is reasonable to ask whether this join can be taken in time that is linear in the size of the input to that Reduce task. While more complex joins might not be computable in linear time, the join of our running example can be executed at each Reduce process efficiently. First, create an index on $R.B$, to organize the R-tuples received. Likewise, create an index on $T.C$ for the T-tuples. Then, consider each received S-tuple, $S(v, w)$. Use the index on $R.B$ to find all R-tuples with $R.B = v$ and use the index on $T.C$ to find all T-tuples with $T.C = w$.

We must select b and c, subject to the constraint $bc = k$, to minimize $s+cr+bt$. We shall use the technique of Lagrangean multipliers to find the place where the function $s + cr + bt - \lambda(bc - k)$ has its derivatives with respect to b and c equal to 0. That is, we must solve the equations $r - \lambda b = 0$ and $t - \lambda c = 0$. Since $r = \lambda b$ and $t = \lambda c$, we may multiply corresponding sides of these equations to get $rt = \lambda^2 bc$. Since $bc = k$, we get $rt = \lambda^2 k$, or $\lambda = \sqrt{rt/k}$. Thus, the minimum communication cost is obtained when $c = t/\lambda = \sqrt{kt/r}$, and $b = r/\lambda = \sqrt{kr/t}$.

If we substitute these values into the formula $s + cr + bt$, we get $s + 2\sqrt{krt}$. That is the communication cost for the Reduce tasks, to which we must add the cost $s + r + t$ for the communication cost of the Map tasks. The latter term typically will be smaller than the first term by a factor $O(\sqrt{k})$, so we can neglect it in most situations, as long as the number of Reduce tasks is reasonably large.

EXAMPLE 2.10   Let us see under what circumstances the 3-way join has lower communication cost than the cascade of two 2-way joins. To make matters simple, let us assume that R, S, and T are all the same relation R, which represents the "friends" relation in a social network like Facebook. There are roughly 300,000,000 subscribers on Facebook, with an average of 300 friends each, so relation R has $r = 9 \times 10^{10}$ tuples. Suppose we want to compute $R \bowtie R \bowtie R$, perhaps as part of a calculation to find the number of friends of friends of friends each subscriber has, or perhaps just the person with the largest number of friends of friends of friends.[8] The cost of the 3-way join of R with itself is $4r + 2r\sqrt{k}$; $3r$ represents the cost of the Map tasks, and $r + 2\sqrt{kr^2}$ is the cost of the Reduce tasks. Since we assume $r = 9 \times 10^{10}$, this cost is $3.6 \times 10^{11} + 1.8 \times 10^{11}\sqrt{k}$.

Now consider the communication cost of joining R with itself, and then joining the result with R again. The Map and Reduce tasks for the first join each have a cost of $2r$, so the first join only costs $4r = 3.6 \times 10^{11}$. But the size of $R \bowtie R$ is large. We cannot say exactly how large, since friends tend to fall into cliques, and therefore a person with 300 friends will have many fewer than the maximum possible number of friends of friends, which is 90,000. Let us estimate conservatively that the size of $R \bowtie R$ is not $300r$, but only $30r$, or 2.7×10^{12}. The communication

---

[8] This person, or more generally, people with large extended circles of friends, are good people to use to start a marketing campaign by giving them free samples.

Star Joins

A common structure for data mining of commercial data is the *star join*. For example, a chain store like Walmart keeps a *fact table* whose tuples each represent a single sale. This relation looks like $F(A_1, A_2, \ldots)$, where each attribute A_i is a key representing one of the important components of the sale, such as the purchaser, the item purchased, the store branch, or the date. For each key attribute there is a *dimension table* giving information about the participant. For instance, the dimension table $D(A_1, B_{11}, B_{12}, \ldots)$ might represent purchasers. A_1 is the purchaser ID, the key for this relation. The B_{1i}'s might give the purchaser's name, address, phone, and so on. Typically, the fact table is much larger than the dimension tables. For instance, there might be a fact table of a billion tuples and ten dimension tables of a million tuples each.

Analysts mine this data by asking *analytic queries* that typically join the fact table with several of the dimension tables (a "star join") and then aggregate the result into a useful form. For instance, an analyst might ask "give me a table of sales of pants, broken down by region and color, for each month of 2010." Under the communication-cost model of this section, joining the fact table and dimension tables by a multiway join is almost certain to be more efficient than joining the relations in pairs. In fact, it may make sense to store the fact table over however many compute nodes are available, and replicate the dimension tables permanently in exactly the same way as we would replicate them should we take the join of the fact table and all the dimension tables. In this special case, only the key attributes (the A's above) are hashed to buckets, and the number of buckets for each key attribute is inversely proportional to the size of its dimension table.

---

cost for the second join of $(R \bowtie R) \bowtie R$ is thus $5.4 \times 10^{12} + 1.8 \times 10^{11}$. The total cost of the two joins is therefore $3.6 \times 10^{11} + 5.4 \times 10^{12} + 1.8 \times 10^{11} = 5.94 \times 10^{12}$.

We must ask whether the cost of the 3-way join, which is

$$3.6 \times 10^{11} + 1.8 \times 10^{11} \sqrt{k}$$

is less than 5.94×10^{12}. That is so, provided $1.8 \times 10^{11} \sqrt{k} < 5.58 \times 10^{12}$, or $\sqrt{k} < 31$. That is, the 3-way join will be preferable provided we use no more than $31^2 = 961$ Reduce tasks.

2.5.4   Exercises for Section 2.5

EXERCISE 2.5.1   What is the communication cost of each of the following algorithms, as a function of the size of the relations, matrices, or vectors to which they are applied?

(a) The matrix-vector multiplication algorithm of Section 2.3.2.
(b) The union algorithm of Section 2.3.6.
(c) The aggregation algorithm of Section 2.3.9.
(d) The matrix-multiplication algorithm of Section 2.3.11.

! EXERCISE 2.5.2   Suppose relations R, S, and T have sizes r, s, and t, respectively, and we want to take the 3-way join $R(A, B) \bowtie S(B, C) \bowtie T(A, C)$, using k Reduce tasks. We shall hash values of attributes A, B, and C to a, b, and c buckets, respectively, where $abc = k$. Each Reduce task is associated with a vector of buckets, one for each of the three hash functions. Find, as a function of r, s, t, and k, the values of a, b, and c that minimize the communication cost of the algorithm.

! EXERCISE 2.5.3   Suppose we take a star join of a fact table $F(A_1, A_2, \ldots, A_m)$ with dimension tables $D_i(A_i, B_i)$ for $i = 1, 2, \ldots, m$. Let there be k Reduce tasks, each associated with a vector of buckets, one for each of the key attributes $A_1, A_2, \ldots, A_m$. Suppose the number of buckets into which we hash A_i is a_i. Naturally, $a_1 a_2 \cdots a_m = k$. Finally, suppose each dimension table D_i has size d_i, and the size of the fact table is much larger than any of these sizes. Find the values of the a_i's that minimize the cost of taking the star join as one map-reduce operation.

2.6   Summary of Chapter 2

✦ *Cluster Computing*: A common architecture for very large-scale applications is a cluster of compute nodes (processor chip, main memory, and disk). Compute nodes are mounted in racks, and the nodes on a rack are connected, typically by gigabit Ethernet. Racks are also connected by a high-speed network or switch.

✦ *Distributed File Systems*: An architecture for very large-scale file systems has developed recently. Files are composed of chunks of about 64 megabytes, and each chunk is replicated several times, on different compute nodes or racks.

✦ *Map-Reduce*: This programming system allows one to exploit parallelism inherent in cluster computing, and manages the hardware failures that can occur during a long computation on many nodes. Many Map tasks and many Reduce tasks are managed by a Master process. Tasks on a failed compute node are rerun by the Master.

✦ *The Map Function*: This function is written by the user. It takes a collection of input objects and turns each into zero or more key-value pairs. Key values are not necessarily unique.

✦ *The Reduce Function*: A map-reduce programming system sorts all the key-value pairs produced by all the Map tasks, forms all the values associated with a given key into a list and distributes key-list pairs to Reduce tasks. Each reduce task combines the elements on each list, by applying the function written by the user. The results produced by all the Reduce tasks form the output of the map-reduce process.

✦ *Hadoop*: This programming system is an open-source implementation of a distributed file system (HDFS, the Hadoop Distributed File System) and map-reduce (Hadoop itself). It is available through the Apache Foundation.

✦ *Managing Compute-Node Failures*: Map-reduce systems support restart of tasks that fail because their compute node, or the rack containing that node, fail. Because Map and Reduce tasks deliver their output only after they finish, it is possible to restart a failed task without concern for possible repetition of the effects of that task. It is necessary to restart the entire job only if the node at which the Master executes fails.

✦ *Applications of Map-Reduce*: While not all parallel algorithms are suitable for implementation in the map-reduce framework, there are simple implementations of matrix-vector and matrix-matrix multiplication. Also, the principal operators of relational algebra are easily implemented in map-reduce.

✦ *Workflow Systems*: Map-reduce has been generalized to systems that support any acyclic collection of functions, each of which can be instantiated by any number of tasks, each responsible for executing that function on a portion of the data. Clustera and Hyracks are examples of such systems.

✦ *Recursive Workflows*: When implementing a recursive collection of functions, it is not always possible to preserve the ability to restart any failed task, because recursive tasks may have produced output that was consumed by another task before the failure. A number of schemes for checkpointing parts of the computation to allow restart of single tasks, or restart all tasks from a recent point, have been proposed.

✦ *The Communication-Cost Model*: Many applications of map-reduce or similar systems do very simple things for each task. Then, the dominant cost is usually the cost of transporting data from where it is created to where it is used. In these cases, efficiency of an algorithm can be estimated by calculating the sum of the sizes of the inputs to all the tasks.

✦ *Multiway Joins*: It is sometimes more efficient to replicate tuples of the relations involved in a join and have the join of three or more relations computed as a single map-reduce job. The technique of Lagrangean multipliers can be used to optimize the degree of replication for each of the participating relations.

✦ *Star Joins*: Analytic queries often involve a very large fact table joined with smaller dimension tables. These joins can always be done efficiently by the multiway-join technique. An alternative is to distribute the fact table and replicate the dimension tables permanently, using the same strategy as would be used if we were taking the multiway join of the fact table and every dimension table.

2.7   References for Chapter 2

GFS, the Google File System, was described in [(10)]. The paper on Google's map-reduce is [(8)]. Information about Hadoop and HDFS can be found at [(11)]. More detail on relations and relational algebra can be found in [(16)].

Clustera is covered in [(9)]. Hyracks (previously called Hyrax) is from [(4)]. The Dryad system [(13)] has similar capabilities, but requires user creation of parallel tasks. That responsibility was automated through the introduction of DryadLINQ [(17)]. For a discussion of cluster implementation of recursion, see [(1)]. Pregel is from [(14)].

A different approach to recursion was taken in Haloop [(5)]. There, recursion is seen as an iteration, with the output of one round being input to the next round. Efficiency is obtained by managing the location of the intermediate data and the tasks that implement each round.

The communication-cost model for algorithms comes from [(2)]. [(3)] discusses optimal implementations of multiway joins using a map-reduce system.

There are a number of other systems built on a distributed file system and/or map-reduce, which have not been covered here, but may be worth knowing about. [(6)] describes *BigTable*, a Google implementation of an object store of very large size. A somewhat different direction was taken at Yahoo! with *Pnuts* [(7)]. The latter supports a limited form of transaction processing, for example.

PIG [(15)] is an implementation of relational algebra on top of Hadoop. Similarly, *Hive* [(12)] implements a restricted form of SQL on top of Hadoop.

(1) F.N. Afrati, V. Borkar, M. Carey, A. Polyzotis, and J.D. Ullman, "Cluster computing, recursion, and Datalog," to appear in *Proc. Datalog 2.0 Workshop*, Elsevier, 2011.

(2) F.N. Afrati and J.D. Ullman, "A new computation model for cluster computing," `http://ilpubs.stanford.edu:8090/953`, Stanford Dept. of CS Technical Report, 2009.

(3) F.N. Afrati and J.D. Ullman, "Optimizing joins in a map-reduce environment," *Proc. Thirteenth Intl. Conf. on Extending Database Technology*, 2010.

(4) V. Borkar and M. Carey, "Hyrax: demonstrating a new foundation for data-parallel computation,"

`http://asterix.ics.uci.edu/pub/hyraxdemo.pdf`

Univ. of California, Irvine, 2010.

(5) Y. Bu, B. Howe, M. Balazinska, and M. Ernst, "HaLoop: efficient iterative data processing on large clusters," *Proc. Intl. Conf. on Very Large Databases*, 2010.

(6) F. Chang, J. Dean, S. Ghemawat, W.C. Hsieh, D.A. Wallach, M. Burrows, T. Chandra, A. Fikes, and R.E. Gruber, "Bigtable: a distributed storage

system for structured data," *ACM Transactions on Computer Systems* **26**:2, pp. 1–26, 2008.

(7) B.F. Cooper, R. Ramakrishnan, U. Srivastava, A. Silberstein, P. Bohannon, H.-A. Jacobsen, N. Puz, D. Weaver, and R. Yerneni, "Pnuts: Yahoo!'s hosted data serving platform," *PVLDB* **1**:2, pp. 1277–1288, 2008.

(8) J. Dean and S. Ghemawat, "Mapreduce: simplified data processing on large clusters," *Comm. ACM* **51**:1, pp. 107–113, 2008.

(9) D.J. DeWitt, E. Paulson, E. Robinson, J.F. Naughton, J. Royalty, S. Shankar, and A. Krioukov, "Clustera: an integrated computation and data management system," *PVLDB* **1**:1, pp. 28–41, 2008.

(10) S. Ghemawat, H. Gobioff, and S.-T. Leung, "The Google file system," *19th ACM Symposium on Operating Systems Principles*, 2003.

(11) `hadoop.apache.org`, Apache Foundation.

(12) `hadoop.apache.org/hive`, Apache Foundation.

(13) M. Isard, M. Budiu, Y. Yu, A. Birrell, and D. Fetterly. "Dryad: distributed data-parallel programs from sequential building blocks," *Proceedings of the 2nd ACM SIGOPS/EuroSys European Conference on Computer Systems*, pp. 59–72, ACM, 2007.

(14) G. Malewicz, M.N. Austern, A.J.C. Sik, J.C. Denhert, H. Horn, N. Leiser, and G. Czajkowski, "Pregel: a system for large-scale graph processing," *Proc. ACM SIGMOD Conference*, 2010.

(15) C. Olston, B. Reed, U. Srivastava, R. Kumar, and A. Tomkins, "Pig latin: a not-so-foreign language for data processing," *Proc. ACM SIGMOD Conference*, pp. 1099–1110, 2008.

(16) J.D. Ullman and J. Widom, *A First Course in Database Systems*, Third Edition, Prentice-Hall, Upper Saddle River, NJ, 2008.

(17) Y. Yu, M. Isard, D. Fetterly, M. Budiu, I. Erlingsson, P.K. Gunda, and J. Currey, "DryadLINQ: a system for general-purpose distributed data-parallel computing using a high-level language," *OSDI*, pp. 1–14, USENIX Association, 2008.

3 Finding Similar Items

A fundamental data-mining problem is to examine data for "similar" items. We shall take up applications in Section 3.1, but an example would be looking at a collection of Web pages and finding near-duplicate pages. These pages could be plagiarisms, for example, or they could be mirrors that have almost the same content but differ in information about the host and about other mirrors.

We begin by phrasing the problem of similarity as one of finding sets with a relatively large intersection. We show how the problem of finding textually similar documents can be turned into such a set problem by the technique known as "shingling." Then, we introduce a technique called "minhashing," which compresses large sets in such a way that we can still deduce the similarity of the underlying sets from their compressed versions. Other techniques that work when the required degree of similarity is very high are covered in Section 3.9.

Another important problem that arises when we search for similar items of any kind is that there may be far too many pairs of items to test each pair for their degree of similarity, even if computing the similarity of any one pair can be made very easy. That concern motivates a technique called "locality-sensitive hashing," for focusing our search on pairs that are most likely to be similar.

Finally, we explore notions of "similarity" that are not expressible as intersection of sets. This study leads us to consider the theory of distance measures in arbitrary spaces. It also motivates a general framework for locality-sensitive hashing that applies for other definitions of "similarity."

3.1 Applications of Near-Neighbor Search

We shall focus initially on a particular notion of "similarity": the similarity of sets by looking at the relative size of their intersection. This notion of similarity is called "Jaccard similarity," and will be introduced in Section 3.1.1. We then examine some of the uses of finding similar sets. These include finding textually similar documents and collaborative filtering by finding similar customers and similar products. In order to turn the problem of textual similarity of documents into one of set intersection, we use a technique called "shingling," which is introduced in Section 3.2.

3.1.1   Jaccard Similarity of Sets

The *Jaccard similarity* of sets S and T is $|S \cap T|/|S \cup T|$, that is, the ratio of the size of the intersection of S and T to the size of their union. We shall denote the Jaccard similarity of S and T by $\text{SIM}(S,T)$.

EXAMPLE 3.1   In Fig. 3.1 we see two sets S and T. There are three elements in their intersection and a total of eight elements that appear in S or T or both. Thus, $\text{SIM}(S,T) = 3/8$.

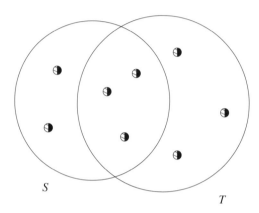

Figure 3.1 Two sets with Jaccard similarity 3/8

3.1.2   Similarity of Documents

An important class of problems that Jaccard similarity addresses well is that of finding textually similar documents in a large corpus such as the Web or a collection of news articles. We should understand that the aspect of similarity we are looking at here is character-level similarity, not "similar meaning," which requires us to examine the words in the documents and their uses. That problem is also interesting but is addressed by other techniques, which we hinted at in Section 1.3.1. However, textual similarity also has important uses. Many of these involve finding duplicates or near duplicates. First, let us observe that testing whether two documents are exact duplicates is easy; just compare the two documents character-by-character, and if they ever differ then they are not the same. However, in many applications, the documents are not identical, yet they share large portions of their text. Here are some examples:

Plagiarism

Finding plagiarized documents tests our ability to find textual similarity. The plagiarizer may extract only some parts of a document for his own. He may alter a few words and may alter the order in which sentences of the original appear. Yet the resulting document may still contain 50% or more of the original. No simple process of comparing documents character by character will detect a sophisticated plagiarism.

Mirror Pages

It is common for important or popular Web sites to be duplicated at a number of hosts, in order to share the load. The pages of these *mirror* sites will be quite similar, but are rarely identical. For instance, they might each contain information associated with their particular host, and they might each have links to the other mirror sites but not to themselves. A related phenomenon is the appropriation of pages from one class to another. These pages might include class notes, assignments, and lecture slides. Similar pages might change the name of the course, year, and make small changes from year to year. It is important to be able to detect similar pages of these kinds, because search engines produce better results if they avoid showing two pages that are nearly identical within the first page of results.

Articles from the Same Source

It is common for one reporter to write a news article that gets distributed, say through the Associated Press, to many newspapers, which then publish the article on their Web sites. Each newspaper changes the article somewhat. They may cut out paragraphs, or even add material of their own. They most likely will surround the article by their own logo, ads, and links to other articles at their site. However, the core of each newspaper's page will be the original article. News aggregators, such as Google News, try to find all versions of such an article, in order to show only one, and that task requires finding when two Web pages are textually similar, although not identical.[1]

3.1.3 Collaborative Filtering as a Similar-Sets Problem

Another class of applications where similarity of sets is very important is called *collaborative filtering*, a process whereby we recommend to users items that were liked by other users who have exhibited similar tastes. We shall investigate collaborative filtering in detail in Section 9.3, but for the moment let us see some common examples.

On-Line Purchases

Amazon.com has millions of customers and sells millions of items. Its database records which items have been bought by which customers. We can say two customers are similar if their sets of purchased items have a high Jaccard similarity. Likewise, two items that have sets of purchasers with high Jaccard similarity will be deemed similar. Note that, while we might expect mirror sites to have Jaccard similarity above 90%, it is unlikely that any two customers have Jaccard

---

[1] News aggregation also involves finding articles that are about the same topic, even though not textually similar. This problem too can yield to a similarity search, but it requires techniques other than Jaccard similarity of sets.

similarity that high (unless they have purchased only one item). Even a Jaccard similarity like 20% might be unusual enough to identify customers with similar tastes. The same observation holds for items; Jaccard similarities need not be very high to be significant.

Collaborative filtering requires several tools, in addition to finding similar customers or items, as we discuss in Chapter 9. For example, two Amazon customers who like science-fiction might each buy many science-fiction books, but only a few of these will be in common. However, by combining similarity-finding with clustering (Chapter 7), we might be able to discover that science-fiction books are mutually similar and put them in one group. Then, we can get a more powerful notion of customer-similarity by asking whether they made purchases within many of the same groups.

Movie Ratings

NetFlix records which movies each of its customers rented, and also the ratings assigned to those movies by the customers. We can see movies as similar if they were rented or rated highly by many of the same customers, and see customers as similar if they rented or rated highly many of the same movies. The same observations that we made for Amazon above apply in this situation: similarities need not be high to be significant, and clustering movies by genre will make things easier.

In addition, the matter of ratings introduces a new element. Some options are:

(1) Ignore low-rated customer/movie pairs; that is, treat these events as if the customer never rented the movie.
(2) When comparing customers, imagine two set elements for each movie, "liked" and "hated." If a customer rated a movie highly, put the "liked" for that movie in the customer's set. If they gave a low rating to a movie, put "hated" for that movie in their set. Then, we can look for high Jaccard similarity among these sets. We can do a similar trick when comparing movies.
(3) If ratings are 1-to-5-stars, put a movie in a customer's set n times if they rated the movie n-stars. Then, use *Jaccard similarity for bags* when measuring the similarity of customers. The Jaccard similarity for bags B and C is defined by counting an element n times in the intersection if n is the minimum of the number of times the element appears in B and C. In the union, we count the element the sum of the number of times it appears in B and in C.

EXAMPLE 3.2   The bag-similarity of bags $\{a, a, a, b\}$ and $\{a, a, b, b, c\}$ is 1/3. The intersection counts a twice and b once, so its size is 3. The size of the union of two bags is always the sum of the sizes of the two bags, or 9 in this case.

3.1.4   Exercises for Section 3.1

EXERCISE 3.1.1   Compute the Jaccard similarities of each pair of the following three sets: $\{1, 2, 3, 4\}$, $\{2, 3, 5, 7\}$, and $\{2, 4, 6\}$.

EXERCISE 3.1.2 Compute the Jaccard bag similarity of each pair of the following three bags: $\{1, 1, 1, 2\}$, $\{1, 1, 2, 2, 3\}$, and $\{1, 2, 3, 4\}$.

!! EXERCISE 3.1.3 Suppose we have a universal set U of n elements, and we choose two subsets S and T at random, each with m of the n elements. What is the expected value of the Jaccard similarity of S and T?

3.2 Shingling of Documents

The most effective way to represent documents as sets, for the purpose of identifying lexically similar documents is to construct from the document the set of short strings that appear within it. If we do so, then documents that share pieces as short as sentences or even phrases will have many common elements in their sets, even if those sentences appear in different orders in the two documents. In this section, we introduce the simplest and most common approach, shingling, as well as an interesting variation.

3.2.1 k-Shingles

A document is a string of characters. Define a k-shingle for a document to be any substring of length k found within the document. Then, we may associate with each document the set of k-shingles that appear one or more times within that document.

EXAMPLE 3.3 Suppose our document D is the string `abcdabd`, and we pick $k = 2$. Then the set of 2-shingles for D is $\{\texttt{ab}, \texttt{bc}, \texttt{cd}, \texttt{da}, \texttt{bd}\}$.

Note that the substring `ab` appears twice within D, but appears only once as a shingle. A variation of shingling produces a bag, rather than a set, so each shingle would appear in the result as many times as it appears in the document. However, we shall not use bags of shingles here.

There are several options regarding how white space (blank, tab, newline, etc.) is treated. It probably makes sense to replace any sequence of one or more whitespace characters by a single blank. That way, we distinguish shingles that cover two or more words from those that do not.

EXAMPLE 3.4 If we use $k = 9$, but eliminate whitespace altogether, then we would see some lexical similarity in the sentences "The plane was ready for touch down". and "The quarterback scored a touchdown". However, if we retain the blanks, then the first has shingles `touch dow` and `ouch down`, while the second has `touchdown`. If we eliminated the blanks, then both would have `touchdown`.

3.2.2   Choosing the Shingle Size

We can pick k to be any constant we like. However, if we pick k too small, then we would expect most sequences of k characters to appear in most documents. If so, then we could have documents whose shingle-sets had high Jaccard similarity, yet the documents had none of the same sentences or even phrases. As an extreme example, if we use $k = 1$, most Web pages will have most of the common characters and few other characters, so almost all Web pages will have high similarity.

How large k should be depends on how long typical documents are and how large the set of typical characters is. The important thing to remember is:

- k should be picked large enough that the probability of any given shingle appearing in any given document is low.

Thus, if our corpus of documents is emails, picking $k = 5$ should be fine. To see why, suppose that only letters and a general white-space character appear in emails (although in practice, most of the printable ASCII characters can be expected to appear occasionally). If so, then there would be $27^5 = 14,348,907$ possible shingles. Since the typical email is much smaller than 14 million characters long, we would expect $k = 5$ to work well, and indeed it does.

However, the calculation is a bit more subtle. Surely, more than 27 characters appear in emails, However, all characters do not appear with equal probability. Common letters and blanks dominate, while "z" and other letters that have high point-value in Scrabble are rare. Thus, even short emails will have many 5-shingles consisting of common letters, and the chances of unrelated emails sharing these common shingles is greater than would be implied by the calculation in the paragraph above. A good rule of thumb is to imagine that there are only 20 characters and estimate the number of k-shingles as 20^k. For large documents, such as research articles, choice $k = 9$ is considered safe.

3.2.3   Hashing Shingles

Instead of using substrings directly as shingles, we can pick a hash function that maps strings of length k to some number of buckets and treat the resulting bucket number as the shingle. The set representing a document is then the set of integers that are bucket numbers of one or more k-shingles that appear in the document. For instance, we could construct the set of 9-shingles for a document and then map each of those 9-shingles to a bucket number in the range 0 to $2^{32} - 1$. Thus, each shingle is represented by four bytes instead of nine. Not only has the data been compacted, but we can now manipulate (hashed) shingles by single-word machine operations.

Notice that we can differentiate documents better if we use 9-shingles and hash them down to four bytes than to use 4-shingles, even though the space used to represent a shingle is the same. The reason was touched upon in Section 3.2.2. If we use 4-shingles, most sequences of four bytes are unlikely or impossible to find in typical documents. Thus, the effective number of different shingles is much less than $2^{32} - 1$. If, as in Section 3.2.2, we assume only 20 characters are frequent in English text, then the number of different 4-shingles that are likely to occur is only $(20)^4 = 160,000$. However, if we use 9-shingles, there are many more than 2^{32} likely shingles. When we hash them down to four bytes, we can expect almost any sequence of four bytes to be possible, as was discussed in Section 1.3.2.

3.2.4   Shingles Built from Words

An alternative form of shingle has proved effective for the problem of identifying similar news articles, mentioned in Section 3.1.2. The exploitable distinction for this problem is that the news articles are written in a rather different style than are other elements that typically appear on the page with the article. News articles, and most prose, have a lot of stop words (see Section 1.3.1), the most common words such as "and," "you," "to," and so on. In many applications, we want to ignore stop words, since they don't tell us anything useful about the article, such as its topic.

However, for the problem of finding similar news articles, it was found that defining a shingle to be a stop word followed by the next two words, regardless of whether or not they were stop words, formed a useful set of shingles. The advantage of this approach is that the news article would then contribute more shingles to the set representing the Web page than would the surrounding elements. Recall that the goal of the exercise is to find pages that had the same articles, regardless of the surrounding elements. By biasing the set of shingles in favor of the article, pages with the same article and different surrounding material have higher Jaccard similarity than pages with the same surrounding material but with a different article.

EXAMPLE 3.5   An ad might have the simple text "Buy Sudzo." However, a news article with the same idea might read something like "*A* spokesperson *for the* Sudzo Corporation revealed today *that* studies *have* shown *it is* good *for* people *to* buy Sudzo products." Here we have italicized all the likely stop words, although there is no set number of the most frequent words that should be considered stop words. The first three shingles made from a stop word and the next two following are:

```
A spokesperson for
for the Sudzo
the Sudzo Corporation
```

There are nine shingles from the sentence, but none from the "ad."

3.2.5   Exercises for Section 3.2

EXERCISE 3.2.1   What are the first ten 3-shingles in the first sentence of Section 3.2?

EXERCISE 3.2.2   If we use the stop-word-based shingles of Section 3.2.4, and we take the stop words to be all the words of three or fewer letters, then what are the shingles in the first sentence of Section 3.2?

EXERCISE 3.2.3   What is the largest number of k-shingles a document of n bytes can have? You may assume that the size of the alphabet is large enough that the number of possible strings of length k is at least as n.

3.3   Similarity-Preserving Summaries of Sets

Sets of shingles are large. Even if we hash them to four bytes each, the space needed to store a set is still roughly four times the space taken by the document. If we have millions of documents, it may well not be possible to store all the shingle-sets in main memory.[2]

Our goal in this section is to replace large sets by much smaller representations called "signatures." The important property we need for signatures is that we can compare the signatures of two sets and estimate the Jaccard similarity of the underlying sets from the signatures alone. It is not possible that the signatures give the exact similarity of the sets they represent, but the estimates they provide are close, and the larger the signatures the more accurate the estimates. For example, if we replace the 200,000-byte hashed-shingle sets that derive from 50,000-byte documents by signatures of 1000 bytes, we can usually get within a few percent.

3.3.1   Matrix Representation of Sets

Before explaining how it is possible to construct small signatures from large sets, it is helpful to visualize a collection of sets as their *characteristic matrix*. The columns of the matrix correspond to the sets, and the rows correspond to elements of the universal set from which elements of the sets are drawn. There is a 1 in row r and column c if the element for row r is a member of the set for column c. Otherwise the value in position (r, c) is 0.

EXAMPLE 3.6   In Fig. 3.2 is an example of a matrix representing sets chosen from the universal set $\{a, b, c, d, e\}$. Here, $S_1 = \{a, d\}$, $S_2 = \{c\}$, $S_3 = \{b, d, e\}$, and $S_4 = \{a, c, d\}$. The top row and leftmost columns are not part of the matrix, but are present only to remind us what the rows and columns represent.

It is important to remember that the characteristic matrix is unlikely to be the way the data is stored, but it is useful as a way to visualize the data. For one reason not to store data as a matrix, these matrices are almost always *sparse* (they have many more 0's than 1's) in practice. It saves space to represent a

---

[2] There is another serious concern: even if the sets fit in main memory, the number of pairs may be too great for us to evaluate the similarity of each pair. We take up the solution to this problem in Section 3.4.

Element	S_1	S_2	S_3	S_4
a	1	0	0	1
b	0	0	1	0
c	0	1	0	1
d	1	0	1	1
e	0	0	1	0

Figure 3.2 A matrix representing four sets

sparse matrix of 0's and 1's by the positions in which the 1's appear. For another reason, the data is usually stored in some other format for other purposes.

As an example, if rows are products, and columns are customers, represented by the set of products they bought, then this data would really appear in a database table of purchases. A tuple in this table would list the item, the purchaser, and probably other details about the purchase, such as the date and the credit card used.

3.3.2 Minhashing

The signatures we desire to construct for sets are composed of the results of a large number of calculations, say several hundred, each of which is a "minhash" of the characteristic matrix. In this section, we shall learn how a minhash is computed in principle, and in later sections we shall see how a good approximation to the minhash is computed in practice.

To *minhash* a set represented by a column of the characteristic matrix, pick a permutation of the rows. The minhash value of any column is the number of the first row, in the permuted order, in which the column has a 1.

EXAMPLE 3.7   Let us suppose we pick the order of rows *beadc* for the matrix of Fig. 3.2. This permutation defines a minhash function h that maps sets to rows. Let us compute the minhash value of set S_1 according to h. The first column, which is the column for set S_1, has 0 in row b, so we proceed to row e, the second in the permuted order. There is again a 0 in the column for S_1, so we proceed to row a, where we find a 1. Thus. $h(S_1) = a$.

Element	S_1	S_2	S_3	S_4
b	0	0	1	0
e	0	0	1	0
a	1	0	0	1
d	1	0	1	1
c	0	1	0	1

Figure 3.3 A permutation of the rows of Fig. 3.2

Although it is not physically possible to permute very large characteristic matrices, the minhash function h implicitly reorders the rows of the matrix of Fig. 3.2 so it becomes the matrix of Fig. 3.3. In this matrix, we can read off the values of h by scanning from the top until we come to a 1. Thus, we see that $h(S_2) = c$, $h(S_3) = b$, and $h(S_4) = a$.

3.3.3   Minhashing and Jaccard Similarity

There is a remarkable connection between minhashing and Jaccard similarity of the sets that are minhashed.

- The probability that the minhash function for a random permutation of rows produces the same value for two sets equals the Jaccard similarity of those sets.

To see why, we need to picture the columns for those two sets. If we restrict ourselves to the columns for sets S_1 and S_2, then rows can be divided into three classes:

(1) Type X rows have 1 in both columns.
(2) Type Y rows have 1 in one of the columns and 0 in the other.
(3) Type Z rows have 0 in both columns.

Since the matrix is sparse, most rows are of type Z. However, it is the ratio of the numbers of type X and type Y rows that determine both $\text{SIM}(S_1, S_2)$ and the probability that $h(S_1) = h(S_2)$. Let there be x rows of type X and y rows of type Y. Then $\text{SIM}(S_1, S_2) = x/(x+y)$. The reason is that x is the size of $S_1 \cap S_2$ and $x + y$ is the size of $S_1 \cup S_2$.

Now, consider the probability that $h(S_1) = h(S_2)$. If we imagine the rows permuted randomly, and we proceed from the top, the probability that we shall meet a type X row before we meet a type Y row is $x/(x+y)$. But if the first row from the top other than type Z rows is a type X row, then surely $h(S_1) = h(S_2)$. On the other hand, if the first row other than a type Z row that we meet is a type Y row, then the set with a 1 gets that row as its minhash value. However the set with a 0 in that row surely gets some row further down the permuted list. Thus, we know $h(S_1) \neq h(S_2)$ if we first meet a type Y row. We conclude the probability that $h(S_1) = h(S_2)$ is $x/(x+y)$, which is also the Jaccard similarity of S_1 and S_2.

3.3.4   Minhash Signatures

Again think of a collection of sets represented by their characteristic matrix M. To represent sets, we pick at random some number n of permutations of the rows of M. Perhaps 100 permutations or several hundred permutations will do. Call the minhash functions determined by these permutations $h_1, h_2, \ldots, h_n$. From the column representing set S, construct the *minhash signature* for S, the vector $[h_1(S), h_2(S), \ldots, h_n(S)]$. We normally represent this list of hash-values as a column. Thus, we can form from matrix M a *signature matrix*, in which the ith column of M is replaced by the minhash signature for (the set of) the ith column.

Note that the signature matrix has the same number of columns as M but only n rows. Even if M is not represented explicitly, but in some compressed form suitable for a sparse matrix (e.g., by the locations of its 1's), it is normal for the signature matrix to be much smaller than M.

3.3.5   Computing Minhash Signatures

It is not feasible to permute a large characteristic matrix explicitly. Even picking a random permutation of millions or billions of rows is time-consuming, and the necessary sorting of the rows would take even more time. Thus, permuted matrices like that suggested by Fig. 3.3, while conceptually appealing, are not implementable.

Fortunately, it is possible to simulate the effect of a random permutation by a random hash function that maps row numbers to as many buckets as there are rows. A hash function that maps integers $0, 1, \ldots, k-1$ to bucket numbers 0 through $k-1$ typically will map some pairs of integers to the same bucket and leave other buckets unfilled. However, the difference is unimportant as long as k is large and there are not too many collisions. We can maintain the fiction that our hash function h "permutes" row r to position $h(r)$ in the permuted order.

Thus, instead of picking n random permutations of rows, we pick n randomly chosen hash functions $h_1, h_2, \ldots, h_n$ on the rows. We construct the signature matrix by considering each row in their given order. Let $\text{SIG}(i, c)$ be the element of the signature matrix for the ith hash function and column c. Initially, set $\text{SIG}(i, c)$ to ∞ for all i and c. We handle row r by doing the following:

(1) Compute $h_1(r), h_2(r), \ldots, h_n(r)$.
(2) For each column c do the following:
   (a) If c has 0 in row r, do nothing.
   (b) However, if c has 1 in row r, then for each $i = 1, 2, \ldots, n$ set $\text{SIG}(i, c)$ to the smaller of the current value of $\text{SIG}(i, c)$ and $h_i(r)$.

Row	S_1	S_2	S_3	S_4	$x+1 \mod 5$	$3x+1 \mod 5$
0	1	0	0	1	1	1
1	0	0	1	0	2	4
2	0	1	0	1	3	2
3	1	0	1	1	4	0
4	0	0	1	0	0	3

Figure 3.4 Hash functions computed for the matrix of Fig. 3.2

EXAMPLE 3.8   Let us reconsider the characteristic matrix of Fig. 3.2, which we reproduce with some additional data as Fig. 3.4. We have replaced the letters naming the rows by integers 0 through 4. We have also chosen two hash functions: $h_1(x) = x + 1 \mod 5$ and $h_2(x) = 3x + 1 \mod 5$. The values of these two functions applied to the row numbers are given in the last two columns of Fig. 3.4. Notice that these simple hash functions are true permutations of the rows, but a true permutation is only possible because the number of rows, 5, is a prime. In general, there will be collisions, where two rows get the same hash value.

Now, let us simulate the algorithm for computing the signature matrix. Initially, this matrix consists of all ∞'s:

	S_1	S_2	S_3	S_4
h_1	∞	∞	∞	∞
h_2	∞	∞	∞	∞

First, we consider row 0 of Fig. 3.4. We see that the values of $h_1(0)$ and $h_2(0)$ are both 1. The row numbered 0 has 1's in the columns for sets S_1 and S_4, so only these columns of the signature matrix can change. As 1 is less than ∞, we do in fact change both values in the columns for S_1 and S_4. The current estimate of the signature matrix is thus:

	S_1	S_2	S_3	S_4
h_1	1	∞	∞	1
h_2	1	∞	∞	1

Now, we move to the row numbered 1 in Fig. 3.4. This row has 1 only in S_3, and its hash values are $h_1(1) = 2$ and $h_2(1) = 4$. Thus, we set SIG$(1, 3)$ to 2 and SIG$(2, 3)$ to 4. All other signature entries remain as they are because their columns have 0 in the row numbered 1. The new signature matrix:

	S_1	S_2	S_3	S_4
h_1	1	∞	2	1
h_2	1	∞	4	1

The row of Fig. 3.4 numbered 2 has 1's in the columns for S_2 and S_4, and its hash values are $h_1(2) = 3$ and $h_2(2) = 2$. We could change the values in the signature for S_4, but the values in this column of the signature matrix, $[1, 1]$, are each less than the corresponding hash values $[3, 2]$. However, since the column for S_2 still has ∞'s, we replace it by $[3, 2]$, resulting in:

	S_1	S_2	S_3	S_4
h_1	1	3	2	1
h_2	1	2	4	1

Next comes the row numbered 3 in Fig. 3.4. Here, all columns but S_2 have 1, and the hash values are $h_1(3) = 4$ and $h_2(3) = 0$. The value 4 for h_1 exceeds what is already in the signature matrix for all the columns, so we shall not change any values in the first row of the signature matrix. However, the value 0 for h_2 is less than what is already present, so we lower $\text{SIG}(2,1)$, $\text{SIG}(2,3)$ and $\text{SIG}(2,4)$ to 0. Note that we cannot lower $\text{SIG}(2,2)$ because the column for S_2 in Fig. 3.4 has 0 in the row we are currently considering. The resulting signature matrix:

	S_1	S_2	S_3	S_4
h_1	1	3	2	1
h_2	0	2	0	0

Finally, consider the row of Fig. 3.4 numbered 4. $h_1(4) = 0$ and $h_2(4) = 3$. Since row 4 has 1 only in the column for S_3, we only compare the current signature column for that set, $[2,0]$ with the hash values $[0,3]$. Since $0 < 2$, we change $\text{SIG}(1,3)$ to 0, but since $3 > 0$ we do not change $\text{SIG}(2,3)$. The final signature matrix is:

	S_1	S_2	S_3	S_4
h_1	1	3	0	1
h_2	0	2	0	0

We can estimate the Jaccard similarities of the underlying sets from this signature matrix. Notice that columns 1 and 4 are identical, so we guess that $\text{SIM}(S_1, S_4) = 1.0$. If we look at Fig. 3.4, we see that the true Jaccard similarity of S_1 and S_4 is $2/3$. Remember that the fraction of rows that agree in the signature matrix is only an estimate of the true Jaccard similarity, and this example is much too small for the law of large numbers to assure that the estimates are close. For additional examples, the signature columns for S_1 and S_3 agree in half the rows (true similarity $1/4$), while the signatures of S_1 and S_2 estimate 0 as their Jaccard similarity (the correct value).

3.3.6   Exercises for Section 3.3

EXERCISE 3.3.1   Verify the theorem from Section 3.3.3, which relates the Jaccard similarity to the probability of minhashing to equal values, for the particular case of Fig. 3.2.

(a) Compute the Jaccard similarity of each of the pairs of columns in Fig. 3.2.

! (b) Compute, for each pair of columns of that figure, the fraction of the 120 permutations of the rows that make the two columns hash to the same value.

EXERCISE 3.3.2   Using the data from Fig. 3.4, add to the signatures of the columns the values of the following hash functions:

(a) $h_3(x) = 2x + 4$.
(b) $h_4(x) = 3x - 1$.

EXERCISE 3.3.3   In Fig. 3.5 is a matrix with six rows.

Element	S_1	S_2	S_3	S_4
0	0	1	0	1
1	0	1	0	0
2	1	0	0	1
3	0	0	1	0
4	0	0	1	1
5	1	0	0	0

Figure 3.5 Matrix for Exercise 3.3.3

(a) Compute the minhash signature for each column if we use the following three hash functions: $h_1(x) = 2x+1 \mod 6$; $h_2(x) = 3x+2 \mod 6$; $h_3(x) = 5x+2 \mod 6$.

(b) Which of these hash functions are true permutations?

(c) How close are the estimated Jaccard similarities for the six pairs of columns to the true Jaccard similarities?

! EXERCISE 3.3.4   Now that we know Jaccard similarity is related to the probability that two sets minhash to the same value, reconsider Exercise 3.1.3. Can you use this relationship to simplify the problem of computing the expected Jaccard similarity of randomly chosen sets?

! EXERCISE 3.3.5   Prove that if the Jaccard similarity of two columns is 0, then then minhashing always gives a correct estimate of the Jaccard similarity.

!! EXERCISE 3.3.6   One might expect that we could estimate the Jaccard similarity of columns without using all possible permutations of rows. For example, we could only allow cyclic permutations; i.e., start at a randomly chosen row r, which becomes the first in the order, followed by rows $r + 1$, $r + 2$, and so on, down to the last row, and then continuing with the first row, second row, and so on, down to row $r - 1$. There are only n such permutations if there are n rows. However, these permutations are not sufficient to estimate the Jaccard similarity correctly. Give an example of a two-column matrix where averaging over all the cyclic permutations does not give the Jaccard similarity.

! EXERCISE 3.3.7   Suppose we want to use a map-reduce framework to compute minhash signatures. If the matrix is stored in chunks that correspond to some columns, then it is quite easy to exploit parallelism. Each Map task gets some of the columns and all the hash functions, and computes the minhash signatures of its given columns. However, suppose the matrix were chunked by rows, so that a Map task is given the hash functions and a set of rows to work on. Design Map and Reduce functions to exploit map-reduce with data in this form.

3.4   Locality-Sensitive Hashing for Documents

Even though we can use minhashing to compress large documents into small
signatures and preserve the expected similarity of any pair of documents, it still
may be impossible to find the pairs with greatest similarity efficiently. The reason
is that the number of pairs of documents may be too large, even if there are not
too many documents.

EXAMPLE 3.9   Suppose we have a million documents, and we use signatures of
length 250. Then we use 1000 bytes per document for the signatures, and the
entire data fits in a gigabyte – less than a typical main memory of a laptop.
However, there are $\binom{1,000,000}{2}$ or half a trillion pairs of documents. If it takes a
microsecond to compute the similarity of two signatures, then it takes almost six
days to compute all the similarities on that laptop.

If our goal is to compute the similarity of every pair, there is nothing we can do
to reduce the work, although parallelism can reduce the elapsed time. However,
often we want only the most similar pairs or all pairs that are above some lower
bound in similarity. If so, then we need to focus our attention only on pairs that
are likely to be similar, without investigating every pair. There is a general theory
of how to provide such focus, called *locality-sensitive hashing* (LSH) or *near-
neighbor search*. In this section we shall consider a specific form of LSH, designed
for the particular problem we have been studying: documents, represented by
shingle-sets, then minhashed to short signatures. In Section 3.6 we present the
general theory of locality-sensitive hashing and a number of applications and
related techniques.

3.4.1   LSH for Minhash Signatures

One general approach to LSH is to "hash" items several times, in such a way that
similar items are more likely to be hashed to the same bucket than dissimilar
items are. We then consider any pair that hashed to the same bucket for any
of the hashings to be a *candidate pair*. We check only the candidate pairs for
similarity. The hope is that most of the dissimilar pairs will never hash to the
same bucket, and therefore will never be checked. Those dissimilar pairs that do
hash to the same bucket are *false positives*; we hope these will be only a small
fraction of all pairs. We also hope that most of the truly similar pairs will hash
to the same bucket under at least one of the hash functions. Those that do not
are *false negatives*; we hope these will be only a small fraction of the truly similar
pairs.

If we have minhash signatures for the items, an effective way to choose the
hashings is to divide the signature matrix into b bands consisting of r rows
each. For each band, there is a hash function that takes vectors of r integers
(the portion of one column within that band) and hashes them to some large
number of buckets. We can use the same hash function for all the bands, but we

use a separate bucket array for each band, so columns with the same vector in different bands will not hash to the same bucket.

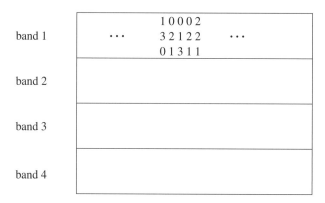

Figure 3.6 Dividing a signature matrix into four bands of three rows per band

EXAMPLE 3.10   Figure 3.6 shows part of a signature matrix of 12 rows divided into four bands of three rows each. The second and fourth of the explicitly shown columns each have the column vector $[0, 2, 1]$ in the first band, so they will definitely hash to the same bucket in the hashing for the first band. Thus, regardless of what those columns look like in the other three bands, this pair of columns will be a candidate pair. It is possible that other columns, such as the first two shown explicitly, will also hash to the same bucket according to the hashing of the first band. However, since their column vectors are different, $[1, 3, 0]$ and $[0, 2, 1]$, and there are many buckets for each hashing, we expect the chances of an accidental collision to be very small. We shall normally assume that two vectors hash to the same bucket if and only if they are identical.

Two columns that do not agree in band 1 have three other chances to become a candidate pair; they might be identical in any one of these other bands. However, observe that the more similar two columns are, the more likely it is that they will be identical in some band. Thus, intuitively the banding strategy makes similar columns much more likely to be candidate pairs than dissimilar pairs.

3.4.2   Analysis of the Banding Technique

Suppose we use b bands of r rows each, and suppose that a particular pair of documents have Jaccard similarity s. Recall from Section 3.3.3 that the probability the minhash signatures for these documents agree in any one particular row of the signature matrix is s. We can calculate the probability that these documents (or rather their signatures) become a candidate pair as follows:

(1) The probability that the signatures agree in all rows of one particular band is s^r.

(2) The probability that the signatures do not agree in at least one row of a particular band is $1 - s^r$.

(3) The probability that the signatures do not agree in all rows of any of the bands is $(1 - s^r)^b$.

(4) The probability that the signatures agree in all the rows of at least one band, and therefore become a candidate pair, is $1 - (1 - s^r)^b$.

It may not be obvious, but regardless of the chosen constants b and r, this function has the form of an *S-curve*, as suggested in Fig. 3.7. The *threshold*, that is, the value of similarity s at which the rise becomes steepest, is a function of b and r. An approximation to the threshold is $(1/b)^{1/r}$. For example, if $b = 16$ and $r = 4$, then the threshold is approximately $1/2$, since the 4th root of 16 is 2.

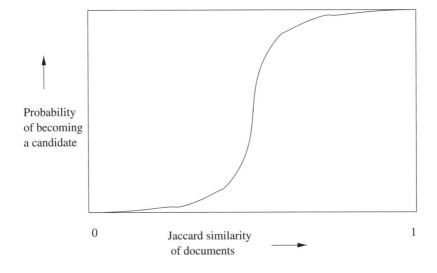

Figure 3.7 The S-curve

EXAMPLE 3.11   Let us consider the case $b = 20$ and $r = 5$. That is, we suppose we have signatures of length 100, divided into twenty bands of five rows each. Figure 3.8 tabulates some of the values of the function $1 - (1 - s^5)^{20}$. Notice that the threshold, the value of s at which the curve has risen halfway, is just slightly more than 0.5. Also notice that the curve is not exactly the ideal step function that jumps from 0 to 1 at the threshold, but the slope of the curve in the middle is significant. For example, it rises by more than 0.6 going from $s = 0.4$ to $s = 0.6$, so the slope in the middle is greater than 3.

For example, at $s = 0.8$, $1 - (0.8)^5$ is about 0.328. If you raise this number to the 20th power, you get about 0.00035. Subtracting this fraction from 1 yields 0.99965. That is, if we consider two documents with 80% similarity, then in any one band, they have only about a 33% chance of agreeing in all five rows and thus

s	$1 - (1 - s^r)^b$
.2	.006
.3	.047
.4	.186
.5	.470
.6	.802
.7	.975
.8	.9996

Figure 3.8 Values of the S-curve for $b = 20$ and $r = 5$

becoming a candidate pair. However, there are 20 bands and thus 20 chances to become a candidate. Only roughly one in 3000 pairs that are as high as 80% similar will fail to become a candidate pair and thus be a false negative.

3.4.3   Combining the Techniques

We can now give an approach to finding the set of candidate pairs for similar documents and then discovering the truly similar documents among them. It must be emphasized that this approach can produce false negatives – pairs of similar documents that are not identified as such because they never become a candidate pair. There will also be false positives – candidate pairs that are evaluated, but are found not to be sufficiently similar.

(1) Pick a value of k and construct from each document the set of k-shingles. Optionally, hash the k-shingles to shorter bucket numbers.

(2) Sort the document-shingle pairs to order them by shingle.

(3) Pick a length n for the minhash signatures. Feed the sorted list to the algorithm of Section 3.3.5 to compute the minhash signatures for all the documents.

(4) Choose a threshold t that defines how similar documents have to be in order for them to be regarded as a desired "similar pair." Pick a number of bands b and a number of rows r such that $br = n$, and the threshold t is approximately $(1/b)^{1/r}$. If avoidance of false negatives is important, you may wish to select b and r to produce a threshold lower than t; if speed is important and you wish to limit false positives, select b and r to produce a higher threshold.

(5) Construct candidate pairs by applying the LSH technique of Section 3.4.1.

(6) Examine each candidate pair's signatures and determine whether the fraction of components in which they agree is at least t.

(7) Optionally, if the signatures are sufficiently similar, go to the documents themselves and check that they are truly similar, rather than documents that, by luck, had similar signatures.

3.4.4   Exercises for Section 3.4

EXERCISE 3.4.1   Evaluate the S-curve $1 - (1 - s^r)^b$ for $s = 0.1, 0.2, \ldots, 0.9$, for the following values of r and b:

- $r = 3$ and $b = 10$.
- $r = 6$ and $b = 20$.
- $r = 5$ and $b = 50$.

! EXERCISE 3.4.2   For each of the (r, b) pairs in Exercise 3.4.1, compute the threshold, that is, the value of s for which the value of $1 - (1 - s^r)^b$ is exactly $1/2$. How does this value compare with the estimate of $(1/b)^{1/r}$ that was suggested in Section 3.4.2?

! EXERCISE 3.4.3   Use the techniques explained in Section 1.3.5 to approximate the S-curve $1 - (1 - s^r)^b$ when s^r is very small.

! EXERCISE 3.4.4   Suppose we wish to implement LSH by map-reduce. Specifically, assume chunks of the signature matrix consist of columns, and elements are key-value pairs where the key is the column number and the value is the signature itself (i.e., a vector of values).

(a) Show how to produce the buckets for all the bands as output of a single map-reduce process. *Hint*: Remember that a Map function can produce several key-value pairs from a single element.

(b) Show how another map-reduce process can convert the output of (a) to a list of pairs that need to be compared. Specifically, for each column i, there should be a list of those columns $j > i$ with which i needs to be compared.

3.5   Distance Measures

We now take a short detour to study the general notion of distance measures. The Jaccard similarity is a measure of how close sets are, although it is not really a distance measure. That is, the closer sets are, the higher the Jaccard similarity. Rather, 1 minus the Jaccard similarity is a distance measure, as we shall see; it is called the *Jaccard distance.*

However, Jaccard distance is not the only measure of closeness that makes sense. We shall examine in this section some other distance measures that have applications. Then, in Section 3.6 we see how some of these distance measures also have an LSH technique that allows us to focus on nearby points without comparing all points. Other applications of distance measures will appear when we study clustering in Chapter 7.

3.5.1   Definition of a Distance Measure

Suppose we have a set of points, called a *space*. A *distance measure* on this space is a function $d(x, y)$ that takes two points in the space as arguments and produces a real number, and satisfies the following axioms:

(1) $d(x, y) \geq 0$ (no negative distances).
(2) $d(x, y) = 0$ if and only if $x = y$ (distances are positive, except for the distance from a point to itself).
(3) $d(x, y) = d(y, x)$ (distance is symmetric).
(4) $d(x, y) \leq d(x, z) + d(z, y)$ (the *triangle inequality*).

The triangle inequality is the most complex condition. It says, intuitively, that to travel from x to y, we cannot obtain any benefit if we are forced to travel via some particular third point z. The triangle-inequality axiom is what makes all distance measures behave as if distance describes the length of a shortest path from one point to another.

3.5.2   Euclidean Distances

The most familiar distance measure is the one we normally think of as "distance." An *n-dimensional Euclidean space* is one where points are vectors of n real numbers. The conventional distance measure in this space, which we shall refer to as the L_2-*norm*, is defined:

$$d([x_1, x_2, \ldots, x_n], [y_1, y_2, \ldots, y_n]) = \sqrt{\sum_{i=1}^{n}(x_i - y_i)^2}$$

That is, we square the distance in each dimension, sum the squares, and take the positive square root.

It is easy to verify the first three requirements for a distance measure are satisfied. The Euclidean distance between two points cannot be negative, because the positive square root is intended. Since all squares of real numbers are nonnegative, any i such that $x_i \neq y_i$ forces the distance to be strictly positive. On the other hand, if $x_i = y_i$ for all i, then the distance is clearly 0. Symmetry follows because $(x_i - y_i)^2 = (y_i - x_i)^2$. The triangle inequality requires a good deal of algebra to verify. However, it is well understood to be a property of Euclidean space: the sum of the lengths of any two sides of a triangle is no less than the length of the third side.

There are other distance measures that have been used for Euclidean spaces. For any constant r, we can define the L_r-*norm* to be the distance measure d defined by:

$$d([x_1, x_2, \ldots, x_n], [y_1, y_2, \ldots, y_n]) = (\sum_{i=1}^{n}|x_i - y_i|^r)^{1/r}$$

The case $r = 2$ is the usual L_2-norm just mentioned. Another common distance measure is the L_1-norm, or *Manhattan distance*. There, the distance between two points is the sum of the magnitudes of the differences in each dimension. It is called "Manhattan distance" because it is the distance one would have to travel between points if one were constrained to travel along grid lines, as on the streets of a city such as Manhattan.

Another interesting distance measure is the L_∞-norm, which is the limit as r approaches infinity of the L_r-norm. As r gets larger, only the dimension with the largest difference matters, so formally, the L_∞-norm is defined as the maximum of $|x_i - y_i|$ over all dimensions i.

EXAMPLE 3.12   Consider the two-dimensional Euclidean space (the customary plane) and the points $(2, 7)$ and $(6, 4)$. The L_2-norm gives a distance of $\sqrt{(2-6)^2 + (7-4)^2} = \sqrt{4^2 + 3^2} = 5$. The L_1-norm gives a distance of $|2-6| + |7-4| = 4 + 3 = 7$. The L_∞-norm gives a distance of

$$\max(|2-6|, |7-4|) = \max(4, 3) = 4$$

3.5.3   Jaccard Distance

As mentioned at the beginning of the section, we define the *Jaccard distance* of sets by $d(x, y) = 1 - \text{SIM}(x, y)$. That is, the Jaccard distance is 1 minus the ratio of the sizes of the intersection and union of sets x and y. We must verify that this function is a distance measure.

(1) $d(x, y)$ is nonnegative because the size of the intersection cannot exceed the size of the union.

(2) $d(x, y) = 0$ if $x = y$, because $x \cup x = x \cap x = x$. However, if $x \neq y$, then the size of $x \cap y$ is strictly less than the size of $x \cup y$, so $d(x, y)$ is strictly positive.

(3) $d(x, y) = d(y, x)$ because both union and intersection are symmetric; i.e., $x \cup y = y \cup x$ and $x \cap y = y \cap x$.

(4) For the triangle inequality, recall from Section 3.3.3 that $\text{SIM}(x, y)$ is the probability a random minhash function maps x and y to the same value. Thus, the Jaccard distance $d(x, y)$ is the probability that a random minhash function *does not* send x and y to the same value. We can therefore translate the condition $d(x, y) \leq d(x, z) + d(z, y)$ to the statement that if h is a random minhash function, then the probability that $h(x) \neq h(y)$ is no greater than the sum of the probability that $h(x) \neq h(z)$ and the probability that $h(z) \neq h(y)$. However, this statement is true because whenever $h(x) \neq h(y)$, at least one of $h(x)$ and $h(y)$ must be different from $h(z)$. They could not both be $h(z)$, because then $h(x)$ and $h(y)$ would be the same.

.

3.5.4   Cosine Distance

The *cosine distance* makes sense in spaces that have dimensions, including Euclidean spaces and discrete versions of Euclidean spaces, such as spaces where points are vectors with integer components or boolean (0 or 1) components. In such a space, points may be thought of as directions. We do not distinguish between a vector and a multiple of that vector. Then the cosine distance between two points is the angle that the vectors to those points make. This angle will be in the range 0 to 180 degrees, regardless of how many dimensions the space has.

We can calculate the cosine distance by first computing the cosine of the angle, and then applying the arc-cosine function to translate to an angle in the 0-180 degree range. Given two vectors x and y, the cosine of the angle between them is the dot product $x.y$ divided by the L_2-norms of x and y (i.e., their Euclidean distances from the origin). Recall that the dot product of vectors $[x_1, x_2, \ldots, x_n].[y_1, y_2, \ldots, y_n]$ is $\sum_{i=1}^{n} x_i y_i$.

EXAMPLE 3.13   Let our two vectors be $x = [1, 2, -1]$ and $= [2, 1, 1]$. The dot product $x.y$ is $1 \times 2 + 2 \times 1 + (-1) \times 1 = 3$. The L_2-norm of both vectors is $\sqrt{6}$. For example, x has L_2-norm $\sqrt{1^2 + 2^2 + (-1)^2} = \sqrt{6}$. Thus, the cosine of the angle between x and y is $3/(\sqrt{6}\sqrt{6})$ or $1/2$. The angle whose cosine is $1/2$ is 60 degrees, so that is the cosine distance between x and y.

We must show that the cosine distance is indeed a distance measure. We have defined it so the values are in the range 0 to 180, so no negative distances are possible. Two vectors have angle 0 if and only if they are the same direction.[3] Symmetry is obvious: the angle between x and y is the same as the angle between y and x. The triangle inequality is best argued by physical reasoning. One way to rotate from x to y is to rotate to z and thence to y. The sum of those two rotations cannot be less than the rotation directly from x to y.

3.5.5   Edit Distance

This distance makes sense when points are strings. The distance between two strings $x = x_1 x_2 \cdots x_n$ and $y = y_1 y_2 \cdots y_m$ is the smallest number of insertions and deletions of single characters that will convert x to y.

EXAMPLE 3.14   The edit distance between the strings $x = $ abcde and $y = $ acfdeg is 3. To convert x to y:

(1) Delete b.
(2) Insert f after c.
(3) Insert g after e.

---

[3] Notice that to satisfy the second axiom, we have to treat vectors that are multiples of one another, e.g. $[1, 2]$ and $[3, 6]$, as the same direction, which they are. If we regarded these as different vectors, we would give them distance 0 and thus violate the condition that only $d(x, x)$ is 0.

Non-Euclidean Spaces

Notice that several of the distance measures introduced in this section are not Euclidean spaces. A property of Euclidean spaces that we shall find important when we take up clustering in Chapter 7 is that the average of points in a Euclidean space always exists and is a point in the space. However, consider the space of sets for which we defined the Jaccard distance. The notion of the "average" of two sets makes no sense. Likewise, the space of strings, where we can use the edit distance, does not let us take the "average" of strings.

Vector spaces, for which we suggested the cosine distance, may or may not be Euclidean. If the components of the vectors can be any real numbers, then the space is Euclidean. However, if we restrict components to be integers, then the space is not Euclidean. Notice that, for instance, we cannot find an average of the vectors $[1, 2]$ and $[3, 1]$ in the space of vectors with two integer components, although if we treated them as members of the two-dimensional Euclidean space, then we could say that their average was $[2.0, 1.5]$.

No sequence of fewer than three insertions and/or deletions will convert x to y. Thus, $d(x, y) = 3$.

Another way to define and calculate the edit distance $d(x, y)$ is to compute a *longest common subsequence* (LCS) of x and y. An LCS of x and y is a string that is constructed by deleting positions from x and y, and that is as long as any string that can be constructed that way. The edit distance $d(x, y)$ can be calculated as the length of x plus the length of y minus twice the length of their LCS.

EXAMPLE 3.15 The strings $x =$ abcde and $y =$ acfdeg from Example 3.14 have a unique LCS, which is acde. We can be sure it is the longest possible, because it contains every symbol appearing in both x and y. Fortunately, these common symbols appear in the same order in both strings, so we are able to use them all in an LCS. Note that the length of x is 5, the length of y is 6, and the length of their LCS is 4. The edit distance is thus $5 + 6 - 2 \times 4 = 3$, which agrees with the direct calculation in Example 3.14.

For another example, consider $x =$ aba and $y =$ bab. Their edit distance is 2. For example, we can convert x to y by deleting the first a and then inserting b at the end. There are two LCS's: ab and ba. Each can be obtained by deleting one symbol from each string. As must be the case for multiple LCS's of the same pair of strings, both LCS's have the same length. Therefore, we may compute the edit distance as $3 + 3 - 2 \times 2 = 2$.

Edit distance is a distance measure. Surely no edit distance can be negative, and only two identical strings have an edit distance of 0. To see that edit distance is symmetric, note that a sequence of insertions and deletions can be reversed, with each insertion becoming a deletion, and vice-versa. The triangle inequality is also straightforward. One way to turn a string s into a string t is to turn s

into some string u and then turn u into t. Thus, the number of edits made going from s to u, plus the number of edits made going from u to t cannot be less than the smallest number of edits that will turn s into t.

3.5.6   Hamming Distance

Given a space of vectors, we define the *Hamming distance* between two vectors to be the number of components in which they differ. It should be obvious that Hamming distance is a distance measure. Clearly the Hamming distance cannot be negative, and if it is zero, then the vectors are identical. The distance does not depend on which of two vectors we consider first. The triangle inequality should also be evident. If x and z differ in m components, and z and y differ in n components, then x and y cannot differ in more than $m + n$ components. Most commonly, Hamming distance is used when the vectors are boolean; they consist of 0's and 1's only. However, in principle, the vectors can have components from any set.

EXAMPLE 3.16   The Hamming distance between the vectors 10101 and 11110 is 3. That is, these vectors differ in the second, fourth, and fifth components, while they agree in the first and third components.

3.5.7   Exercises for Section 3.5

! EXERCISE 3.5.1   On the space of nonnegative integers, which of the following functions are distance measures? If so, prove it; if not, prove that it fails to satisfy one or more of the axioms.

(a) $\max(x, y) =$ the larger of x and y.
(b) $\mathrm{diff}(x, y) = |x - y|$ (the absolute magnitude of the difference between x and y).
(c) $\mathrm{sum}(x, y) = x + y$.

EXERCISE 3.5.2   Find the L_1 and L_2 distances between the points $(5, 6, 7)$ and $(8, 2, 4)$.

!! EXERCISE 3.5.3   Prove that if i and j are any positive integers, and $i < j$, then the L_i norm between any two points is greater than the L_j norm between those same two points.

EXERCISE 3.5.4   Find the Jaccard distances between the following pairs of sets:

(a) $\{1, 2, 3, 4\}$ and $\{2, 3, 4, 5\}$.
(b) $\{1, 2, 3\}$ and $\{4, 5, 6\}$.

EXERCISE 3.5.5   Compute the cosines of the angles between each of the following pairs of vectors.[4]

---

[4] Note that what we are asking for is not precisely the cosine distance, but from the cosine of an angle, you can compute the angle itself, perhaps with the aid of a table or library function.

(a) $(3, -1, 2)$ and $(-2, 3, 1)$.
(b) $(1, 2, 3)$ and $(2, 4, 6)$.
(c) $(5, 0, -4)$ and $(-1, -6, 2)$.
(d) $(0, 1, 1, 0, 1, 1)$ and $(0, 0, 1, 0, 0, 0)$.

! EXERCISE 3.5.6   Prove that the cosine distance between any two vectors of 0's and 1's, of the same length, is at most 90 degrees.

EXERCISE 3.5.7   Find the edit distances (using only insertions and deletions) between the following pairs of strings.

(a) `abcdef` and `bdaefc`.
(b) `abccdabc` and `acbdcab`.
(c) `abcdef` and `baedfc`.

! EXERCISE 3.5.8   There are a number of other notions of edit distance available. For instance, we can allow, in addition to insertions and deletions, the following operations:

(a) *Mutation*, where one symbol is replaced by another symbol. Note that a mutation can always be performed by an insertion followed by a deletion, but if we allow mutations, then this change counts for only 1, not 2, when computing the edit distance.
(b) *Transposition*, where two adjacent symbols have their positions swapped. Like a mutation, we can simulate a transposition by one insertion followed by one deletion, but here we count only 1 for these two steps.

Repeat Exercise 3.5.7 if edit distance is defined to be the number of insertions, deletions, mutations, and transpositions needed to transform one string into another.

! EXERCISE 3.5.9   Prove that the edit distance discussed in Exercise 3.5.8 is indeed a distance measure.

EXERCISE 3.5.10   Find the Hamming distances between each pair of the following vectors: 000000, 110011, 010101, and 011100.

3.6   The Theory of Locality-Sensitive Functions

The LSH technique developed in Section 3.4 is one example of a family of functions (the minhash functions) that can be combined (by the banding technique) to distinguish strongly between pairs at a low distance from pairs at a high distance. The steepness of the S-curve in Fig. 3.7 reflects how effectively we can avoid false positives and false negatives among the candidate pairs.

Now, we shall explore other families of functions, besides the minhash functions, that can serve to produce candidate pairs efficiently. These functions can apply to the space of sets and the Jaccard distance, or to another space and/or another distance measure. There are three conditions that we need for a family of functions:

(1) They must be more likely to make close pairs be candidate pairs than distant pairs. We make this notion precise in Section 3.6.1.
(2) They must be statistically independent, in the sense that it is possible to estimate the probability that two or more functions will all give a certain response by the product rule for independent events.
(3) They must be efficient, in two ways:
  (a) They must be able to identify candidate pairs in time much less than the time it takes to look at all pairs. For example, minhash functions have this capability, since we can hash sets to minhash values in time proportional to the size of the data, rather than the square of the number of sets in the data. Since sets with common values are colocated in a bucket, we have implicitly produced the candidate pairs for a single minhash function in time much less than the number of pairs of sets.
  (b) They must be combinable to build functions that are better at avoiding false positives and negatives, and the combined functions must also take time that is much less than the number of pairs. For example, the banding technique of Section 3.4.1 takes single minhash functions, which satisfy condition (3)(a) but do not, by themselves have the S-curve behavior we want, and produces from a number of minhash functions a combined function that has the S-curve shape.

Our first step is to define "locality-sensitive functions" generally. We then see how the idea can be applied in several applications. Finally, we discuss how to apply the theory to arbitrary data with either a cosine distance or a Euclidean distance measure.

3.6.1   Locality-Sensitive Functions

For the purposes of this section, we shall consider functions that take two items and render a decision about whether these items should be a candidate pair. In many cases, the function f will "hash" items, and the decision will be based on whether or not the result is equal. Because it is convenient to use the notation $f(x) = f(y)$ to mean that $f(x, y)$ is "yes; make x and y a candidate pair," we shall use $f(x) = f(y)$ as a shorthand with this meaning. We also use $f(x) \neq f(y)$ to mean "do not make x and y a candidate pair unless some other function concludes we should do so."

A collection of functions of this form will be called a *family* of functions. For example, the family of minhash functions, each based on one of the possible permutations of rows of a characteristic matrix, form a family.

Let $d_1 < d_2$ be two distances according to some distance measure d. A family **F** of functions is said to be (d_1, d_2, p_1, p_2)-*sensitive* if for every f in **F**:

(1) If $d(x, y) \leq d_1$, then the probability that $f(x) = f(y)$ is at least p_1.

(2) If $d(x, y) \geq d_2$, then the probability that $f(x) = f(y)$ is at most p_2.

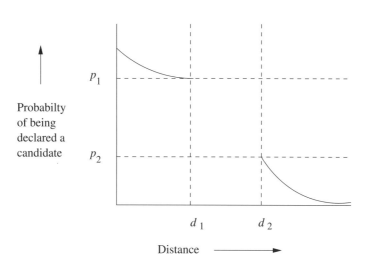

Figure 3.9 Behavior of a (d_1, d_2, p_1, p_2)-sensitive function

Figure 3.9 illustrates what we expect about the probability that a given function in a (d_1, d_2, p_1, p_2)-sensitive family will declare two items to be a candidate pair. Notice that we say nothing about what happens when the distance between the items is strictly between d_1 and d_2, but we can make d_1 and d_2 as close as we wish. The penalty is that typically p_1 and p_2 are then close as well. As we shall see, it is possible to drive p_1 and p_2 apart while keeping d_1 and d_2 fixed.

3.6.2   Locality-Sensitive Families for Jaccard Distance

For the moment, we have only one way to find a family of locality-sensitive functions: use the family of minhash functions, and assume that the distance measure is the Jaccard distance. As before, we interpret a minhash function h to make x and y a candidate pair if and only if $h(x) = h(y)$.

- The family of minhash functions is a $(d_1, d_2, 1 - d_1, 1 - d_2)$-sensitive family for any d_1 and d_2, where $0 \leq d_1 < d_2 \leq 1$.

The reason is that if $d(x, y) \leq d_1$, where d is the Jaccard distance, then $\mathrm{SIM}(x, y) = 1 - d(x, y) \geq 1 - d_1$. But we know that the Jaccard similarity of x and y is equal to the probability that a minhash function will hash x and y to the same value. A similar argument applies to d_2 or any distance.

EXAMPLE 3.17   We could let $d_1 = 0.3$ and $d_2 = 0.6$. Then we can assert that the family of minhash functions is a $(0.3, 0.6, 0.7, 0.4)$-sensitive family. That is, if the Jaccard distance between x and y is at most 0.3 (i.e., $\mathrm{SIM}(x, y) \geq 0.7$) then there is at least a 0.7 chance that a minhash function will send x and y to the same value, and if the Jaccard distance between x and y is at least 0.6 (i.e., $\mathrm{SIM}(x, y) \le 0.4$), then there is at most a 0.4 chance that x and y will be sent to the same value. Note that we could make the same assertion with another choice of d_1 and d_2; only $d_1 < d_2$ is required.

3.6.3   Amplifying a Locality-Sensitive Family

Suppose we are given a (d_1, d_2, p_1, p_2)-sensitive family $\mathbf{F}$. We can construct a new family $\mathbf{F'}$ by the *AND-construction* on $\mathbf{F}$, which is defined as follows. Each member of $\mathbf{F'}$ consists of r members of $\mathbf{F}$ for some fixed r. If f is in $\mathbf{F'}$, and f is constructed from the set $\{f_1, f_2, \ldots, f_r\}$ of members of $\mathbf{F}$, we say $f(x) = f(y)$ if and only if $f_i(x) = f_i(y)$ for all $i = 1, 2, \ldots, r$. Notice that this construction mirrors the effect of the r rows in a single band: the band makes x and y a candidate pair if every one of the r rows in the band say that x and y are equal (and therefore a candidate pair according to that row).

Since the members of $\mathbf{F}$ are independently chosen to make a member of $\mathbf{F'}$, we can assert that $\mathbf{F'}$ is a $(d_1, d_2, (p_1)^r, (p_2)^r)$-sensitive family. That is, for any p, if p is the probability that a member of $\mathbf{F}$ will declare (x, y) to be a candidate pair, then the probability that a member of $\mathbf{F'}$ will so declare is p^r.

There is another construction, which we call the *OR-construction*, that turns a (d_1, d_2, p_1, p_2)-sensitive family $\mathbf{F}$ into a $(d_1, d_2, 1 - (1 - p_1)^b, 1 - (1 - p_2)^b)$-sensitive family $\mathbf{F'}$. Each member f of $\mathbf{F'}$ is constructed from b members of $\mathbf{F}$, say $f_1, f_2, \ldots, f_b$. We define $f(x) = f(y)$ if and only if $f_i(x) = f_i(y)$ for one or more values of i. The OR-construction mirrors the effect of combining several bands: x and y become a candidate pair if any band makes them a candidate pair.

If p is the probability that a member of $\mathbf{F}$ will declare (x, y) to be a candidate pair, then $1 - p$ is the probability it will not so declare. $(1 - p)^b$ is the probability that none of $f_1, f_2, \ldots, f_b$ will declare (x, y) a candidate pair, and $1 - (1 - p)^b$ is the probability that at least one f_i will declare (x, y) a candidate pair, and therefore that f will declare (x, y) to be a candidate pair.

Notice that the AND-construction lowers all probabilities, but if we choose $\mathbf{F}$ and r judiciously, we can make the small probability p_2 get very close to 0, while the higher probability p_1 stays significantly away from 0. Similarly, the OR-construction makes all probabilities rise, but by choosing $\mathbf{F}$ and b judiciously, we can make the larger probability approach 1 while the smaller probability remains bounded away from 1. We can cascade AND- and OR-constructions in any order to make the low probability close to 0 and the high probability close to 1. Of course the more constructions we use, and the higher the values of r and b that we pick, the larger the number of functions from the original family that we are forced to use. Thus, the better the final family of functions is, the longer it takes to apply the functions from this family.

EXAMPLE 3.18   Suppose we start with a family $\mathbf{F}$. We use the AND-construction with $r = 4$ to produce a family $\mathbf{F}_1$. We then apply the OR-construction to

$\mathbf{F}_1$ with $b = 4$ to produce a third family $\mathbf{F}_2$. Note that the members of $\mathbf{F}_2$ each are built from 16 members of $\mathbf{F}$, and the situation is analogous to starting with 16 minhash functions and treating them as four bands of four rows each.

p	$1 - (1 - p^4)^4$
0.2	0.0064
0.3	0.0320
0.4	0.0985
0.5	0.2275
0.6	0.4260
0.7	0.6666
0.8	0.8785
0.9	0.9860

Figure 3.10 Effect of the 4-way AND-construction followed by the 4-way OR-construction

The 4-way AND-function converts any probability p into p^4. When we follow it by the 4-way OR-construction, that probability is further converted into $1 - (1 - p^4)^4$. Some values of this transformation are indicated in Fig. 3.10. This function is an S-curve, staying low for a while, then rising steeply (although not too steeply; the slope never gets much higher than 2), and then leveling off at high values. Like any S-curve, it has a *fixedpoint*, the value of p that is left unchanged when we apply the function of the S-curve. In this case, the fixedpoint is the value of p for which $p = 1 - (1 - p^4)^4$. We can see that the fixedpoint is somewhere between 0.7 and 0.8. Below that value, probabilities are decreased, and above it they are increased. Thus, if we pick a high probability above the fixedpoint and a low probability below it, we shall have the desired effect that the low probability is decreased and the high probability is increased.

Suppose $\mathbf{F}$ is the minhash functions, regarded as a $(0.2, 0.6, 0.8, 0.4)$-sensitive family. Then $\mathbf{F}_2$, the family constructed by a 4-way AND followed by a 4-way OR, is a $(0.2, 0.6, 0.8785, 0.0985)$-sensitive family, as we can read from the rows for 0.2 and 0.6 in Fig. 3.10. By replacing $\mathbf{F}$ by $\mathbf{F}_2$, we have reduced both the false-negative and false-positive rates, at the cost of making application of the functions take 16 times as long.

EXAMPLE 3.19 For the same cost, we can apply a 4-way OR-construction followed by a 4-way AND-construction. Figure 3.11 gives the transformation on probabilities implied by this construction. For instance, suppose that $\mathbf{F}$ is a $(0.2, 0.6, 0.8, 0.4)$-sensitive family. Then the constructed family is a

$$(0.2, 0.6, 0.9936, 0.5740)\text{-sensitive}$$

family. This choice is not necessarily the best. Although the higher probability has moved much closer to 1, the lower probability has also raised, increasing the number of false positives.

p	$\left(1-(1-p)^4\right)^4$
0.1	0.0140
0.2	0.1215
0.3	0.3334
0.4	0.5740
0.5	0.7725
0.6	0.9015
0.7	0.9680
0.8	0.9936

Figure 3.11 Effect of the 4-way OR-construction followed by the 4-way AND-construction

EXAMPLE 3.20   We can cascade constructions as much as we like. For example, we could use the construction of Example 3.18 on the family of minhash functions and then use the construction of Example 3.19 on the resulting family. The constructed family would then have functions each built from 256 minhash functions. It would, for instance transform a $(0.2, 0.8, 0.8, 0.2)$-sensitive family into a $(0.2, 0.8, 0.99999996, 0.0008715)$-sensitive family.

3.6.4   Exercises for Section 3.6

EXERCISE 3.6.1   What is the effect on probability of starting with the family of minhash functions and applying:

(a) A 2-way AND construction followed by a 3-way OR construction.
(b) A 3-way OR construction followed by a 2-way AND construction.
(c) A 2-way AND construction followed by a 2-way OR construction, followed by a 2-way AND construction.
(d) A 2-way OR construction followed by a 2-way AND construction, followed by a 2-way OR construction followed by a 2-way AND construction.

EXERCISE 3.6.2   Find the fixedpoints for each of the functions constructed in Exercise 3.6.1.

! EXERCISE 3.6.3   Any function of probability p, such as that of Fig. 3.10, has a slope given by the derivative of the function. The maximum slope is where that derivative is a maximum. Find the value of p that gives a maximum slope for the S-curves given by Fig. 3.10 and Fig. 3.11. What are the values of these maximum slopes?

!! EXERCISE 3.6.4   Generalize Exercise 3.6.3 to give, as a function of r and b, the point of maximum slope and the value of that slope, for families of functions defined from the minhash functions by:

(a) An r-way AND construction followed by a b-way OR construction.
(b) A b-way OR construction followed by an r-way AND construction.

3.7   LSH Families for Other Distance Measures

There is no guarantee that a distance measure has a locality-sensitive family of hash functions. So far, we have only seen such families for the Jaccard distance. In this section, we shall show how to construct locality-sensitive families for Hamming distance, the cosine distance and for the normal Euclidean distance.

3.7.1   LSH Families for Hamming Distance

It is quite simple to build a locality-sensitive family of functions for the Hamming distance. Suppose we have a space of d-dimensional vectors, and $h(x, y)$ denotes the Hamming distance between vectors x and y. If we take any one position of the vectors, say the ith position, we can define the function $f_i(x)$ to be the ith bit of vector x. Then $f_i(x) = f_i(y)$ if and only if vectors x and y agree in the ith position. Then the probability that $f_i(x) = f_i(y)$ for a randomly chosen i is exactly $1 - h(x, y)/d$; i.e., it is the fraction of positions in which x and y agree.

This situation is almost exactly like the one we encountered for minhashing. Thus, the family $\mathbf{F}$ consisting of the functions $\{f_1, f_2, \ldots, f_d\}$ is a

$$(d_1, d_2, 1 - d_1/d, 1 - d_2/d)\text{-sensitive}$$

family of hash functions, for any $d_1 < d_2$. There are only two differences between this family and the family of minhash functions.

(1) While Jaccard distance runs from 0 to 1, the Hamming distance on a vector space of dimension d runs from 0 to d. It is therefore necessary to scale the distances by dividing by d, to turn them into probabilities.
(2) While there is essentially an unlimited supply of minhash functions, the size of the family $\mathbf{F}$ for Hamming distance is only d.

The first point is of no consequence; it only requires that we divide by d at appropriate times. The second point is more serious. If d is relatively small, then we are limited in the number of functions that can be composed using the AND and OR constructions, thereby limiting how steep we can make the S-curve be.

3.7.2   Random Hyperplanes and the Cosine Distance

Recall from Section 3.5.4 that the cosine distance between two vectors is the angle between the vectors. For instance, we see in Fig. 3.12 two vectors x and y that make an angle θ between them. Note that these vectors may be in a space of many dimensions, but they always define a plane, and the angle between them is measured in this plane. Figure 3.12 is a "top-view" of the plane containing x and y.

Suppose we pick a hyperplane through the origin. This hyperplane intersects the plane of x and y in a line. Figure 3.12 suggests two possible hyperplanes, one whose intersection is the dashed line and the other's intersection is the dotted

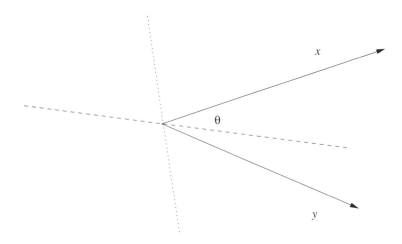

Figure 3.12 Two vectors make an angle θ

line. To pick a random hyperplane, we actually pick the normal vector to the hyperplane, say v. The hyperplane is then the set of points whose dot product with v is 0.

First, consider a vector v that is normal to the hyperplane whose projection is represented by the dashed line in Fig. 3.12; that is, x and y are on different sides of the hyperplane. Then the dot products $v.x$ and $v.y$ will have different signs. If we assume, for instance, that v is a vector whose projection onto the plane of x and y is above the dashed line in Fig. 3.12, then $v.x$ is positive, while $v.y$ is negative. The normal vector v instead might extend in the opposite direction, below the dashed line. In that case $v.x$ is negative and $v.y$ is positive, but the signs are still different.

On the other hand, the randomly chosen vector v could be normal to a hyperplane like the dotted line in Fig. 3.12. In that case, both $v.x$ and $v.y$ have the same sign. If the projection of v extends to the right, then both dot products are positive, while if v extends to the left, then both are negative.

What is the probability that the randomly chosen vector is normal to a hyperplane that looks like the dashed line rather than the dotted line? All angles for the line that is the intersection of the random hyperplane and the plane of x and y are equally likely. Thus, the hyperplane will look like the dashed line with probability $\theta/180$ and will look like the dotted line otherwise.

Thus, each hash function f in our locality-sensitive family $\mathbf{F}$ is built from a randomly chosen vector v_f. Given two vectors x and y, say $f(x) = f(y)$ if and only if the dot products $v_f.x$ and $v_f.y$ have the same sign. Then $\mathbf{F}$ is a locality-sensitive family for the cosine distance. The parameters are essentially the same as for the Jaccard-distance family described in Section 3.6.2, except the scale of distances is 0–180 rather than 0–1. That is, $\mathbf{F}$ is a

$$(d_1, d_2, (180 - d_1)/180, d_2/180)\text{-sensitive}$$

family of hash functions. From this basis, we can amplify the family as we wish, just as for the minhash-based family.

3.7.3 Sketches

Instead of chosing a random vector from all possible vectors, it turns out to be sufficiently random if we restrict our choice to vectors whose components are $+1$ and -1. The dot product of any vector x with a vector v of $+1$'s and -1's is formed by adding the components of x where v is $+1$ and then subtracting the other components of x – those where v is -1.

If we pick a collection of random vectors, say $v_1, v_2, \ldots, v_n$, then we can apply them to an arbitrary vector x by computing $v_1.x, v_2.x, \ldots, v_n.x$ and then replacing any positive value by $+1$ and any negative value by -1. The result is called the *sketch* of x. You can handle 0's arbitrarily, e.g., by chosing a result $+1$ or -1 at random. Since there is only a tiny probability of a zero dot product, the choice has essentially no effect.

EXAMPLE 3.21   Suppose our space consists of 4-dimensional vectors, and we pick three random vectors: $v_1 = [+1, -1, +1, +1]$, $v_2 = [-1, +1, -1, +1]$, and $v_3 = [+1, +1, -1, -1]$. For the vector $x = [3, 4, 5, 6]$, the sketch is $[+1, +1, -1]$. That is, $v_1.x = 3 - 4 + 5 + 6 = 10$. Since the result is positive, the first component of the sketch is $+1$. Similarly, $v_2.x = 3$ and $v_3.x = -4$, so the second component of the sketch is $+1$ and the third component is -1.

Consider the vector $y = [4, 3, 2, 1]$. We can similarly compute its sketch to be $[+1, -1, +1]$. Since the sketches for x and y agree in 1/3 of the positions, we estimate that the angle between them is 120 degrees. That is, a randomly chosen hyperplane is twice as likely to look like the dashed line in Fig. 3.12 than like the dotted line.

The above conclusion turns out to be quite wrong. We can calculate the cosine of the angle between x and y to be $x.y$, which is

$$6 \times 1 + 5 \times 2 + 4 \times 3 + 3 \times 4 = 40$$

divided by the magnitudes of the two vectors. These magnitudes are

$$\sqrt{6^2 + 5^2 + 4^2 + 3^2} = 9.274$$

and $\sqrt{1^2 + 2^2 + 3^2 + 4^2} = 5.477$. Thus, the cosine of the angle between x and y is 0.7875, and this angle is about 38 degrees. However, if you look at all 16 different vectors v of length 4 that have $+1$ and -1 as components, you find that there are only four of these whose dot products with x and y have a different sign, namely v_2, v_3, and their complements $[+1, -1, +1, -1]$ and $[-1, -1, +1, +1]$. Thus, had we picked all sixteen of these vectors to form a sketch, the estimate of the angle would have been $180/4 = 45$ degrees.

3.7.4   LSH Families for Euclidean Distance

Now, let us turn to the Euclidean distance (Section 3.5.2), and see if we can develop a locality-sensitive family of hash functions for this distance. We shall start with a 2-dimensional Euclidean space. Each hash function f in our family **F** will be associated with a randomly chosen line in this space. Pick a constant a and divide the line into segments of length a, as suggested by Fig. 3.13, where the "random" line has been oriented to be horizontal.

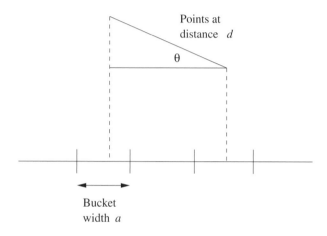

Figure 3.13 Two points at distance $d \gg a$ have a small chance of being hashed to the same bucket

The segments of the line are the buckets into which function f hashes points. A point is hashed to the bucket in which its projection onto the line lies. If the distance d between two points is small compared with a, then there is a good chance the two points hash to the same bucket, and thus the hash function f will declare the two points equal. For example, if $d = a/2$, then there is at least a 50% chance the two points will fall in the same bucket. In fact, if the angle θ between the randomly chosen line and the line connecting the points is large, then there is an even greater chance that the two points will fall in the same bucket. For instance, if θ is 90 degrees, then the two points are certain to fall in the same bucket.

However, suppose d is larger than a. In order for there to be any chance of the two points falling in the same bucket, we need $d \cos \theta \le a$. The diagram of Fig. 3.13 suggests why this requirement holds. Note that even if $d \cos \theta \ll a$ it is still not certain that the two points will fall in the same bucket. However, we can guarantee the following. If $d \ge 2a$, then there is no more than a 1/3 chance the two points fall in the same bucket. The reason is that for $d \cos \theta$ to be less than 1/2, we need to have θ in the range 60 to 90 degrees. If θ is in the range 0 to 60 degrees, then $\cos \theta$ is more than 1/2. But since θ is the smaller angle between two randomly chosen lines in the plane, θ is twice as likely to be between 0 and 60 as it is to be between 60 and 90.

We conclude that the family $\mathbf{F}$ just described forms a $(a/2, 2a, 1/2, 1/3)$-sensitive family of hash functions. That is, for distances up to $a/2$ the probability is at least $1/2$ that two points at that distance will fall in the same bucket, while for distances at least $2a$ the probability points at that distance will fall in the same bucket is at most $1/3$. We can amplify this family as we like, just as for the other examples of locality-sensitive hash functions we have discussed.

3.7.5 More LSH Families for Euclidean Spaces

There is something unsatisfying about the family of hash functions developed in Section 3.7.4. First, the technique was only described for two-dimensional Euclidean spaces. What happens if our data is points in a space with many dimensions? Second, for Jaccard and cosine distances, we were able to develop locality-sensitive families for any pair of distances d_1 and d_2 as long as $d_1 < d_2$. In Section 3.7.4 we appear to need the stronger condition $d_1 < 4d_2$.

However, we claim that there is a locality-sensitive family of hash functions for any $d_1 < d_2$ and for any number of dimensions. The family's hash functions still derive from random lines through the space and a bucket size a that partitions the line. We still hash points by projecting them onto the line. Given that $d_1 < d_2$, we may not know what the probability p_1 is that two points at distance d_1 hash to the same bucket, but we can be certain that it is greater than p_2, the probability that two points at distance d_2 hash to the same bucket. The reason is that this probability surely grows as the distance shrinks. Thus, even if we cannot calculate p_1 and p_2 easily, we know that there is a (d_1, d_2, p_1, p_2)-sensitive family of hash functions for any $d_1 < d_2$ and any given number of dimensions.

Using the amplification techniques of Section 3.6.3, we can then adjust the two probabilities to surround any particular value we like, and to be as far apart as we like. Of course, the further apart we want the probabilities to be, the larger the number of basic hash functions in $\mathbf{F}$ we must use.

3.7.6 Exercises for Section 3.7

EXERCISE 3.7.1 Suppose we construct the basic family of six locality-sensitive functions for vectors of length six. For each pair of the vectors 000000, 110011, 010101, and 011100, which of the six functions makes them candidates?

EXERCISE 3.7.2 Let us compute sketches using the following four "random" vectors:

$$v_1 = [+1, +1, +1, -1] \quad v_2 = [+1, +1, -1, +1]$$
$$v_3 = [+1, -1, +1, +1] \quad v_4 = [-1, +1, +1, +1]$$

Compute the sketches of the following vectors.

(a) $[2, 3, 4, 5]$.

(b) $[-2, 3, -4, 5]$.

(c) $[2, -3, 4, -5]$.

For each pair, what is the estimated angle between them, according to the sketches? What are the true angles?

EXERCISE 3.7.3   Suppose we form sketches by using all sixteen of the vectors of length 4, whose components are each $+1$ or -1. Compute the sketches of the three vectors in Exercise 3.7.2. How do the estimates of the angles between each pair compare with the true angles?

EXERCISE 3.7.4   Suppose we form sketches using the four vectors from Exercise 3.7.2.

! (a) What are the constraints on a, b, c, and d that will cause the sketch of the vector $[a, b, c, d]$ to be $[+1, +1, +1, +1]$?

!! (b) Consider two vectors $[a, b, c, d]$ and $[e, f, g, h]$. What are the conditions on $a, b, \ldots, h$ that will make the sketches of these two vectors be the same?

EXERCISE 3.7.5   Suppose we have points in a 3-dimensional Euclidean space: $p_1 = (1, 2, 3)$, $p_2 = (0, 2, 4)$, and $p_3 = (4, 3, 2)$. Consider the three hash functions defined by the three axes (to make our calculations very easy). Let buckets be of length a, with one bucket the interval $[0, a)$ (i.e., the set of points x such that $0 \le x < a$), the next $[a, 2a)$, the previous one $[-a, 0)$, and so on.

(a) For each of the three lines, assign each of the points to buckets, assuming $a = 1$.

(b) Repeat part (a), assuming $a = 2$.

(c) What are the candidate pairs for the cases $a = 1$ and $a = 2$?

! (d) For each pair of points, for what values of a will that pair be a candidate pair?

3.8   Applications of Locality-Sensitive Hashing

In this section, we shall explore three examples of how LSH is used in practice. In each case, the techniques we have learned must be modified to meet certain constraints of the problem. The three subjects we cover are:

(1) *Entity Resolution*: This term refers to matching data records that refer to the same real-world entity, e.g., the same person. The principal problem addressed here is that the similarity of records does not match exactly either the similar-sets or similar-vectors models of similarity on which the theory is built.

(2) *Matching Fingerprints*: It is possible to represent fingerprints as sets. However, we shall explore a different family of locality-sensitive hash functions from the one we get by minhashing.

(3) *Matching Newspaper Articles*: Here, we consider a different notion of shingling that focuses attention on the core article in an on-line newspaper's Web page, ignoring all the extraneous material such as ads and newspaper-specific material.

3.8.1   Entity Resolution

It is common to have several data sets available, and to know that they refer to some of the same entities. For example, several different bibliographic sources provide information about many of the same books or papers. In the general case, we have records describing entities of some type, such as people or books. The records may all have the same format, or they may have different formats, with different kinds of information.

There are many reasons why information about an entity may vary, even if the field in question is supposed to be the same. For example, names may be expressed differently in different records because of misspellings, absence of a middle initial, use of a nickname, and many other reasons. For example, "Bob S. Jomes" and "Robert Jones Jr." may or may not be the same person. If records come from different sources, the fields may differ as well. One source's records may have an "age" field, while another does not. The second source might have a "date of birth" field, or it may have no information at all about when a person was born.

3.8.2   An Entity-Resolution Example

We shall examine a real example of how LSH was used to deal with an entity-resolution problem. Company A was engaged by Company B to solicit customers for B. Company B would pay A a yearly fee, as long as the customer maintained their subscription. They later quarreled and disagreed over how many customers A had provided to B. Each had about 1,000,000 records, some of which described the same people; those were the customers A had provided to B. The records had different data fields, but unfortunately none of those fields was "this is a customer that A had provided to B." Thus, the problem was to match records from the two sets to see if a pair represented the same person.

Each record had fields for the name, address, and phone number of the person. However, the values in these fields could differ for many reasons. Not only were there the misspellings and other naming differences mentioned in Section 3.8.1, but there were other opportunities to disagree as well. A customer might give their home phone to A and their cell phone to B. Or they might move, and tell B but not A (because they no longer had need for a relationship with A). Area codes of phones sometimes change.

The strategy for identifying records involved scoring the differences in three fields: name, address, and phone. To create a *score* describing the likelihood that two records, one from A and the other from B, described the same person, 100 points was assigned to each of the three fields, so records with exact matches in all three fields got a score of 300. However, there were deductions for mismatches in each of the three fields. As a first approximation, edit-distance (Section 3.5.5) was used, but the penalty grew quadratically with the distance. Then, certain publicly available tables were used to reduce the penalty in appropriate situations. For example, "Bill" and "William" were treated as if they differed in only one letter, even though their edit-distance is 5.

However, it is not feasible to score all one trillion pairs of records. Thus, a simple LSH was used to focus on likely candidates. Three "hash functions" were used. The first sent records to the same bucket only if they had identical names; the second did the same but for identical addresses, and the third did the same for phone numbers. In practice, there was no hashing; rather the records were sorted by name, so records with identical names would appear consecutively and get scored for overall similarity of the name, address, and phone. Then the records were sorted by address, and those with the same address were scored. Finally, the records were sorted a third time by phone, and records with identical phones were scored.

This approach missed a record pair that truly represented the same person but none of the three fields matched exactly. Since the goal was to prove in a court of law that the persons were the same, it is unlikely that such a pair would have been accepted by a judge as sufficiently similar anyway.

3.8.3   Validating Record Matches

What remains is to determine how high a score indicates that two records truly represent the same individual. In the example at hand, there was an easy way to make that decision, and the technique can be applied in many similar situations. It was decided to look at the creation-dates for the records at hand, and to assume that 90 days was an absolute maximum delay between the time the service was bought at Company A and registered at B. Thus, a proposed match between two records that were chosen at random, subject only to the constraint that the date on the B-record was between 0 and 90 days after the date on the A-record, would have an average delay of 45 days.

It was found that of the pairs with a perfect 300 score, the average delay was 10 days. If you assume that 300-score pairs are surely correct matches, then you can look at the pool of pairs with any given score s, and compute the average delay of those pairs. Suppose that the average delay is x, and the fraction of true matches among those pairs with score s is f. Then $x = 10f + 45(1 - f)$, or $x = 45 - 35f$. Solving for f, we find that the fraction of the pairs with score s that are truly matches is $(45 - x)/35$.

The same trick can be used whenever:

(1) There is a scoring system used to evaluate the likelihood that two records represent the same entity, and

---

When Are Record Matches Good Enough?

While every case will be different, it may be of interest to know how the experiment of Section 3.8.3 turned out on the data of Section 3.8.2. For scores down to 185, the value of x was very close to 10; i.e., these scores indicated that the likelihood of the records representing the same person was essentially 1. Note that a score of 185 in this example represents a situation where one field is the same (as would have to be the case, or the records would never even be scored), one field was completely different, and the third field had a small discrepancy. Moreover, for scores as low as 115, the value of x was noticeably less than 45, meaning that some of these pairs did represent the same person. Note that a score of 115 represents a case where one field is the same, but there is only a slight similarity in the other two fields.

---

(2) There is some field, not used in the scoring, from which we can derive a measure that differs, on average, for true pairs and false pairs.

For instance, suppose there were a "height" field recorded by both companies A and B in our running example. We can compute the average difference in height for pairs of random records, and we can compute the average difference in height for records that have a perfect score (and thus surely represent the same entities). For a given score s, we can evaluate the average height difference of the pairs with that score and estimate the probability of the records representing the same entity. That is, if h_0 is the average height difference for the perfect matches, h_1 is the average height difference for random pairs, and h is the average height difference for pairs of score s, then the fraction of good pairs with score s is $(h_1 - h)/(h_1 - h_0)$.

3.8.4 Matching Fingerprints

When fingerprints are matched by computer, the usual representation is not an image, but a set of locations in which *minutiae* are located. A minutia, in the context of fingerprint descriptions, is a place where something unusual happens, such as two ridges merging or a ridge ending. If we place a grid over a fingerprint, we can represent the fingerprint by the set of grid squares in which minutiae are located.

Ideally, before overlaying the grid, fingerprints are normalized for size and orientation, so that if we took two images of the same finger, we would find minutiae lying in exactly the same grid squares. We shall not consider here the best ways to normalize images. Let us assume that some combination of techniques, including choice of grid size and placing a minutia in several adjacent grid squares if it lies close to the border of the squares enables us to assume that grid squares from two images have a significantly higher probability of agreeing in the presence or absence of a minutia than if they were from images of different fingers.

Thus, fingerprints can be represented by sets of grid squares – those where their minutiae are located – and compared like any sets, using the Jaccard similarity or distance. There are two versions of fingerprint comparison, however.

- The *many-one* problem is the one we typically expect. A fingerprint has been found on a gun, and we want to compare it with all the fingerprints in a large database, to see which one matches.
- The *many-many* version of the problem is to take the entire database, and see if there are any pairs that represent the same individual.

While the many-many version matches the model that we have been following for finding similar items, the same technology can be used to speed up the many-one problem.

3.8.5   A LSH Family for Fingerprint Matching

We could minhash the sets that represent a fingerprint, and use the standard LSH technique from Section 3.4. However, since the sets are chosen from a relatively small set of grid points (perhaps 1000), the need to minhash them into more succinct signatures is not clear. We shall study here another form of locality-sensitive hashing that works well for data of the type we are discussing.

Suppose for an example that the probability of finding a minutia in a random grid square of a random fingerprint is 20%. Also, assume that if two fingerprints come from the same finger, and one has a minutia in a given grid square, then the probability that the other does too is 80%. We can define a locality-sensitive family of hash functions as follows. Each function f in this family $\mathbf{F}$ is defined by three grid squares. Function f says "yes" for two fingerprints if both have minutiae in all three grid squares, and otherwise f says "no." Put another way, we may imagine that f sends to a single bucket all fingerprints that have minutiae in all three of f's grid points, and sends each other fingerprint to a bucket of its own. In what follows, we shall refer to the first of these buckets as "the" bucket for f and ignore the buckets that are required to be singletons.

If we want to solve the many-one problem, we can use many functions from the family $\mathbf{F}$ and precompute their buckets of fingerprints to which they answer "yes." Then, given a new fingerprint that we want to match, we determine which of these buckets it belongs to and compare it with all the fingerprints found in any of those buckets. To solve the many-many problem, we compute the buckets for each of the functions and compare all fingerprints in each of the buckets.

Let us consider how many functions we need to get a reasonable probability of catching a match, without having to compare the fingerprint on the gun with each of the millions of fingerprints in the database. First, the probability that two fingerprints from different fingers would be in the bucket for a function f in $\mathbf{F}$ is $(0.2)^6 = 0.000064$. The reason is that they will both go into the bucket only if they each have a minutia in each of the three grid points associated with f, and the probability of each of those six independent events is 0.2.

Now, consider the probability that two fingerprints from the same finger wind up in the bucket for f. The probability that the first fingerprint has minutiae in each of the three squares belonging to f is $(0.2)^3 = 0.008$. However, if it does, then the probability is $(0.8)^3 = 0.512$ that the other fingerprint will as well. Thus, if the fingerprints are from the same finger, there is a $0.008 \times 0.512 = 0.004096$ probability that they will both be in the bucket of f. That is not much; it is about one in 200. However, if we use many functions from $\mathbf{F}$, but not too many, then we can get a good probability of matching fingerprints from the same finger while not having too many false positives – fingerprints that must be considered but do not match.

EXAMPLE 3.22   For a specific example, let us suppose that we use 1024 functions chosen randomly from $\mathbf{F}$. Next, we shall construct a new family $\mathbf{F}_1$ by performing a 1024-way OR on $\mathbf{F}$. Then the probability that $\mathbf{F}_1$ will put fingerprints from the same finger together in at least one bucket is $1 - (1 - 0.004096)^{1024} = 0.985$. On the other hand, the probability that two fingerprints from different fingers will be placed in the same bucket is $(1 - (1 - 0.000064)^{1024} = 0.063$. That is, we get about 1.5% false negatives and about 6.3% false positives.

The result of Example 3.22 is not the best we can do. While it offers only a 1.5% chance that we shall fail to identify the fingerprint on the gun, it does force us to look at 6.3% of the entire database. Increasing the number of functions from $\mathbf{F}$ will increase the number of false positives, with only a small benefit of reducing the number of false negatives below 1.5%. On the other hand, we can also use the AND construction, and in so doing, we can greatly reduce the probability of a false positive, while making only a small increase in the false-negative rate. For instance, we could take 2048 functions from $\mathbf{F}$ in two groups of 1024. Construct the buckets for each of the functions. However, given a fingerprint P on the gun:

(1) Find the buckets from the first group in which P belongs, and take the union of these buckets.

(2) Do the same for the second group.

(3) Take the intersection of the two unions.

(4) Compare P only with those fingerprints in the intersection.

Note that we still have to take unions and intersections of large sets of fingerprints, but we compare only a small fraction of those. It is the comparison of fingerprints that takes the bulk of the time; in steps (1) and (2) fingerprints can be represented by their integer indices in the database.

If we use this scheme, the probability of detecting a matching fingerprint is $(0.985)^2 = 0.970$; that is, we get about 3% false negatives. However, the probability of a false positive is $(0.063)^2 = 0.00397$. That is, we only have to examine about 1/250th of the database.

3.8.6   Similar News Articles

Our last case study concerns the problem of organizing a large repository of on-line news articles by grouping together Web pages that were derived from the same basic text. It is common for organizations like The Associated Press to produce a news item and distribute it to many newspapers. Each newspaper puts the story in its on-line edition, but surrounds it by information that is special to that newspaper, such as the name and address of the newspaper, links to related articles, and links to ads. In addition, it is common for the newspaper to modify the article, perhaps by leaving off the last few paragraphs or even deleting text from the middle. As a result, the same news article can appear quite different at the Web sites of different newspapers.

The problem looks very much like the one that was suggested in Section 3.4: find documents whose shingles have a high Jaccard similarity. Note that this problem is different from the problem of finding news articles that tell about the same events. The latter problem requires other techniques, typically examining the set of important words in the documents (a concept we discussed briefly in Section 1.3.1) and clustering them to group together different articles about the same topic.

However, an interesting variation on the theme of shingling was found to be more effective for data of the type described. The problem is that shingling as we described it in Section 3.2 treats all parts of a document equally. However, we wish to ignore parts of the document, such as ads or the headlines of other articles to which the newspaper added a link, that are not part of the news article. It turns out that there is a noticeable difference between text that appears in prose and text that appears in ads or headlines. Prose has a much greater frequency of stop words, the very frequent words such as "the" or "and." The total number of words that are considered stop words varies with the application, but it is common to use a list of several hundred of the most frequent words.

EXAMPLE 3.23   A typical ad might say simply "Buy Sudzo." On the other hand, a prose version of the same thought that might appear in an article is "I recommend that you buy Sudzo for your laundry." In the latter sentence, it would be normal to treat "I," "that," "you," "for," and "your" as stop words.

Suppose we define a *shingle* to be a stop word followed by the next two words. Then the ad "Buy Sudzo" from Example 3.23 has no shingles and would not be reflected in the representation of the Web page containing that ad. On the other hand, the sentence from Example 3.23 would be represented by five shingles: "I recommend that," "that you buy," "you buy Sudzo," "for your laundry," and "your laundry x," where x is whatever word follows that sentence.

Suppose we have two Web pages, each of which consists of half news text and half ads or other material that has a low density of stop words. If the news text is the same but the surrounding material is different, then we would expect that a large fraction of the shingles of the two pages would be the same. They might have a Jaccard similarity of 75%. However, if the surrounding material is the same but the news content is different, then the number of common shingles would be small, perhaps 25%. If we were to use the conventional shingling, where shingles are (say) sequences of 10 consecutive characters, we would expect the two documents to share half their shingles (i.e., a Jaccard similarity of 1/3), regardless of whether it was the news or the surrounding material that they shared.

3.8.7 Exercises for Section 3.8

EXERCISE 3.8.1 Suppose we are trying to perform entity resolution among bibliographic references, and we score pairs of references based on the similarities of their titles, list of authors, and place of publication. Suppose also that all references include a year of publication, and this year is equally likely to be any of the ten most recent years. Further, suppose that we discover that among the pairs of references with a perfect score, there is an average difference in the publication year of 0.1.[5] Suppose that the pairs of references with a certain score s are found to have an average difference in their publication dates of 2. What is the fraction of pairs with score s that truly represent the same publication? *Note*: Do not make the mistake of assuming the average difference in publication date between random pairs is 5 or 5.5. You need to calculate it exactly, and you have enough information to do so.

EXERCISE 3.8.2 Suppose we use the family $\mathbf{F}$ of functions described in Section 3.8.5, where there is a 20% chance of a minutia in an grid square, an 80% chance of a second copy of a fingerprint having a minutia in a grid square where the first copy does, and each function in $\mathbf{F}$ being formed from three grid squares. In Example 3.22, we constructed family $\mathbf{F}_1$ by using the OR construction on 1024 members of $\mathbf{F}$. Suppose we instead used family $\mathbf{F}_2$ that is a 2048-way OR of members of $\mathbf{F}$.

(a) Compute the rates of false positives and false negatives for $\mathbf{F}_2$.
(b) How do these rates compare with what we get if we organize the same 2048 functions into a 2-way AND of members of $\mathbf{F}_1$, as was discussed at the end of Section 3.8.5?

EXERCISE 3.8.3 Suppose fingerprints have the same statistics outlined in Exercise 3.8.2, but we use a base family of functions $\mathbf{F}'$ defined like $\mathbf{F}$, but using only two randomly chosen grid squares. Construct another set of functions $\mathbf{F}'_1$ from $\mathbf{F}'$ by taking the n-way OR of functions from $\mathbf{F}'$. What, as a function of n, are the false positive and false negative rates for $\mathbf{F}'_1$?

EXERCISE 3.8.4 Suppose we use the functions $\mathbf{F}_1$ from Example 3.22, but we want to solve the many-many problem.

---

[5] We might expect the average to be 0, but in practice, errors in publication year do occur.

(a) If two fingerprints are from the same finger, what is the probability that they will not be compared (i.e., what is the false negative rate)?

(b) What fraction of the fingerprints from different fingers will be compared (i.e., what is the false positive rate)?

! EXERCISE 3.8.5   Assume we have the set of functions $\mathbf{F}$ as in Exercise 3.8.2, and we construct a new set of functions $\mathbf{F}_3$ by an n-way OR of functions in $\mathbf{F}$. For what value of n is the sum of the false positive and false negative rates minimized?

3.9   Methods for High Degrees of Similarity

LSH-based methods appear most effective when the degree of similarity we accept is relatively low. When we want to find sets that are almost identical, there are other methods that can be faster. Moreover, these methods are exact, in that they find every pair of items with the desired degree of similarity. There are no false negatives, as there can be with LSH.

3.9.1   Finding Identical Items

The extreme case is finding identical items, for example, Web pages that are identical, character-for-character. It is straightforward to compare two documents and tell whether they are identical, but we still must avoid having to compare every pair of documents. Our first thought would be to hash documents based on their first few characters, and compare only those documents that fell into the same bucket. That scheme should work well, unless all the documents begin with the same characters, such as an HTML header.

Our second thought would be to use a hash function that examines the entire document. That would work, and if we use enough buckets, it would be very rare that two documents went into the same bucket, yet were not identical. The downside of this approach is that we must examine every character of every document. If we limit our examination to a small number of characters, then we never have to examine a document that is unique and falls into a bucket of its own.

A better approach is to pick some fixed random positions for all documents, and make the hash function depend only on these. This way, we can avoid a problem where there is a common prefix for all or most documents, yet we need not examine entire documents unless they fall into a bucket with another document. One problem with selecting fixed positions is that if some documents are short, they may not have some of the selected positions. However, if we are looking for highly similar documents, we never need to compare two documents that differ significantly in their length. We exploit this idea in Section 3.9.3.

3.9.2   Representing Sets as Strings

Now, let us focus on the harder problem of finding, in a large collection of sets, all pairs that have a high Jaccard similarity, say at least 0.9. We can represent a set by sorting the elements of the universal set in some fixed order, and representing any set by listing its elements in this order. The list is essentially a string of "characters," where the characters are the elements of the universal set. These strings are unusual, however, in that:

(1) No character appears more than once in a string, and

(2) If two characters appear in two different strings, then they appear in the same order in both strings.

EXAMPLE 3.24   Suppose the universal set consists of the 26 lower-case letters, and we use the normal alphabetical order. Then the set $\{d, a, b\}$ is represented by the string abd.

In what follows, we shall assume all strings represent sets in the manner just described. Thus, we shall talk about the Jaccard similarity of strings, when strictly speaking we mean the similarity of the sets that the strings represent. Also, we shall talk of the length of a string, as a surrogate for the number of elements in the set that the string represents.

Note that the documents discussed in Section 3.9.1 do not exactly match this model, even though we can see documents as strings. To fit the model, we would shingle the documents, assign an order to the shingles, and represent each document by its list of shingles in the selected order.

3.9.3   Length-Based Filtering

The simplest way to exploit the string representation of Section 3.9.2 is to sort the strings by length. Then, each string s is compared with those strings t that follow s in the list, but are not too long. Suppose the upper bound on Jaccard distance between two strings is J. For any string x, denote its length by L_x. Note that $L_s \leq L_t$. The intersection of the sets represented by s and t cannot have more than L_s members, while their union has at least L_t members. Thus, the Jaccard similarity of s and t, which we denote $\text{SIM}(s, t)$, is at most L_s/L_t. That is, in order for s and t to require comparison, it must be that $J \leq L_s/L_t$, or equivalently, $L_t \leq L_s/J$.

EXAMPLE 3.25   Suppose that s is a string of length 9, and we are looking for strings with at least 0.9 Jaccard similarity. Then we have only to compare s with strings following it in the length-based sorted order that have length at most $9/0.9 = 10$. That is, we compare s with those strings of length 9 that follow it in order, and all strings of length 10. We have no need to compare s with any other string.

Suppose the length of s were 8 instead. Then s would be compared with

---

> ### A Better Ordering for Symbols
>
> Instead of using the obvious order for elements of the universal set, e.g., lexicographic order for shingles, we can order symbols rarest first. That is, determine how many times each element appears in the collection of sets, and order them by this count, lowest first. The advantage of doing so is that the symbols in prefixes will tend to be rare. Thus, they will cause that string to be placed in index buckets that have relatively few members. Then, when we need to examine a string for possible matches, we shall find few other strings that are candidates for comparison.

following strings of length up to $8/0.9 = 8.89$. That is, a string of length 9 would be too long to have a Jaccard similarity of 0.9 with s, so we only have to compare s with the strings that have length 8 but follow it in the sorted order.

3.9.4   Prefix Indexing

In addition to length, there are several other features of strings that can be exploited to limit the number of comparisons that must be made to identify all pairs of similar strings. The simplest of these options is to create an index for each symbol; recall a symbol of a string is any one of the elements of the universal set. For each string s, we select a prefix of s consisting of the first p symbols of s. How large p must be depends on L_s and J, the lower bound on Jaccard distance. We add string s to the index for each of its first p symbols.

In effect, the index for each symbol becomes a bucket of strings that must be compared. We must be certain that any other string t such that $\text{SIM}(s,t) \geq J$ will have at least one symbol in its prefix that also appears in the prefix of s.

Suppose not; rather $\text{SIM}(s,t) \geq J$, but t has none of the first p symbols of s. Then the highest Jaccard similarity that s and t can have occurs when t is a suffix of s, consisting of everything but the first p symbols of s. The Jaccard similarity of s and t would then be $(L_s - p)/L_s$. To be sure that we do not have to compare s with t, we must be certain that $J > (L_s - p)/L_s$. That is, p must be at least $\lfloor (1-J)L_s \rfloor + 1$. Of course we want p to be as small as possible, so we do not index string s in more buckets than we need to. Thus, we shall hereafter take $p = \lfloor (1-J)L_s \rfloor + 1$ to be the length of the prefix that gets indexed.

EXAMPLE 3.26   Suppose $J = 0.9$. If $L_s = 9$, then $p = \lfloor 0.1 \times 9 \rfloor + 1 = \lfloor 0.9 \rfloor + 1 = 1$. That is, we need to index s under only its first symbol. Any string t that does not have the first symbol of s in a position such that t is indexed by that symbol will have Jaccard similarity with s that is less than 0.9. Suppose s is bcdefghij. Then s is indexed under b only. Suppose t does not begin with b. There are two cases to consider.

(1) If t begins with a, and $\text{SIM}(s,t) \geq 0.9$, then it can only be that t is abcdefghij. But if that is the case, t will be indexed under both a and b. The reason is

that $L_t = 10$, so t will be indexed under the symbols of its prefix of length $\lfloor 0.1 \times 10 \rfloor + 1 = 2$.

(2) If t begins with c or a later letter, then the maximum value of $\text{SIM}(s,t)$ occurs when t is cdefghij. But then $\text{SIM}(s,t) = 8/9 < 0.9$.

In general, with $J = 0.9$, strings of length up to 9 are indexed by their first symbol, strings of lengths 10–19 are indexed under their first two symbols, strings of length 20–29 are indexed under their first three symbols, and so on.

We can use the indexing scheme in two ways, depending on whether we are trying to solve the many-many problem or a many-one problem; recall the distinction was introduced in Section 3.8.4. For the many-one problem, we create the index for the entire database. To query for matches to a new set S, we convert that set to a string s, which we call the *probe* string. Determine the length of the prefix that must be considered, that is, $\lfloor (1-J)L_s \rfloor + 1$. For each symbol appearing in one of the prefix positions of s, we look in the index bucket for that symbol, and we compare s with all the strings appearing in that bucket.

If we want to solve the many-many problem, start with an empty database of strings and indexes. For each set S, we treat S as a new set for the many-one problem. We convert S to a string s, which we treat as a probe string in the many-one problem. However, after we examine an index bucket, we also add s to that bucket, so s will be compared with later strings that could be matches.

3.9.5   Using Position Information

Consider the strings $s = $ acdefghijk and $t = $ bcdefghijk, and assume $J = 0.9$. Since both strings are of length 10, they are indexed under their first two symbols. Thus, s is indexed under a and c, while t is indexed under b and c. Whichever is added last will find the other in the bucket for c, and they will be compared. However, since c is the second symbol of both, we know there will be two symbols, a and b in this case, that are in the union of the two sets but not in the intersection. Indeed, even though s and t are identical from c to the end, their intersection is 9 symbols and their union is 11; thus $\text{SIM}(s,t) = 9/11$, which is less than 0.9.

If we build our index based not only on the symbol, but on the position of the symbol within the string, we could avoid comparing s and t above. That is, let our index have a bucket for each pair (x, i), containing the strings that have symbol x in position i of their prefix. Given a string s, and assuming J is the minimum desired Jaccard distance, we look at the prefix of s, that is, the positions 1 through $\lfloor (1-J)L_s \rfloor + 1$. If the symbol in position i of the prefix is x, add s to the index bucket for (x, i).

Now consider s as a probe string. With what buckets must it be compared? We shall visit the symbols of the prefix of s from the left, and we shall take advantage of the fact that we only need to find a possible matching string t if none of the previous buckets we have examined for matches held t. That is, we only need to find a candidate match once. Thus, if we find that the ith symbol of s is x, then we need look in the bucket (x, j) for certain small values of j.

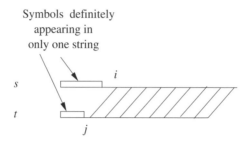

Figure 3.14 Strings s and t begin with $i - 1$ and $j - 1$ unique symbols, respectively, and then agree beyond that

To compute the upper bound on j, suppose t is a string none of whose first $j - 1$ symbols matched anything in s, but the ith symbol of s is the same as the jth symbol of t. The highest value of $\text{SIM}(s, t)$ occurs if s and t are identical beyond their ith and jth symbols, respectively, as suggested by Fig. 3.14. If that is the case, the size of their intersection is $L_s - i + 1$, since that is the number of symbols of s that could possibly be in t. The size of their union is at least $L_s + j - 1$. That is, s surely contributes L_s symbols to the union, and there are also at least $j - 1$ symbols of t that are not in s. The ratio of the sizes of the intersection and union must be at least J, so we must have:

$$\frac{L_s - i + 1}{L_s + j - 1} \geq J$$

If we isolate j in this inequality, we have $j \leq \big(L_s(1 - J) - i + 1 + J\big)/J$.

EXAMPLE 3.27 Consider the string $s = \texttt{acdefghijk}$ with $J = 0.9$ discussed at the beginning of this section. Suppose s is now a probe string. We already established that we need to consider the first two positions; that is, i can be 1 or 2. Suppose $i = 1$. Then $j \leq (10 \times 0.1 - 1 + 1 + 0.9)/0.9$. That is, we only have to compare the symbol $\texttt{a}$ with strings in the bucket for $(\texttt{a}, j)$ if $j \leq 2.11$. Thus, j can be 1 or 2, but nothing higher.

Now suppose $i = 2$. Then we require $j \leq (10 \times 0.1 - 2 + 1 + 0.9)/0.9$, Or $j \leq 1$. We conclude that we must look in the buckets for $(\texttt{a}, 1)$, $(\texttt{a}, 2)$, and $(\texttt{c}, 1)$, but in no other bucket. In comparison, using the buckets of Section 3.9.4, we would look into the buckets for $\texttt{a}$ and $\texttt{c}$, which is equivalent to looking to all buckets $(\texttt{a}, j)$ and $(\texttt{c}, j)$ for any j.

3.9.6   Using Position and Length in Indexes

When we considered the upper limit on j in the previous section, we assumed that what follows positions i and j were as in Fig. 3.14, where what followed these positions in strings s and t matched exactly. We do not want to build an index that involves every symbol in the strings, because that makes the total work excessive. However, we can add to our index a summary of what follows the positions being indexed. Doing so expands the number of buckets, but not beyond reasonable bounds, and yet enables us to eliminate many candidate matches without comparing entire strings. The idea is to use index buckets corresponding to a symbol, a position, and the *suffix length*, that is, the number of symbols following the position in question.

EXAMPLE 3.28 The string $s = \texttt{acdefghijk}$, with $J = 0.9$, would be indexed in the buckets for $(\texttt{a}, 1, 9)$ and $(\texttt{c}, 2, 8)$. That is, the first position of s has symbol $\texttt{a}$, and its suffix is of length 9. The second position has symbol $\texttt{c}$ and its suffix is of length 8.

Figure 3.14 assumes that the suffixes for position i of s and position j of t have the same length. If not, then we can either get a smaller upper bound on the size of the intersection of s and t (if t is shorter) or a larger lower bound on the size of the union (if t is longer). Suppose s has prefix length p and t has prefix length q.

Case 1: $p \geq q$. Here, the maximum size of the intersection is

$$L_s - i + 1 - (p - q)$$

Since $L_s = i + p$, we can write the above expression for the intersection size as $q + 1$. The minimum size of the union is $L_s + j - 1$, as it was when we did not take suffix length into account. Thus, we require

$$\frac{q + 1}{L_s + j - 1} \geq J$$

whenever $p \geq q$.

Case 2: $p < q$. Here, the maximum size of the intersection is $L_s - i + 1$, as when suffix length was not considered. However, the minimum size of the union is now $L_s + j - 1 + q - p$. If we again use the relationship $L_s = i + p$, we can replace $L_s - p$ by i and get the formula $i + j - 1 + q$ for the size of the union. If the Jaccard similarity is at least J, then

$$\frac{L_s - i + 1}{i + j - 1 + q} \geq J$$

whenever $p < q$.

EXAMPLE 3.29 Let us again consider the string $s = \texttt{acdefghijk}$, but to make the example show some details, let us choose $J = 0.8$ instead of 0.9. We know that $L_s = 10$. Since $\lfloor (1 - J)L_s \rfloor + 1 = 3$, we must consider prefix positions $i = 1$, 2, and 3 in what follows. As before, let p be the suffix length of s and q the suffix length of t.

First, consider the case $p \geq q$. The additional constraint we have on q and j is $(q+1)/(9+j) \geq 0.8$. We can enumerate the pairs of values of j and q for each i between 1 and 3, as follows.

$i = 1$: Here, $p = 9$, so $q \leq 9$. Let us consider the possible values of q:

$q = 9$: We must have $10/(9+j) \geq 0.8$. Thus, we can have $j = 1$, $j = 2$, or $j = 3$. Note that for $j = 4$, $10/13 > 0.8$.

$q = 8$: We must have $9/(9+j) \geq 0.8$. Thus, we can have $j = 1$ or $j = 2$. For $j = 3$, $9/12 > 0.8$.

$q = 7$: We must have $8/(9+j) \geq 0.8$. Only $j = 1$ satisfies this inequality.

$q = 6$: There are no possible values of j, since $7/(9+j) > 0.8$ for every positive integer j. The same holds for every smaller value of q.

$i = 2$: Here, $p = 8$, so we require $q \leq 8$. Since the constraint $(q+1)/(9+j \geq 0.8$ does not depend on i,[6] we can use the analysis from the above case, but exclude the case $q = 9$. Thus, the only possible values of j and q when $i = 2$ are

(1) $q = 8$; $j = 1$.
(2) $q = 8$; $j = 2$.
(3) $q = 7$; $j = 1$.

$i = 3$: Now, $p = 7$ and the constraints are $q \leq 7$ and $(q+1)/(9+j) \geq 0.8$. The only option is $q = 7$ and $j = 1$.

Next, we must consider the case $p < q$. The additional constraint is

$$\frac{11 - i}{i + j + q - 1} \geq 0.8$$

Again, consider each possible value of i.

$i = 1$: Then $p = 9$, so we require $q \geq 10$ and $10/(q+j) \geq 0.8$. The possible values of q and j are

(1) $q = 10$; $j = 1$.
(2) $q = 10$; $j = 2$.
(3) $q = 11$; $j = 1$.

$i = 2$: Now, $p = 10$, so we require $q \geq 11$ and $9/(q+j+1) \geq 0.8$. there are no solutions, since j must be a positive integer.

$i = 3$: As for $i = 2$, there are no solutions.

When we accumulate the possible combinations of i, j, and q, we see that the set of index buckets in which we must look forms a pyramid. Figure 3.15 shows the buckets in which we must search. That is, we must look in those buckets (x, j, q) such that the ith symbol of the string s is x, j is the position associated with the bucket and q the suffix length.

---

[6] Note that i does influence the value of p, and through p, puts a limit on q.

q	$j = 1$	$j = 2$	$j = 3$
7	x		
8	x	x	
$i = 1$ 9	x	x	x
10	x	x	
11	x		
7	x		
$i = 2$ 8	x	x	
9	x		
$i = 3$ 7	x		

Figure 3.15 The buckets that must be examined to find possible matches for the string $s = $ acdefghijk with $J = 0.8$ are marked with an x

3.9.7 Exercises for Section 3.9

EXERCISE 3.9.1   Suppose our universal set is the lower-case letters, and the order of elements is taken to be the vowels, in alphabetic order, followed by the consonants in reverse alphabetic order. Represent the following sets as strings.

(a) $\{q, w, e, r, t, y\}$.
(b) $\{a, s, d, f, g, h, j, u, i\}$.

EXERCISE 3.9.2   Suppose we filter candidate pairs based only on length, as in Section 3.9.3. If s is a string of length 20, with what strings is s compared when J, the lower bound on Jaccard similarity has the following values:

(a) $J = 0.85$;
(b) $J = 0.95$;
(c) $J = 0.98$?

EXERCISE 3.9.3   Suppose we have a string s of length 15, and we wish to index its prefix as in Section 3.9.4.

(a) How many positions are in the prefix if $J = 0.85$?
(b) How many positions are in the prefix if $J = 0.95$?
! (c) For what range of values of J will s be indexed under its first four symbols, but no more?

EXERCISE 3.9.4   Suppose s is a string of length 12. With what symbol-position pairs will s be compared with if we use the indexing approach of Section 3.9.5, and

(a) $J = 0.75$;
(b) $J = 0.95$?

! EXERCISE 3.9.5   Suppose we use position information in our index, as in Section 3.9.5. Strings s and t are both chosen at random from a universal set of 100 elements. Assume $J = 0.9$. What is the probability that s and t will be compared if

(a) s and t are both of length 9.
(b) s and t are both of length 10.

EXERCISE 3.9.6   Suppose we use indexes based on both position and suffix length, as in Section 3.9.6. If s is a string of length 20, with what symbol-position-length triples will s be compared with, if

(a) $J = 0.8$;
(b) $J = 0.9$?

3.10   Summary of Chapter 3

✦   *Jaccard Similarity*: The Jaccard similarity of sets is the ratio of the size of the intersection of the sets to the size of the union. This measure of similarity is suitable for many applications, including textual similarity of documents and similarity of buying habits of customers.

✦   *Shingling*: A k-shingle is any k characters that appear consecutively in a document. If we represent a document by its set of k-shingles, then the Jaccard similarity of the shingle sets measures the textual similarity of documents. Sometimes, it is useful to hash shingles to bit strings of shorter length, and use sets of hash values to represent documents.

✦   *Minhashing*: A minhash function on sets is based on a permutation of the universal set. Given any such permutation, the minhash value for a set is that element of the set that appears first in the permuted order.

✦   *Minhash Signatures*: We may represent sets by picking some list of permutations and computing for each set its minhash signature, which is the sequence of minhash values obtained by applying each permutation on the list to that set. Given two sets, the expected fraction of the permutations that will yield the same minhash value is exactly the Jaccard similarity of the sets.

✦   *Efficient Minhashing*: Since it is not really possible to generate random permutations, it is normal to simulate a permutation by picking a random hash function and taking the minhash value for a set to be the least hash value of any of the set's members.

✦   *Locality-Sensitive Hashing for Signatures*: This technique allows us to avoid computing the similarity of every pair of sets or their minhash signatures. If we are given signatures for the sets, we may divide them into bands, and only measure the similarity of a pair of sets if they are identical in at least one band. By choosing the size of bands appropriately, we can eliminate from consideration most of the pairs that do not meet our threshold of similarity.

✦ *Distance Measures*: A distance measure is a function on pairs of points in a space that satisfy certain axioms. The distance between two points is 0 if the points are the same, but greater than 0 if the points are different. The distance is symmetric; it does not matter in which order we consider the two points. A distance measure must satisfy the triangle inequality: the distance between two points is never more than the sum of the distances between those points and some third point.

✦ *Euclidean Distance*: The most common notion of distance is the Euclidean distance in an n-dimensional space. This distance, sometimes called the L_2-norm, is the square root of the sum of the squares of the differences between the points in each dimension. Another distance suitable for Euclidean spaces, called Manhattan distance or the L_1-norm is the sum of the magnitudes of the differences between the points in each dimension.

✦ *Jaccard Distance*: One minus the Jaccard similarity is a distance measure, called the Jaccard distance.

✦ *Cosine Distance*: The angle between vectors in a vector space is the cosine distance measure. We can compute the cosine of that angle by taking the dot product of the vectors and dividing by the lengths of the vectors.

✦ *Edit Distance*: This distance measure applies to a space of strings, and is the number of insertions and/or deletions needed to convert one string into the other. The edit distance can also be computed as the sum of the lengths of the strings minus twice the length of the longest common subsequence of the strings.

✦ *Hamming Distance*: This distance measure applies to a space of vectors. The Hamming distance between two vectors is the number of positions in which the vectors differ.

✦ *Generalized Locality-Sensitive Hashing*: We may start with any collection of functions, such as the minhash functions, that can render a decision as to whether or not a pair of items should be candidates for similarity checking. The only constraint on these functions is that they provide a lower bound on the probability of saying "yes" if the distance (according to some distance measure) is below a given limit, and an upper bound on the probability of saying "yes" if the distance is above another given limit. We can then increase the probability of saying "yes" for nearby items and at the same time decrease the probability of saying "yes" for distant items to as great an extent as we wish, by applying an AND construction and an OR construction.

✦ *Random Hyperplanes and LSH for Cosine Distance*: We can get a set of basis functions to start a generalized LSH for the cosine distance measure by identifying each function with a list of randomly chosen vectors. We apply a function to a given vector v by taking the dot product of v with each vector on the list. The result is a sketch consisting of the signs (+1 or −1) of the dot products. The fraction of positions in which the sketches of two vectors agree, multiplied by 180, is an estimate of the angle between the two vectors.

✦ *LSH For Euclidean Distance*: A set of basis functions to start LSH for Euclidean distance can be obtained by choosing random lines and projecting points onto those lines. Each line is broken into fixed-length intervals, and the function answers "yes" to a pair of points that fall into the same interval.

✦ *High-Similarity Detection by String Comparison*: An alternative approach to finding similar items, when the threshold of Jaccard similarity is close to 1, avoids using minhashing and LSH. Rather, the universal set is ordered, and sets are represented by strings, consisting their elements in order. The simplest way to avoid comparing all pairs of sets or their strings is to note that highly similar sets will have strings of approximately the same length. If we sort the strings, we can compare each string with only a small number of the immediately following strings.

✦ *Character Indexes*: If we represent sets by strings, and the similarity threshold is close to 1, we can index all strings by their first few characters. The prefix whose characters must be indexed is approximately the length of the string times the maximum Jaccard distance (1 minus the minimum Jaccard similarity).

✦ *Position Indexes*: We can index strings not only on the characters in their prefixes, but on the position of that character within the prefix. We reduce the number of pairs of strings that must be compared, because if two strings share a character that is not in the first position in both strings, then we know that either there are some preceding characters that are in the union but not the intersection, or there is an earlier symbol that appears in both strings.

✦ *Suffix Indexes*: We can also index strings based not only on the characters in their prefixes and the positions of those characters, but on the length of the character's suffix – the number of positions that follow it in the string. This structure further reduces the number of pairs that must be compared, because a common symbol with different suffix lengths implies additional characters that must be in the union but not in the intersection.

3.11   References for Chapter 3

The technique we called shingling is attributed to [(10)]. The use in the manner we discussed here is from [(2)]. Minhashing comes from [(3)]. The original works on locality-sensitive hashing were [(9)] and [(7)]. [(1)] is a useful summary of ideas in this field.

[(4)] introduces the idea of using random-hyperplanes to summarize items in a way that respects the cosine distance. [(8)] suggests that random hyperplanes plus LSH can be more accurate at detecting similar documents than minhashing plus LSH.

Techniques for summarizing points in a Euclidean space are covered in [(6)]. [(11)] presented the shingling technique based on stop words.

The length and prefix-based indexing schemes for high-similarity matching comes from [(5)]. The technique involving suffix length is from [(12)].

(1) A. Andoni and P. Indyk, "Near-optimal hashing algorithms for approximate nearest neighbor in high dimensions," *Comm. ACM* **51**:1, pp. 117–122, 2008.

(2) A.Z. Broder, "On the resemblance and containment of documents," *Proc. Compression and Complexity of Sequences*, pp. 21–29, Positano Italy, 1997.

(3) A.Z. Broder, M. Charikar, A.M. Frieze, and M. Mitzenmacher, "Min-wise independent permutations," *ACM Symposium on Theory of Computing*, pp. 327–336, 1998.

(4) M.S. Charikar, "Similarity estimation techniques from rounding algorithms," *ACM Symposium on Theory of Computing*, pp. 380–388, 2002.

(5) S. Chaudhuri, V. Ganti, and R. Kaushik, "A primitive operator for similarity joins in data cleaning," *Proc. Intl. Conf. on Data Engineering*, 2006.

(6) M. Datar, N. Immorlica, P. Indyk, and V.S. Mirrokni, "Locality-sensitive hashing scheme based on p-stable distributions," *Symposium on Computational Geometry* pp. 253–262, 2004.

(7) A. Gionis, P. Indyk, and R. Motwani, "Similarity search in high dimensions via hashing," *Proc. Intl. Conf. on Very Large Databases*, pp. 518–529, 1999.

(8) M. Henzinger, "Finding near-duplicate web pages: a large-scale evaluation of algorithms," *Proc. 29th SIGIR Conf.*, pp. 284–291, 2006.

(9) P. Indyk and R. Motwani. "Approximate nearest neighbor: towards removing the curse of dimensionality," *ACM Symposium on Theory of Computing*, pp. 604–613, 1998.

(10) U. Manber, "Finding similar files in a large file system," *Proc. USENIX Conference*, pp. 1–10, 1994.

(11) M. Theobald, J. Siddharth, and A. Paepcke, "SpotSigs: robust and efficient near duplicate detection in large web collections," *31st Annual ACM SIGIR Conference*, July, 2008, Singapore.

(12) C. Xiao, W. Wang, X. Lin, and J.X. Yu, "Efficient similarity joins for near duplicate detection," *Proc. WWW Conference*, pp. 131-140, 2008.

4 Mining Data Streams

Most of the algorithms described in this book assume that we are mining a database. That is, all our data is available when and if we want it. In this chapter, we shall make another assumption: data arrives in a stream or streams, and if it is not processed immediately or stored, then it is lost forever. Moreover, we shall assume that the data arrives so rapidly that it is not feasible to store it all in active storage (i.e., in a conventional database), and then interact with it at the time of our choosing.

The algorithms for processing streams each involve summarization of the stream in some way. We shall start by considering how to make a useful sample of a stream and how to filter a stream to eliminate most of the "undesirable" elements. We then show how to estimate the number of different elements in a stream using much less storage than would be required if we listed all the elements we have seen.

Another approach to summarizing a stream is to look at only a fixed-length "window" consisting of the last n elements for some (typically large) n. We then query the window as if it were a relation in a database. If there are many streams and/or n is large, we may not be able to store the entire window for every stream, so we need to summarize even the windows. We address the fundamental problem of maintaining an approximate count on the number of 1's in the window of a bit stream, while using much less space than would be needed to store the entire window itself. This technique generalizes to approximating various kinds of sums.

4.1 The Stream Data Model

Let us begin by discussing the elements of streams and stream processing. We explain the difference between streams and databases and the special problems that arise when dealing with streams. Some typical applications where the stream model applies will be examined.

4.1.1 A Data-Stream-Management System

In analogy to a database-management system, we can view a stream processor as a kind of data-management system, the high-level organization of which is suggested in Fig. 4.1. Any number of streams can enter the system. Each stream

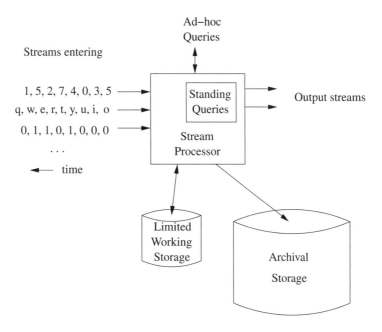

Streams entering

Ad–hoc
Queries

1, 5, 2, 7, 4, 0, 3, 5

q, w, e, r, t, y, u, i, o

0, 1, 1, 0, 1, 0, 0, 0

. . .

← time

Standing
Queries

Stream
Processor

Output streams

Limited
Working
Storage

Archival

Storage

Figure 4.1 A data-stream-management system

can provide elements at its own schedule; they need not have the same data rates
or data types, and the time between elements of one stream need not be uniform.
The fact that the rate of arrival of stream elements is not under the control of
the system distinguishes stream processing from the processing of data that goes
on within a database-management system. The latter system controls the rate
at which data is read from the disk, and therefore never has to worry about data
getting lost as it attempts to execute queries.

Streams may be archived in a large *archival store*, but we assume it is not
possible to answer queries from the archival store. It could be examined only
under special circumstances using time-consuming retrieval processes. There is
also a *working store*, into which summaries or parts of streams may be placed,
and which can be used for answering queries. The working store might be disk,
or it might be main memory, depending on how fast we need to process queries.
But either way, it is of sufficiently limited capacity that it cannot store all the
data from all the streams.

4.1.2   Examples of Stream Sources

Before proceeding, let us consider some of the ways in which stream data arises
naturally.

Sensor Data

Imagine a temperature sensor bobbing about in the ocean, sending back to a
base station a reading of the surface temperature each hour. The data produced

by this sensor is a stream of real numbers. It is not a very interesting stream, since the data rate is so low. It would not stress modern technology, and the entire stream could be kept in main memory, essentially forever.

Now, give the sensor a GPS unit, and let it report surface height instead of temperature. The surface height varies quite rapidly compared with temperature, so we might have the sensor send back a reading every tenth of a second. If it sends a 4-byte real number each time, then it produces 3.5 megabytes per day. It will still take some time to fill up main memory, let alone a single disk.

But one sensor might not be that interesting. To learn something about ocean behavior, we might want to deploy a million sensors, each sending back a stream, at the rate of ten per second. A million sensors isn't very many; there would be one for every 150 square miles of ocean. Now we have 3.5 terabytes arriving every day, and we definitely need to think about what can be kept in working storage and what can only be archived.

Image Data

Satellites often send down to earth streams consisting of many terabytes of images per day. Surveillance cameras produce images with lower resolution than satellites, but there can be many of them, each producing a stream of images at intervals like one second. London is said to have six million such cameras, each producing a stream.

Internet and Web Traffic

A switching node in the middle of the Internet receives streams of IP packets from many inputs and routes them to its outputs. Normally, the job of the switch is to transmit data and not to retain it or query it. But there is a tendency to put more capability into the switch, e.g., the ability to detect denial-of-service attacks or the ability to reroute packets based on information about congestion in the network.

Web sites receive streams of various types. For example, Google receives several hundred million search queries per day. Yahoo! accepts billions of "clicks" per day on its various sites. Many interesting things can be learned from these streams. For example, an increase in queries like "sore throat" enables us to track the spread of viruses. A sudden increase in the click rate for a link could indicate some news connected to that page, or it could mean that the link is broken and needs to be repaired.

4.1.3   Stream Queries

There are two ways that queries get asked about streams. We show in Fig. 4.1 a place within the processor where *standing queries* are stored. These queries are, in a sense, permanently executing, and produce outputs at appropriate times.

EXAMPLE 4.1   The stream produced by the ocean-surface-temperature sensor mentioned at the beginning of Section 4.1.2 might have a standing query to output an alert whenever the temperature exceeds 25 degrees centigrade. This query is easily answered, since it depends only on the most recent stream element.

Alternatively, we might have a standing query that, each time a new reading arrives, produces the average of the 24 most recent readings. That query also can be answered easily, if we store the 24 most recent stream elements. When a new stream element arrives, we can drop from the working store the 25th most recent element, since it will never again be needed (unless there is some other standing query that requires it).

Another query we might ask is the maximum temperature ever recorded by that sensor. We can answer this query by retaining a simple summary: the maximum of all stream elements ever seen. It is not necessary to record the entire stream. When a new stream element arrives, we compare it with the stored maximum, and set the maximum to whichever is larger. We can then answer the query by producing the current value of the maximum. Similarly, if we want the average temperature over all time, we have only to record two values: the number of readings ever sent in the stream and the sum of those readings. We can adjust these values easily each time a new reading arrives, and we can produce their quotient as the answer to the query.

The other form of query is *ad-hoc*, a question asked once about the current state of a stream or streams. If we do not store all streams in their entirety, as normally we can not, then we cannot expect to answer arbitrary queries about streams. If we have some idea what kind of queries will be asked through the ad-hoc query interface, then we can prepare for them by storing appropriate parts or summaries of streams as in Example 4.1.

If we want the facility to ask a wide variety of ad-hoc queries, a common approach is to store a *sliding window* of each stream in the working store. A sliding window can be the most recent n elements of a stream, for some n, or it can be all the elements that arrived within the last t time units, e.g., one day. If we regard each stream element as a tuple, we can treat the window as a relation and query it with any SQL query. Of course the stream-management system must keep the window fresh, deleting the oldest elements as new ones come in.

EXAMPLE 4.2 Web sites often like to report the number of unique users over the past month. If we think of each login as a stream element, we can maintain a window that is all logins in the most recent month. We must associate the arrival time with each login, so we know when it no longer belongs to the window. If we think of the window as a relation `Logins(name, time)`, then it is simple to get the number of unique users over the past month. The SQL query is:

```
SELECT COUNT(DISTINCT(name))
FROM Logins
WHERE time >= t;
```

Here, t is a constant that represents the time one month before the current time.

Note that we must be able to maintain the entire stream of logins for the past month in working storage. However, for even the largest sites, that data is not more than a few terabytes, and so surely can be stored on disk.

4.1.4   Issues in Stream Processing

Before proceeding to discuss algorithms, let us consider the constraints under which we work when dealing with streams. First, streams often deliver elements very rapidly. We must process elements in real time, or we lose the opportunity to process them at all, without accessing the archival storage. Thus, it often is important that the stream-processing algorithm is executed in main memory, without access to secondary storage or with only rare accesses to secondary storage. Moreover, even when streams are "slow," as in the sensor-data example of Section 4.1.2, there may be many such streams. Even if each stream by itself can be processed using a small amount of main memory, the requirements of all the streams together can easily exceed the amount of available main memory.

Thus, many problems about streaming data would be easy to solve if we had enough memory, but become rather hard and require the invention of new techniques in order to execute them at a realistic rate on a machine of realistic size. Here are two generalizations about stream algorithms worth bearing in mind as you read through this chapter:

- Often, it is much more efficient to get an approximate answer to our problem than an exact solution.
- As in Chapter 3, a variety of techniques related to hashing turn out to be useful. Generally, these techniques introduce useful randomness into the algorithm's behavior, in order to produce an approximate answer that is very close to the true result.

4.2   Sampling Data in a Stream

As our first example of managing streaming data, we shall look at extracting reliable samples from a stream. As with many stream algorithms, the "trick" involves using hashing in a somewhat unusual way.

4.2.1   A Motivating Example

The general problem we shall address is selecting a subset of a stream so that we can ask queries about the selected subset and have the answers be statistically representative of the stream as a whole. If we know what queries are to be asked, then there are a number of methods that might work, but we are looking for a technique that will allow ad-hoc queries on the sample. We shall look at a particular problem, from which the general idea will emerge.

Our running example is the following. A search engine receives a stream of queries, and it would like to study the behavior of typical users.[1] We assume the stream consists of tuples (user, query, time). Suppose that we want to answer queries such as "What fraction of the typical user's queries were repeated over the past month?" Assume also that we wish to store only 1/10th of the stream elements.

The obvious approach would be to generate a random number, say an integer from 0 to 9, in response to each search query. Store the tuple if and only if the random number is 0. If we do so, each user has, on average, 1/10th of their queries stored. Statistical fluctuations will introduce some noise into the data, but if users issue many queries, the law of large numbers will assure us that most users will have a fraction quite close to 1/10th of their queries stored.

However, this scheme gives us the wrong answer to the query asking for the average number of duplicate queries for a user. Suppose a user has issued s search queries one time in the past month, d search queries twice, and no search queries more than twice. If we have a 1/10th sample, of queries, we shall see in the sample for that user an expected $s/10$ of the search queries issued once. Of the d search queries issued twice, only $d/100$ will appear twice in the sample; that fraction is d times the probability that both occurrences of the query will be in the 1/10th sample. Of the queries that appear twice in the full stream, $18d/100$ will appear exactly once. To see why, note that $18/100$ is the probability that one of the two occurrences will be in the 1/10th of the stream that is selected, while the other is in the 9/10th that is not selected.

The correct answer to the query about the fraction of repeated searches is $d/(s+d)$. However, the answer we shall obtain from the sample is $d/(10s+19d)$. To derive the latter formula, note that $d/100$ appear twice, while $s/10 + 18d/100$ appear once. Thus, the fraction appearing twice in the sample is $d/100$ divided by $d/100 + s/10 + 18d/100$. This ratio is $d/(10s + 19d)$. for no positive values of s and d is $d/(s + d) = d/(10s + 19d)$.

4.2.2 Obtaining a Representative Sample

The query of Section 4.2.1, like many queries about the statistics of typical users, cannot be answered by taking a sample of each user's search queries. Thus, we must strive to pick 1/10th of the users, and take all their searches for the sample, while taking none of the searches from other users. If we can store a list of all users, and whether or not they are in the sample, then we could do the following. Each time a search query arrives in the stream, we look up the user to see whether or not they are in the sample. If so, we add this search query to the sample, and if not, then not. However, if we have no record of ever having seen this user before, then we generate a random integer between 0 and 9. If the number is 0,

---

[1] While we shall refer to "users," the search engine really receives URL's from which the search query was issued. We shall assume that these URL's identify unique users, which is approximately true, but not exactly true.

we add this user to our list with value "in," and if the number is other than 0, we add the user with the value "out."

That method works as long as we can afford to keep the list of all users and their in/out decision in main memory, because there isn't time to go to disk for every search that arrives. By using a hash function, one can avoid keeping the list of users. That is, we hash each user name to one of ten buckets, 0 through 9. If the user hashes to bucket 0, then accept this search query for the sample, and if not, then not.

Note we do not actually store the user in the bucket; in fact, there is no data in the buckets at all. Effectively, we use the hash function as a random-number generator, with the important property that, when applied to the same user several times, we always get the same "'random" number. That is, without storing the in/out decision for any user, we can reconstruct that decision any time a search query by that user arrives.

More generally, we can obtain a sample consisting of any rational fraction a/b of the users by hashing user names to b buckets, 0 through $b-1$. Add the search query to the sample if the hash value is less than a.

4.2.3   The General Sampling Problem

The running example is typical of the following general problem. Our stream consists of tuples with n components. A subset of the components are the *key* components, on which the selection of the sample will be based. In our running example, there are three components – user, query, and time – of which only *user* is in the key. However, we could also take a sample of queries by making *query* be the key, or even take a sample of user-query pairs by making both those components form the key.

To take a sample of size a/b, we hash the key value for each tuple to b buckets, and accept the tuple for the sample if the hash value is less than a. If the key consists of more than one component, the hash function needs to combine the values for those components to make a single hash-value. The result will be a sample consisting of all tuples with certain key values. The selected key values will be approximately a/b of all the key values appearing in the stream.

4.2.4   Varying the Sample Size

Often, the sample will grow as more of the stream enters the system. In our running example, we retain all the search queries of the selected 1/10th of the users, forever. As time goes on, more searches for the same users will be accumulated, and new users that are selected for the sample will appear in the stream.

If we have a budget for how many tuples from the stream can be stored as the sample, then the fraction of key values must vary, lowering as time goes on. In order to assure that at all times, the sample consists of all tuples from a subset of the key values, we choose a hash function h from key values to a very large number of values $0, 1, \ldots, B - 1$. We maintain a *threshold* t, which initially can be the largest bucket number, $B - 1$. At all times, the sample consists of those tuples whose key K satisfies $h(K) \leq t$. New tuples from the stream are added to the sample if and only if they satisfy the same condition.

If the number of stored tuples of the sample exceeds the allotted space, we lower t to $t - 1$ and remove from the sample all those tuples whose key K hashes to t. For efficiency, we can lower t by more than 1, and remove the tuples with several of the highest hash values, whenever we need to throw some key values out of the sample. Further efficiency is obtained by maintaining an index on the hash value, so we can find all those tuples whose keys hash to a particular value quickly.

4.2.5 Exercises for Section 4.2

EXERCISE 4.2.1   Suppose we have a stream of tuples with the schema

$$\text{Grades(university, courseID, studentID, grade)}$$

Assume universities are unique, but a courseID is unique only within a university (i.e., different universities may have different courses with the same ID, e.g., "CS101") and likewise, studentID's are unique only within a university (different universities may assign the same ID to different students). Suppose we want to answer certain queries approximately from a 1/20th sample of the data. For each of the queries below, indicate how you would construct the sample. That is, tell what the key attributes should be.

(a) For each university, estimate the average number of students in a course.
(b) Estimate the fraction of students who have a GPA of 3.5 or more.
(c) Estimate the fraction of courses where at least half the students got "A."

4.3 Filtering Streams

Another common process on streams is selection, or filtering. We want to accept those tuples in the stream that meet a criterion. Accepted tuples are passed to another process as a stream, while other tuples are dropped. If the selection criterion is a property of the tuple that can be calculated (e.g., the first component is less than 10), then the selection is easy to do. The problem becomes harder when the criterion involves lookup for membership in a set. It is especially hard, when that set is too large to store in main memory. In this section, we shall discuss the technique known as "Bloom filtering" as a way to eliminate most of the tuples that do not meet the criterion.

4.3.1 A Motivating Example

Again let us start with a running example that illustrates the problem and what we can do about it. Suppose we have a set S of one billion allowed email addresses – those that we will allow through because we believe them not to be spam. The stream consists of pairs: an email address and the email itself. Since the typical email address is 20 bytes or more, it is not reasonable to store S in main memory. Thus, we can either use disk accesses to determine whether or not to let through any given stream element, or we can devise a method that requires no more main memory than we have available, and yet will filter most of the undesired stream elements.

Suppose for argument's sake that we have one gigabyte of available main memory. In the technique known as *Bloom filtering*, we use that main memory as a bit array. In this case, we have room for eight billion bits, since one byte equals eight bits. Devise a hash function h from email addresses to eight billion buckets. Hash each member of S to a bit, and set that bit to 1. All other bits of the array remain 0.

Since there are one billion members of S, approximately 1/8th of the bits will be 1. The exact fraction of bits set to 1 will be slightly less than 1/8th, because it is possible that two members of S hash to the same bit. We shall discuss the exact fraction of 1's in Section 4.3.3. When a stream element arrives, we hash its email address. If the bit to which that email address hashes is 1, then we let the email through. But if the email address hashes to a 0, we are certain that the address is not in S, so we can drop this stream element.

Unfortunately, some spam email will get through. Approximately 1/8th of the stream elements whose email address is not in S will happen to hash to a bit whose value is 1 and will be let through. Nevertheless, since the majority of emails are spam (about 80% according to some reports), eliminating 7/8th of the spam is a significant benefit. Moreover, if we want to eliminate every spam, we need only check for membership in S those good and bad emails that get through the filter. Those checks will require the use of secondary memory to access S itself. There are also other options, as we shall see when we study the general Bloom-filtering technique. As a simple example, we could use a cascade of filters, each of which would eliminate 7/8th of the remaining spam.

4.3.2   The Bloom Filter

A *Bloom filter* consists of:

(1) An array of n bits, initially all 0's.
(2) A collection of hash functions $h_1, h_2, \ldots, h_k$. Each hash function maps "key" values to n buckets, corresponding to the n bits of the bit-array.
(3) A set S of m key values.

The purpose of the Bloom filter is to allow through all stream elements whose keys are in S, while rejecting most of the stream elements whose keys are not in S.

To initialize the bit array, begin with all bits 0. Take each key value in S and hash it using each of the k hash functions. Set to 1 each bit that is $h_i(K)$ for some hash function h_i and some key value K in S.

To test a key K that arrives in the stream, check that all of

$$h_1(K), h_2(K), \ldots, h_k(K)$$

are 1's in the bit-array. If all are 1's, then let the stream element through. If one or more of these bits are 0, then K could not be in S, so reject the stream element.

4.3.3   Analysis of Bloom Filtering

If a key value is in S, then the element will surely pass through the Bloom filter. However, if the key value is not in S, it might still pass. We need to understand how to calculate the probability of a *false positive*, as a function of n, the bit-array length, m the number of members of S, and k, the number of hash functions.

The model to use is throwing darts at targets. Suppose we have x targets and y darts. Any dart is equally likely to hit any target. After throwing the darts, how many targets can we expect to be hit at least once? The analysis is similar to the analysis in Section 3.4.2, and goes as follows:

- The probability that a given dart will not hit a given target is $(x-1)/x$.
- The probability that none of the y darts will hit a given target is $\left(\frac{x-1}{x}\right)^y$. We can write this expression as $(1 - \frac{1}{x})^{x(\frac{y}{x})}$.
- Using the approximation $(1-\epsilon)^{1/\epsilon} = 1/e$ for small ϵ (recall Section 1.3.5), we conclude that the probability that none of the y darts hit a given target is $e^{-y/x}$.

EXAMPLE 4.3   Consider the running example of Section 4.3.1. We can use the above calculation to get the true expected number of 1's in the bit array. Think of each bit as a target, and each member of S as a dart. Then the probability that a given bit will be 1 is the probability that the corresponding target will be hit by one or more darts. Since there are one billion members of S, we have $y = 10^9$ darts. As there are eight billion bits, there are $x = 8 \times 10^9$ targets. Thus, the probability that a given target is not hit is $e^{-y/x} = e^{-1/8}$ and the probability that it *is* hit is $1 - e^{-1/8}$. That quantity is about 0.1175. In Section 4.3.1 we suggested that $1/8 = 0.125$ is a good approximation, which it is, but now we have the exact calculation.

We can apply the rule to the more general situation, where set S has m members, the array has n bits, and there are k hash functions. The number of targets is $x = n$, and the number of darts is $y = km$. Thus, the probability that a bit remains 0 is $e^{-km/n}$. We want the fraction of 0 bits to be fairly large, or else the probability that a nonmember of S will hash at least once to a 0 becomes too small, and there are too many false positives. For example, we might choose k, the number of hash functions to be n/m or less. Then the probability of a 0 is at least e^{-1} or 37%. In general, the probability of a false positive is the probability of a 1 bit, which is $1 - e^{-km/n}$, raised to the kth power, i.e., $(1 - e^{-km/n})^k$.

EXAMPLE 4.4   In Example 4.3 we found that the fraction of 1's in the array of our running example is 0.1175, and this fraction is also the probability of a false positive. That is, a nonmember of S will pass through the filter if it hashes to a 1, and the probability of it doing so is 0.1175.

Suppose we used the same S and the same array, but used two different hash functions. This situation corresponds to throwing two billion darts at eight billion targets, and the probability that a bit remains 0 is $e^{-1/4}$. In order to be a false positive, a nonmember of S must hash twice to bits that are 1, and this probability is $(1 - e^{-1/4})^2$, or approximately 0.0493. Thus, adding a second hash function for our running example is an improvement, reducing the false-positive rate from 0.1175 to 0.0493.

4.3.4   Exercises for Section 4.3

EXERCISE 4.3.1   For the situation of our running example (8 billion bits, 1 billion members of the set S), calculate the false-positive rate if we use three hash functions? What if we use four hash functions?

! EXERCISE 4.3.2   Suppose we have n bits of memory available, and our set S has m members. Instead of using k hash functions, we could divide the n bits into k arrays, and hash once to each array. As a function of n, m, and k, what is the probability of a false positive? How does it compare with using k hash functions into a single array?

!! EXERCISE 4.3.3   As a function of n, the number of bits and m the number of members in the set S, what number of hash functions minimizes the false-positive rate?

4.4   Counting Distinct Elements in a Stream

In this section we look at a third simple kind of processing we might want to do on a stream. As with the previous examples – sampling and filtering – it is somewhat tricky to do what we want in a reasonable amount of main memory, so we use a variety of hashing and a randomized algorithm to get approximately what we want with little space needed per stream.

4.4.1   The Count-Distinct Problem

Suppose stream elements are chosen from some universal set. We would like to know how many different elements have appeared in the stream, counting either from the beginning of the stream or from some known time in the past.

EXAMPLE 4.5   As a useful example of this problem, consider a Web site gathering statistics on how many unique users it has seen in each given month. The universal set is the set of logins for that site, and a stream element is generated each time someone logs in. This measure is appropriate for a site like Amazon, where the typical user logs in with their unique login name.

A similar problem is a Web site like Google that does not require login to issue a search query, and may be able to identify users only by the URL from which they send the query. Here, the universal set of possible URL's could be thought of as all logical host names (e.g., `infolab.stanford.edu`), which is essentially infinite. Technically, there are only 4 billion URL's, so that could be considered the universal set as well.

The obvious way to solve the problem is to keep in main memory a list of all the elements seen so far in the stream. Keep them in an efficient search structure such as a hash table or search tree, so one can quickly add new elements and check whether or not the element that just arrived on the stream was already seen. As long as the number of distinct elements is not too great, this structure can fit in main memory and there is little problem obtaining an exact answer to the question how many distinct elements appear in the stream.

However, if the number of distinct elements is too great, or if there are too many streams that need to be processed at once (e.g., Yahoo! wants to count the number of unique users viewing each of its pages in a month), then we cannot store the needed data in main memory. There are several options. We could use more machines, each machine handling only one or several of the streams. We could store most of the data structure in secondary memory and batch stream elements so whenever we brought a disk block to main memory there would be many tests and updates to be performed on the data in that block. Or we could use the strategy to be discussed in this section, where we only estimate the number of distinct elements but use much less memory than the number of distinct elements.

4.4.2   The Flajolet-Martin Algorithm

It is possible to estimate the number of distinct elements by hashing the elements of the universal set to a bit-string that is sufficiently long. The length of the bit-string must be sufficient that there are more possible results of the hash function than there are elements of the universal set. For example, 64 bits is sufficient to hash URL's. We shall pick many different hash functions and hash each element of the stream using these hash functions. The important property of a hash function is that when applied to the same element, it always produces the same result. Notice that this property was also essential for the sampling technique of Section 4.2.

The idea behind the Flajolet-Martin Algorithm is that the more different elements we see in the stream, the more different hash-values we shall see. As we see more different hash-values, it becomes more likely that one of these values will be "unusual." The particular unusual property we shall exploit is that the value ends in many 0's, although many other options exist.

Whenever we apply a hash function h to a stream element a, the bit string $h(a)$ will end in some number of 0's, possibly none. Call this number the *tail length* for a and h. Let R be the maximum tail length of any a seen so far in the stream. Then we shall use estimate 2^R for the number of distinct elements seen in the stream.

This estimate makes intuitive sense. The probability that a given stream element a has $h(a)$ ending in at least r 0's is 2^{-r}. Suppose there are m distinct elements in the stream. Then the probability that none of them has tail length at least r is $(1 - 2^{-r})^m$. This sort of expression should be familiar by now. We can rewrite it as $\left((1 - 2^{-r})^{2^r}\right)^{m2^{-r}}$. Assuming r is reasonably large, the inner expression is of the form $(1 - \epsilon)^{1/\epsilon}$, which is approximately $1/e$. Thus, the probability of not finding a stream element with as many as r 0's at the end of its hash value is $e^{-m2^{-r}}$. We can conclude:

(1) If m is much larger than 2^r, then the probability that we shall find a tail of length at least r approaches 1.

(2) If m is much less than 2^r, then the probability of finding a tail length at least r approaches 0.

We conclude from these two points that the proposed estimate of m, which is 2^R (recall R is the largest tail length for any stream element) is unlikely to be either much too high or much too low.

4.4.3   Combining Estimates

Unfortunately, there is a trap regarding the strategy for combining the estimates of m, the number of distinct elements, that we obtain by using many different hash functions. Our first assumption would be that if we take the average of the values 2^R that we get from each hash function, we shall get a value that approaches the true m, the more hash functions we use. However, that is not the case, and the reason has to do with the influence an overestimate has on the average.

Consider a value of r such that 2^r is much larger than m. There is some probability p that we shall discover r to be the largest number of 0's at the end of the hash value for any of the m stream elements. Then the probability of finding $r + 1$ to be the largest number of 0's instead is at least $p/2$. However, if we do increase by 1 the number of 0's at the end of a hash value, the value of 2^R doubles. Consequently, the contribution from each possible large R to the expected value of 2^R grows as R grows, and the expected value of 2^R is actually infinite.[2]

---

[2] Technically, since the hash value is a bit-string of finite length, there is no contribution to 2^R for R's that are larger than the length of the hash value. However, this effect is not enough to avoid the conclusion that the expected value of 2^R is much too large.

Another way to combine estimates is to take the median of all estimates. The median is not affected by the occasional outsized value of 2^R, so the worry described above for the average should not carry over to the median. Unfortunately, the median suffers from another defect: it is always a power of 2. Thus, no matter how many hash functions we use, should the correct value of m be between two powers of 2, say 400, then it will be impossible to obtain a close estimate.

There is a solution to the problem, however. We can combine the two methods. First, group the hash functions into small groups, and take their average. Then, take the median of the averages. It is true that an occasional outsized 2^R will bias some of the groups and make them too large. However, taking the median of group averages will reduce the influence of this effect almost to nothing. Moreover, if the groups themselves are large enough, then the averages can be essentially any number, which enables us to approach the true value m as long as we use enough hash functions. In order to guarantee that any possible average can be obtained, groups should be of size at least a small multiple of $\log_2 m$.

4.4.4 Space Requirements

Observe that as we read the stream it is not necessary to store the elements seen. The only thing we need to keep in main memory is one integer per hash function; this integer records the largest tail length seen so far for that hash function and any stream element. If we are processing only one stream, we could use millions of hash functions, which is far more than we need to get a close estimate. Only if we are trying to process many streams at the same time would main memory constrain the number of hash functions we could associate with any one stream. In practice, the time it takes to compute hash values for each stream element would be the more significant limitation on the number of hash functions we use.

4.4.5 Exercises for Section 4.4

EXERCISE 4.4.1 Suppose our stream consists of the integers 3, 1, 4, 1, 5, 9, 2, 6, 5. Our hash functions will all be of the form $h(x) = ax + b \mod 32$ for some a and b. You should treat the result as a 5-bit binary integer. Determine the tail length for each stream element and the resulting estimate of the number of distinct elements if the hash function is:

(a) $h(x) = 2x + 1 \mod 32$.
(b) $h(x) = 3x + 7 \mod 32$.
(c) $h(x) = 4x \mod 32$.

! EXERCISE 4.4.2 Do you see any problems with the choice of hash functions in Exercise 4.4.1? What advice could you give someone who was going to use a hash function of the form $h(x) = ax + b \mod 2^k$?

4.5   Estimating Moments

In this section we consider a generalization of the problem of counting distinct elements in a stream. The problem, called computing "moments," involves the distribution of frequencies of different elements in the stream. We shall define moments of all orders and concentrate on computing second moments, from which the general algorithm for all moments is a simple extension.

4.5.1   Definition of Moments

Suppose a stream consists of elements chosen from a universal set. Assume the universal set is ordered so we can speak of the ith element for any i. Let m_i be the number of occurrences of the ith element for any i. Then the *kth-order moment* (or just kth moment) of the stream is the sum over all i of $(m_i)^k$.

EXAMPLE 4.6   The 0th moment is the sum of 1 for each m_i that is greater than 0.[3] That is, the 0th moment is a count of the number of distinct elements in the stream. We can use the method of Section 4.4 to estimate the 0th moment of a stream.

The 1st moment is the sum of the m_i's, which must be the length of the stream. Thus, first moments are especially easy to compute; just count the length of the stream seen so far.

The second moment is the sum of the squares of the m_i's. It is sometimes called the *surprise number*, since it measures how uneven the distribution of elements in the the stream is. To see the distinction, suppose we have a stream of length 100, in which eleven different elements appear. The most even distribution of these eleven elements would have one appearing 10 times and the other ten appearing 9 times each. In this case, the surprise number is $10^2 + 10 \times 9^2 = 910$. At the other extreme, one of the eleven elements could appear 90 times and the other ten appear 1 time each. Then, the surprise number would be $90^2 + 10 \times 1^2 = 8110$.

As in Section 4.4, there is no problem computing moments of any order if we can afford to keep in main memory a count for each element that appears in the stream. However, also as in that section, if we cannot afford to use that much memory, then we need to estimate the kth moment by keeping a limited number of values in main memory and computing an estimate from these values. For the case of distinct elements, each of these values were counts of the longest tail produced by a single hash function. We shall see another form of value that is useful for second and higher moments.

---

[3] Technically, since m_i could be 0 for some elements in the universal set, we need to make explicit in the definition of "moment" that 0^0 is taken to be 0. For moments 1 and above, the contribution of m_i's that are 0 is surely 0.

4.5.2   The Alon-Matias-Szegedy Algorithm for Second
         Moments

For now, let us assume that a stream has a particular length n. We shall show
how to deal with growing streams in the next section. Suppose we do not have
enough space to count all the m_i's for all the elements of the stream. We can still
estimate the second moment of the stream using a limited amount of space; the
more space we use, the more accurate the estimate will be. We compute some
number of *variables*. For each variable X, we store:

(1) A particular element of the universal set, which we refer to as $X.element$,
    and

(2) An integer $X.value$, which is the *value* of the variable. To determine the
    value of a variable X, we choose a position in the stream between 1 and n,
    uniformly and at random. Set $X.element$ to be the element found there, and
    initialize $X.value$ to 1. As we read the stream, add 1 to $X.value$ each time
    we encounter another occurrence of $X.element$.

EXAMPLE 4.7   Suppose the stream is $a, b, c, b, d, a, c, d, a, b, d, c, a, a, b$. The length
of the stream is $n = 15$. Since a appears 5 times, b appears 4 times, and c and d
appear three times each, the second moment for the stream is $5^2 + 4^2 + 3^2 + 3^2 =$
59. Suppose we keep three variables, X_1, X_2, and X_3. Also, assume that at "random" we pick the 3rd, 8th, and 13th positions to define these three variables.

When we reach position 3, we find element c, so we set $X_1.element = c$ and
$X_1.value = 1$. Position 4 holds b, so we do not change X_1. Likewise, nothing
happens at positions 5 or 6. At position 7, we see c again, so we set $X_1.value = 2$.

At position 8 we find d, and so set $X_2.element = d$ and $X_2.value = 1$. Positions
9 and 10 hold a and b, so they do not affect X_1 or X_2. Position 11 holds d so we set
$X_2.value = 2$, and position 12 holds c so we set $X_1.value = 3$. At position 13, we
find element a, and so set $X_3.element = a$ and $X_3.value = 1$. Then, at position 14
we see another a and so set $X_3.value = 2$. Position 15, with element b does not
affect any of the variables, so we are done, with final values $X_1.value = 3$ and
$X_2.value = X_3.value = 2$.

We can derive an estimate of the second moment from any variable X. This
estimate is $n \times (2 \times X.value - 1)$.

EXAMPLE 4.8   Consider the three variables from Example 4.7. From X_1 we
derive the estimate $n \times (2 \times X_1.value - 1) = 15 \times (2 \times 3 - 1) = 75$. The other
two variables, X_2 and X_3, each have value 2 at the end, so their estimates are
$15 \times (2 \times 2 - 1) = 45$. Recall that the true value of the second moment for this
stream is 59. On the other hand, the average of the three estimates is 55, a fairly
close approximation.

4.5.3   Why the Alon-Matias-Szegedy Algorithm Works

We can prove that the expected value of any variable constructed as in Section 4.5.2 is the second moment of the stream from which it is constructed. Some notation will make the argument easier to follow. Let $e(i)$ be the stream element that appears at position i in the stream, and let $c(i)$ be the number of times element $e(i)$ appears in the stream among positions $i, i+1, \ldots, n$.

EXAMPLE 4.9   Consider the stream of Example 4.7. $e(6) = a$, since the 6th position holds a. Also, $c(6) = 4$, since a appears at positions 9, 13, and 14, as well as at position 6. Note that a also appears at position 1, but that fact does not contribute to $c(6)$.

The expected value of $X.value$ is the average over all positions i between 1 and n of $n \times (2 \times c(i) - 1)$, that is

$$E(X.value) = \frac{1}{n} \sum_{i=1}^{n} n \times (2 \times c(i) - 1)$$

We can simplify the above by canceling factors $1/n$ and n, to get

$$E(X.value) = \sum_{i=1}^{n} \big(2c(i) - 1\big)$$

However, to make sense of the formula, we need to change the order of summation by grouping all those positions that have the same element. For instance, concentrate on some element a that appears m_a times in the stream. The term for the last position in which a appears must be $2 \times 1 - 1 = 1$. The term for the next-to-last position in which a appears is $2 \times 2 - 1 = 3$. The positions with a before that yield terms 5, 7, and so on, up to $2m_a - 1$, which is the term for the first position in which a appears. That is, the formula for the expected value of $X.value$ can be written:

$$E(X.value) = \sum_{a} 1 + 3 + 5 + \cdots + (2m_a - 1)$$

Note that $1 + 3 + 5 + \cdots + (2m_a - 1) = (m_a)^2$. The proof is an easy induction on the number of terms in the sum. Thus, $E(X.value) = \sum_a (m_a)^2$, which is the definition of the second moment.

4.5.4   Higher-Order Moments

We estimate kth moments, for $k > 2$, in essentially the same way as we estimate second moments. The only thing that changes is the way we derive an estimate from a variable. In Section 4.5.2 we used the formula $n \times (2v - 1)$ to turn a value v, the count of the number of occurrences of some particular stream element a, into an estimate of the second moment. Then, in Section 4.5.3 we saw why this formula works: the terms $2v - 1$, for $v = 1, 2, \ldots, m$ sum to m^2, where m is the number of times a appears in the stream.

Notice that $2v-1$ is the difference between v^2 and $(v-1)^2$. Suppose we wanted the third moment rather than the second. Then all we have to do is replace $2v-1$ by $v^3-(v-1)^3 = 3v^2-3v+1$. Then $\sum_{v=1}^{m} 3v^2-3v+1 = m^3$, so we can use as our estimate of the third moment the formula $n \times (3v^2 - 3v + 1)$, where $v = X.value$ is the value associated with some variable X. More generally, we can estimate kth moments for any $k \geq 2$ by turning value $v = X.value$ into $n \times \left(v^k - (v-1)^k\right)$.

4.5.5 Dealing With Infinite Streams

Technically, the estimate we used for second and higher moments assumes that n, the stream length, is a constant. In practice, n grows with time. That fact, by itself, doesn't cause problems, since we store only the values of variables and multiply some function of that value by n when it is time to estimate the moment. If we count the number of stream elements seen and store this value, which only requires $\log n$ bits, then we have n available whenever we need it.

A more serious problem is that we must be careful how we select the positions for the variables. If we do this selection once and for all, then as the stream gets longer, we are biased in favor of early positions, and the estimate of the moment will be too large. On the other hand, if we wait too long to pick positions, then early in the stream we do not have many variables and so will get an unreliable estimate.

The proper technique is to maintain as many variables as we can store at all times, and to throw some out as the stream grows. The discarded variables are replaced by new ones, in such a way that at all times, the probability of picking any one position for a variable is the same as that of picking any other position. Suppose we have space to store s variables. Then the first s positions of the stream are each picked as the position of one of the s variables.

Inductively, suppose we have seen n stream elements, and the probability of any particular position being the position of a variable is uniform, that is s/n. When the $(n+1)$st element arrives, pick that position with probability $s/(n+1)$. If not picked, then the s variables keep their same positions. However, if the $(n+1)$st position is picked, then throw out one of the current s variables, with equal probability. Replace the one discarded by a new variable whose element is the one at position $n+1$ and whose value is 1.

Surely, the probability that position $n+1$ is selected for a variable is what it should be: $s/(n+1)$. However, the probability of every other position also is $s/(n+1)$, as we can prove by induction on n. By the inductive hypothesis, before the arrival of the $(n+1)$st stream element, this probability was s/n. With probability $1-s/(n+1)$ the $(n+1)$st position will not be selected, and the probability of each of the first n positions remains s/n. However, with probability $s/(n+1)$, the $(n+1)$st position is picked, and the probability for each of the first n positions is reduced by factor $(s-1)/s$. Considering the two cases, the

> ### A General Stream-Sampling Problem
>
> Notice that the technique described in Section 4.5.5 actually solves a more general problem. It gives us a way to maintain a sample of s stream elements so that at all times, all stream elements are equally likely to be selected for the sample.
>
> As an example of where this technique can be useful, recall that in Section 4.2 we arranged to select all the tuples of a stream having key value in a randomly selected subset. Suppose that, as time goes on, there are too many tuples associated with any one key. We can arrange to limit the number of tuples for any key K to a fixed constant s by using the technique of Section 4.5.5 whenever a new tuple for key K arrives.

probability of selecting each of the first n positions is

$$\left(1 - \frac{s}{n+1}\right)\left(\frac{s}{n}\right) + \left(\frac{s}{n+1}\right)\left(\frac{s-1}{s}\right)\left(\frac{s}{n}\right)$$

This expression simplifies to

$$\left(1 - \frac{s}{n+1}\right)\left(\frac{s}{n}\right) + \left(\frac{s-1}{n+1}\right)\left(\frac{s}{n}\right)$$

and then to

$$\left(\left(1 - \frac{s}{n+1}\right) + \left(\frac{s-1}{n+1}\right)\right)\left(\frac{s}{n}\right)$$

which in turn simplifies to

$$\left(\frac{n}{n+1}\right)\left(\frac{s}{n}\right) = \frac{s}{n+1}$$

Thus, we have shown by induction on the stream length n that all positions have equal probability s/n of being chosen as the position of a variable.

4.5.6   Exercises for Section 4.5

EXERCISE 4.5.1   Compute the surprise number (second moment) for the stream 3, 1, 4, 1, 3, 4, 2, 1, 2. What is the third moment of this stream?

! **EXERCISE 4.5.2**   If a stream has n elements, of which m are distinct, what are the minimum and maximum possible surprise number, as a function of m and n?

EXERCISE 4.5.3   Suppose we are given the stream of Exercise 4.5.1, to which we apply the Alon-Matias-Szegedy Algorithm to estimate the surprise number. For each possible value of i, if X_i is a variable starting position i, what is the value of $X_i.value$?

EXERCISE 4.5.4   Repeat Exercise 4.7 if the intent of the variables is to compute third moments. What is the value of each variable at the end? What estimate of the third moment do you get from each variable? How does the average of these estimates compare with the true value of the third moment?

EXERCISE 4.5.5   Prove by induction on n that $1 + 3 + 5 + \cdots + (2m - 1) = m^2$.

EXERCISE 4.5.6   If we wanted to compute fourth moments, how would we convert $X.value$ to an estimate of the fourth moment?

4.6   Counting Ones in a Window

We now turn our attention to counting problems for streams. Suppose we have a window of length N on a binary stream. We want at all times to be able to answer queries of the form "how many 1's are there in the last k bits?" for any $k \le N$. As in previous sections, we focus on the situation where we cannot afford to store the entire window. After showing an approximate algorithm for the binary case, we discuss how this idea can be extended to summing numbers.

4.6.1   The Cost of Exact Counts

To begin, suppose we want to be able to count exactly the number of 1's in the last k bits for any $k \le N$. Then we claim it is necessary to store all N bits of the window, as any representation that used fewer than N bits could not work. In proof, suppose we have a representation that uses fewer than N bits to represent the N bits in the window. Since there are 2^N sequences of N bits, but fewer than 2^N representations, there must be two different bit strings w and x that have the same representation. Since $w \ne x$, they must differ in at least one bit. Let the last $k - 1$ bits of w and x agree, but let them differ on the kth bit from the right end.

EXAMPLE 4.10   If $w = 0101$ and $x = 1010$, then $k = 1$, since scanning from the right, they first disagree at position 1. If $w = 1001$ and $x = 0101$, then $k = 3$, because they first disagree at the third position from the right.

Suppose the data representing the contents of the window is whatever sequence of bits represents both w and x. Ask the query "how many 1's are in the last k bits?" The query-answering algorithm will produce the same answer, whether the window contains w or x, because the algorithm can only see their representation. But the correct answers are surely different for these two bit-strings. Thus, we have proved that we must use at least N bits to answer queries about the last k bits for any k.

In fact, we need N bits, even if the only query we can ask is "how many 1's are in the entire window of length N?" The argument is similar to that used above. Suppose we use fewer than N bits to represent the window, and therefore we can find w, x, and k as above. It might be that w and x have the same number of 1's, as they did in both cases of Example 4.10. However, if we follow the current window by any $N - k$ bits, we will have a situation where the true window contents resulting from w and x are identical except for the leftmost bit, and therefore, their counts of 1's are unequal. However, since the representations of w and x are the same, the representation of the window must still be the same if we feed the same bit sequence to these representations. Thus, we can force the answer to the query "how many 1's in the window?" to be incorrect for one of the two possible window contents.

4.6.2   The Datar-Gionis-Indyk-Motwani Algorithm

We shall present the simplest case of an algorithm called DGIM. This version of the algorithm uses $O(\log^2 N)$ bits to represent a window of N bits, and allows us to estimate the number of 1's in the window with an error of no more than 50%. Later, we shall discuss an improvement of the method that limits the error to any fraction $\epsilon > 0$, and still uses only $O(\log^2 N)$ bits (although with a constant factor that grows as ϵ shrinks).

To begin, each bit of the stream has a *timestamp*, the position in which it arrives. The first bit has timestamp 1, the second has timestamp 2, and so on. Since we only need to distinguish positions within the window of length N, we shall represent timestamps modulo N, so they can be represented by $\log_2 N$ bits. If we also store the total number of bits ever seen in the stream (i.e., the most recent timestamp) modulo N, then we can determine from a timestamp modulo N where in the current window the bit with that timestamp is.

We divide the window into *buckets*,[4] consisting of:

(1) The timestamp of its right (most recent) end.
(2) The number of 1's in the bucket. This number must be a power of 2, and we refer to the number of 1's as the *size* of the bucket.

To represent a bucket, we need $\log_2 N$ bits to represent the timestamp (modulo N) of its right end. To represent the number of 1's we only need $\log_2 \log_2 N$ bits. The reason is that we know this number i is a power of 2, say 2^j, so we can represent i by coding j in binary. Since j is at most $\log_2 N$, it requires $\log_2 \log_2 N$ bits. Thus, $O(\log N)$ bits suffice to represent a bucket.

There are five rules that must be followed when representing a stream by buckets.

- The right end of a bucket is always a position with a 1.
- No position is in more than one bucket.
- There are one or two buckets of any given size, up to some maximum size.
- All sizes must be a power of 2.
- Buckets cannot decrease in size as we move to the left (back in time).

---

[4] Do not confuse these "buckets" with the "buckets" discussed in connection with hashing.

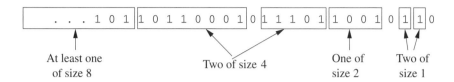

Figure 4.2 A bit-stream divided into buckets following the DGIM rules

EXAMPLE 4.11   Figure 4.2 shows a bit stream divided into buckets in a way that satisfies the DGIM rules. At the right (most recent) end we see two buckets of size 1. To its left we see one bucket of size 2. Note that this bucket covers four positions, but only two of them are 1. Proceeding left, we see two buckets of size 4, and we suggest that a bucket of size 8 exists further left.

Notice that it is OK for some 0's to lie between buckets. Also, observe from Fig. 4.2 that the buckets do not overlap; there are one or two of each size up to the largest size, and sizes only increase moving left.

In the next sections, we shall explain the following about the DGIM algorithm:

(1) Why the number of buckets representing a window must be small.
(2) How to estimate the number of 1's in the last k bits for any k, with an error no greater than 50%.
(3) How to maintain the DGIM conditions as new bits enter the stream.

4.6.3   Storage Requirements for the DGIM Algorithm

We observed that each bucket can be represented by $O(\log n)$ bits. If the window has length N, then there are no more than N 1's, surely. Suppose the largest bucket is of size 2^j. Then j cannot exceed $\log_2 N$, or else there are more 1's in this bucket than there are 1's in the entire window. Thus, there are at most two buckets of all sizes from $\log_2 N$ down to 1, and no buckets of larger sizes.

We conclude that there are $O(\log N)$ buckets. Since each bucket can be represented in $O(\log N)$ bits, the total space required for all the buckets representing a window of size N is $O(\log^2 N)$.

4.6.4   Query Answering in the DGIM Algorithm

Suppose we are asked how many 1's there are in the last k bits of the window, for some $1 \le k \le N$. Find the bucket b with the highest timestamp that includes at least some of the k most recent bits. Estimate the number of 1's to be the sum of the sizes of all the buckets to the right (more recent) than bucket b, plus half the size of b itself.

EXAMPLE 4.12   Suppose the stream is that of Fig. 4.2, and $k = 10$. Then the query asks for the number of 1's in the ten rightmost bits, which happen to be 0110010110. Let the current timestamp (time of the rightmost bit) be t. Then the two buckets with one 1, having timestamps $t - 1$ and $t - 2$ are completely included in the answer. The bucket of size 2, with timestamp $t - 4$, is also completely included. However, the rightmost bucket of size 4, with timestamp $t - 8$ is only partly included. We know it is the last bucket to contribute to the answer, because the next bucket to its left has timestamp less than $t - 9$ and thus is completely out of the window. On the other hand, we know the buckets to its right are completely inside the range of the query because of the existence of a bucket to their left with timestamp $t - 9$ or greater.

Our estimate of the number of 1's in the last ten positions is thus 6. This number is the two buckets of size 1, the bucket of size 2, and half the bucket of size 4 that is partially within range. Of course the correct answer is 5.

Suppose the above estimate of the answer to a query involves a bucket b of size 2^j that is partially within the range of the query. Let us consider how far from the correct answer c our estimate could be. There are two cases: the estimate could be larger or smaller than c.

Case 1: The estimate is less than c. In the worst case, all the 1's of b are actually within the range of the query, so the estimate misses half bucket b, or 2^{j-1} 1's. But in this case, c is at least 2^j; in fact it is at least $2^{j+1} - 1$, since there is at least one bucket of each of the sizes $2^{j-1}, 2^{j-2}, \ldots, 1$. We conclude that our estimate is at least 50% of c.

Case 2: The estimate is greater than c. In the worst case, only the rightmost bit of bucket b is within range, and there is only one bucket of each of the sizes smaller than b. Then $c = 1 + 2^{j-1} + 2^{j-2} + \cdots + 1 = 2^j$ and the estimate we give is $2^{j-1} + 2^{j-1} + 2^{j-2} + \cdots + 1 = 2^j + 2^{j-1} - 1$. We see that the estimate is no more than 50% greater than c.

4.6.5   Maintaining the DGIM Conditions

Suppose we have a window of length N properly represented by buckets that satisfy the DGIM conditions. When a new bit comes in, we may need to modify the buckets, so they continue to represent the window and continue to satisfy the DGIM conditions. First, whenever a new bit enters:

- Check the leftmost (earliest) bucket. If its timestamp has now reached the current timestamp minus N, then this bucket no longer has any of its 1's in the window. Therefore, drop it from the list of buckets.

Now, we must consider whether the new bit is 0 or 1. If it is 0, then no further change to the buckets is needed. If the new bit is a 1, however, we may need to make several changes. First:

- Create a new bucket with the current timestamp and size 1.

If there was only one bucket of size 1, then nothing more needs to be done. However, if there are now three buckets of size 1, that is one too many. We fix this problem by combining the leftmost (earliest) two buckets of size 1.

• To combine any two adjacent buckets of the same size, replace them by one bucket of twice the size. The timestamp of the new bucket is the timestamp of the rightmost (later in time) of the two buckets.

Combining two buckets of size 1 may create a third bucket of size 2. If so, we combine the leftmost two buckets of size 2 into a bucket of size 4. That, in turn, may create a third bucket of size 4, and if so we combine the leftmost two into a bucket of size 8. This process may ripple through the bucket sizes, but there are at most $\log_2 N$ different sizes, and the combination of two adjacent buckets of the same size only requires constant time. As a result, any new bit can be processed in $O(\log N)$ time.

EXAMPLE 4.13 Suppose we start with the buckets of Fig. 4.2 and a 1 enters. First, the leftmost bucket evidently has not fallen out of the window, so we do not drop any buckets. We create a new bucket of size 1 with the current timestamp, say t. There are now three buckets of size 1, so we combine the leftmost two. They are replaced with a single bucket of size 2. Its timestamp is $t - 2$, the timestamp of the bucket on the right (i.e., the rightmost bucket that actually appears in Fig. 4.2.

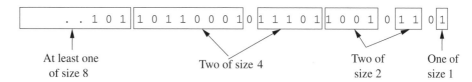

Figure 4.3 Modified buckets after a new 1 arrives in the stream

There are now two buckets of size 2, but that is allowed by the DGIM rules. Thus, the final sequence of buckets after the addition of the 1 is as shown in Fig. 4.3.

4.6.6 Reducing the Error

Instead of allowing either one or two of each size bucket, suppose we allow either $r - 1$ or r of each of the exponentially growing sizes $1, 2, 4, \ldots$, for some integer $r > 2$. In order to represent any possible number of 1's, we must relax this condition for the buckets of the largest size present; there may be any number, from 1 to r, of these.

The rule for combining buckets is essentially the same as in Section 4.6.5. If we get $r + 1$ buckets of size 2^j, combine the leftmost two into a bucket of size

---

Bucket Sizes and Ripple-Carry Adders

There is a pattern to the distribution of bucket sizes as we execute the basic algorithm of Section 4.6.5. Think of two buckets of size 2^j as a "1" in position j and one bucket of size 2^j as a "0" in that position. Then as 1's arrive in the stream, the bucket sizes after each 1 form consecutive binary integers. The occasional long sequences of bucket combinations are analogous to the occasional long rippling of carries as we go from an integer like 101111 to 110000.

2^{j+1}. That may, in turn, cause there to be $r + 1$ buckets of size 2^{j+1}, and if so we continue combining buckets of larger sizes.

The argument used in Section 4.6.4 can also be used here. However, because there are more buckets of smaller sizes, we can get a stronger bound on the error. We saw there that the largest relative error occurs when only one 1 from the leftmost bucket b is within the query range, and we therefore overestimate the true count. Suppose bucket b is of size 2^j. Then the true count is at least $1 + (r - 1)(2^{j-1} + 2^{j-2} + \cdots + 1) = 1 + (r - 1)(2^j - 1)$. The overestimate is $2^{j-1} - 1$. Thus, the fractional error is

$$\frac{2^{j-1} - 1}{1 + (r - 1)(2^j - 1)}$$

No matter what j is, this fraction is upper bounded by $1/(r-1)$. Thus, by picking r sufficiently large, we can limit the error to any desired $\epsilon > 0$.

4.6.7 Extensions to the Counting of Ones

It is natural to ask whether we can extend the technique of this section to handle aggregations more general than counting 1's in a binary stream. An obvious direction to look is to consider streams of integers and ask if we can estimate the sum of the last k integers for any $1 \leq k \leq N$, where N, as usual, is the window size.

It is unlikely that we can use the DGIM approach to streams containing both positive and negative integers. We could have a stream containing both very large positive integers and very large negative integers, but with a sum in the window that is very close to 0. Any imprecision in estimating the values of these large integers would have a huge effect on the estimate of the sum, and so the fractional error could be unbounded.

For example, suppose we broke the stream into buckets as we have done, but represented the bucket by the sum of the integers therein, rather than the count of 1's. If b is the bucket that is partially within the query range, it could be that b has, in its first half, very large negative integers and in its second half, equally large positive integers, with a sum of 0. If we estimate the contribution of b by half its sum, that contribution is essentially 0. But the actual contribution of that part of bucket b that is in the query range could be anything from 0 to the sum of all the positive integers. This difference could be far greater than the actual query answer, and so the estimate would be meaningless.

On the other hand, some other extensions involving integers do work. Suppose that the stream consists of only positive integers in the range 1 to 2^m for some m. We can treat each of the m bits of each integer as if it were a separate stream. We then use the DGIM method to count the 1's in each bit. Suppose the count of the ith bit (assuming bits count from the low-order end, starting at 0) is c_i. Then the sum of the integers is

$$\sum_{i=0}^{m-1} c_i 2^i$$

If we use the technique of Section 4.6.6 to estimate each c_i with fractional error at most ϵ, then the estimate of the true sum has error at most ϵ. The worst case occurs when all the c_i's are overestimated or all are underestimated by the same fraction.

4.6.8 Exercises for Section 4.6

EXERCISE 4.6.1 Suppose the window is as shown in Fig. 4.2. Estimate the number of 1's the the last k positions, for $k = $ (a) 5 (b) 15. In each case, how far off the correct value is your estimate?

! EXERCISE 4.6.2 There are several ways that the bit-stream 1001011011101 could be partitioned into buckets. Find all of them.

EXERCISE 4.6.3 Describe what happens to the buckets if three more 1's enter the window represented by Fig. 4.3. You may assume none of the 1's shown leave the window.

4.7 Decaying Windows

We have assumed that a sliding window held a certain tail of the stream, either the most recent N elements for fixed N, or all the elements that arrived after some time in the past. Sometimes we do not want to make a sharp distinction between recent elements and those in the distant past, but want to weight the recent elements more heavily. In this section, we consider "exponentially decaying windows," and an application where they are quite useful: finding the most common "recent" elements.

4.7.1 The Problem of Most-Common Elements

Suppose we have a stream whose elements are the movie tickets purchased all over the world, with the name of the movie as part of the element. We want to keep a summary of the stream that is the most popular movies "currently."

While the notion of "currently" is imprecise, intuitively, we want to discount the popularity of a movie like *Star Wars–Episode 4*, which sold many tickets, but most of these were sold decades ago. On the other hand, a movie that sold n tickets in each of the last 10 weeks is probably more popular than a movie that sold $2n$ tickets last week but nothing in previous weeks.

One solution would be to imagine a bit stream for each movie, and give it value 1 if the ticket is for that movie, and 0 otherwise. Pick a window size N, which is the number of most recent tickets that would be considered in evaluating popularity. Then, use the method of Section 4.6 to estimate the number of tickets for each movie, and rank movies by their estimated counts. This technique might work for movies, because there are only thousands of movies, but it would fail if we were instead recording the popularity of items sold at Amazon, or the rate at which different Twitter-users tweet, because there are too many Amazon products and too many tweeters. Further, it only offers approximate answers.

4.7.2   Definition of the Decaying Window

An alternative approach is to redefine the question so that we are not asking for a count of 1's in a window. Rather, let us compute a smooth aggregation of all the 1's ever seen in the stream, with decaying weights, so the further back in the stream, the less weight is given. Formally, let a stream currently consist of the elements $a_1, a_2, \ldots, a_t$, where a_1 is the first element to arrive and a_t is the current element. Let c be a small constant, such as 10^{-6} or 10^{-9}. Define the *exponentially decaying window* for this stream to be the sum

$$\sum_{i=0}^{t-1} a_{t-i}(1-c)^i$$

The effect of this definition is to spread out the weights of the stream elements as far back in time as the stream goes. In contrast, a fixed window with the same sum of the weights, $1/c$, would put equal weight 1 on each of the most recent $1/c$ elements to arrive and weight 0 on all previous elements. The distinction is suggested by Fig. 4.4.

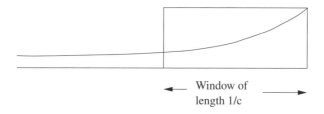

Figure 4.4 A decaying window and a fixed-length window of equal weight

It is much easier to adjust the sum in an exponentially decaying window than in a sliding window of fixed length. In the sliding window, we have to worry about the element that falls out of the window each time a new element arrives. That forces us to keep the exact elements along with the sum, or to use an approximation scheme such as DGIM. However, when a new element a_{t+1} arrives at the stream input, all we need to do is:

(1) Multiply the current sum by $1 - c$.
(2) Add a_{t+1}.

The reason this method works is that each of the previous elements has now moved one position further from the current element, so its weight is multiplied by $1 - c$. Further, the weight on the current element is $(1 - c)^0 = 1$, so adding a_{t+1} is the correct way to include the new element's contribution.

4.7.3   Finding the Most Popular Elements

Let us return to the problem of finding the most popular movies in a stream of ticket sales.[5] We shall use an exponentially decaying window with a constant c, which you might think of as 10^{-9}. That is, we approximate a sliding window holding the last one billion ticket sales. For each movie, we imagine a separate stream with a 1 each time a ticket for that movie appears in the stream, and a 0 each time a ticket for some other movie arrives. The decaying sum of the 1's measures the current popularity of the movie.

We imagine that the number of possible movies in the stream is huge, so we do not want to record values for the unpopular movies. Therefore, we establish a threshold, say $1/2$, so that if the popularity score for a movie goes below this number, its score is dropped from the counting. For reasons that will become obvious, the threshold must be less than 1, although it can be any number less than 1. When a new ticket arrives on the stream, do the following:

(1) For each movie whose score we are currently maintaining, multiply its score by $(1 - c)$.
(2) Suppose the new ticket is for movie M. If there is currently a score for M, add 1 to that score. If there is no score for M, create one and initialize it to 1.
(3) If any score is below the threshold $1/2$, drop that score.

It may not be obvious that the number of movies whose scores are maintained at any time is limited. However, note that the sum of all scores is $1/c$. There cannot be more than $2/c$ movies with score of $1/2$ or more, or else the sum of the scores would exceed $1/c$. Thus, $2/c$ is a limit on the number of movies being counted at any time. Of course in practice, the ticket sales would be concentrated on only a small number of movies at any time, so the number of actively counted movies would be much less than $2/c$.

---

[5] This example should be taken with a grain of salt, because, as we pointed out, there aren't enough different movies for this technique to be essential. Imagine, if you will, that the number of movies is extremely large, so counting ticket sales of each one separately is not feasible.

4.8   Summary of Chapter 4

✦ *The Stream Data Model*: This model assumes data arrives at a processing engine at a rate that makes it infeasible to store everything in active storage. One strategy to dealing with streams is to maintain summaries of the streams, sufficient to answer the expected queries about the data. A second approach is to maintain a sliding window of the most recently arrived data.

✦ *Sampling of Streams*: To create a sample of a stream that is usable for a class of queries, we identify a set of key attributes for the stream. By hashing the key of any arriving stream element, we can use the hash value to decide consistently whether all or none of the elements with that key will become part of the sample.

✦ *Bloom Filters*: This technique allows us to filter streams so elements that belong to a particular set are allowed through, while most nonmembers are deleted. We use a large bit array, and several hash functions. Members of the selected set are hashed to buckets, which are bits in the array, and those bits are set to 1. To test a stream element for membership, we hash the element to a set of bits using each of the hash functions, and only accept the element if all these bits are 1.

✦ *Counting Distinct Elements*: To estimate the number of different elements appearing in a stream, we can hash elements to integers, interpreted as binary numbers. 2 raised to the power that is the longest sequence of 0's seen in the hash value of any stream element is an estimate of the number of different elements. By using many hash functions and combining these estimates, first by taking averages within groups, and then taking the median of the averages, we get a reliable estimate.

✦ *Moments of Streams*: The kth moment of a stream is the sum of the kth powers of the counts of each element that appears at least once in the stream. The 0th moment is the number of distinct elements, and the 1st moment is the length of the stream.

✦ *Estimating Second Moments*: A good estimate for the second moment, or surprise number, is obtained by choosing a random position in the stream, taking twice the number of times this element appears in the stream from that position onward, subtracting 1, and multiplying by the length of the stream. Many random variables of this type can be combined like the estimates for counting the number of distinct elements, to produce a reliable estimate of the second moment.

✦ *Estimating Higher Moments*: The technique for second moments works for kth moments as well, as long as we replace the formula $2x - 1$ (where x is the number of times the element appears at or after the selected position) by $x^k - (x - 1)^k$.

✦ *Estimating the Number of 1's in a Window*: We can estimate the number of 1's in a window of 0's and 1's by grouping the 1's into buckets. Each bucket has a number of 1's that is a power of 2; there are one or two buckets of each size, and sizes never decrease as we go back in time. If we record only the position and size of the buckets, we can represent the contents of a window of size N with $O(\log^2 N)$ space.

✦ *Answering Queries About Numbers of 1's*: If we want to know the approximate numbers of 1's in the most recent k elements of a binary stream, we find the earliest bucket B that is at least partially within the last k positions of the window and estimate the number of 1's to be the sum of the sizes of each of the more recent buckets plus half the size of B. This estimate can never be off by more that 50% of the true count of 1's.

✦ *Closer Approximations to the Number of 1's*: By changing the rule for how many buckets of a given size can exist in the representation of a binary window, so that either r or $r-1$ of a given size may exist, we can assure that the approximation to the true number of 1's is never off by more than $1/r$.

✦ *Exponentially Decaying Windows*: Rather than fixing a window size, we can imagine that the window consists of all the elements that ever arrived in the stream, but with the element that arrived t time units ago weighted by e^{-ct} for some time-constant c. Doing so allows us to maintain certain summaries of an exponentially decaying window easily. For instance, the weighted sum of elements can be recomputed, when a new element arrives, by multiplying the old sum by $1-c$ and then adding the new element.

✦ *Maintaining Frequent Elements in an Exponentially Decaying Window*: We can imagine that each item is represented by a binary stream, where 0 means the item was not the element arriving at a given time, and 1 means that it was. We can find the elements whose sum of their binary stream is at least $1/2$. When a new element arrives, multiply all recorded sums by 1 minus the time constant, add 1 to the count of the item that just arrived, and delete from the record any item whose sum has fallen below $1/2$.

4.9 References for Chapter 4

Many ideas associated with stream management appear in the "chronicle data model" of [(8)]. An early survey of research in stream-management systems is [(2)]. Also, [(6)] is a recent book on the subject of stream management.

The sampling technique of Section 4.2 is from [(7)]. The Bloom Filter is generally attributed to [(3)], although essentially the same technique appeared as "superimposed codes" in [(9)].

The algorithm for counting distinct elements is essentially that of [(5)], although the particular method we described appears in [(1)]. The latter is also the source for the algorithm for calculating the surprise number and higher moments. However, the technique for maintaining a uniformly chosen sample of positions in the stream is called "reservoir sampling" and comes from [(10)].

The technique for approximately counting 1's in a window is from [(4)].

(1) N. Alon, Y. Matias, and M. Szegedy, "The space complexity of approximating frequency moments," *28th ACM Symposium on Theory of Computing,* pp. 20–29, 1996.

(2) B. Babcock, S. Babu, M. Datar, R. Motwani, and J. Widom, "Models and issues in data stream systems," *Symposium on Principles of Database Systems,* pp. 1–16, 2002.

(3) B.H. Bloom, "Space/time trade-offs in hash coding with allowable errors," *Comm. ACM* **13**:7, pp. 422–426, 1970.

(4) M. Datar, A. Gionis, P. Indyk, and R. Motwani, "Maintaining stream statistics over sliding windows," *SIAM J. Computing* **31**, pp. 1794–1813, 2002.

(5) P. Flajolet and G.N. Martin, "Probabilistic counting for database applications," *24th Symposium on Foundations of Computer Science,* pp. 76–82, 1983.

(6) M. Garofalakis, J. Gehrke, and R. Rastogi (editors), *Data Stream Management,* Springer, 2009.

(7) P.B. Gibbons, "Distinct sampling for highly-accurate answers to distinct values queries and event reports," *Intl. Conf. on Very Large Databases,* pp. 541–550, 2001.

(8) H.V. Jagadish, I.S. Mumick, and A. Silberschatz, "View maintenance issues for the chronicle data model," *Proc. ACM Symp. on Principles of Database Systems,* pp. 113–124, 1995.

(9) W.H. Kautz and R.C. Singleton, "Nonadaptive binary superimposed codes," *IEEE Transactions on Information Theory* **10**, pp. 363–377, 1964.

(10) J. Vitter, "Random sampling with a reservoir," *ACM Transactions on Mathematical Software* **11**:1, pp. 37–57, 1985.

5   Link Analysis

One of the biggest changes in our lives in the decade following the turn of the century was the availability of efficient and accurate Web search, through search engines such as Google. While Google was not the first search engine, it was the first able to defeat the spammers who had made search almost useless. Moreover, the innovation provided by Google was a nontrivial technological advance, called "PageRank." We shall begin the chapter by explaining what PageRank is and how it is computed efficiently.

Yet the war between those who want to make the Web useful and those who would exploit it for their own purposes is never over. When PageRank was established as an essential technique for a search engine, spammers invented ways to manipulate the PageRank of a Web page, often called link spam.[1] That development led to the response of TrustRank and other techniques for preventing spammers from attacking PageRank. We shall discuss TrustRank and other approaches to detecting link spam.

Finally, this chapter also covers some variations on PageRank. These techniques include topic-sensitive PageRank (which can also be adapted for combating link spam) and the HITS, or "hubs and authorities" approach to evaluating pages on the Web.

5.1   PageRank

We begin with a portion of the history of search engines, in order to motivate the definition of PageRank,[2] a tool for evaluating the importance of Web pages in a way that it is not easy to fool. We introduce the idea of "random surfers," to explain why PageRank is effective. We then introduce the technique of "taxation" or recycling of random surfers, in order to avoid certain Web structures that present problems for the simple version of PageRank.

---

[1] Link spammers sometimes try to make their unethicality less apparent by referring to what they do as "search-engine optimization."

[2] The term PageRank comes from Larry Page, the inventor of the idea and a founder of Google.

5.1.1   Early Search Engines and Term Spam

There were many search engines before Google. Largely, they worked by crawling the Web and listing the *terms* (words or other strings of characters other than white space) found in each page, in an inverted index. An *inverted index* is a data structure that makes it easy, given a term, to find (pointers to) all the places where that term occurs.

When a *search query* (list of terms) was issued, the pages with those terms were extracted from the inverted index and ranked in a way that reflected the use of the terms within the page. Thus, presence of a term in a header of the page made the page more relevant than would the presence of the term in ordinary text, and large numbers of occurrences of the term would add to the assumed relevance of the page for the search query.

As people began to use search engines to find their way around the Web, unethical people saw the opportunity to fool search engines into leading people to their page. Thus, if you were selling shirts on the Web, all you cared about was that people would see your page, regardless of what they were looking for. Thus, you could add a term like "movie" to your page, and do it thousands of times, so a search engine would think you were a terribly important page about movies. When a user issued a search query with the term "movie," the search engine would list your page first. To prevent the thousands of occurrences of "movie" from appearing on your page, you could give it the same color as the background. And if simply adding "movie" to your page didn't do the trick, then you could go to the search engine, give it the query "movie," and see what page *did* come back as the first choice. Then, copy that page into your own, again using the background color to make it invisible.

Techniques for fooling search engines into believing your page is about something it is not, are called *term spam*. The ability of term spammers to operate so easily rendered early search engines almost useless. To combat term spam, Google introduced two innovations:

(1) PageRank was used to simulate where Web surfers, starting at a random page, would tend to congregate if they followed randomly chosen outlinks from the page at which they were currently located, and this process were allowed to iterate many times. Pages that would have a large number of surfers were considered more "important" than pages that would rarely be visited. Google prefers important pages to unimportant pages when deciding which pages to show first in response to a search query.

(2) The content of a page was judged not only by the terms appearing on that page, but by the terms used in or near the links to that page. Note that while it is easy for a spammer to add false terms to a page they control, they cannot as easily get false terms added to the pages that link to their own page, if they do not control those pages.

These two techniques together make it very hard for the hypothetical shirt

---

> ## Simplified PageRank Doesn't Work
>
> As we shall see, computing PageRank by simulating random surfers is a time-consuming process. One might think that simply counting the number of in-links for each page would be a good approximation to where random surfers would wind up. However, if that is all we did, then the hypothetical shirt-seller could simply create a "spam farm" of a million pages, each of which linked to his shirt page. Then, the shirt page looks very important indeed, and a search engine would be fooled.

vendor to fool Google. While the shirt-seller can still add "movie" to his page, the fact that Google believed what other pages say about him, over what he says about himself would negate the use of false terms. The obvious countermeasure is for the shirt seller to create many pages of his own, and link to his shirt-selling page with a link that says "movie." But those pages would not be given much importance by PageRank, since other pages would not link to them. The shirt-seller could create many links among his own pages, but none of these pages would get much importance according to the PageRank algorithm, and therefore, he still would not be able to fool Google into thinking his page was about movies.

It is reasonable to ask why simulation of random surfers should allow us to approximate the intuitive notion of the "importance" of pages. There are two related motivations that inspired this approach.

- Users of the Web "vote with their feet." They tend to place links to pages they think are good or useful pages to look at, rather than bad or useless pages.
- The behavior of a random surfer indicates which pages users of the Web are likely to visit. Users are more likely to visit useful pages than useless pages.

But regardless of the reason, the PageRank measure has been proved empirically to work, and so we shall study in detail how it is computed.

5.1.2 Definition of PageRank

PageRank is a function that assigns a real number to each page in the Web (or at least to that portion of the Web that has been crawled and its links discovered). The intent is that the higher the PageRank of a page, the more "important" it is. There is not one fixed algorithm for assignment of PageRank, and in fact variations on the basic idea can alter the relative PageRank of any two pages. We begin by defining the basic, idealized PageRank, and follow it by modifications that are necessary for dealing with some real-world problems concerning the structure of the Web.

Think of the Web as a directed graph, where pages are the nodes, and there is an arc from page p_1 to page p_2 if there are one or more links from p_1 to p_2. Figure 5.1 is an example of a tiny version of the Web, where there are only four pages. Page A has links to each of the other three pages; page B has links to A and D only; page C has a link only to A, and page D has links to B and C only.

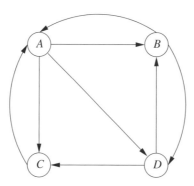

Figure 5.1 A hypothetical example of the Web

Suppose a random surfer starts at page A in Fig. 5.1. There are links to B, C, and D, so this surfer will next be at each of those pages with probability $1/3$, and has zero probability of being at A. A random surfer at B has, at the next step, probability $1/2$ of being at A, $1/2$ of being at D, and 0 of being at B or C.

In general, we can define the *transition matrix of the Web* to describe what happens to random surfers after one step. This matrix M has n rows and columns, if there are n pages. The element m_{ij} in row i and column j has value $1/k$ if page j has k arcs out, and one of them is to page i. Otherwise, $m_{ij} = 0$.

EXAMPLE 5.1   The transition matrix for the Web of Fig. 5.1 is

$$M = \begin{bmatrix} 0 & 1/2 & 1 & 0 \\ 1/3 & 0 & 0 & 1/2 \\ 1/3 & 0 & 0 & 1/2 \\ 1/3 & 1/2 & 0 & 0 \end{bmatrix}$$

In this matrix, the order of the pages is the natural one, A, B, C, and D. Thus, the first column expresses the fact, already discussed, that a surfer at A has a $1/3$ probability of next being at each of the other pages. The second column expresses the fact that a surfer at B has a $1/2$ probability of being next at A and the same of being at D. The third column says a surfer at C is certain to be at A next. The last column says a surfer at D has a $1/2$ probability of being next at B and the same at C.

The probability distribution for the location of a random surfer can be described by a column vector whose jth component is the probability that the surfer is at page j. This probability is the (idealized) *PageRank* function.

Suppose we start a random surfer at any of the n pages of the Web with equal probability. Then the initial vector $\mathbf{v}_0$ will have $1/n$ for each component. If M is the transition matrix of the Web, then after one step, the distribution of the surfer will be $M\mathbf{v}_0$, after two steps it will be $M(M\mathbf{v}_0) = M^2\mathbf{v}_0$, and so on. In general, multiplying the initial vector $\mathbf{v}_0$ by M a total of i times will give us the distribution of the surfer after i steps.

To see why multiplying a distribution vector $\mathbf{v}$ by M gives the distribution $\mathbf{x} = M\mathbf{v}$ at the next step, we reason as follows. The probability $\mathbf{x}_i$ that a random surfer will be at node i at the next step, is $\sum_j m_{ij}\mathbf{v}_j$. Here, m_{ij} is the probability that a surfer at node j will move to node i at the next step (often 0 because there is no link from j to i), and $\mathbf{v}_j$ is the probability that the surfer was at node j at the previous step.

This sort of behavior is an example of the ancient theory of *Markov processes*. It is known that the distribution of the surfer approaches a limiting distribution $\mathbf{v}$ that satisfies $\mathbf{v} = M\mathbf{v}$, provided two conditions are met:

(1) The graph is *strongly connected*; that is, it is possible to get from any node to any other node.
(2) There are no *dead ends*: nodes that have no arcs out.

Note that Fig. 5.1 satisfies both these conditions.

The limit is reached when multiplying the distribution by M another time does not change the distribution. In other terms, the limiting $\mathbf{v}$ is an eigenvector of M (an *eigenvector* of a matrix M is a vector $\mathbf{v}$ that satisfies $\mathbf{v} = \lambda M\mathbf{v}$ for some constant *eigenvalue* λ). In fact, because M is *stochastic*, meaning that its columns each add up to 1, $\mathbf{v}$ is the *principal* eigenvector (its associated eigenvalue is the largest of all eigenvalues). Note also that, because M is stochastic, the eigenvalue associated with the principal eigenvector is 1.

The principal eigenvector of M tells us where the surfer is most likely to be after a long time. Recall that the intuition behind PageRank is that the more likely a surfer is to be at a page, the more important the page is. We can compute the principal eigenvector of M by starting with the initial vector $\mathbf{v}_0$ and multiplying by M some number of times, until the vector we get shows little change at each round. In practice, for the Web itself, 50–75 iterations are sufficient to converge to within the error limits of double-precision arithmetic.

EXAMPLE 5.2 Suppose we apply the process described above to the matrix M from Example 5.1. Since there are four nodes, the initial vector $\mathbf{v}_0$ has four components, each $1/4$. The sequence of approximations to the limit that we get by multiplying at each step by M is:

$$\begin{bmatrix} 1/4 \\ 1/4 \\ 1/4 \\ 1/4 \end{bmatrix} \begin{bmatrix} 9/24 \\ 5/24 \\ 5/24 \\ 5/24 \end{bmatrix} \begin{bmatrix} 15/48 \\ 11/48 \\ 11/48 \\ 11/48 \end{bmatrix} \begin{bmatrix} 11/32 \\ 7/32 \\ 7/32 \\ 7/32 \end{bmatrix} \cdots \begin{bmatrix} 3/9 \\ 2/9 \\ 2/9 \\ 2/9 \end{bmatrix}$$

Notice that in this example, the probabilities for B, C, and D remain the same. It is easy to see that B and C must always have the same values at any iteration, because their rows in M are identical. To show that their values are

---

Solving Linear Equations

If you look at the 4-node "Web" of Example 5.2, you might think that the way to solve the equation $\mathbf{v} = M\mathbf{v}$ is by Gaussian elimination. Indeed, in that example, we argued what the limit would be essentially by doing so. However, in realistic examples, where there are tens or hundreds of billions of nodes, Gaussian elimination is not feasible. The reason is that Gaussian elimination takes time that is cubic in the number of equations. Thus, the only way to solve equations on this scale is to iterate as we have suggested. Even that iteration is quadratic at each round, but we can speed it up by taking advantage of the fact that the matrix M is very sparse; there are on average about ten links per page, i.e., ten nonzero entries per column.

Moreover, there is another difference between PageRank calculation and solving linear equations. The equation $\mathbf{v} = M\mathbf{v}$ has an infinite number of solutions, since we can take any solution $\mathbf{v}$, multiply its components by any fixed constant c, and get another solution to the same equation. When we include the constraint that the sum of the components is 1, as we have done, then we get a unique solution.

---

also the same as the value for D, an inductive proof works, and we leave it as an exercise. Given that the last three values of the limiting vector must be the same, it is easy to discover the limit of the above sequence. The first row of M tells us that the probability of A must be 3/2 the other probabilities, so the limit has the probability of A equal to 3/9, or 1/3, while the probability for the other three nodes is 2/9.

This difference in probability is not great. But in the real Web, with billions of nodes of greatly varying importance, the true probability of being at a node like `www.amazon.com` is orders of magnitude greater than the probability of typical nodes.

5.1.3   Structure of the Web

It would be nice if the Web were strongly connected like Fig. 5.1. However, it is not, in practice. An early study of the Web found it to have the structure shown in Fig. 5.2. There was a large strongly connected component (SCC), but there were several other portions that were almost as large.

(1) The *in-component*, consisting of pages that could reach the SCC by following links, but were not reachable from the SCC.
(2) The *out-component*, consisting of pages reachable from the SCC but unable to reach the SCC.
(3) *Tendrils*, which are of two types. Some tendrils consist of pages reachable from the in-component but not able to reach the in-component. The other tendrils can reach the out-component, but are not reachable from the out-component.

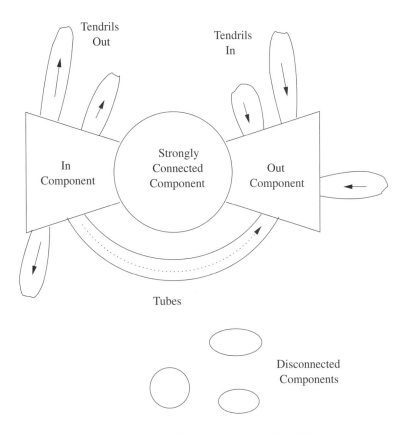

Figure 5.2 The "bowtie" picture of the Web

In addition, there were small numbers of pages found either in

(a) *Tubes*, which are pages reachable from the in-component and able to reach the out-component, but unable to reach the SCC or be reached from the SCC.

(b) Isolated components that are unreachable from the large components (the SCC, in- and out-compunents) and unable to reach those components.

Several of these structures violate the assumptions needed for the Markov-process iteration to converge to a limit. For example, when a random surfer enters the out-component, they can never leave. As a result, surfers starting in either the SCC or in-component are going to wind up in either the out-component or a tendril off the in-component. Thus, no page in the SCC or in-component winds up with any probability of a surfer being there. If we interpret this probability as measuring the importance of a page, then we conclude falsely that nothing in the SCC or in-component is of any importance.

As a result, PageRank is usually modified to prevent such anomalies. There are really two problems we need to avoid. First is the dead end, a page that has no links out. Surfers reaching such a page disappear, and the result is that in the limit no page that can reach a dead end can have any PageRank at all. The second problem is groups of pages that all have outlinks but they never link to any other pages. These structures are called *spider traps*.[3] Both these problems are solved by a method called "taxation," where we assume a random surfer has a finite probability of leaving the Web at any step, and new surfers are started at each page. We shall illustrate this process as we study each of the two problem cases.

5.1.4   Avoiding Dead Ends

Recall that a page with no link out is called a dead end. If we allow dead ends, the transition matrix of the Web is no longer stochastic, since some of the columns will sum to 0 rather than 1. A matrix whose column sums are at most 1 is called *substochastic*. If we compute $M^i \mathbf{v}$ for increasing powers of a substochastic matrix M, then some or all of the components of the vector go to 0. That is, importance "drains out" of the Web, and we get no information about the relative importance of pages.

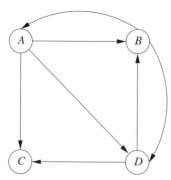

Figure 5.3 C is now a dead end

EXAMPLE 5.3   In Fig. 5.3 we have modified Fig. 5.1 by removing the arc from C to A. Thus, C becomes a dead end. In terms of random surfers, when a surfer reaches C they disappear at the next round. The matrix M that describes Fig. 5.3 is

$$M = \begin{bmatrix} 0 & 1/2 & 0 & 0 \\ 1/3 & 0 & 0 & 1/2 \\ 1/3 & 0 & 0 & 1/2 \\ 1/3 & 1/2 & 0 & 0 \end{bmatrix}$$

Note that it is substochastic, but not stochastic, because the sum of the third column, for C, is 0, not 1. Here is the sequence of vectors that result by starting

---

[3] They are so called because the programs that crawl the Web, recording pages and links, are often referred to as "spiders." Once a spider enters a spider trap, it can never leave.

with the vector with each component $1/4$, and repeatedly multiplying the vector by M:

$$\begin{bmatrix} 1/4 \\ 1/4 \\ 1/4 \\ 1/4 \end{bmatrix} \begin{bmatrix} 3/24 \\ 5/24 \\ 5/24 \\ 5/24 \end{bmatrix} \begin{bmatrix} 5/48 \\ 7/48 \\ 7/48 \\ 7/48 \end{bmatrix} \begin{bmatrix} 21/288 \\ 31/288 \\ 31/288 \\ 31/288 \end{bmatrix} \cdots \begin{bmatrix} 0 \\ 0 \\ 0 \\ 0 \end{bmatrix}$$

As we see, the probability of a surfer being anywhere goes to 0, as the number of steps increase.

There are two approaches to dealing with dead ends.

(1) We can drop the dead ends from the graph, and also drop their incoming arcs. Doing so may create more dead ends, which also have to be dropped, recursively. However, eventually we wind up with a strongly-connected component, none of whose nodes are dead ends. In terms of Fig. 5.2, recursive deletion of dead ends will remove parts of the out-component, tendrils, and tubes, but leave the SCC and the in-component, as well as parts of any small isolated components.[4]

(2) We can modify the process by which random surfers are assumed to move about the Web. This method, which we refer to as "taxation," also solves the problem of spider traps, so we shall defer it to Section 5.1.5.

If we use the first approach, recursive deletion of dead ends, then we solve the remaining graph G by whatever means are appropriate, including the taxation method if there might be spider traps in G. Then, we restore the graph, but keep the PageRank values for the nodes of G. Nodes not in G, but with predecessors all in G can have their PageRank computed by summing, over all predecessors p, the PageRank of p divided by the number of successors of p in the full graph. Now there may be other nodes, not in G, that have the PageRank of all their predecessors computed. These may have their own PageRank computed by the same process. Eventually, all nodes outside G will have their PageRank computed; they can surely be computed in the order opposite to that in which they were deleted.

EXAMPLE 5.4 Figure 5.4 is a variation on Fig. 5.3, where we have introduced a successor E for C. But E is a dead end, and when we remove it, and the arc entering from C, we find that C is now a dead end. After removing C, no more nodes can be removed, since each of A, B, and D have arcs leaving. The resulting graph is shown in Fig. 5.5.

---

[4] You might suppose that the entire out-component and all the tendrils will be removed, but remember that they can have within them smaller strongly connected components, including spider traps, which cannot be deleted.

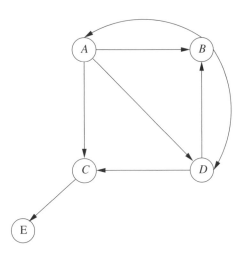

Figure 5.4 A graph with two levels of dead ends

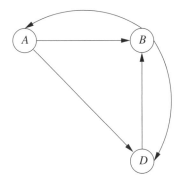

Figure 5.5 The reduced graph with no dead ends

The matrix for the graph of Fig. 5.5 is

$$M = \begin{bmatrix} 0 & 1/2 & 0 \\ 1/2 & 0 & 1 \\ 1/2 & 1/2 & 0 \end{bmatrix}$$

The rows and columns correspond to A, B, and D in that order. To get the PageRanks for this matrix, we start with a vector with all components equal to $1/3$, and repeatedly multiply by M. The sequence of vectors we get is

$$\begin{bmatrix} 1/3 \\ 1/3 \\ 1/3 \end{bmatrix} \begin{bmatrix} 1/6 \\ 3/6 \\ 2/6 \end{bmatrix} \begin{bmatrix} 3/12 \\ 5/12 \\ 4/12 \end{bmatrix} \begin{bmatrix} 5/24 \\ 11/24 \\ 8/24 \end{bmatrix} \cdots \begin{bmatrix} 2/9 \\ 4/9 \\ 3/9 \end{bmatrix}$$

We now know that the PageRank of A is $2/9$, the PageRank of B is $4/9$, and the PageRank of D is $3/9$. We still need to compute PageRanks for C and E, and we do so in the order opposite to that in which they were deleted. Since C was last to be deleted, we know all its predecessors have PageRanks computed. These predecessors are A and D. In Fig. 5.4, A has three successors, so it contributes $1/3$ of its PageRank to C. Page D has two successors in Fig. 5.4, so it contributes half its PageRank to C. Thus, the PageRank of C is $\frac{1}{3} \times \frac{2}{9} + \frac{1}{2} \times \frac{3}{9} = 13/54$.

Now we can compute the PageRank for E. That node has only one predecessor, C, and C has only one successor. Thus, the PageRank of E is the same as that of C. Note that the sums of the PageRanks exceed 1, and they no longer represent the distribution of a random surfer. Yet they do represent decent estimates of the relative importance of the pages.

5.1.5 Spider Traps and Taxation

As we mentioned, a spider trap is a set of nodes with no dead ends but no arcs out. These structures can appear intentionally or unintentionally on the Web, and they cause the PageRank calculation to place all the PageRank within the spider traps.

EXAMPLE 5.5   Consider Fig. 5.6, which is Fig. 5.1 with the arc out of C changed to point to C itself. That change makes C a simple spider trap of one node. Note that in general spider traps can have many nodes, and as we shall see in Section 5.4, there are spider traps with millions of nodes that spammers construct intentionally.

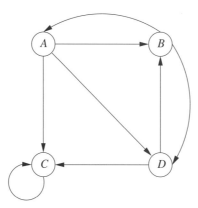

Figure 5.6 A graph with a one-node spider trap

The transition matrix for Fig. 5.6 is

$$M = \begin{bmatrix} 0 & 1/2 & 0 & 0 \\ 1/3 & 0 & 0 & 1/2 \\ 1/3 & 0 & 1 & 1/2 \\ 1/3 & 1/2 & 0 & 0 \end{bmatrix}$$

If we perform the usual iteration to compute the PageRank of the nodes, we get

$$
\begin{bmatrix} 1/4 \\ 1/4 \\ 1/4 \\ 1/4 \end{bmatrix}
\begin{bmatrix} 3/24 \\ 5/24 \\ 11/24 \\ 5/24 \end{bmatrix}
\begin{bmatrix} 5/48 \\ 7/48 \\ 29/48 \\ 7/48 \end{bmatrix}
\begin{bmatrix} 21/288 \\ 31/288 \\ 205/288 \\ 31/288 \end{bmatrix}
\cdots
\begin{bmatrix} 0 \\ 0 \\ 1 \\ 0 \end{bmatrix}
$$

As predicted, all the PageRank is at C, since once there a random surfer can never leave.

To avoid the problem illustrated by Example 5.5, we modify the calculation of PageRank by allowing each random surfer a small probability of *teleporting* to a random page, rather than following an out-link from their current page. The iterative step, where we compute a new vector estimate of PageRanks $\mathbf{v}'$ from the current PageRank estimate $\mathbf{v}$ and the transition matrix M is

$$
\mathbf{v}' = \beta M \mathbf{v} + (1 - \beta)\mathbf{e}/n
$$

where β is a chosen constant, usually in the range 0.8 to 0.9, $\mathbf{e}$ is a vector of all 1's with the appropriate number of components, and n is the number of nodes in the Web graph. The term $\beta M \mathbf{v}$ represents the case where, with probability β, the random surfer decides to follow an out-link from their present page. The term $(1 - \beta)\mathbf{e}/n$ is a vector each of whose components has value $(1 - \beta)/n$ and represents the introduction, with probability $1 - \beta$, of a new random surfer at a random page.

Note that if the graph has no dead ends, then the probability of introducing a new random surfer is exactly equal to the probability that the random surfer will decide *not* to follow a link from their current page. In this case, it is reasonable to visualize the surfer as deciding either to follow a link or teleport to a random page. However, if there are dead ends, then there is a third possibility, which is that the surfer goes nowhere. Since the term $(1 - \beta)\mathbf{e}/n$ does not depend on the sum of the components of the vector $\mathbf{v}$, there will always be some fraction of a surfer operating on the Web. That is, when there are dead ends, the sum of the components of $\mathbf{v}$ may be less than 1, but it will never reach 0.

EXAMPLE 5.6 Let us see how the new approach to computing PageRank fares on the graph of Fig. 5.6. We shall use $\beta = 0.8$ in this example. Thus, the equation for the iteration becomes

$$
\mathbf{v}' = \begin{bmatrix} 0 & 2/5 & 0 & 0 \\ 4/15 & 0 & 0 & 2/5 \\ 4/15 & 0 & 4/5 & 2/5 \\ 4/15 & 2/5 & 0 & 0 \end{bmatrix} \mathbf{v} + \begin{bmatrix} 1/20 \\ 1/20 \\ 1/20 \\ 1/20 \end{bmatrix}
$$

Notice that we have incorporated the factor β into M by multiplying each of its elements by 4/5. The components of the vector $(1 - \beta)\mathbf{e}/n$ are each 1/20, since

$1 - \beta = 1/5$ and $n = 4$. Here are the first few iterations:

$$\begin{bmatrix} 1/4 \\ 1/4 \\ 1/4 \\ 1/4 \end{bmatrix} \begin{bmatrix} 9/60 \\ 13/60 \\ 25/60 \\ 13/60 \end{bmatrix} \begin{bmatrix} 41/300 \\ 53/300 \\ 153/300 \\ 53/300 \end{bmatrix} \begin{bmatrix} 543/4500 \\ 707/4500 \\ 2543/4500 \\ 707/4500 \end{bmatrix} \cdots \begin{bmatrix} 15/148 \\ 19/148 \\ 95/148 \\ 19/148 \end{bmatrix}$$

By being a spider trap, C has managed to get more than half of the PageRank for itself. However, the effect has been limited, and each of the nodes gets some of the PageRank.

5.1.6   Using PageRank in a Search Engine

Having seen how to calculate the PageRank vector for the portion of the Web that a search engine has crawled, we should examine how this information is used. Each search engine has a secret formula that decides the order in which to show pages to the user in response to a search query consisting of one or more search terms (words). Google is said to use over 250 different properties of pages, from which a linear order of pages is decided.

First, in order to be considered for the ranking at all, a page has to have at least one of the search terms in the query. Normally, the weighting of properties is such that unless all the search terms are present, a page has very little chance of being in the top ten that are normally shown first to the user. Among the qualified pages, a score is computed for each, and an important component of this score is the PageRank of the page. Other components include the presence or absence of search terms in prominent places, such as headers or the links to the page itself.

5.1.7   Exercises for Section 5.1

EXERCISE 5.1.1   Compute the PageRank of each page in Fig. 5.7, assuming no taxation.

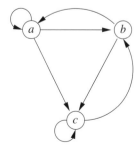

Figure 5.7 An example graph for exercises

EXERCISE 5.1.2   Compute the PageRank of each page in Fig. 5.7, assuming $\beta = 0.8$.

! EXERCISE 5.1.3   Suppose the Web consists of a *clique* (set of nodes with all possible arcs from one to another) of n nodes and a single additional node that is the successor of each of the n nodes in the clique. Figure 5.8 shows this graph for the case $n = 4$. Determine the PageRank of each page, as a function of n and β.

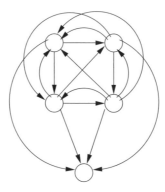

Figure 5.8 Example of graphs discussed in Exercise 5.1.3

!! EXERCISE 5.1.4   Construct, for any integer n, a Web such that, depending on β, any of the n nodes can have the highest PageRank among those n. It is allowed for there to be other nodes in the Web besides these n.

! EXERCISE 5.1.5   Show by induction on n that if the second, third, and fourth components of a vector $\mathbf{v}$ are equal, and M is the transition matrix of Example 5.1, then the second, third, and fourth components are also equal in $M^n\mathbf{v}$ for any $n \geq 0$.

Figure 5.9 A chain of dead ends

EXERCISE 5.1.6   Suppose we recursively eliminate dead ends from the graph, solve the remaining graph, and estimate the PageRank for the dead-end pages as described in Section 5.1.4. Suppose the graph is a chain of dead ends, headed by a node with a self-loop, as suggested in Fig. 5.9. What would be the PageRank assigned to each of the nodes?

EXERCISE 5.1.7   Repeat Exercise 5.1.6 for the tree of dead ends suggested by

Fig. 5.10. That is, there is a single node with a self-loop, which is also the root of a complete binary tree of n levels.

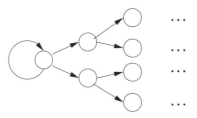

Figure 5.10 A tree of dead ends

5.2   Efficient Computation of PageRank

To compute the PageRank for a large graph representing the Web, we have to perform a matrix–vector multiplication on the order of 50 times, until the vector is close to unchanged at one iteration. To a first approximation, the map-reduce method given in Section 2.3.1 is suitable. However, we must deal with two issues:

(1) The transition matrix of the Web M is very sparse. Thus, representing it by all its elements is highly inefficient. Rather, we want to represent the matrix by its nonzero elements.

(2) We may not be using map-reduce, or for efficiency reasons we may wish to use a combiner (see Section 2.2.4) with the Map tasks to reduce the amount of data that must be passed from Map tasks to Reduce tasks. In this case, the striping approach discussed in Section 2.3.1 is not sufficient to avoid heavy use of disk (thrashing).

We discuss the solution to these two problems in this section.

5.2.1   Representing Transition Matrices

The transition matrix is very sparse, since the average Web page has about 10 out-links. If, say, we are analyzing a graph of ten billion pages, then only one in a billion entries is not 0. The proper way to represent any sparse matrix is to list the locations of the nonzero entries and their values. If we use 4-byte integers for coordinates of an element and an 8-byte double-precision number for the value, then we need 16 bytes per nonzero entry. That is, the space needed is linear in the number of nonzero entries, rather than quadratic in the side of the matrix.

However, for a transition matrix of the Web, there is one further compression that we can do. If we list the nonzero entries by column, then we know what each nonzero entry is; it is 1 divided by the out-degree of the page. We can thus represent a column by one integer for the out-degree, and one integer per nonzero entry in that column, giving the row number where that entry is located. Thus, we need slightly more than 4 bytes per nonzero entry to represent a transition matrix.

EXAMPLE 5.7   Let us reprise the example Web graph from Fig. 5.1, whose transition matrix is

$$M = \begin{bmatrix} 0 & 1/2 & 1 & 0 \\ 1/3 & 0 & 0 & 1/2 \\ 1/3 & 0 & 0 & 1/2 \\ 1/3 & 1/2 & 0 & 0 \end{bmatrix}$$

Recall that the rows and columns represent nodes A, B, C, and D, in that order. In Fig. 5.11 is a compact representation of this matrix.[5]

Source	Degree	Destinations
A	3	B, C, D
B	2	A, D
C	1	A
D	2	B, C

Figure 5.11 Represent a transition matrix by the out-degree of each node and the list of its successors

For instance, the entry for A has degree 3 and a list of three successors. From that row of Fig. 5.11 we can deduce that the column for A in matrix M has 0 in the row for A (since it is not on the list of destinations) and $1/3$ in the rows for B, C, and D. We know that the value is $1/3$ because the degree column in Fig. 5.11 tells us there are three links out of A.

5.2.2   PageRank Iteration Using Map-Reduce

One iteration of the PageRank algorithm involves taking an estimated PageRank vector $\mathbf{v}$ and computing the next estimate $\mathbf{v}'$ by

$$\mathbf{v}' = \beta M \mathbf{v} + (1 - \beta)\mathbf{e}/n$$

Recall β is a constant slightly less than 1, $\mathbf{e}$ is a vector of all 1's, and n is the number of nodes in the graph that transition matrix M represents.

If n is small enough that each Map task can store the full vector $\mathbf{v}$ in main memory and also have room in main memory for the result vector $\mathbf{v}'$, then there is little more here than a matrix–vector multiplication. The additional steps are

---

[5] Because M is not sparse, this representation is not very useful for M. However, the example illustrates the process of representing matrices in general, and the sparser the matrix is, the more this representation will save.

to multiply each component of $M\mathbf{v}$ by constant β and to add $(1 - \beta)/n$ to each component.

However, it is likely, given the size of the Web today, that $\mathbf{v}$ is much too large to fit in main memory. As we discussed in Section 2.3.1, the method of striping, where we break M into vertical stripes (see Fig. 2.4) and break $\mathbf{v}$ into corresponding horizontal stripes, will allow us to execute the map-reduce process efficiently, with no more of $\mathbf{v}$ at any one Map task than can conveniently fit in main memory.

5.2.3 Use of Combiners to Consolidate the Result Vector

There are two reasons the method of Section 5.2.2 might not be adequate.

(1) We might wish to add terms for $\mathbf{v}'_i$, the ith component of the result vector $\mathbf{v}$, at the Map tasks. This improvement is the same as using a combiner, since the Reduce function simply adds terms with a common key. Recall that for a map-reduce implementation of matrix–vector multiplication, the key is the value of i for which a term $m_{ij}\mathbf{v}_j$ is intended.

(2) We might not be using map-reduce at all, but rather executing the iteration step at a single machine or a collection of machines.

We shall assume that we are trying to implement a combiner in conjunction with a Map task; the second case uses essentially the same idea.

Suppose that we are using the stripe method to partition a matrix and vector that do not fit in main memory. Then a vertical stripe from the matrix M and a horizontal stripe from the vector $\mathbf{v}$ will contribute to all components of the result vector $\mathbf{v}'$. Since that vector is the same length as $\mathbf{v}$, it will not fit in main memory either. Moreover, as M is stored column-by-column for efficiency reasons, a column can affect any of the components of $\mathbf{v}'$. As a result, it is unlikely that when we need to add a term to some component $\mathbf{v}'_i$, that component will already be in main memory. Thus, most terms will require that a page be brought into main memory to add it to the proper component. That situation, called *thrashing*, takes orders of magnitude too much time to be feasible.

An alternative strategy is based on partitioning the matrix into k^2 blocks, while the vectors are still partitioned into k stripes. A picture, showing the division for $k = 4$, is in Fig. 5.12. Note that we have not shown the multiplication of the matrix by β or the addition of $(1-\beta)\mathbf{e}/n$, because these steps are straightforward, regardless of the strategy we use.

In this method, we use k^2 Map tasks. Each task gets one square of the matrix M, say M_{ij}, and one stripe of the vector $\mathbf{v}$, which must be $\mathbf{v}_j$. Notice that each stripe of the vector is sent to k different Map tasks; $\mathbf{v}_j$ is sent to the task handling M_{ij} for each of the k possible values of i. Thus, $\mathbf{v}$ is transmitted over the network k times. However, each piece of the matrix is sent only once. Since the size of the matrix, properly encoded as described in Section 5.2.1, can be expected to be several times the size of the vector, the transmission cost is not too much greater

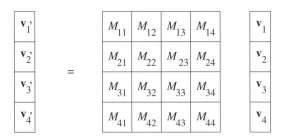

Figure 5.12 Partitioning a matrix into square blocks

than the minimum possible. And because we are doing considerable combining at the Map tasks, we save as data is passed from the Map tasks to the Reduce tasks.

The advantage of this approach is that we can keep both the jth stripe of $\mathbf{v}$ and the ith stripe of $\mathbf{v}'$ in main memory as we process M_{ij}. Note that all terms generated from M_{ij} and $\mathbf{v}_j$ contribute to $\mathbf{v}'_i$ and no other stripe of $\mathbf{v}'$.

5.2.4   Representing Blocks of the Transition Matrix

Since we are representing transition matrices in the special way described in Section 5.2.1, we need to consider how the blocks of Fig. 5.12 are represented. Unfortunately, the space required for a column of blocks (a "stripe" as we called it earlier) is greater than the space needed for the stripe as a whole, but not too much greater.

For each block, we need data about all those columns that have at least one nonzero entry within the block. If k, the number of stripes in each dimension, is large, then most columns will have nothing in most blocks of its stripe. For a given block, we not only have to list those rows that have a nonzero entry for that column, but we must repeat the out-degree for the node represented by the column. Consequently, it is possible that the out-degree will be repeated as many times as the out-degree itself. That observation bounds from above the space needed to store the blocks of a stripe at twice the space needed to store the stripe as a whole.

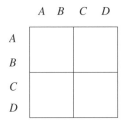

Figure 5.13 A four-node graph is divided into four 2-by-2 blocks

EXAMPLE 5.8 Let us suppose the matrix from Example 5.7 is partitioned into blocks, with $k = 2$. That is, the upper-left quadrant represents links from A or B to A or B, the upper-right quadrant represents links from C or D to A or B, and so on. It turns out that in this small example, the only entry that we can avoid is the entry for C in M_{22}, because C has no arcs to either C or D. The tables representing each of the four blocks are shown in Fig. 5.14.

Source	Degree	Destinations
A	3	B
B	2	A

(a) Representation of M_{11} connecting A and B to A and B

Source	Degree	Destinations
C	1	A
D	2	B

(b) Representation of M_{12} connecting C and D to A and B

Source	Degree	Destinations
A	3	C, D
B	2	D

(c) Representation of M_{21} connecting A and B to C and D

Source	Degree	Destinations
D	2	C

(d) Representation of M_{22} connecting C and D to C and D

Figure 5.14 Sparse representation of the blocks of a matrix

If we examine Fig. 5.14(a), we see the representation of the upper-left quadrant. Notice that the degrees for A and B are the same as in Fig. 5.11, because we need to know the entire number of successors, not the number of successors within the relevant block. However, each successor of A or B is represented in Fig. 5.14(a) or Fig. 5.14(c), but not both. Notice also that in Fig. 5.14(d), there is no entry for C, because there are no successors of C within the lower half of the matrix (rows C and D).

5.2.5   Other Efficient Approaches to PageRank Iteration

The algorithm discussed in Section 5.2.3 is not the only option. We shall discuss several other approaches that use fewer processors. These algorithms share with the algorithm of Section 5.2.3 the good property that the matrix M is read only once, although the vector $\mathbf{v}$ is read k times, where the parameter k is chosen so that $1/k$th of the vectors $\mathbf{v}$ and $\mathbf{v}'$ can be held in main memory. Recall that the algorithm of Section 5.2.3 uses k^2 processors, assuming all Map tasks are executed in parallel at different processors.

We can assign all the blocks in one row of blocks to a single Map task, and thus reduce the number of Map tasks to k. For instance, in Fig. 5.12, M_{11}, M_{12}, M_{13}, and M_{14} would be assigned to a single Map task. If we represent the blocks as in Fig. 5.14, we can read the blocks in a row of blocks one-at-a-time, so the matrix does not consume a significant amount of main-memory. At the same time that we read M_{ij}, we must read the vector stripe $\mathbf{v}_j$. As a result, each of the k Map tasks reads the entire vector $\mathbf{v}$, along with $1/k$th of the matrix.

The work reading M and $\mathbf{v}$ is thus the same as for the algorithm of Section 5.2.3, but the advantage of this approach is that each Map task can combine all the terms for the portion $\mathbf{v}'_i$ for which it is exclusively responsible. In other words, the Reduce tasks have nothing to do but to concatenate the pieces of $\mathbf{v}'$ received from the k Map tasks.

We can extend this idea to an environment in which map-reduce is not used. Suppose we have a single processor, with M and $\mathbf{v}$ stored on its disk, using the same sparse representation for M that we have discussed. We can first simulate the first Map task, the one that uses blocks M_{11} through M_{1k} and all of $\mathbf{v}$ to compute $\mathbf{v}'_1$. Then we simulate the second Map task, reading M_{21} through M_{2k} and all of $\mathbf{v}$ to compute $\mathbf{v}'_2$, and so on. As for the previous algorithms, we thus read M once and $\mathbf{v}$ k times. We can make k as small as possible, subject to the constraint that there is enough main memory to store $1/k$th of $\mathbf{v}$ and $1/k$th of $\mathbf{v}'$, along with as small a portion of M as we can read from disk (typically, one disk block).

5.2.6   Exercises for Section 5.2

EXERCISE 5.2.1   Suppose we wish to store an $n \times n$ boolean matrix (0 and 1 elements only). We could represent it by the bits themselves, or we could represent the matrix by listing the positions of the 1's as pairs of integers, each integer requiring $\lceil \log_2 n \rceil$ bits. The former is suitable for dense matrices; the latter is suitable for sparse matrices. How sparse must the matrix be (i.e., what fraction of the elements should be 1's) for the sparse representation to save space?

EXERCISE 5.2.2   Using the method of Section 5.2.1, represent the transition matrices of the following graphs:

(a) Figure 5.4.
(b) Figure 5.7.

EXERCISE 5.2.3   Using the method of Section 5.2.4, represent the transition matrices of the graph of Fig. 5.3, assuming blocks have side 2.

EXERCISE 5.2.4   Consider a Web graph that is a chain, like Fig. 5.9, with n nodes. As a function of k, which you may assume divides n, describe the representation of the transition matrix for this graph, using the method of Section 5.2.4

5.3   Topic-Sensitive PageRank

There are several improvements we can make to PageRank. One, to be studied in this section, is that we can weight certain pages more heavily because of their topic. The mechanism for enforcing this weighting is to alter the way random surfers behave, having them prefer to land on a page that is known to cover the chosen topic. In the next section, we shall see how the topic-sensitive idea can also be applied to negate the effects of a new kind of spam, called "'link spam," that has developed to try to fool the PageRank algorithm.

5.3.1   Motivation for Topic-Sensitive Page Rank

Different people have different interests, and sometimes distinct interests are expressed using the same term in a query. The canonical example is the search query `jaguar`, which might refer to the animal, the automobile, a version of the MAC operating system, or even an ancient game console. If a search engine can deduce that the user is interested in automobiles, for example, then it can do a better job of returning relevant pages to the user.

Ideally, each user would have a private PageRank vector that gives the importance of each page to that user. It is not feasible to store a vector of length many billions for each of a billion users, so we need to do something simpler. The *topic-sensitive PageRank* approach creates one vector for each of some small number of topics, biasing the PageRank to favor pages of that topic. We then endeavour to classify users according to the degree of their interest in each of the selected topics. While we surely lose some accuracy, the benefit is that we store only a short vector for each user, rather than an enormous vector for each user.

EXAMPLE 5.9   One useful topic set is the 16 top-level categories (sports, medicine, etc.) of the Open Directory (DMOZ).[6]   We could create 16 PageRank vectors, one for each topic. If we could determine that the user is interested in one of these topics, perhaps by the content of the pages they have recently viewed, then we could use the PageRank vector for that topic when deciding on the ranking of pages.

---

[6] This directory, found at `www.dmoz.org`, is a collection of human-classified Web pages.

5.3.2   Biased Random Walks

Suppose we have identified some pages that represent a topic such as "sports." To create a topic-sensitive PageRank for sports, we can arrange that the random surfers are introduced only to a random sports page, rather than to a random page of any kind. The consequence of this choice is that random surfers are likely to be at an identified sports page, or a page reachable along a short path from one of these known sports pages. Our intuition is that pages linked to by sports pages are themselves likely to be about sports. The pages they link to are also likely to be about sports, although the probability of being about sports surely decreases as the distance from an identified sports page increases.

The mathematical formulation for the iteration that yields topic-sensitive PageRank is similar to the equation we used for general PageRank. The only difference is how we add the new surfers. Suppose S is a set of integers consisting of the row/column numbers for the pages we have identified as belonging to a certain topic (called the *teleport set*). Let $\mathbf{e}_S$ be a vector that has 1 in the components in S and 0 in other components. Then the *topic-sensitive PageRank for S* is the limit of the iteration

$$\mathbf{v}' = \beta M \mathbf{v} + (1 - \beta)\mathbf{e}_S/|S|$$

Here, as usual, M is the transition matrix of the Web, and $|S|$ is the size of set S.

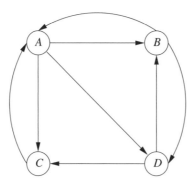

Figure 5.15 Repeat of example Web graph

EXAMPLE 5.10   Let us reconsider the original Web graph we used in Fig. 5.1, which we reproduce as Fig. 5.15. Suppose we use $\beta = 0.8$. Then the transition matrix for this graph, multiplied by β, is

$$\beta M = \begin{bmatrix} 0 & 2/5 & 4/5 & 0 \\ 4/15 & 0 & 0 & 2/5 \\ 4/15 & 0 & 0 & 2/5 \\ 4/15 & 2/5 & 0 & 0 \end{bmatrix}$$

Suppose that our topic is represented by the teleport set $S = \{B, D\}$. Then the vector $(1-\beta)\mathbf{e}_S/|S|$ has $1/10$ for its second and fourth components and 0 for the other two components. The reason is that $1-\beta=1/5$, the size of S is 2, and $\mathbf{e}_S$ has 1 in the components for B and D and 0 in the components for A and C. Thus, the equation that must be iterated is

$$\mathbf{v}' = \begin{bmatrix} 0 & 2/5 & 4/5 & 0 \\ 4/15 & 0 & 0 & 2/5 \\ 4/15 & 0 & 0 & 2/5 \\ 4/15 & 2/5 & 0 & 0 \end{bmatrix} \mathbf{v} + \begin{bmatrix} 0 \\ 1/10 \\ 0 \\ 1/10 \end{bmatrix}$$

Here are the first few iterations of this equation. We have also started with the surfers only at the pages in the teleport set. Although the initial distribution has no effect on the limit, it may help the computation to converge faster.

$$\begin{bmatrix} 0/2 \\ 1/2 \\ 0/2 \\ 1/2 \end{bmatrix} \begin{bmatrix} 2/10 \\ 3/10 \\ 2/10 \\ 3/10 \end{bmatrix} \begin{bmatrix} 42/150 \\ 41/150 \\ 26/150 \\ 41/150 \end{bmatrix} \begin{bmatrix} 62/250 \\ 71/250 \\ 46/250 \\ 71/250 \end{bmatrix} \cdots \begin{bmatrix} 54/210 \\ 59/210 \\ 38/210 \\ 59/210 \end{bmatrix}$$

Notice that because of the concentration of surfers at B and D, these nodes get a higher PageRank than they did in Example 5.2. In that example, A was the node of highest PageRank.

5.3.3 Using Topic-Sensitive PageRank

In order to integrate topic-sensitive PageRank into a search engine, we must:

(1) Decide on the topics for which we shall create specialized PageRank vectors.
(2) Pick a teleport set for each of these topics, and use that set to compute the topic-sensitive PageRank vector for that topic.
(3) Find a way of determining the topic or set of topics that are most relevant for a particular search query.
(4) Use the PageRank vectors for that topic or topics in the ordering of the responses to the search query.

We have mentioned one way of selecting the topic set: use the top-level topics of the Open Directory. Other approaches are possible, but there is probably a need for human classification of at least some pages.

The third step is probably the trickiest, and several methods have been proposed. Some possibilities:

(a) Allow the user to select a topic from a menu.
(b) Infer the topic(s) by the words that appear in the Web pages recently searched by the user, or recent queries issued by the user. We need to discuss how one goes from a collection of words to a topic, and we shall do so in Section 5.3.4
(c) Infer the topic(s) by information about the user, e.g., their bookmarks or their stated interests on Facebook.

5.3.4   Inferring Topics from Words

The question of classifying documents by topic is a subject that has been studied for decades, and we shall not go into great detail here. Suffice it to say that topics are characterized by words that appear surprisingly often in documents on that topic. For example, neither `fullback` nor `measles` appear very often in documents on the Web. But `fullback` will appear far more often than average in pages about sports, and `measles` will appear far more often than average in pages about medicine.

If we examine the entire Web, or a large, random sample of the Web, we can get the background frequency of each word. Suppose we then go to a large sample of pages known to be about a certain topic, say the pages classified under sports by the Open Directory. Examine the frequencies of words in the sports sample, and identify the words that appear significantly more frequently in the sports sample than in the background. In making this judgment, we must be careful to avoid some extremely rare word that appears in the sports sample with relatively higher frequency. This word is probably a misspelling that happened to appear only in one or a few of the sports pages. Thus, we probably want to put a floor on the number of times a word appears, before it can be considered characteristic of a topic.

Once we have identified a large collection of words that appear much more frequently in the sports sample than in the background, and we do the same for all the topics on our list, we can examine other pages and classify them by topic. Here is a simple approach. Suppose that $S_1, S_2, \ldots, S_k$ are the sets of words that have been determined to be characteristic of each of the topics on our list. Let P be the set of words that appear in a given page P. Compute the Jaccard similarity (recall Section 3.1.1) between P and each of the S_i's. Classify the page as that topic with the highest Jaccard similarity. Note that all Jaccard similarities may be very low, especially if the sizes of the sets S_i are small. Thus, it is important to pick reasonably large sets S_i to make sure that we cover all aspects of the topic represented by the set.

We can use this method, or a number of variants, to classify the pages the user has most recently retrieved. We could say the user is interested in the topic into which the largest number of these pages fall. Or we could blend the topic-sensitive PageRank vectors in proportion to the fraction of these pages that fall into each topic, thus constructing a single PageRank vector that reflects the user's current blend of interests. We could also use the same procedure on the pages that the user currently has bookmarked, or combine the bookmarked pages with the recently viewed pages.

5.3.5   Exercises for Section 5.3

EXERCISE 5.3.1   Compute the topic-sensitive PageRank for the graph of Fig. 5.15, assuming the teleport set is:

(a) A only.

(b) A and C.

5.4   Link Spam

When it became apparent that PageRank and other techniques used by Google made term spam ineffective, spammers turned to methods designed to fool the PageRank algorithm into overvaluing certain pages. The techniques for artificially increasing the PageRank of a page are collectively called *link spam*. In this section we shall first examine how spammers create link spam, and then see several methods for decreasing the effectiveness of these spamming techniques, including TrustRank and measurement of spam mass.

5.4.1   Architecture of a Spam Farm

A collection of pages whose purpose is to increase the PageRank of a certain page or pages is called a *spam farm*. Figure 5.16 shows the simplest form of spam farm. From the point of view of the spammer, the Web is divided into three parts:

(1) *Inaccessible pages*: the pages that the spammer cannot affect. Most of the Web is in this part.
(2) *Accessible pages*: those pages that, while they are not controlled by the spammer, can be affected by the spammer.
(3) *Own pages*: the pages that the spammer owns and controls.

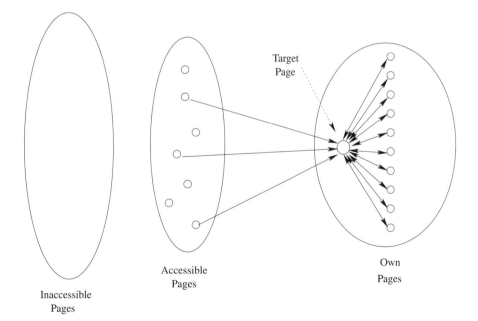

Figure 5.16 The Web from the point of view of the link spammer

The spam farm consists of the spammer's own pages, organized in a special way as seen on the right, and some links from the accessible pages to the spammer's pages. Without some links from the outside, the spam farm would be useless, since it would not even be crawled by a typical search engine.

Concerning the accessible pages, it might seem surprising that one can affect a page without owning it. However, today there are many sites, such as blogs or newspapers that invite others to post their comments on the site. In order to get as much PageRank flowing to his own pages from outside, the spammer posts many comments such as "I agree. Please see my article at www.mySpamFarm.com."

In the spam farm, there is one page t, the *target page*, at which the spammer attempts to place as much PageRank as possible. There are a large number m of *supporting* pages, that accumulate the portion of the PageRank that is distributed equally to all pages (the fraction $1-\beta$ of the PageRank that represents surfers going to a random page). The supporting pages also prevent the Page-Rank of t from being lost, to the extent possible, since some will be taxed away at each round. Notice that t has a link to every supporting page, and every supporting page links only to t.

5.4.2 Analysis of a Spam Farm

Suppose that PageRank is computed using a taxation parameter β, typically around 0.85. That is, β is the fraction of a page's PageRank that gets distributed to its successors at the next round. Let there be n pages on the Web in total, and let some of them be a spam farm of the form suggested in Fig. 5.16, with a target page t and m supporting pages. Let x be the amount of PageRank contributed by the accessible pages. That is, x is the sum, over all accessible pages p with a link to t, of the PageRank of p times β, divided by the number of successors of p. Finally, let y be the unknown PageRank of t. We shall solve for y.

First, the PageRank of each supporting page is

$$\beta y/m + (1-\beta)/n$$

The first term represents the contribution from t. The PageRank y of t is taxed, so only βy is distributed to t's successors. That PageRank is divided equally among the m supporting pages. The second term is the supporting page's share of the fraction $1 - \beta$ of the PageRank that is divided equally among all pages on the Web.

Now, let us compute the PageRank y of target page t. Its PageRank comes from three sources:

(1) Contribution x from outside, as we have assumed.
(2) β times the PageRank of every supporting page; that is,

$$\beta\big(\beta y/m + (1-\beta)/n\big)$$

(3) $(1 - \beta)/n$, the share of the fraction $1 - \beta$ of the PageRank that belongs to t. This amount is negligible and will be dropped to simplify the analysis.

Thus, from (1) and (2) above, we can write

$$y = x + \beta m \left(\frac{\beta y}{m} + \frac{1 - \beta}{n} \right) = x + \beta^2 y + \beta(1 - \beta)\frac{m}{n}$$

We may solve the above equation for y, yielding

$$y = \frac{x}{1 - \beta^2} + c\frac{m}{n}$$

where $c = \beta(1 - \beta)/(1 - \beta^2) = \beta/(1 + \beta)$.

EXAMPLE 5.11 If we choose $\beta = 0.85$, then $1/(1 - \beta^2) = 3.6$, and $c = \beta/(1 + \beta) = 0.46$. That is, the structure has amplified the external PageRank contribution by 360%, and also obtained an amount of PageRank that is 46% of the fraction m/n that represents the portion of the Web m/n that is in the spam farm.

5.4.3 Combating Link Spam

It has become essential for search engines to detect and eliminate link spam, just as it was necessary in the previous decade to eliminate term spam. There are two approaches to link spam. One is to look for structures such as the spam farm in Fig. 5.16, where one page links to a very large number of pages, each of which links back to it. Search engines surely search for such structures and eliminate those pages from their index. That causes spammers to develop different structures that have essentially the same effect of capturing PageRank for a target page or pages. There is essentially no end to variations of Fig. 5.16, so this war between the spammers and the search engines will likely go on for a long time.

However, there is another approach to eliminating link spam that doesn't rely on locating the spam farms. Rather, a search engine can modify its definition of PageRank to lower the rank of link-spam pages automatically. We shall consider two different formulas:

(1) *TrustRank*, a variation of topic-sensitive PageRank designed to lower the score of spam pages.
(2) *Spam mass*, a calculation that identifies the pages that are likely to be spam and allows the search engine to eliminate those pages or to lower their Page-Rank strongly.

5.4.4 TrustRank

TrustRank is topic-sensitive PageRank, where the "topic" is a set of pages believed to be trustworthy (not spam). The theory is that while a spam page might easily be made to link to a trustworthy page, it is unlikely that a trustworthy page would link to a spam page. The borderline area is a site with blogs or other opportunities for spammers to create links, as was discussed in Section 5.4.1. These pages cannot be considered trustworthy, even if their own content is highly reliable, as would be the case for a reputable newspaper that allowed readers to post comments.

To implement TrustRank, we need to develop a suitable teleport set of trustworthy pages. Two approaches that have been tried are:

(1) Let humans examine a set of pages and decide which of them are trustworthy. For example, we might pick the pages of highest PageRank to examine, on the theory that, while link spam can raise a page's rank from the bottom to the middle of the pack, it is essentially impossible to give a spam page a PageRank near the top of the list.

(2) Pick a domain whose membership is controlled, on the assumption that it is hard for a spammer to get their pages into these domains. For example, we could pick the .edu domain, since university pages are unlikely to be spam farms. We could likewise pick .mil, or .gov. However, the problem with these specific choices is that they are almost exclusively US sites. To get a good distribution of trustworthy Web pages, we should include the analogous sites from foreign countries, e.g., ac.il, or edu.sg.

It is likely that search engines today implement a strategy of the second type routinely, so that what we think of as PageRank really is a form of TrustRank.

5.4.5 Spam Mass

The idea behind spam mass is that we measure the fraction of its PageRank that comes from spam. We do so by computing both the ordinary PageRank and the TrustRank based on some teleport set of trustworthy pages. Suppose page p has PageRank r and TrustRank t. Then the *spam mass* of p is $(r - t)/r$. A negative or small positive spam mass means that p is probably not a spam page, while a spam mass close to 1 suggests that the page probably is spam. It is possible to eliminate pages with a high spam mass from the index of Web pages used by a search engine, thus eliminating a great deal of the link spam without having to identify particular structures that spam farmers use.

EXAMPLE 5.12   Let us consider both the PageRank and topic-sensitive PageRank that were computed for the graph of Fig. 5.1 in Examples 5.2 and 5.10, respectively. In the latter case, the teleport set was nodes B and D, so let us assume those are the trusted pages. Figure 5.17 tabulates the PageRank, TrustRank, and spam mass for each of the four nodes.

In this simple example, the only conclusion is that the nodes B and D, which were a priori determined not to be spam, have negative spam mass and are therefore not spam. The other two nodes, A and C, each have a positive spam mass, since their PageRanks are higher than their TrustRanks. For instance, the

Node	PageRank	TrustRank	Spam Mass
A	3/9	54/210	0.229
B	2/9	59/210	-0.264
C	2/9	38/210	0.186
D	2/9	59/210	-0.264

Figure 5.17 Calculation of spam mass

spam mass of A is computed by taking the difference $3/9 - 54/210 = 8/105$ and dividing $8/105$ by the PageRank $3/9$ to get $8/35$ or about 0.229. However, their spam mass is still closer to 0 than to 1, so it is probable that they are not spam.

5.4.6 Exercises for Section 5.4

EXERCISE 5.4.1 In Section 5.4.2 we analyzed the spam farm of Fig. 5.16, where every supporting page links back to the target page. Repeat the analysis for a spam farm in which:

(a) Each supporting page links to itself instead of to the target page.
(b) Each supporting page links nowhere.
(c) Each supporting page links both to itself and to the target page.

EXERCISE 5.4.2 For the original Web graph of Fig. 5.1, assuming only B is a trusted page:

(a) Compute the TrustRank of each page.
(b) Compute the spam mass of each page.

! EXERCISE 5.4.3 Suppose two spam farmers agree to link their spam farms. How would you link the pages in order to increase as much as possible the Page-Rank of each spam farm's target page? Is there an advantage to linking spam farms?

5.5 Hubs and Authorities

An idea called "hubs and authorities' was proposed shortly after PageRank was first implemented. The algorithm for computing hubs and authorities bears some resemblance to the computation of PageRank, since it also deals with the iterative computation of a fixedpoint involving repeated matrix–vector multiplication. However, there are also significant differences between the two ideas, and neither can substitute for the other.

   This hubs-and-authorities algorithm, sometimes called *HITS* (*hyperlink-induced topic search*), was originally intended not as a preprocessing step before handling search queries, as PageRank is, but as a step to be done along with the processing of a search query, to rank only the responses to that query. We shall, however, describe it as a technique for analyzing the entire Web, or the portion crawled by a search engine. There is reason to believe that something like this approach is, in fact, used by the Ask search engine.

5.5.1   The Intuition Behind HITS

While PageRank assumes a one-dimensional notion of importance for pages, HITS views important pages as having two flavors of importance.

(1) Certain pages are valuable because they provide information about a topic. These pages are called *authorities*.

(2) Other pages are valuable not because they provide information about any topic, but because they tell you where to go to find out about that topic. These pages are called *hubs*.

EXAMPLE 5.13   A typical department at a university maintains a Web page listing all the courses offered by the department, with links to a page for each course, telling about the course – the instructor, the text, an outline of the course content, and so on. If you want to know about a certain course, you need the page for that course; the departmental course list will not do. The course page is an authority for that course. However, if you want to find out what courses the department is offering, it is not helpful to search for each courses' page; you need the page with the course list first. This page is a hub for information about courses.

Just as PageRank uses the recursive definition of importance that "a page is important if important pages link to it," HITS uses a mutually recursive definition of two concepts: "a page is a good hub if it links to good authorities, and a page is a good authority if it is linked to by good hubs."

5.5.2   Formalizing Hubbiness and Authority

To formalize the above intuition, we shall assign two scores to each Web page. One score represents the *hubbiness* of a page – that is, the degree to which it is a good hub, and the second score represents the degree to which the page is a good authority. Assuming that pages are enumerated, we represent these scores by vectors $\mathbf{h}$ and $\mathbf{a}$. The ith component of $\mathbf{h}$ gives the hubbiness of the ith page, and the ith component of $\mathbf{a}$ gives the authority of the same page.

While importance is divided among the successors of a page, as expressed by the transition matrix of the Web, the normal way to describe the computation of hubbiness and authority is to add the authority of successors to estimate hubbiness and to add hubbiness of predecessors to estimate authority. If that is all we did, then the hubbiness and authority values would typically grow beyond bounds. Thus, we normally scale the values of the vectors $\mathbf{h}$ and $\mathbf{a}$ so that the largest component is 1. An alternative is to scale so that the sum of components is 1.

To describe the iterative computation of **h** and **a** formally, we use the *link matrix of the Web*, L. If we have n pages, then L is an $n \times n$ matrix, and $L_{ij} = 1$ if there is a link from page i to page j, and $L_{ij} = 0$ if not. We shall also have need for L^{T}, the *transpose* of L. That is, $L_{ij}^{\mathrm{T}} = 1$ if there is a link from page j to page i, and $L_{ij}^{\mathrm{T}} = 0$ otherwise. Notice that L^{T} is similar to the matrix M that we used for PageRank, but where L^{T} has 1, M has a fraction – 1 divided by the number of out-links from the page represented by that column.

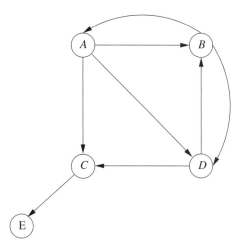

Figure 5.18 Sample data used for HITS examples

EXAMPLE 5.14   For a running example, we shall use the Web of Fig. 5.4, which we reproduce here as Fig. 5.18. An important observation is that dead ends or spider traps do not prevent the HITS iteration from converging to a meaningful pair of vectors. Thus, we can work with Fig. 5.18 directly, with no "taxation" or alteration of the graph needed. The link matrix L and its transpose are shown in Fig. 5.19.

$$L = \begin{bmatrix} 0 & 1 & 1 & 1 & 0 \\ 1 & 0 & 0 & 1 & 0 \\ 0 & 0 & 0 & 0 & 1 \\ 0 & 1 & 1 & 0 & 0 \\ 0 & 0 & 0 & 0 & 0 \end{bmatrix} \qquad L^{\mathrm{T}} = \begin{bmatrix} 0 & 1 & 0 & 0 & 0 \\ 1 & 0 & 0 & 1 & 0 \\ 1 & 0 & 0 & 1 & 0 \\ 1 & 1 & 0 & 0 & 0 \\ 0 & 0 & 1 & 0 & 0 \end{bmatrix}$$

Figure 5.19 The link matrix for the Web of Fig. 5.18 and its transpose

The fact that the hubbiness of a page is proportional to the sum of the authority of its successors is expressed by the equation $\mathbf{h} = \lambda L \mathbf{a}$, where λ is an unknown constant representing the scaling factor needed. Likewise, the fact that the authority of a page is proportional to the sum of the hubbinesses of its predecessors is expressed by $\mathbf{a} = \mu L^{\mathrm{T}}\mathbf{h}$, where μ is another scaling constant. These equations allow us to compute the hubbiness and authority independently, by substituting one equation in the other, as:

- $\mathbf{h} = \lambda\mu LL^{\mathrm{T}}\mathbf{h}$.
- $\mathbf{a} = \lambda\mu L^{\mathrm{T}}L\mathbf{a}$.

However, since LL^{T} and $L^{\mathrm{T}}L$ are not as sparse as L and L^{T}, we are usually better off computing $\mathbf{h}$ and $\mathbf{a}$ in a true mutual recursion. That is, start with $\mathbf{h}$ a vector of all 1's.

(1) Compute $\mathbf{a} = L^{\mathrm{T}}\mathbf{h}$ and then scale so the largest component is 1.
(2) Next, compute $\mathbf{h} = L\mathbf{a}$ and scale again.

Now, we have a new $\mathbf{h}$ and can repeat steps (1) and (2) until at some iteration the changes to the two vectors are sufficiently small that we can stop and accept the current values as the limit.

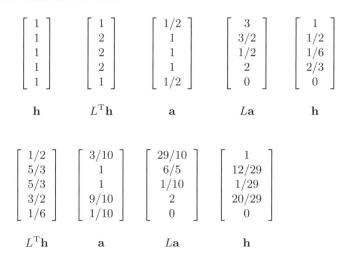

Figure 5.20 First two iterations of the HITS algorithm

EXAMPLE 5.15   Let us perform the first two iterations of the HITS algorithm on the Web of Fig. 5.18. In Fig. 5.20 we see the succession of vectors computed. The first column is the initial $\mathbf{h}$, all 1's. In the second column, we have estimated the relative authority of pages by computing $L^{\mathrm{T}}\mathbf{h}$, thus giving each page the sum of the hubbinesses of its predecessors. The third column gives us the first estimate of $\mathbf{a}$. It is computed by scaling the second column; in this case we have divided each component by 2, since that is the largest value in the second column.

The fourth column is $L\mathbf{a}$. That is, we have estimated the hubbiness of each page by summing the estimate of the authorities of each of its successors. Then, the fifth column scales the fourth column. In this case, we divide by 3, since that is the largest value in the fourth column. Columns six through nine repeat the process outlined in our explanations for columns two through five, but with the better estimate of hubbiness given by the fifth column.

The limit of this process may not be obvious, but it can be computed by a simple program. The limits are:

$$
\mathbf{h} = \begin{bmatrix} 1 \\ 0.3583 \\ 0 \\ 0.7165 \\ 0 \end{bmatrix}
\qquad
\mathbf{a} = \begin{bmatrix} 0.2087 \\ 1 \\ 1 \\ 0.7913 \\ 0 \end{bmatrix}
$$

This result makes sense. First, we notice that the hubbiness of E is surely 0, since it leads nowhere. The hubbiness of C depends only on the authority of E and vice versa, so it should not surprise us that both are 0. A is the greatest hub, since it links to the three biggest authorities, B, C, and D. Also, B and C are the greatest authorities, since they are linked to by the two biggest hubs, A and D.

For Web-sized graphs, the only way of computing the solution to the hubs-and-authorities equations is iteratively. However, for this tiny example, we can compute the solution by solving equations. We shall use the equations $\mathbf{h} = \lambda\mu LL^{\mathrm{T}}\mathbf{h}$. First, LL^{T} is

$$
LL^{\mathrm{T}} = \begin{bmatrix}
3 & 1 & 0 & 2 & 0 \\
1 & 2 & 0 & 0 & 0 \\
0 & 0 & 1 & 0 & 0 \\
2 & 0 & 0 & 2 & 0 \\
0 & 0 & 0 & 0 & 0
\end{bmatrix}
$$

Let $\nu = 1/(\lambda\mu)$ and let the components of $\mathbf{h}$ for nodes A through E be a through e, respectively. Then the equations for $\mathbf{h}$ can be written

$$
\begin{aligned}
\nu a &= 3a + b + 2d & \nu b &= a + 2b \\
\nu c &= c & \nu d &= 2a + 2d \\
\nu e &= 0
\end{aligned}
$$

The equation for b tells us $b = a/(\nu - 2)$ and the equation for d tells us $d = 2a/(\nu - 2)$. If we substitute these expressions for b and d in the equation for a, we get $\nu a = a\big(3 + 5/(\nu - 2)\big)$. From this equation, since a is a factor of both sides, we are left with a quadratic equation for ν which simplifies to $\nu^2 - 5\nu + 1 = 0$. The positive root is $\nu = (5 + \sqrt{21})/2 = 4.791$. Now that we know ν is neither 0 or 1, the equations for c and e tell us immediately that $c = e = 0$.

Finally, if we recognize that a is the largest component of $\mathbf{h}$ and set $a = 1$, we get $b = 0.3583$ and $d = 0.7165$. Along with $c = e = 0$, these values give us the limiting value of h. The value of $\mathbf{a}$ can be computed from $\mathbf{h}$ by multiplying by A^{T} and scaling.

5.5.3   Exercises for Section 5.5

EXERCISE 5.5.1   Compute the hubbiness and authority of each of the nodes in our original Web graph of Fig. 5.1.

! EXERCISE 5.5.2   Suppose our graph is a chain of n nodes, as was suggested by Fig. 5.9. Compute the hubs and authorities vectors, as a function of n.

5.6   Summary of Chapter 5

◆   *Term Spam*: Early search engines were unable to deliver relevant results because they were vulnerable to term spam – the introduction into Web pages of words that misrepresented what the page was about.

◆   *The Google Solution to Term Spam*: Google was able to counteract term spam by two techniques. First was the PageRank algorithm for determining the relative importance of pages on the Web. The second was a strategy of believing what other pages said about a given page, in or near their links to that page, rather than believing only what the page said about itself.

◆   *PageRank*: PageRank is an algorithm that assigns a real number, called its PageRank, to each page on the Web. The PageRank of a page is a measure of how important the page is, or how likely it is to be a good response to a search query. In its simplest form, PageRank is a solution to the recursive equation "a page is important if important pages link to it."

◆   *Transition Matrix of the Web*: We represent links in the Web by a matrix whose ith row and ith column represent the ith page of the Web. If there are one or more links from page j to page i, then the entry in row i and column j is $1/k$, where k is the number of pages to which page j links. Other entries of the transition matrix are 0.

◆   *Computing PageRank on Strongly Connected Web Graphs*: For strongly connected Web graphs (those where any node can reach any other node), Page-Rank is the principal eigenvector of the transition matrix. We can compute PageRank by starting with any nonzero vector and repeatedly multiplying the current vector by the transition matrix, to get a better estimate.[7] After about 50 iterations, the estimate will be very close to the limit, which is the true PageRank.

◆   *The Random Surfer Model*: Calculation of PageRank can be thought of as simulating the behavior of many random surfers, who each start at a random page and at any step move, at random, to one of the pages to which their current page links. The limiting probability of a surfer being at a given page is the PageRank of that page. The intuition is that people tend to create

---

[7] Technically, the condition for this method to work is more restricted than simply "strongly connected." However, the other necessary conditions will surely be met by any large strongly connected component of the Web that was not artificially constructed.

links to the pages they think are useful, so random surfers will tend to be at a useful page.

✦ *Dead Ends*: A dead end is a Web page with no links out. The presence of dead ends will cause the PageRank of some or all of the pages to go to 0 in the iterative computation, including pages that are not dead ends. We can eliminate all dead ends before undertaking a PageRank calculation by recursively dropping nodes with no arcs out. Note that dropping one node can cause another, which linked only to it, to become a dead end, so the process must be recursive.

✦ *Spider Traps*: A spider trap is a set of nodes that, while they may link to each other, have no links out to other nodes. In an iterative calculation of Page-Rank, the presence of spider traps cause all the PageRank to be captured within that set of nodes.

✦ *Taxation Schemes*: To counter the effect of spider traps (and of dead ends, if we do not eliminate them), PageRank is normally computed in a way that modifies the simple iterative multiplication by the transition matrix. A parameter β is chosen, typically around 0.85. Given an estimate of the PageRank, the next estimate is computed by multiplying the estimate by β times the transition matrix, and then adding $(1 - \beta)/n$ to the estimate for each page, where n is the total number of pages.

✦ *Taxation and Random Surfers*: The calculation of PageRank using taxation parameter β can be thought of as giving each random surfer a probability $1 - \beta$ of leaving the Web, and introducing an equivalent number of surfers randomly throughout the Web.

✦ *Efficient Representation of Transition Matrices*: Since a transition matrix is very sparse (almost all entries are 0), it saves both time and space to represent it by listing its nonzero entries. However, in addition to being sparse, the nonzero entries have a special property: they are all the same in any given column; the value of each nonzero entry is the inverse of the number of nonzero entries in that column. Thus, the preferred representation is column-by-column, where the representation of a column is the number of nonzero entries, followed by a list of the rows where those entries occur.

✦ *Very Large-Scale Matrix–Vector Multiplication*: For Web-sized graphs, it may not be feasible to store the entire PageRank estimate vector in the main memory of one machine. Thus, we can break the vector into k segments and break the transition matrix into k^2 squares, called blocks, assigning each square to one machine. The vector segments are each sent to k machines, so there is a small additional cost in replicating the vector.

✦ *Representing Blocks of a Transition Matrix*: When we divide a transition matrix into square blocks, the columns are divided into k segments. To represent a segment of a column, nothing is needed if there are no nonzero entries in that segment. However, if there are one or more nonzero entries, then we need to represent the segment of the column by the total number of nonzero entries in the column (so we can tell what value the nonzero entries have) followed by a list of the rows with nonzero entries.

✦ *Topic-Sensitive PageRank*: If we know the queryer is interested in a certain topic, then it makes sense to bias the PageRank in favor of pages on that topic. To compute this form of PageRank, we identify a set of pages known to be on that topic, and we use it as a "teleport set." The PageRank calculation is modified so that only the pages in the teleport set are given a share of the tax, rather than distributing the tax among all pages on the Web.

✦ *Creating Teleport Sets*: For topic-sensitive PageRank to work, we need to identify pages that are very likely to be about a given topic. One approach is to start with the pages that the open directory (DMOZ) identifies with that topic. Another is to identify words known to be associated with the topic, and select for the teleport set those pages that have an unusually high number of occurrences of such words.

✦ *Link Spam*: To fool the PageRank algorithm, unscrupulous actors have created spam farms. These are collections of pages whose purpose is to concentrate high PageRank on a particular target page.

✦ *Structure of a Spam Farm*: Typically, a spam farm consists of a target page and very many supporting pages. The target page links to all the supporting pages, and the supporting pages link only to the target page. In addition, it is essential that some links from outside the spam farm be created. For example, the spammer might introduce links to their target page by writing comments in other people's blogs or discussion groups.

✦ *TrustRank*: One way to ameliorate the effect of link spam is to compute a topic-sensitive PageRank called TrustRank, where the teleport set is a collection of trusted pages. For example, the home pages of universities could serve as the trusted set. This technique avoids sharing the tax in the PageRank calculation with the large numbers of supporting pages in spam farms and thus preferentially reduces their PageRank.

✦ *Spam Mass*: To identify spam farms, we can compute both the conventional PageRank and the TrustRank for all pages. Those pages that have much lower TrustRank than PageRank are likely to be part of a spam farm.

✦ *Hubs and Authorities*: While PageRank gives a one-dimensional view of the importance of pages, an algorithm called HITS tries to measure two different aspects of importance. Authorities are those pages that contain valuable information. Hubs are pages that, while they do not themselves contain the information, link to places where the information can be found.

✦ *Recursive Formulation of the HITS Algorithm*: Calculation of the hubs and authorities scores for pages depends on solving the recursive equations: "a hub links to many authorities, and an authority is linked to by many hubs." The solution to these equations is essentially an iterated matrix–vector multiplication, just like PageRank's. However, the existence of dead ends or spider traps does not affect the solution to the HITS equations in the way they do for PageRank, so no taxation scheme is necessary.

5.7   References for Chapter 5

The PageRank algorithm was first expressed in [(1)]. The experiments on the structure of the Web, which we used to justify the existence of dead ends and spider traps, were described in [(2)]. The block-stripe method for performing the PageRank iteration is taken from [(5)].

Topic-sensitive PageRank is taken from [(6)]. TrustRank is described in [(4)], and the idea of spam mass is taken from [(3)].

The HITS (hubs and authorities) idea was described in [(7)].

(1) S. Brin and L. Page, "Anatomy of a large-scale hypertextual web search engine," *Proc. 7th Intl. World-Wide-Web Conference*, pp. 107–117, 1998.

(2) A. Broder, R. Kumar, F. Maghoul, P. Raghavan, S. Rajagopalan, R. Stata, A. Tomkins, and J. Weiner, "Graph structure in the web," *Computer Networks* **33**:1–6, pp. 309–320, 2000.

(3) Z. Gyöngi, P. Berkhin, H. Garcia-Molina, and J. Pedersen, "Link spam detection based on mass estimation," *Proc. 32nd Intl. Conf. on Very Large Databases*, pp. 439–450, 2006.

(4) Z. Gyöngi, H. Garcia-Molina, and J. Pedersen, "Combating link spam with trustrank," *Proc. 30th Intl. Conf. on Very Large Databases*, pp. 576–587, 2004.

(5) T.H. Haveliwala, "Efficient computation of PageRank," Stanford Univ. Dept. of Computer Science technical report, Sept., 1999. Available as

    http://infolab.stanford.edu/~taherh/papers/efficient-pr.pdf

(6) T.H. Haveliwala, "Topic-sensitive PageRank," *Proc. 11th Intl. World-Wide-Web Conference*, pp. 517–526, 2002

(7) J.M. Kleinberg, "Authoritative sources in a hyperlinked environment," *J. ACM* **46**:5, pp. 604–632, 1999.

6 Frequent Itemsets

We turn in this chapter to one of the major families of techniques for characterizing data: the discovery of frequent itemsets. This problem is often viewed as the discovery of "association rules," although the latter is a more complex characterization of data, whose discovery depends fundamentally on the discovery of frequent itemsets.

To begin, we introduce the "market-basket" model of data, which is essentially a many-many relationship between two kinds of elements, called "items" and "baskets," but with some assumptions about the shape of the data. The frequent-itemsets problem is that of finding sets of items that appear in (are related to) many of the same baskets.

The problem of finding frequent itemsets differs from the similarity search discussed in Chapter 3. Here we are interested in the absolute number of baskets that contain a particular set of items. In Chapter 3 we wanted items that have a large fraction of their baskets in common, even if the absolute number of baskets is small.

The difference leads to a new class of algorithms for finding frequent itemsets. We begin with the A-Priori Algorithm, which works by eliminating most large sets as candidates by looking first at smaller sets and recognizing that a large set cannot be frequent unless all its subsets are. We then consider various improvements to the basic A-Priori idea, concentrating on very large data sets that stress the available main memory.

Next, we consider approximate algorithms that work faster but are not guaranteed to find all frequent itemsets. Also in this class of algorithms are those that exploit parallelism, including the parallelism we can obtain through a map-reduce formulation. Finally, we discuss briefly how to find frequent itemsets in a data stream.

6.1   The Market-Basket Model

The *market-basket* model of data is used to describe a common form of many-many relationship between two kinds of objects. On the one hand, we have *items*, and on the other we have *baskets*, sometimes called "transactions." Each basket consists of a set of items (an *itemset*), and usually we assume that the number of items in a basket is small – much smaller than the total number of items. The number of baskets is usually assumed to be very large, bigger than what can fit in main memory. The data is assumed to be represented in a file consisting of a sequence of baskets. In terms of the distributed file system described in Section 2.1, the baskets are the objects of the file, and each basket is of type "set of items."

6.1.1   Definition of Frequent Itemsets

Intuitively, a set of items that appears in many baskets is said to be "frequent." To be formal, we assume there is a number s, called the *support threshold*. If I is a set of items, the *support* for I is the number of baskets for which I is a subset. We say I is *frequent* if its support is s or more.

EXAMPLE 6.1   In Fig. 6.1 are sets of words. Each set is a basket, and the words are items. We took these sets by googling cat dog and taking snippets from the highest-ranked pages. Do not be concerned if a word appears twice in a basket, as baskets are sets, and in principle items can appear only once. Also, ignore capitalization.

(1) {Cat, and, dog, bites}
(2) {Yahoo, news, claims, a, cat, mated, with, a, dog, and, produced, viable, offspring}
(3) {Cat, killer, likely, is, a, big, dog}
(4) {Professional, free, advice, on, dog, training, puppy, training}
(5) {Cat, and, kitten, training, and, behavior}
(6) {Dog, &, Cat, provides, dog, training, in, Eugene, Oregon}
(7) { "Dog, and, cat", is, a, slang, term, used, by, police, officers, for, a, male–female, relationship}
(8) {Shop, for, your, show, dog, grooming, and, pet, supplies}

Figure 6.1 Here are eight baskets, each consisting of items that are words

Since the empty set is a subset of any set, the support for $\emptyset$ is 8. However, we shall not generally concern ourselves with the empty set, since it tells us nothing.

Among the singleton sets, obviously {cat} and {dog} are quite frequent. "Dog" appears in all but basket (5), so its support is 7, while "cat" appears in all but (4) and (8), so its support is 6. The word "and" is also quite frequent; it appears in (1), (2), (5), (7), and (8), so its support is 5. The words "a" and "training" appear in three sets, while "for" and "is" appear in two each. No other word appears more than once.

Suppose that we set our threshold at $s = 3$. Then there are five frequent singleton itemsets: {dog}, {cat}, {and}, {a}, and {training}.

Now, let us look at the doubletons. A doubleton cannot be frequent unless both items in the set are frequent by themselves. Thus, there are only ten possible frequent doubletons. Fig. 6.2 is a table indicating which baskets contain which doubletons.

	training	a	and	cat
dog	4, 6	2, 3, 7	1, 2, 8	1, 2, 3, 6, 7
cat	5, 6	2, 7	1, 2, 5	
and	5	2, 3		
a	none			

Figure 6.2 Occurrences of doubletons

For example, we see from the table of Fig. 6.2 that doubleton {dog, training} appears only in baskets (4) and (6). Therefore, its support is 2, and it is not frequent. There are four frequent doubletons if $s = 3$; they are

$$\{\text{dog, a}\} \quad \{\text{dog, and}\}$$
$$\{\text{dog, cat}\} \quad \{\text{cat, and}\}$$

Each appears exactly three times, except for {dog, cat}, which appears five times.

Next, let us see if there are frequent triples. In order to be a frequent triple, each pair of elements in the set must be a frequent doubleton. For example, {dog, a, and} cannot be a frequent itemset, because if it were, then surely {a, and} would be frequent, but it is not. The triple {dog, cat, and} might be frequent, because each of its doubleton subsets is frequent. Unfortunately, the three words appear together only in baskets (1) and (2), so there are in fact no frequent triples. If there are no frequent triples, then there surely are no frequent quadruples or larger sets.

6.1.2   Applications of Frequent Itemsets

The original application of the market-basket model was in the analysis of true market baskets. That is, supermarkets and chain stores record the contents of every market basket (physical shopping cart) brought to the register for checkout. Here the "items" are the different products that the store sells, and the "baskets" are the sets of items in a single market basket. A major chain might sell 100,000 different items and collect data about millions of market baskets.

By finding frequent itemsets, a retailer can learn what is commonly bought together. Especially important are pairs or larger sets of items that occur much more frequently than would be expected were the items bought independently. We shall discuss this aspect of the problem in Section 6.1.3, but for the moment let us simply consider the search for frequent itemsets. We will discover by this analysis that many people buy bread and milk together, but that is of little interest, since we already knew that these were popular items individually.

On-Line versus Brick-and-Mortar Retailing

We suggested in Section 3.1.3 that an on-line retailer would use similarity measures for items to find pairs items that, while they might not be bought by many customers, had a significant fraction of their customers in common. An on-line retailer could then advertise one item of the pair to the few customers who had bought the other item of the pair. This methodology makes no sense for a bricks-and-mortar retailer, because unless lots of people buy an item, it cannot be cost effective to advertise a sale on the item. Thus, the techniques of Chapter 3 are not often useful for brick-and-mortar retailers.

Conversely, the on-line retailer has little need for the analysis we discuss in this chapter, since it is designed to search for itemsets that appear frequently. If the on-line retailer was limited to frequent itemsets, they would miss all the opportunities that are present in the "'long tail" to select advertisements for each customer individually.

We might discover that many people buy hot dogs and mustard together. That, again, should be no surprise to people who like hot dogs, but it offers the super-market an opportunity to do some clever marketing. They can advertise a sale on hot dogs and raise the price of mustard. When people come to the store for the cheap hot dogs, they often will remember that they need mustard, and buy that too. Either they will not notice the price is high, or they reason that it is not worth the trouble to go somewhere else for cheaper mustard.

The famous example of this type is "diapers and beer." One would hardly expect these two items to be related, but through data analysis one chain store discovered that people who buy diapers are unusually likely to buy beer. The theory is that if you buy diapers, you probably have a baby at home, and if you have a baby, then you are unlikely to be drinking at a bar; hence you are more likely to bring beer home. The same sort of marketing ploy that we suggested for hot dogs and mustard could be used for diapers and beer.

However, applications of frequent-itemset analysis is not limited to market baskets. The same model can be used to mine many other kinds of data. Some examples are:

(1) *Related concepts*: Let items be words, and let baskets be documents (e.g., Web pages, blogs, tweets). A basket/document contains those items/words that are present in the document. If we look for sets of words that appear together in many documents, the sets will be dominated by the most common words (stop words), as we saw in Example 6.1. There, even though the intent was to find snippets that talked about cats and dogs, the stop words "and" and "a" were prominent among the frequent itemsets. However, if we ignore all the most common words, then we would hope to find among the frequent pairs some pairs of words that represent a joint concept. For exam-

ple, we would expect a pair like {Brad, Angelina} to appear with surprising frequency.

(2) *Plagiarism*: Let the items be documents and the baskets be sentences. An item/document is "in" a basket/sentence if the sentence is in the document. This arrangement appears backwards, but it is exactly what we need, and we should remember that the relationship between items and baskets is an arbitrary many-many relationship. That is, "in" need not have its conventional meaning: "part of." In this application, we look for pairs of items that appear together in several baskets. If we find such a pair, then we have two documents that share several sentences in common. In practice, even one or two sentences in common is a good indicator of plagiarism.

(3) *Biomarkers*: Let the items be of two types – biomarkers such as genes or blood proteins, and diseases. Each basket is the set of data about a patient: their genome and blood-chemistry analysis, as well as their medical history of disease. A frequent itemset that consists of one disease and one or more biomarkers suggests a test for the disease.

6.1.3   Association Rules

While the subject of this chapter is extracting frequent sets of items from data, this information is often presented as a collection of if–then rules, called *association rules*. The form of an association rule is $I \rightarrow j$, where I is a set of items and j is an item. The implication of this association rule is that if all of the items in I appear in some basket, then j is "likely" to appear in that basket as well.

We formalize the notion of "likely" by defining the *confidence* of the rule $I \rightarrow j$ to be the ratio of the support for $I \cup \{j\}$ to the support for I. That is, the confidence of the rule is the fraction of the baskets with all of I that also contain j.

EXAMPLE 6.2   Consider the baskets of Fig. 6.1. The confidence of the rule $\{cat, dog\} \rightarrow and$ is 2/5. The words "cat" and "dog" appear in five baskets: (1), (2), (3), (6), and (7). Of these, "and" appears in only (1) and (2), or 2/5 of the baskets.

For another illustration, the confidence of $\{cat\} \rightarrow kitten$ is 1/6. The word "cat" appears in six baskets, (1), (2), (3), (5), (6), and (7). Of these, only (5) has the word "kitten."

Confidence alone can be useful, provided the support for the left side of the rule is fairly large. For example, we don't need to know that people are unusually likely to buy mustard when they buy hot dogs, as long as we know that many people buy hot dogs, and many people buy both hot dogs and mustard. We can still use the sale-on-hot-dogs trick discussed in Section 6.1.2. However, there is often more value to an association rule if it reflects a true relationship, where the item or items on the left somehow affect the item on the right.

Thus, we define the *interest* of an association rule $I \rightarrow j$ to be the difference between its confidence and the fraction of baskets that contain j. That its, if I has no influence on j, then we would expect that the fraction of baskets including I that contain j would be exactly the same as the fraction of all baskets that contain j. Such a rule has interest 0. However, it is interesting, in both the informal and technical sense, if a rule has either high interest, meaning that the presence of I in a basket somehow causes the presence of j, or highly negative interest, meaning that the presence of I discourages the presence of j.

EXAMPLE 6.3   The story about bear and diapers is really a claim that the association rule $\{diapers\} \rightarrow beer$ has high interest. That is, the fraction of diaper-buyers who buy beer is significantly greater than the fraction of all customers that buy beer. An example of a rule with negative interest is $\{coke\} \rightarrow pepsi$. That is, people who buy Coke are unlikely to buy Pepsi as well, even though a good fraction of all people buy Pepsi – people typically prefer one or the other, but not both. Similarly, the rule $\{pepsi\} \rightarrow coke$ can be expected to have negative interest.

For some numerical calculations, let us return to the data of Fig. 6.1. The rule $\{dog\} \rightarrow cat$ has confidence 5/7, since "dog" appears in seven baskets, of which five have "cat." However, "cat" appears in six out of the eight baskets, so we would expect that 75% of the seven baskets with "dog" would have "cat" as well. Thus, the interest of the rule is $5/7 - 3/4 = -0.036$, which is essentially 0. The rule $\{cat\} \rightarrow kitten$ has interest $1/6 - 1/8 = 0.042$. The justification is that one out of the six baskets with "cat" have "kitten" as well, while "kitten" appears in only one of the eight baskets. This interest, while positive, is close to 0 and therefore indicates the association rule is not very "interesting."

6.1.4   Finding Association Rules with High Confidence

Identifying useful association rules is not much harder than finding frequent itemsets. We shall take up the problem of finding frequent itemsets in the balance of this chapter, but for the moment, assume it is possible to find those frequent itemsets whose support is at or above a support threshold s.

If we are looking for association rules $I \rightarrow j$ that apply to a reasonable fraction of the baskets, then the support of I must be reasonably high. In practice, such as for marketing in brick-and-mortar stores, "reasonably high" is often around 1% of the baskets. We also want the confidence of the rule to be reasonably high, perhaps 50%, or else the rule has little practical effect. As a result, the set $I \cup \{j\}$ will also have fairly high support.

Suppose we have found all itemsets that meet a threshold of support, and that we have the exact support calculated for each of these itemsets. We can find within them all the association rules that have both high support and high confidence. That is, if J is a set of n items that is found to be frequent, there are only n possible association rules involving this set of items, namely $J - \{j\} \rightarrow j$ for each j in J. If J is frequent, $J - \{j\}$ must be at least as frequent. Thus, it too is a frequent itemset, and we have already computed the support of both J and $J - \{j\}$. Their ratio is the confidence of the rule $J - \{j\} \rightarrow j$.

It must be assumed that there are not too many frequent itemsets and thus not too many candidates for high-support, high-confidence association rules. The reason is that each one found must be acted upon. If we give the store manager a million association rules that meet our thresholds for support and confidence, they cannot even read them, let alone act on them. Likewise, if we produce a million candidates for biomarkers, we cannot afford to run the experiments needed to check them out. Thus, it is normal to adjust the support threshold so that we do not get too many frequent itemsets. This assumption leads, in later sections, to important consequences about the efficiency of algorithms for finding frequent itemsets.

6.1.5   Exercises for Section 6.1

EXERCISE 6.1.1   Suppose there are 100 items, numbered 1 to 100, and also 100 baskets, also numbered 1 to 100. Item i is in basket b if and only if i divides b with no remainder. Thus, item 1 is in all the baskets, item 2 is in all fifty of the even-numbered baskets, and so on. Basket 12 consists of items $\{1, 2, 3, 4, 6, 12\}$, since these are all the integers that divide 12. Answer the following questions:

(a) If the support threshold is 5, which items are frequent?

! (b) If the support threshold is 5, which pairs of items are frequent?

! (c) What is the sum of the sizes of all the baskets?

! EXERCISE 6.1.2   For the item-basket data of Exercise 6.1.1, which basket is the largest?

EXERCISE 6.1.3   Suppose there are 100 items, numbered 1 to 100, and also 100 baskets, also numbered 1 to 100. Item i is in basket b if and only if b divides i with no remainder. For example, basket 12 consists of items

$$\{12, 24, 36, 48, 60, 72, 84, 96\}$$

Repeat Exercise 6.1.1 for this data.

! EXERCISE 6.1.4   This question involves data from which nothing interesting can be learned about frequent itemsets, because there are no sets of items that are correlated. Suppose the items are numbered 1 to 10, and each basket is constructed by including item i with probability $1/i$, each decision being made independently of all other decisions. That is, all the baskets contain item 1, half contain item 2, a third contain item 3, and so on. Assume the number of baskets is sufficiently large that the baskets collectively behave as one would expect statistically. Let the support threshold be 1% of the baskets. Find the frequent itemsets.

EXERCISE 6.1.5   For the data of Exercise 6.1.1, what is the confidence of the following association rules?

(a) $\{5, 7\} \rightarrow 2$.

(b) $\{2, 3, 4\} \rightarrow 5$.

EXERCISE 6.1.6   For the data of Exercise 6.1.3, what is the confidence of the following association rules?

(a) $\{24, 60\} \rightarrow 8$.

(b) $\{2, 3, 4\} \rightarrow 5$.

!! EXERCISE 6.1.7   Describe all the association rules that have 100% confidence for the market-basket data of:

(a) Exercise 6.1.1.

(b) Exercise 6.1.3.

! EXERCISE 6.1.8   Prove that in the data of Exercise 6.1.4 there are no interesting association rules; i.e., the interest of every association rule is 0.

6.2 Market Baskets and the A-Priori Algorithm

We shall now begin a discussion of how to find frequent itemsets or information derived from them, such as association rules with high support and confidence. The original improvement on the obvious algorithms, known as "A-Priori," from which many variants have been developed, will be covered here. The next two sections will discuss certain further improvements. Before discussing the A-priori Algorithm itself, we begin the section with an outline of the assumptions about how data is stored and manipulated when searching for frequent itemsets.

6.2.1   Representation of Market-Basket Data

As we mentioned, we assume that market-basket data is stored in a file basket-by-basket. Possibly, the data is in a distributed file system as in Section 2.1, and the baskets are the objects the file contains. Or the data may be stored in a conventional file, with a character code to represent the baskets and their items.

EXAMPLE 6.4   We could imagine that such a file begins:

```
{23,456,1001}{3,18,92,145}{...
```

Here, the character { begins a basket and the character } ends it. The items in a basket are represented by integers and are separated by commas. Thus, the first basket contains items 23, 456, and 1001; the second basket contains items 3, 18, 92, and 145.

It may be that one machine receives the entire file. Or we could be using map-reduce or a similar tool to divide the work among many processors, in which case each processor receives only a part of the file. It turns out that combining the work of parallel processors to get the exact collection of itemsets that meet a global support threshold is hard, and we shall address this question only in Section 6.4.4.

We also assume that the size of the file of baskets is sufficiently large that it does not fit in main memory. Thus, a major cost of any algorithm is the time it takes to read the baskets from disk. Once a disk block full of baskets is in main memory, we can expand it, generating all the subsets of size k. Since one of the assumptions of our model is that the average size of a basket is small, generating all the pairs in main memory should take time that is much less than the time it took to read the basket from disk. For example, if there are 20 items in a basket, then there are $\binom{20}{2} = 190$ pairs of items in the basket, and these can be generated easily in a pair of nested for-loops.

As the size of the subsets we want to generate gets larger, the time required grows larger; in fact takes approximately time $n^k/k!$ to generate all the subsets of size k for a basket with n items. Eventually, this time dominates the time needed to transfer the data from disk. However:

(1) Often, we need only small frequent itemsets, so k never grows beyond 2 or 3.
(2) And when we do need the itemsets for a large size k, it is usually possible to eliminate many of the items in each basket as not able to participate in a frequent itemset, so the value of n drops as k increases.

The conclusion we would like to draw is that the work of examining each of the baskets can usually be assumed proportional to the size of the file. We can thus measure the running time of a frequent-itemset algorithm by the number of times that each disk block of the data file is read.

Moreover, all the algorithms we discuss have the property that they read the basket file sequentially. Thus, algorithms can be characterized by the number of passes through the basket file that they make, and their running time is proportional to the product of the number of passes they make through the basket file times the size of that file. Since we cannot control the amount of data, only the number of passes taken by the algorithm matters, and it is that aspect of the algorithm that we shall focus upon when measuring the running time of a frequent-itemset algorithm.

6.2.2   Use of Main Memory for Itemset Counting

There is a second data-related issue that we must examine, however. All frequent-itemset algorithms require us to maintain many different counts as we make a pass through the data. For example, we might need to count the number of times that each pair of items occurs in baskets. If we do not have enough main memory to store each of the counts, then adding 1 to a random count will most likely require us to load a page from disk. In that case, the algorithm will thrash and run many orders of magnitude slower than if we were certain to find each count in main memory. The conclusion is that we cannot count anything that doesn't fit in main memory. Thus, each algorithm has a limit on how many items it can deal with.

EXAMPLE 6.5   Suppose a certain algorithm has to count all pairs of items, and there are n items. We thus need space to store $\binom{n}{2}$ integers, or about $n^2/2$ integers. If integers take 4 bytes, we require $2n^2$ bytes. If our machine has 2 giga-bytes, or 2^{31} bytes of main memory, then we require $n \leq 2^{15}$, or approximately $n < 33{,}000$.

It is not trivial to store the $\binom{n}{2}$ counts in a way that makes it easy to find the count for a pair $\{i, j\}$. First, we have not assumed anything about how items are represented. They might, for instance, be strings like "bread." It is more space-efficient to represent items by consecutive integers from 1 to n, where n is the number of distinct items. Unless items are already represented this way, we need a hash table that translates items as they appear in the file to integers. That is, each time we see an item in the file, we hash it. If it is already in the hash table, we can obtain its integer code from its entry in the table. If the item is not there, we assign it the next available number (from a count of the number of distinct items seen so far) and enter the item and its code into the table.

The Triangular-Matrix Method
Even after coding items as integers, we still have the problem that we must count a pair $\{i, j\}$ in only one place. For example, we could order the pair so that $i < j$, and only use the entry $a[i, j]$ in a two-dimensional array a. That strategy would make half the array useless. A more space-efficient way is to use a one-dimensional *triangular array*. We store in $a[k]$ the count for the pair $\{i, j\}$, with $1 \leq i < j \leq n$, where

$$k = (i - 1)\left(n - \frac{i}{2}\right) + j - i$$

The result of this layout is that the pairs are stored in lexicographic order, that is first $\{1, 2\}$, $\{1, 3\}, \ldots, \{1, n\}$, then $\{2, 3\}$, $\{2, 4\}, \ldots, \{2, n\}$, and so on, down to $\{n - 2, n - 1\}$, $\{n - 2, n\}$, and finally $\{n - 1, n\}$.

The Triples Method
There is another approach to storing counts that may be more appropriate, depending on the fraction of the possible pairs of items that actually appear in some basket. We can store counts as triples $[i, j, c]$, meaning that the count of pair $\{i, j\}$, with $i < j$, is c. A data structure, such as a hash table with i and j as the search key, is used so we can tell if there is a triple for a given i and j and, if so, to find it quickly. We call this approach the *triples method* of storing counts.

Unlike the triangular matrix, the triples method does not require us to store anything if the count for a pair is 0. On the other hand, the triples method requires us to store three integers, rather than one, for every pair that does appear in some basket. In addition, there is the space needed for the hash table or other data structure used to support efficient retrieval. The conclusion is that the triangular matrix will be better if at least 1/3 of the $\binom{n}{2}$ possible pairs actually appear in some basket, while if significantly fewer than 1/3 of the possible pairs occur, we should consider using the triples method.

EXAMPLE 6.6   Suppose there are 100,000 items, and 10,000,000 baskets of 10 items each. Then the triangular-matrix method requires $\binom{100000}{2} = 5 \times 10^9$ (approximately) integer counts.[1] On the other hand, the total number of pairs among all the baskets is $10^7\binom{10}{2} = 4.5 \times 10^8$. Even in the extreme case that every pair of items appeared only once, there could be only 4.5×10^8 pairs with nonzero counts. If we used the triples method to store counts, we would need only three times that number of integers, or 1.35×10^9 integers. Thus, in this case the triples method will surely take much less space than the triangular matrix.

However, even if there were ten or a hundred times as many baskets, it would be normal for there to be a sufficiently uneven distribution of items that we might still be better off using the triples method. That is, some pairs would have very high counts, and the number of different pairs that occurred in one or more baskets would be much less than the theoretical maximum number of such pairs.

6.2.3   Monotonicity of Itemsets

Much of the effectiveness of the algorithms we shall discuss is driven by a single observation, called *monotonicity* for itemsets:

- If a set I of items is frequent, then so is every subset of I.

The reason is simple. Let $J \subseteq I$. Then every basket that contains all the items in I surely contains all the items in J. Thus, the count for J must be at least as great as the count for I, and if the count for I is at least s, then the count for J is at least s. Since J may be contained in some baskets that are missing one or more elements of $I - J$, it is entirely possible that the count for J is strictly greater than the count for I.

In addition to making the A-Priori Algorithm work, monotonicity offers us a way to compact the information about frequent itemsets. If we are given a support threshold s, then we say an itemset is *maximal* if no superset is frequent. If we list only the maximal itemsets, then we know that all subsets of a maximal itemset are frequent, and no set that is not a subset of some maximal itemset can be frequent.

EXAMPLE 6.7   Let us reconsider the data of Example 6.1 with support threshold

---

[1] Here, and throughout the chapter, we shall use the approximation that $\binom{n}{2} = n^2/2$ for large n.

$s = 3$. We found that there were five frequent singletons, those with words "cat," "dog," "a," "and," and "training." Each of these is contained in a frequent doubleton, except for "training," so one maximal frequent itemset is {training}. There are also four frequent doubletons with $s = 3$, namely

$$\{\text{dog, a}\} \quad \{\text{dog, and}\}$$
$$\{\text{dog, cat}\} \quad \{\text{cat, and}\}$$

As there are no frequent triples for support threshold 3, these are all maximal frequent itemsets, and there are no others. Notice that we can deduce from the frequent doubletons that singletons like {dog} are frequent.

6.2.4 Tyranny of Counting Pairs

As you may have noticed, we have focused on the matter of counting pairs in the discussion so far. There is a good reason to do so: in practice the most main memory is required for determining the frequent pairs. The number of items, while possibly very large, is rarely so large we cannot count all the singleton sets in main memory at the same time.

What about larger sets – triples, quadruples, and so on? Recall that in order for frequent-itemset analysis to make sense, the result has to be a small number of sets, or we cannot even *read* them all, let alone consider their significance. Thus, in practice the support threshold is set high enough that it is only a rare set that is frequent. Monotonicity tells us that if there is a frequent triple, then there are three frequent pairs contained within it. And of course there may be frequent pairs contained in no frequent triple as well. Thus, we expect to find more frequent pairs than frequent triples, more frequent triples than frequent quadruples, and so on.

That argument would not be enough were it impossible to avoid counting all the triples, since there are many more triples than pairs. It is the job of the A-Priori Algorithm and related algorithms to avoid counting many triples or larger sets, and they are, as we shall see, effective in doing so. Thus, in what follows, we concentrate on algorithms for computing frequent pairs.

6.2.5 The A-Priori Algorithm

For the moment, let us concentrate on finding the frequent pairs only. If we have enough main memory to count all pairs, using either of the methods discussed in Section 6.2.2 (triangular matrix or triples), then it is a simple matter to read the file of baskets in a single pass. For each basket, we use a double loop to generate all the pairs. Each time we generate a pair, we add 1 to its count. At the end, we examine all pairs and see which have counts that exceed the support threshold s; these are the frequent pairs.

However, this simple approach fails if there are too many pairs of items to count them all in main memory. The *A-Priori* Algorithm is designed to reduce the number of pairs that must be counted, at the expense of performing two passes over data, rather than one pass.

The First Pass of A-Priori

In the first pass, we create two tables. The first table, if necessary, translates item names into integers from 1 to n, as described in Section 6.2.2. The other table is an array of counts; the ith array element counts the occurrences of the item numbered i. Initially, the counts for all the items are 0.

As we read baskets, we look at each item in the basket and translate its name into an integer. Next, we use that integer to index into the array of counts, and we add 1 to the integer found there.

Between the Passes of A-Priori

After the first pass, we examine the counts of the items to determine which of them are frequent as singletons. It might appear surprising that many singletons are not frequent. But remember that we set the threshold s sufficiently high that we do not get too many frequent sets; a typical s would be 1% of the baskets. If we think about our own visits to a supermarket, we surely buy certain things more than 1% of the time: perhaps milk, bread, Coke or Pepsi, and so on. We can even believe that 1% of the customers buy diapers, even though we may not do so. However, many of the items on the shelves are surely not bought by 1% of the customers: Creamy Caesar Salad Dressing for example.

For the second pass of A-Priori, we create a new numbering from 1 to m for just the frequent items. This table is an array indexed 1 to n, and the entry for i is either 0, if item i is not frequent, or a unique integer in the range 1 to m if item i is frequent. We shall refer to this table as the *frequent-items table*.

The Second Pass of A-Priori

During the second pass, we count all the pairs that consist of two frequent items. Recall from Section 6.2.3 that a pair cannot be frequent unless both its members are frequent. Thus, we miss no frequent pairs. The space required on the second pass is $2m^2$, rather than $2n^2$, if we use the triangular-matrix method for counting. Notice that the renumbering of just the frequent items is necessary if we are to use a triangular matrix of the right size. The complete set of main-memory structures used in the first and second passes is shown in Fig. 6.3.

Also notice that the benefit of eliminating infrequent items is amplified; if only half the items are frequent we need one quarter of the space to count. Likewise, if we use the triples method, we need to count only those pairs of two frequent items that occur in at least one basket.

The mechanics of the second pass are as follows.

(1) For each basket, look in the frequent-items table to see which of its items are frequent.
(2) In a double loop, generate all frequent pairs.
(3) For each frequent pair, add one to its count in the data structure used to store counts.

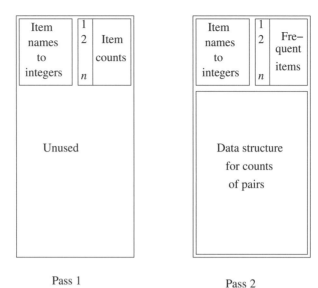

Figure 6.3 Schematic of main-memory use during the two passes of the A-Priori Algorithm

Finally, at the end of the second pass, examine the structure of counts to determine which pairs are frequent.

6.2.6 A-Priori for All Frequent Itemsets

The same technique used for finding frequent pairs without counting all pairs lets us find larger frequent itemsets without an exhaustive count of all sets. In the A-Priori Algorithm, one pass is taken for each set-size k. If no frequent itemsets of a certain size are found, then monotonicity tells us there can be no larger frequent itemsets, so we can stop.

The pattern of moving from one size k to the next size $k+1$ can be summarized as follows. For each size k, there are two sets of itemsets:

(1) C_k is the set of *candidate* itemsets of size k – the itemsets that we must count in order to determine whether they are in fact frequent.
(2) L_k is the set of truly frequent itemsets of size k.

The pattern of moving from one set to the next and one size to the next is suggested by Fig. 6.4.

We start with C_1, which is all singleton itemsets, i.e., the items themselves. That is, before we examine the data, any item could be frequent as far as we know. The first filter step is to count all items, and those whose counts are at least the support threshold s form the set L_1 of frequent items.

The set C_2 of candidate pairs is the set of pairs both of whose items are in L_1; that is, they are frequent items. Note that we do not construct C_2 explicitly.

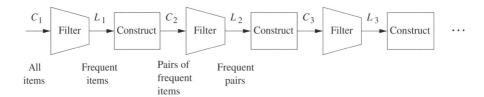

All items — Filter — C_1 — L_1 — Construct — C_2 — Filter — L_2 — Construct — C_3 — Filter — L_3 — Construct — ...

All items | Frequent items | Pairs of frequent items | Frequent pairs

Figure 6.4 The A-Priori Algorithm alternates between constructing candidate sets and filtering to find those that are truly frequent

Rather we use the definition of C_2, and we test membership in C_2 by testing whether both of its members are in L_1. The second pass of the A-Priori Algorithm counts all the candidate pairs and determines which appear at least s times. These pairs form L_2, the frequent pairs.

We can follow this pattern as far as we wish. The set C_3 of candidate triples is constructed (implicitly) as the set of triples, any two of which is a pair in L_2. Our assumption about the sparsity of frequent itemsets, outlined in Section 6.2.4 implies that there will not be too many frequent pairs, so they can be listed in a main-memory table. Likewise, there will not be too many candidate triples, so these can all be counted by a generalization of the triples method. That is, while triples are used to count pairs, we would use quadruples, consisting of the three item codes and the associated count, when we want to count triples. Similarly, we can count sets of size k using tuples with $k + 1$ components, the last of which is the count, and the first k of which are the item codes, in sorted order.

To find L_3 we make a third pass through the basket file. For each basket, we need only look at those items that are in L_1. From these items, we can examine each pair and determine whether or not that pair is in L_2. Any item of the basket that does not appear in at least two frequent pairs, both of which consist of items in the basket, cannot be part of a frequent triple that the basket contains. Thus, we have a fairly limited search for triples that are both contained in the basket and are candidates in C_3. Any such triples found have 1 added to their count.

EXAMPLE 6.8 Suppose our basket consists of items 1 through 10. Of these, 1 through 5 have been found to be frequent items, and the following pairs have been found frequent: $\{1, 2\}$, $\{2, 3\}$, $\{3, 4\}$, and $\{4, 5\}$. At first, we eliminate the nonfrequent items, leaving only 1 through 5. However, 1 and 5 appear in only one frequent pair in the itemset, and therefore cannot contribute to a frequent triple contained in the basket. Thus, we must consider adding to the count of triples that are contained in $\{2, 3, 4\}$. There is only one such triple, of course. However, we shall not find it in C_3, because $\{2, 4\}$ evidently is not frequent.

The construction of the collections of larger frequent itemsets and candidates proceeds in essentially the same manner, until at some pass we find no new frequent itemsets and stop. That is:

(1) Define C_k to be all those itemsets of size k, every $k-1$ of which is an itemset in L_{k-1}.

(2) Find L_k by making a pass through the baskets and counting all and only the itemsets of size k that are in C_k. Those itemsets that have count at least s are in L_k.

6.2.7   Exercises for Section 6.2

EXERCISE 6.2.1   If we use a triangular matrix to count pairs, and n, the number of items, is 20, what pair's count is in $a[100]$?

! EXERCISE 6.2.2   In our description of the triangular-matrix method in Section 6.2.2, the formula for k involves dividing an arbitrary integer i by 2. Yet we need to have k always be an integer. Prove that k will, in fact, be an integer.

! EXERCISE 6.2.3   Let there be I items in a market-basket data set of B baskets. Suppose that every basket contains exactly K items. As a function of I, B, and K:

(a) How much space does the triangular-matrix method take to store the counts of all pairs of items, assuming four bytes per array element?

(b) What is the largest possible number of pairs with a nonzero count?

(c) Under what circumstances can we be certain that the triples method will use less space than the triangular array?

!! EXERCISE 6.2.4   How would you count all itemsets of size 3 by a generalization of the triangular-matrix method? That is, arrange that in a one-dimensional array there is exactly one element for each set of three items.

! EXERCISE 6.2.5   Suppose the support threshold is 5. Find the maximal frequent itemsets for the data of:

(a) Exercise 6.1.1.

(b) Exercise 6.1.3.

EXERCISE 6.2.6   Apply the A-Priori Algorithm with support threshold 5 to the data of:

(a) Exercise 6.1.1.

(b) Exercise 6.1.3.

! EXERCISE 6.2.7   Suppose we have market baskets that satisfy the following assumptions:

(1) The support threshold is 10,000.

(2) There are one million items, represented by the integers $0, 1, \ldots, 999999$.

(3) There are N frequent items, that is, items that occur 10,000 times or more.

(4) There are one million pairs that occur 10,000 times or more.

(5) There are $2M$ pairs that occur exactly once. Of these pairs, M consist of two frequent items; the other M each have at least one nonfrequent item.

(6) No other pairs occur at all.

(7) Integers are always represented by 4 bytes.

Suppose we run the A-Priori Algorithm and can choose on the second pass between the triangular-matrix method for counting candidate pairs and a hash table of item-item-count triples. Neglect in the first case the space needed to translate between original item numbers and numbers for the frequent items, and in the second case neglect the space needed for the hash table. As a function of N and M, what is the minimum number of bytes of main memory needed to execute the A-Priori Algorithm on this data?

6.3   Handling Larger Datasets in Main Memory

The A-Priori Algorithm is fine as long as the step with the greatest requirement for main memory – typically the counting of the candidate pairs C_2 – has enough memory that it can be accomplished without thrashing (repeated moving of data between disk and main memory). Several algorithms have been proposed to cut down on the size of candidate set C_2. Here, we consider the PCY Algorithm, which takes advantage of the fact that in the first pass of A-Priori there is typically lots of main memory not needed for the counting of single items. Then we look at the Multistage Algorithm, which uses the PCY trick and also inserts extra passes to further reduce the size of C_2.

6.3.1   The Algorithm of Park, Chen, and Yu

This algorithm, which we call *PCY* after its authors, exploits the observation that there may be much unused space in main memory on the first pass. If there are a million items and gigabytes of main memory, we do not need more than 10% of the main memory for the two tables suggested in Fig. 6.3 – a translation table from item names to small integers and an array to count those integers. The PCY Algorithm uses that space for an array of integers that generalizes the idea of a Bloom filter (see Section 4.3). The idea is shown schematically in Fig. 6.5.

Think of this array as a hash table, whose buckets hold integers rather than sets of keys (as in an ordinary hash table) or bits (as in a Bloom filter). Pairs of items are hashed to buckets of this hash table. As we examine a basket during the first pass, we not only add 1 to the count for each item in the basket, but we generate all the pairs, using a double loop. We hash each pair, and we add 1 to the bucket into which that pair hashes. Note that the pair itself doesn't go into the bucket; the pair only affects the single integer in the bucket.

At the end of the first pass, each bucket has a count, which is the sum of the counts of all the pairs that hash to that bucket. If the count of a bucket is at

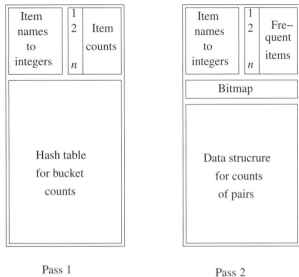

Pass 1   Pass 2

Figure 6.5 Organization of main memory for the first two passes of the PCY Algorithm

least as great as the support threshold s, it is called a *frequent bucket*. We can say nothing about the pairs that hash to a frequent bucket; they could all be frequent pairs from the information available to us. But if the count of the bucket is less than s (an *infrequent bucket*), we know no pair that hashes to this bucket can be frequent, even if the pair consists of two frequent items. That fact gives us an advantage on the second pass. We can define the set of candidate pairs C_2 to be those pairs $\{i, j\}$ such that:

(1) i and j are frequent items.
(2) $\{i, j\}$ hashes to a frequent bucket.

It is the second condition that distinguishes PCY from A-Priori.

EXAMPLE 6.9   Depending on the data and the amount of available main memory, there may or may not be a benefit to using the hash table on pass 1. In the worst case, all buckets are frequent, and the PCY Algorithm counts exactly the same pairs as A-Priori does on the second pass. However, sometimes, we can expect most of the buckets to be infrequent. In that case, PCY reduces the memory requirements of the second pass.

Suppose we have a gigabyte of main memory available for the hash table on the first pass. Suppose also that the data file has a billion baskets, each with ten items. A bucket is an integer, typically 4 bytes, so we can maintain a quarter of a billion buckets. The number of pairs in all the baskets is $10^9 \times \binom{10}{2}$ or 4.5×10^{10} pairs; this number is also the sum of the counts in the buckets. Thus, the average count is $4.5 \times 10^{10}/2.5 \times 10^8$, or 180. If the support threshold s is around 180 or less, we might expect few buckets to be infrequent. However, if s is much larger, say 1000, then it must be that the great majority of the buckets are infrequent. The greatest possible number of frequent buckets is $4.5 \times 10^{10}/1000$, or 45 million out of the 250 million buckets.

Between the passes of PCY, the hash table is summarized as a *bitmap*, with one bit for each bucket. The bit is 1 if the bucket is frequent and 0 if not. Thus integers of 32 bits are replaced by single bits, and the bitmap shown in the second pass in Fig. 6.5 takes up only 1/32 of the space that would otherwise be available to store counts. However, if most buckets are infrequent, we expect that the number of pairs being counted on the second pass will be much smaller than the total number of pairs of frequent items. Thus, PCY can handle some data sets without thrashing during the second pass, while A-Priori would run out of main memory and thrash.

There is another subtlety regarding the second pass of PCY that affects the amount of space needed. While we were able to use the triangular-matrix method on the second pass of A-Priori if we wished, because the frequent items could be renumbered from 1 to some m, we cannot do so for PCY. The reason is that the pairs of frequent items that PCY lets us avoid counting are placed randomly within the triangular matrix; they are the pairs that happen to hash to an infrequent bucket on the first pass. There is no known way of compacting the matrix to avoid leaving space for the uncounted pairs.

Consequently, we are forced to use the triples method in PCY. That restriction may not matter if the fraction of pairs of frequent items that actually appear in buckets were small; we would then want to use triples for A-Priori anyway. However, if most pairs of frequent items appear together in at least one bucket, then we are forced in PCY to use triples, while A-Priori can use a triangular matrix. Thus, unless PCY lets us avoid counting at least 2/3 of the frequent pairs, we cannot gain by using PCY instead of A-Priori.

While the discovery of frequent pairs by PCY differs significantly from A-Priori, the later stages, where we find frequent triples and larger sets if desired, are essentially the same as A-Priori. This statement holds as well for each of the improvements to A-Priori that we cover in this section. As a result, we shall cover only the construction of the frequent pairs from here on.

6.3.2   The Multistage Algorithm

The *multistage Algorithm* improves upon PCY by using several successive hash tables to reduce further the number of candidate pairs. The tradeoff is that Multistage takes more than two passes to find the frequent pairs. An outline of the Multistage Algorithm is shown in Fig. 6.6.

The first pass of Multistage is the same as the first pass of PCY. After that pass, the frequent buckets are identified and summarized by a bitmap, again the same as in PCY. But the second pass of Multistage does not count the candidate pairs. Rather, it uses the available main memory for another hash table, using another hash function. Since the bitmap from the first hash table takes up 1/32

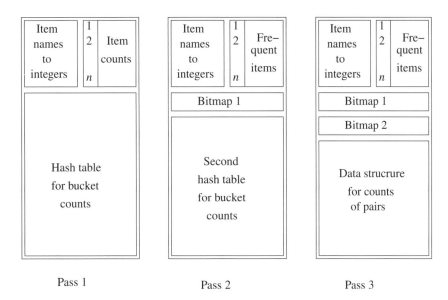

Figure 6.6 The Multistage Algorithm uses additional hash tables to reduce the number of candidate pairs

of the available main memory, the second hash table has almost as many buckets as the first.

On the second pass of Multistage, we again go through the file of baskets. There is no need to count the items again, since we have those counts from the first pass. However, we must retain the information about which items are frequent, since we need it on both the second and third passes. During the second pass, we hash certain pairs of items to buckets of the second hash table. A pair is hashed only if it meets the two criteria for being counted in the second pass of PCY; that is, we hash $\{i, j\}$ if and only if i and j are both frequent, and the pair hashed to a frequent bucket on the first pass. As a result, the sum of the counts in the second hash table should be significantly less than the sum for the first pass. The result is that, even though the second hash table has only 31/32 of the number of buckets that the first table has, we expect there to be many fewer frequent buckets in the second hash table than in the first.

After the second pass, the second hash table is also summarized as a bitmap, and that bitmap is stored in main memory. The two bitmaps together take up slightly less than 1/16th of the available main memory, so there is still plenty of space to count the candidate pairs on the third pass. A pair $\{i, j\}$ is in C_2 if and only if:

(1) i and j are both frequent items.
(2) $\{i, j\}$ hashed to a frequent bucket in the first hash table.
(3) $\{i, j\}$ hashed to a frequent bucket in the second hash table.

The third condition is the distinction between Multistage and PCY.

> ## A Subtle Error in Multistage
>
> Occasionally, an implementation tries to eliminate the second requirement for $\{i, j\}$ to be a candidate – that it hash to a frequent bucket on the first pass. The (false) reasoning is that if it didn't hash to a frequent bucket on the first pass, it wouldn't have been hashed at all on the second pass, and thus would not contribute to the count of its bucket on the second pass. While it is true that the pair is not counted on the second pass, that doesn't mean it wouldn't have hashed to a frequent bucket had it been hashed. Thus, it is entirely possible that $\{i, j\}$ consists of two frequent items and hashes to a frequent bucket on the second pass, yet it did not hash to a frequent bucket on the first pass. Therefore, all three conditions must be checked on the counting pass of Multistage.

It might be obvious that it is possible to insert any number of passes between the first and last in the multistage Algorithm. There is a limiting factor that each pass must store the bitmaps from each of the previous passes. Eventually, there is not enough space left in main memory to do the counts. No matter how many passes we use, the truly frequent pairs will always hash to a frequent bucket, so there is no way to avoid counting them.

6.3.3   The Multihash Algorithm

Sometimes, we can get most of the benefit of the extra passes of the Multistage Algorithm in a single pass. This variation of PCY is called the *Multihash Algorithm*. Instead of using two different hash tables on two successive passes, use two hash functions and two separate hash tables that share main memory on the first pass, as suggested by Fig. 6.7.

The danger of using two hash tables on one pass is that each hash table has half as many buckets as the one large hash table of PCY. As long as the average count of a bucket for PCY is much lower than the support threshold, we can operate two half-sized hash tables and still expect most of the buckets of both hash tables to be infrequent. Thus, in this situation we might well choose the multihash approach.

EXAMPLE 6.10   Suppose that if we run PCY, the average bucket will have a count $s/10$, where s is the support threshold. Then if we used the Multihash approach with two half-sized hash tables, the average count would be $s/5$. As a result, at most 1/5th of the buckets in either hash table could be frequent, and a random infrequent pair has at most probability $(1/5)^2 = 0.04$ of being in a frequent bucket in both hash tables.

By the same reasoning, the upper bound on the infrequent pair being in a frequent bucket in the one PCY hash table is at most 1/10. That is, we might expect to have to count 2.5 times as many infrequent pairs in PCY as in the

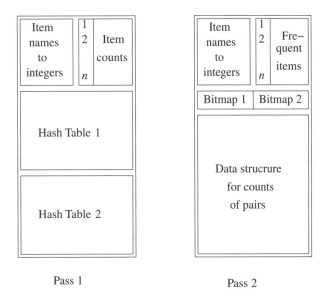

Pass 1   Pass 2

Figure 6.7 The Multihash Algorithm uses several hash tables in one pass

version of Multihash suggested above. We would therefore expect Multihash to have a smaller memory requirement for the second pass than would PCY.

But these upper bounds do not tell the complete story. There may be many fewer frequent buckets than the maximum for either algorithm, since the presence of some very frequent pairs will skew the distribution of bucket counts. However, this analysis is suggestive of the possibility that for some data and support thresholds, we can do better by running several hash functions in main memory at once.

For the second pass of Multihash, each hash table is converted to a bitmap, as usual. Note that the two bitmaps for the two hash functions in Fig. 6.7 occupy exactly as much space as a single bitmap would for the second pass of the PCY Algorithm. The conditions for a pair $\{i, j\}$ to be in C_2, and thus to require a count on the second pass, are the same as for the third pass of Multistage: i and j must both be frequent, and the pair must have hashed to a frequent bucket according to both hash tables.

Just as Multistage is not limited to two hash tables, we can divide the available main memory into as many hash tables as we like on the first pass of Multihash. The risk is that should we use too many hash tables, the average count for a bucket will exceed the support threshold. At that point, there may be very few infrequent buckets in any of the hash tables. Even though a pair must hash to a frequent bucket in every hash table to be counted, we may find that the probability an infrequent pair will be a candidate rises, rather than falls, if we add another hash table.

6.3.4   Exercises for Section 6.3

EXERCISE 6.3.1   Here is a collection of twelve baskets. Each contains three of
the six items 1 through 6.

$$\{1,2,3\} \quad \{2,3,4\} \quad \{3,4,5\} \quad \{4,5,6\}$$
$$\{1,3,5\} \quad \{2,4,6\} \quad \{1,3,4\} \quad \{2,4,5\}$$
$$\{3,5,6\} \quad \{1,2,4\} \quad \{2,3,5\} \quad \{3,4,6\}$$

Suppose the support threshold is 4. On the first pass of the PCY Algorithm we
use a hash table with 11 buckets, and the set $\{i,j\}$ is hashed to bucket $i \times j$
mod 11.

(a) By any method, compute the support for each item and each pair of items.
(b) Which pairs hash to which buckets?
(c) Which buckets are frequent?
(d) Which pairs are counted on the second pass of the PCY Algorithm?

EXERCISE 6.3.2   Suppose we run the Multistage Algorithm on the data of
Exercise 6.3.1, with the same support threshold of 4. The first pass is the same
as in that exercise, and for the second pass, we hash pairs to nine buckets,
using the hash function that hashes $\{i,j\}$ to bucket $i+j$ mod 9. Determine the
counts of the buckets on the second pass. Does the second pass reduce the set
of candidate pairs? Note that all items are frequent, so the only reason a pair
would not be hashed on the second pass is if it hashed to an infrequent bucket
on the first pass.

EXERCISE 6.3.3   Suppose we run the Multihash Algorithm on the data of Exercise 6.3.1. We shall use two hash tables with five buckets each. For one, the
set $\{i,j\}$, is hashed to bucket $2i + 3j + 4$ mod 5, and for the other, the set is
hashed to $i+4j$ mod 5. Since these hash functions are not symmetric in i and j,
order the items so that $i < j$ when evaluating each hash function. Determine the
counts of each of the 10 buckets. How large does the support threshold have to be
for the Multistage Algorithm to eliminate more pairs than the PCY Algorithm
would, using the hash table and function described in Exercise 6.3.1?

! EXERCISE 6.3.4   Suppose we perform the PCY Algorithm to find frequent pairs,
with market-basket data meeting the following specifications:

(1) The support threshold is 10,000.
(2) There are one million items, represented by the integers $0, 1, \ldots, 999999$.
(3) There are 250,000 frequent items, that is, items that occur 10,000 times or
    more.
(4) There are one million pairs that occur 10,000 times or more.
(5) There are P pairs that occur exactly once and consist of two frequent items.
(6) No other pairs occur at all.
(7) Integers are always represented by 4 bytes.

(8) When we hash pairs, they distribute among buckets randomly, but as evenly as possible; i.e., you may assume that each bucket gets exactly its fair share of the P pairs that occur once.

Suppose there are S bytes of main memory. In order to run the PCY Algorithm successfully, the number of buckets must be sufficiently large that most buckets are not frequent. In addition, on the second pass, there must be enough room to count all the candidate pairs. As a function of S, what is the largest value of P for which we can successfully run the PCY Algorithm on this data?

! EXERCISE 6.3.5   Under the assumptions given in Exercise 6.3.4, will the Multihash Algorithm reduce the main-memory requirements for the second pass? As a function of S and P, what is the optimum number of hash tables to use on the first pass?

! EXERCISE 6.3.6   Suppose we perform the 3-pass Multistage Algorithm to find frequent pairs, with market-basket data meeting the following specifications:

(1) The support threshold is 10,000.
(2) There are one million items, represented by the integers $0, 1, \ldots, 999999$. All items are frequent; that is, they occur at least 10,000 times.
(3) There are one million pairs that occur 10,000 times or more.
(4) There are P pairs that occur exactly once.
(5) No other pairs occur at all.
(6) Integers are always represented by 4 bytes.
(7) When we hash pairs, they distribute among buckets randomly, but as evenly as possible; i.e., you may assume that each bucket gets exactly its fair share of the P pairs that occur once.
(8) The hash functions used on the first two passes are completely independent.

Suppose there are S bytes of main memory. As a function of S and P, what is the expected number of candidate pairs on the third pass of the Multistage Algorithm?

6.4   Limited-Pass Algorithms

The algorithms for frequent itemsets discussed so far use one pass for each size of itemset we investigate. If main memory is too small to hold the data and the space needed to count frequent itemsets of one size, there does not seem to be any way to avoid k passes to compute the exact collection of frequent itemsets. However, there are many applications where it is not essential to discover every frequent itemset. For instance, if we are looking for items purchased together at a supermarket, we are not going to run a sale based on every frequent itemset we find, so it is quite sufficient to find most but not all of the frequent itemsets.

    In this section we explore some algorithms that have been proposed to find

---

> ## Why Not Just Pick the First Part of the File?
>
> The risk in selecting a sample from one portion of a large file is that the data is not uniformly distributed in the file. For example, suppose the file were a list of true market-basket contents at a department store, organized by date of sale. If you took only the first baskets in the file, you would have old data. For example, there would be no iPods in these baskets, even though iPods might have become a popular item later.
>
> As another example, consider a file of medical tests performed at different hospitals. If each chunk comes from a different hospital, then picking chunks at random will give us a sample drawn from only a small subset of the hospitals. If hospitals perform different tests or perform them in different ways, the data may be highly biased.

all or most frequent itemsets using at most two passes. We begin with the obvious approach of using a sample of the data rather than the entire dataset. An algorithm called SON uses two passes, gets the exact answer, and lends itself to implementation by map-reduce or another parallel computing regime. Finally, Toivonen's Algorithm uses two passes on average, gets an exact answer, but may, rarely, not terminate in any given amount of time.

6.4.1   The Simple, Randomized Algorithm

Instead of using the entire file of baskets, we could pick a random subset of the baskets and pretend it is the entire dataset. We must adjust the support threshold to reflect the smaller number of baskets. For instance, if the support threshold for the full dataset is s, and we choose a sample of 1% of the baskets, then we should examine the sample for itemsets that appear in at least $s/100$ of the baskets.

The safest way to pick the sample is to read the entire dataset, and for each basket, select that basket for the sample with some fixed probability p. Suppose there are m baskets in the entire file. At the end, we shall have a sample whose size is very close to pm baskets. However, if we have reason to believe that the baskets appear in random order in the file already, then we do not even have to read the entire file. We can select the first pm baskets for our sample. Or, if the file is part of a distributed file system, we can pick some chunks at random to serve as the sample.

Having selected our sample of the baskets, we use part of main memory to store these baskets. The balance of the main memory is used to execute one of the algorithms we have discussed, such as A-Priori, PCY, Multistage, or Multihash. However, the algorithm must run passes over the main-memory sample for each itemset size, until we find a size with no frequent items. There are no disk accesses needed to read the sample, since it resides in main memory. As frequent itemsets of each size are discovered, they can be written out to disk; this operation and the initial reading of the sample from disk are the only disk I/O's the algorithm does.

Of course the algorithm will fail if whichever method from Section 6.2 or 6.3 we choose cannot be run in the amount of main memory left after storing the sample. If we need more main memory, then an option is to read the sample from disk for each pass. Since the sample is much smaller than the full dataset, we still avoid most of the disk I/O's that the algorithms discussed previously would use.

6.4.2   Avoiding Errors in Sampling Algorithms

We should be mindful of the problem with the simple algorithm of Section 6.4.1: it cannot be relied upon either to produce all the itemsets that are frequent in the whole dataset, nor will it produce only itemsets that are frequent in the whole. An itemset that is frequent in the whole but not in the sample is a *false negative*, while an itemset that is frequent in the sample but not the whole is a *false positive*.

If the sample is large enough, there are unlikely to be serious errors. That is, an itemset whose support is much larger than the threshold will almost surely be identified from a random sample, and an itemset whose support is much less than the threshold is unlikely to appear frequent in the sample. However, an itemset whose support in the whole is very close to the threshold is as likely to be frequent in the sample as not.

We can eliminate false positives by making a pass though the full dataset and counting all the itemsets that were identified as frequent in the sample. Retain as frequent only those itemsets that were frequent in the sample and also frequent in the whole. Note that this improvement will eliminate all false positives, but a false negative is not counted and therefore remains undiscovered.

To accomplish this task in a single pass, we need to be able to count all frequent itemsets of all sizes at once, within main memory. If we were able to run the simple algorithm successfully with the main memory available, then there is a good chance we shall be able to count all the frequent itemsets at once, because:

(a) The frequent singletons and pairs are likely to dominate the collection of all frequent itemsets, and we had to count them all in one pass already.

(b) We now have all of main memory available, since we do not have to store the sample in main memory.

We cannot eliminate false negatives completely, but we can reduce their number if the amount of main memory allows it. We have assumed that if s is the support threshold, and the sample is fraction p of the entire dataset, then we use ps as the support threshold for the sample. However, we can use something smaller than that as the threshold for the sample, such a $0.9ps$. Having a lower threshold means that more itemsets of each size will have to be counted, so the main-memory requirement rises. On the other hand, if there is enough main memory, then we shall identify as having support at least $0.9ps$ in the sample almost all those itemsets that have support at least s is the whole. If we then make a complete pass to eliminate those itemsets that were identified as frequent in the sample but are not frequent in the whole, we have no false positives and hopefully have none or very few false negatives.

6.4.3 The Algorithm of Savasere, Omiecinski, and Navathe

Our next improvement avoids both false negatives and false positives, at the cost of making two full passes. It is called the *SON* Algorithm after the authors. The idea is to divide the input file into chunks (which may be "chunks" in the sense of a distributed file system, or simply a piece of the file). Treat each chunk as a sample, and run the algorithm of Section 6.4.1 on that chunk. We use ps as the threshold, if each chunk is fraction p of the whole file, and s is the support threshold. Store on disk all the frequent itemsets found for each chunk.

Once all the chunks have been processed in that way, take the union of all the itemsets that have been found frequent for one or more chunks. These are the *candidate* itemsets. Notice that if an itemset is not frequent in any chunk, then its support is less than ps in each chunk. Since the number of chunks is $1/p$, we conclude that the total support for that itemset is less than $(1/p)ps = s$. Thus, every itemset that is frequent in the whole is frequent in at least one chunk, and we can be sure that all the truly frequent itemsets are among the candidates; i.e., there are no false negatives.

We have made a total of one pass through the data as we read each chunk and processed it. In a second pass, we count all the candidate itemsets and select those that have support at least s as the frequent itemsets.

6.4.4 The SON Algorithm and Map-Reduce

The SON algorithm lends itself well to a parallel-computing environment. Each of the chunks can be processed in parallel, and the frequent itemsets from each chunk combined to form the candidates. We can distribute the candidates to many processors, have each processor count the support for each candidate in a subset of the baskets, and finally sum those supports to get the support for each candidate itemset in the whole dataset. This process does not have to be implemented in map-reduce, but there is a natural way of expressing each of the two passes as a map-reduce operation. We shall summarize this map-reduce-map-reduce sequence below.

First Map Function: Take the assigned subset of the baskets and find the itemsets frequent in the subset using the algorithm of Section 6.4.1. As described there, lower the support threshold from s to ps if each Map task gets fraction p of the total input file. The output is a set of key-value pairs $(F, 1)$, where F is a frequent itemset from the sample. The value is always 1 and is irrelevant.

First Reduce Function: Each Reduce task is assigned a set of keys, which are itemsets. The value is ignored, and the Reduce task simply produces those keys (itemsets) that appear one or more times. Thus, the output of the first Reduce function is the candidate itemsets.

Second Map Function: The Map tasks for the second Map function take all the output from the first Reduce Function (the candidate itemsets) and a portion of the input data file. Each Map task counts the number of occurrences of each of the candidate itemsets among the baskets in the portion of the dataset that it was assigned. The output is a set of key-value pairs (C, v), where C is one of the candidate sets and v is the support for that itemset among the baskets that were input to this Map task.

Second Reduce Function: The Reduce tasks take the itemsets they are given as keys and sum the associated values. The result is the total support for each of the itemsets that the Reduce task was assigned to handle. Those itemsets whose sum of values is at least s are frequent in the whole dataset, so the Reduce task outputs these itemsets with their counts. Itemsets that do not have total support at least s are not transmitted to the output of the Reduce task.[2]

6.4.5   Toivonen's Algorithm

This algorithm uses randomness in a different way from the simple sampling algorithm of Section 6.4.1. Toivonen's Algorithm, given sufficient main memory, will use one pass over a small sample and one full pass over the data. It will give neither false negatives nor positives, but there is a small but finite probability that it will fail to produce any answer at all. In that case it needs to be repeated until it gives an answer. However, the average number of passes needed before it produces all and only the frequent itemsets is a small constant.

Toivonen's algorithm begins by selecting a small sample of the input dataset, and finding from it the candidate frequent itemsets. The process is exactly that of Section 6.4.1, except that it is essential the threshold be set to something less than its proportional value. That is, if the support threshold for the whole dataset is s, and the sample size is fraction p, then when looking for frequent itemsets in the sample, use a threshold such as $0.9ps$ or $0.8ps$. The smaller we make the threshold, the more main memory we need for computing all itemsets that are frequent in the sample, but the more likely we are to avoid the situation where the algorithm fails to provide an answer.

Having constructed the collection of frequent itemsets for the sample, we next construct the *negative border*. This is the collection of itemsets that are not frequent in the sample, but all of their *immediate subsets* (subsets constructed by deleting exactly one item) are frequent in the sample.

---

[2] Strictly speaking, the Reduce function has to produce a value for each key. It can produce 1 as the value for itemsets found frequent and 0 for those not frequent.

EXAMPLE 6.11   Suppose the items are $\{A, B, C, D, E\}$ and we have found the following itemsets to be frequent in the sample: $\{A\}$, $\{B\}$, $\{C\}$, $\{D\}$, $\{B, C\}$, $\{C, D\}$. Note that $\emptyset$ is also frequent, as long as there are at least as many baskets as the support threshold, although technically the algorithms we have described omit this obvious fact. First, $\{E\}$ is in the negative border, because it is not frequent in the sample, but its only immediate subset, $\emptyset$, is frequent.

The sets $\{A, B\}$, $\{A, C\}$, $\{A, D\}$ and $\{B, D\}$ are in the negative border. None of these sets are frequent, and each has two immediate subsets, both of which are frequent. For instance, $\{A, B\}$ has immediate subsets $\{A\}$ and $\{B\}$. Of the other six doubletons, none are in the negative border. The sets $\{B, C\}$ and $\{C, D\}$ are not in the negative border, because they are frequent. The remaining four pairs are each E together with another item, and those are not in the negative border because they have an immediate subset $\{E\}$ that is not frequent.

None of the triples or larger sets are in the negative border. For instance, $\{B, C, D\}$ is not in the negative border because it has an immediate subset $\{B, D\}$ that is not frequent. Thus, the negative border consists of five sets: $\{E\}$, $\{A, B\}$, $\{A, C\}$, $\{A, D\}$ and $\{B, D\}$.

To complete Toivonen's algorithm, we make a pass through the entire dataset, counting all the itemsets that are frequent in the sample or are in the negative border. There are two possible outcomes.

(1) No member of the negative border is frequent in the whole dataset. In this case, the correct set of frequent itemsets is exactly those itemsets from the sample that were found to be frequent in the whole.
(2) Some member of the negative border is frequent in the whole. Then we cannot be sure that there are not some even larger sets, in neither the negative border nor the collection of frequent itemsets for the sample, that are also frequent in the whole. Thus, we can give no answer at this time and must repeat the algorithm with a new random sample.

6.4.6   Why Toivonen's Algorithm Works

Clearly Toivonen's algorithm never produces a false positive, since it only reports as frequent those itemsets that have been counted and found to be frequent in the whole. To argue that it never produces a false negative, we must show that when no member of the negative border is frequent in the whole, then there can be no itemset whatsoever that is:

(1) Frequent in the whole, but
(2) In neither the negative border nor the collection of frequent itemsets for the sample.

Suppose the contrary. That is, there is a set S that is frequent in the whole, but not in the negative border and not frequent in the sample. Also, this round of Toivonen's Algorithm produced an answer, which would certainly not include S

among the frequent itemsets. By monotonicity, all subsets of S are also frequent in the whole. Let T be a subset of S that is of the smallest possible size among all subsets of S that are not frequent in the sample.

We claim that T must be in the negative border. Surely T meets one of the conditions for being in the negative border: it is not frequent in the sample. It also meets the other condition for being in the negative border: each of its immediate subsets is frequent in the sample. For if some immediate subset of T were not frequent in the sample, then there would be a subset of S that is smaller than T and not frequent in the sample, contradicting our selection of T as a subset of S that was not frequent in the sample, yet as small as any such set.

Now we see that T is both in the negative border and frequent in the whole dataset. Consequently, this round of Toivonen's algorithm did not produce an answer.

6.4.7   Exercises for Section 6.4

EXERCISE 6.4.1   Suppose there are eight items, $A, B, \ldots, H$, and the following are the maximal frequent itemsets: $\{A, B\}$, $\{B, C\}$, $\{A, C\}$, $\{A, D\}$, $\{E\}$, and $\{F\}$. Find the negative border.

EXERCISE 6.4.2   Apply Toivonen's Algorithm to the data of Exercise 6.3.1, with a support threshold of 4. Take as the sample the first row of baskets: $\{1, 2, 3\}$, $\{2, 3, 4\}$, $\{3, 4, 5\}$, and $\{4, 5, 6\}$, i.e., one-third of the file. Our scaled-down support theshold will be 1.

(a) What are the itemsets frequent in the sample?
(b) What is the negative border?
(c) What is the outcome of the pass through the full dataset? Are any of the itemsets in the negative border frequent in the whole?

!! EXERCISE 6.4.3   Suppose item i appears exactly s times in a file of n baskets, where s is the support threshold. If we take a sample of $n/100$ baskets, and lower the support threshold for the sample to $s/100$, what is the probability that i will be found to be frequent? You may assume that both s and n are divisible by 100.

6.5   Counting Frequent Items in a Stream

Suppose that instead of a file of baskets we have a stream of baskets, from which we want to mine the frequent itemsets. Recall from Chapter 4 that the difference between a stream and a data file is that stream elements are only available when they arrive, and typically the arrival rate is so great that we cannot store the entire stream in a way that allows easy querying. Further, it is common that streams evolve over time, so the itemsets that are frequent in today's stream may not be frequent tomorrow.

A clear distinction between streams and files, when frequent itemsets are considered, is that there is no end to a stream, so eventually an itemset is going to exceed the support threshold, as long as it appears repeatedly in the stream. As a result, for streams, we must think of the support threshold s as a fraction of the baskets in which an itemset must appear in order to be considered frequent. Even with this adjustment, we still have several options regarding the portion of the stream over which that fraction is measured.

In this section, we shall discuss several ways that we might extract frequent itemsets from a stream. First, we consider ways to use the sampling techniques of the previous section. Then, we consider the decaying-window model from Section 4.7, and extend the method described in Section 4.7.3 for finding "popular" items.

6.5.1   Sampling Methods for Streams

In what follows, we shall assume that stream elements are baskets of items. Perhaps the simplest approach to maintaining a current estimate of the frequent itemsets in a stream is to collect some number of baskets and store it as a file. Run one of the frequent-itemset algorithms discussed in this chapter, meanwhile ignoring the stream elements that arrive, or storing them as another file to be analyzed later. When the frequent-itemsets algorithm finishes, we have an estimate of the frequent itemsets in the stream. We then have several options.

(1) We can use this collection of frequent itemsets for whatever application is at hand, but start running another iteration of the chosen frequent-itemset algorithm immediately. This algorithm can either:

    (a) Use the file that was collected while the first iteration of the algorithm was running. At the same time, collect yet another file to be used at another iteration of the algorithm, when this current iteration finishes.

    (b) Start collecting another file of baskets now, and run the algorithm when an adequate number of baskets has been collected.

(2) We can continue to count the numbers of occurrences of each of these frequent itemsets, along with the total number of baskets seen in the stream, since the counting started. If any itemset is discovered to occur in a fraction of the baskets that is significantly below the threshold fraction s, then this set can be dropped from the collection of frequent itemsets. When computing the fraction, it is important to include the occurrences from the original file of baskets, from which the frequent itemsets were derived. If not, we run the risk that we shall encounter a short period in which a truly frequent itemset does not appear sufficiently frequently and throw it out. We should also allow some way for new frequent itemsets to be added to the current collection. Possibilities include:

(a) Periodically gather a new segment of the baskets in the stream and use it as the data file for another iteration of the chosen frequent-itemsets algorithm. The new collection of frequent items is formed from the result of this iteration and the frequent itemsets from the previous collection that have survived the possibility of having been deleted for becoming infrequent.

(b) Add some random itemsets to the current collection, and count their fraction of occurrences for a while, until one has a good idea of whether or not they are currently frequent. Rather than choosing new itemsets completely at random, one might focus on sets with items that appear in many itemsets already known to be frequent. For example, a good choice is to pick new itemsets from the negative border (Section 6.4.5) of the current set of frequent itemsets.

6.5.2 Frequent Itemsets in Decaying Windows

Recall from Section 4.7 that a decaying window on a stream is formed by picking a small constant c and giving the ith element prior to the most recent element the weight $(1-c)^i$, or approximately e^{-ci}. Section 4.7.3 actually presented a method for computing the frequent items, provided the support threshold is defined in a somewhat different way. That is, we considered, for each item, a stream that had 1 if the item appeared at a certain stream element and 0 if not. We defined the "score" for that element to be the sum of the weights where the stream element was 1. We were constrained to record all items whose score was at least $1/2$. We can not use a score threshold above 1, because we do not initiate a count for an item until the item appears in the stream, and the first time it appears, its score is only 1 (since 1, or $(1-c)^0$, is the weight of the current item).

If we wish to adapt this method to streams of baskets, there are two modifications we must make. The first is simple. Stream elements are baskets rather than individual items, so many items may appear at a given stream element. Treat each of those items as if they were the "current" item and add 1 to their score after multiplying all current scores by $1-c$, as described in Section 4.7.3. If some items in a basket have no current score, initialize the scores of those items to 1.

The second modification is trickier. We want to find all frequent itemsets, not just singleton itemsets. If we were to initialize a count for an itemset whenever we saw it, we would have too many counts. For example, one basket of 20 items has over a million subsets, and all of these would have to be initiated for one basket. On the other hand, as we mentioned, if we use a requirement above 1 for initiating the scoring of an itemset, then we would never get any itemsets started, and the method would not work.

A way of dealing with this problem is to start scoring certain itemsets as soon as we see one instance, but be conservative about which itemsets we start. We may borrow from the A-Priori trick, and only start an itemset I if all its immediate proper subsets are already being scored. The consequence of this restriction is that if I is truly frequent, eventually we shall begin to count it, but we never start an itemset unless it would at least be a candidate in the sense used in the A-Priori Algorithm.

EXAMPLE 6.12   Suppose I is a large itemset, but it appears in the stream periodically, once every $2/c$ baskets. Then its score, and that of its subsets, never falls below $e^{-1/2}$, which is greater than $1/2$. Thus, once a score is created for some subset of I, that subset will continue to be scored forever. The first time I appears, only its singleton subsets will have scores created for them. However, the next time I appears, each of its doubleton subsets will commence scoring, since each of the immediate subsets of those doubletons is already being scored. Likewise, the kth time I appears, its subsets of size $k-1$ are all being scored, so we initiate scores for each of its subsets of size k. Eventually, we reach the size $|I|$, at which time we start scoring I itself.

6.5.3   Hybrid Methods

The approach of Section 6.5.2 offers certain advantages. It requires a limited amount of work each time a stream element arrives, and it always provides an up-to-date picture of what is frequent in the decaying window. Its big disadvantage is that it requires us to maintain scores for each itemset with a score of at least $1/2$. We can limit the number of itemsets being scored by increasing the value of the parameter c. But the larger c is, the smaller the decaying window is. Thus, we could be forced to accept information that tracks the local fluctuations in frequency too closely, rather than integrating over a long period.

We can combine the ideas from Sections 6.5.1 and 6.5.2. For example, we could run a standard algorithm for frequent itemsets on a sample of the stream, with a conventional threshold for support. The itemsets that are frequent by this standard will be treated as if they all arrived at the current time. That is, they each get a score equal to a fixed fraction of their count.

More precisely, suppose the initial sample has b baskets, c is the decay constant for the decaying window, and the minimum score we wish to accept for a frequent itemset in the decaying window is s. Then the support threshold for the initial run of the frequent-itemset algorithm is bcs. If an itemset I is found to have support t in the sample, then it is initially given a score of $t/(bc)$.

EXAMPLE 6.13   Suppose $c = 10^{-6}$ and the minimum score we wish to accept in the decaying window is 10. Suppose also we take a sample of 10^8 baskets from the stream. Then when analyzing that sample, we use a support threshold of $10^8 \times 10^{-6} \times 10 = 1000$.

Consider an itemset I that has support 2000 in the sample. Then the initial score we use for I is $2000/(10^8 \times 10^{-6}) = 20$. After this initiation step, each time a basket arrives in the stream, the current score will be multiplied by $1 - c = 0.999999$. If I is a subset of the current basket, then add 1 to the score.

If the score for I goes below 10, then it is considered to be no longer frequent, so it is dropped from the collection of frequent itemsets.

We do not, sadly, have a reasonable way of initiating the scoring of new itemsets. If we have no score for itemset I, and 10 is the minimum score we want to maintain, there is no way that a single basket can jump its score from 0 to anything more than 1. The best strategy for adding new sets is to run a new frequent-itemsets calculation on a sample from the stream, and add to the collection of itemsets being scored any that meet the threshold for that sample but were not previously being scored.

6.5.4   Exercises for Section 6.5

!! EXERCISE 6.5.1   Suppose we are counting frequent itemsets in a decaying window with a decay constant c. Suppose also that with probability p, a given stream element (basket) contains both items i and j. Additionally, with probability p the basket contains i but not j, and with probability p it contains j but not i. As a function of c and p, what is the fraction of time we shall be scoring the pair $\{i,j\}$?

6.6   Summary of Chapter 6

+ *Market-Basket Data*: This model of data assumes there are two kinds of entities: items and baskets. There is a many–many relationship between items and baskets. Typically, baskets are related to small sets of items, while items may be related to many baskets.
+ *Frequent Itemsets*: The support for a set of items is the number of baskets containing all those items. Itemsets with support that is at least some threshold are called frequent itemsets.
+ *Association Rules*: These are implications that if a basket contains a certain set of items I, then it is likely to contain another particular item j as well. The probability that j is also in a basket containing I is called the confidence of the rule. The interest of the rule is the amount by which the confidence deviates from the fraction of all baskets that contain j.
+ *The Pair-Counting Bottleneck*: To find frequent itemsets, we need to examine all baskets and count the number of occurrences of sets of a certain size. For typical data, with a goal of producing a small number of itemsets that are the most frequent of all, the part that often takes the most main memory is the counting of pairs of items. Thus, methods for finding frequent itemsets typically concentrate on how to minimize the main memory needed to count pairs.
+ *Triangular Matrices*: While one could use a two-dimensional array to count pairs, doing so wastes half the space, because there is no need to count pair $\{i,j\}$ in both the i-j and j-i array elements. By arranging the pairs (i,j) for

which $i < j$ in lexicographic order, we can store only the needed counts in a one-dimensional array with no wasted space, and yet be able to access the count for any pair efficiently.

✦ *Storage of Pair Counts as Triples*: If fewer than $1/3$ of the possible pairs actually occur in baskets, then it is more space-efficient to store counts of pairs as triples (i, j, c), where c is the count of the pair $\{i, j\}$, and $i < j$. An index structure such as a hash table allows us to find the triple for (i, j) efficiently.

✦ *Monotonicity of Frequent Itemsets*: An important property of itemsets is that if a set of items is frequent, then so are all its subsets. We exploit this property to eliminate the need to count certain itemsets by using its contrapositive: if an itemset is not frequent, then neither are its supersets.

✦ *The A-Priori Algorithm for Pairs*: We can find all frequent pairs by making two passes over the baskets. On the first pass, we count the items themselves, and then determine which items are frequent. On the second pass, we count only the pairs of items both of which are found frequent on the first pass. Monotonicity justifies our ignoring other pairs.

✦ *Finding Larger Frequent Itemsets*: A-Priori and many other algorithms allow us to find frequent itemsets larger than pairs, if we make one pass over the baskets for each size itemset, up to some limit. To find the frequent itemsets of size k, monotonicity lets us restrict our attention to only those itemsets such that all their subsets of size $k - 1$ have already been found frequent.

✦ *The PCY Algorithm*: This algorithm improves on A-Priori by creating a hash table on the first pass, using all main-memory space that is not needed to count the items. Pairs of items are hashed, and the hash-table buckets are used as integer counts of the number of times a pair has hashed to that bucket. Then, on the second pass, we only have to count pairs of frequent items that hashed to a frequent bucket (one whose count is at least the support threshold) on the first pass.

✦ *The Multistage Algorithm*: We can insert additional passes between the first and second pass of the PCY Algorithm to hash pairs to other, independent hash tables. At each intermediate pass, we only have to hash pairs of frequent items that have hashed to frequent buckets on all previous passes.

✦ *The Multihash Algorithm*: We can modify the first pass of the PCY Algorithm to divide available main memory into several hash tables. On the second pass, we only have to count a pair of frequent items if they hashed to frequent buckets in all hash tables.

✦ *Randomized Algorithms*: Instead of making passes through all the data, we may choose a random sample of the baskets, small enough that it is possible to store both the sample and the needed counts of itemsets in main memory. The support threshold must be scaled down in proportion. We can then find the frequent itemsets for the sample, and hope that it is a good representation of the data as whole. While this method uses at most one pass through the whole dataset, it is subject to false positives (itemsets that are frequent in the sample but not the whole) and false negatives (itemsets that are frequent in the whole but not the sample).

✦ *The SON Algorithm*: An improvement on the simple randomized algorithm is to divide the entire file of baskets into segments small enough that all frequent itemsets for the segment can be found in main memory. Candidate itemsets are those found frequent for at least one segment. A second pass allows us to count all the candidates and find the exact collection of frequent itemsets. This algorithm is especially appropriate in a map-reduce setting.

✦ *Toivonen's Algorithm*: This algorithm starts by finding frequent itemsets in a sample, but with the threshold lowered so there is little chance of missing an itemset that is frequent in the whole. Next, we examine the entire file of baskets, counting not only the itemsets that are frequent in the sample, but also, the negative border – itemsets that have not been found frequent, but all their immediate subsets are. If no member of the negative border is found frequent in the whole, then the answer is exact. But if a member of the negative border is found frequent, then the whole process has to repeat with another sample.

✦ *Frequent Itemsets in Streams*: If we use a decaying window with constant c, then we can start counting an item whenever we see it in a basket. We start counting an itemset if we see it contained within the current basket, and all its immediate proper subsets already are being counted. As the window is decaying, we multiply all counts by $1 - c$ and eliminate those that are less than $1/2$.

6.7   References for Chapter 6

The market-basket data model, including association rules and the A-Priori Algorithm, are from [(1)] and [(2)].

The PCY Algorithm is from [(4)]. The Multistage and Multihash Algorithms are found in [(3)].

The SON Algorithm is from [(5)]. Toivonen's Algorithm appears in [(6)].

(1) R. Agrawal, T. Imielinski, and A. Swami, "Mining associations between sets of items in massive databases," *Proc. ACM SIGMOD Intl. Conf. on Management of Data*, pp. 207–216, 1993.

(2) R. Agrawal and R. Srikant, "Fast algorithms for mining association rules," *Intl. Conf. on Very Large Databases*, pp. 487–499, 1994.

(3) M. Fang, N. Shivakumar, H. Garcia-Molina, R. Motwani, and J.D. Ullman, "Computing iceberg queries efficiently," *Intl. Conf. on Very Large Databases*, pp. 299-310, 1998.

(4) J.S. Park, M.-S. Chen, and P.S. Yu, "An effective hash-based algorithm for mining association rules," *Proc. ACM SIGMOD Intl. Conf. on Management of Data*, pp. 175–186, 1995.

(5) A. Savasere, E. Omiecinski, and S.B. Navathe, "An efficient algorithm for mining association rules in large databases," *Intl. Conf. on Very Large Databases*, pp. 432–444, 1995.

(6) H. Toivonen, "Sampling large databases for association rules," *Intl. Conf. on Very Large Databases*, pp. 134–145, 1996.

7 Clustering

Clustering is the process of examining a collection of "points," and grouping the points into "clusters" according to some distance measure. The goal is that points in the same cluster have a small distance from one another, while points in different clusters are at a large distance from one another. A suggestion of what clusters might look like was seen in Fig. 1.1. However, there the intent was that there were three clusters around three different road intersections, but two of the clusters blended into one another because they were not sufficiently separated.

Our goal in this chapter is to offer methods for discovering clusters in data. We are particularly interested in situations where the data is very large, and/or where the space either is high-dimensional, or the space is not Euclidean at all. We shall therefore discuss several algorithms that assume the data does not fit in main memory. However, we begin with the basics: the two general approaches to clustering and the methods for dealing with clusters in a non-Euclidean space.

7.1 Introduction to Clustering Techniques

We begin by reviewing the notions of distance measures and spaces. The two major approaches to clustering – hierarchical and agglomerative – are defined. We then turn to a discussion of the "curse of dimensionality," which makes clustering in high-dimensional spaces difficult, but also, as we shall see, enables some simplifications if used correctly in a clustering algorithm.

7.1.1 Points, Spaces, and Distances

A dataset suitable for clustering is a collection of *points*, which are objects belonging to some *space*. In its most general sense, a space is just a universal set of points, from which the points in the dataset are drawn. However, we should be mindful of the common case of a Euclidean space (see Section 3.5.2), which has a number of important properties useful for clustering. In particular, a Euclidean space's points are vectors of real numbers. The length of the vector is the number of dimensions of the space. The components of the vector are commonly called *coordinates* of the represented points.

All spaces for which we can perform a clustering have a distance measure, giving a distance between any two points in the space. We introduced distances in Section 3.5. The common Euclidean distance (square root of the sums of the squares of the differences between the coordinates of the points in each dimension) serves for all Euclidean spaces, although we also mentioned some other options for distance measures in Euclidean spaces, including the Manhattan distance (sum of the magnitudes of the differences in each dimension) and the L_∞-distance (maximum magnitude of the difference in any dimension).

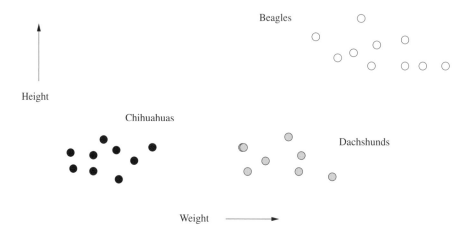

Figure 7.1 Heights and weights of dogs taken from three varieties

EXAMPLE 7.1   Classical applications of clustering often involve low-dimensional Euclidean spaces. For example, Fig. 7.1 shows height and weight measurements of dogs of several varieties. Without knowing which dog is of which variety, we can see just by looking at the diagram that the dogs fall into three clusters, and those clusters happen to correspond to three varieties. With small amounts of data, any clustering algorithm will establish the correct clusters, and simply plotting the points and "eyeballing" the plot will suffice as well.

However, modern clustering problems are not so simple. They may involve Euclidean spaces of very high dimension or spaces that are not Euclidean at all. For example, it is challenging to cluster documents by their topic, based on the occurrence of common, unusual words in the documents. It is challenging to cluster moviegoers by the type or types of movies they like.

We also considered in Section 3.5 distance measures for non-Euclidean spaces. These include the Jaccard distance, cosine distance, Hamming distance, and edit distance. Recall that the requirements for a function on pairs of points to be a distance measure are that

(1) Distances are always nonnegative, and only the distance between a point and itself is 0.

(2) Distance is symmetric; it doesn't matter in which order you consider the points when computing their distance.

(3) Distance measures obey the triangle inequality; the distance from x to y to z is never less than the distance going from x to z directly.

7.1.2   Clustering Strategies

We can divide (cluster!) clustering algorithms into two groups that follow two fundamentally different strategies.

(1) *Hierarchical* or *agglomerative* algorithms start with each point in its own cluster. Clusters are combined based on their "closeness," using one of many possible definitions of "close." Combination stops when further combination leads to clusters that are undesirable for one of several reasons. For example, we may stop when we have a predetermined number of clusters, or we may use a measure of compactness for clusters, and refuse to construct a cluster by combining two smaller clusters if the resulting cluster has points that are spread out over too large a region.

(2) The other class of algorithms involve *point assignment*. Points are considered in some order, and each one is assigned to the cluster into which it best fits. This process is normally preceded by a short phase in which initial clusters are estimated. Variations allow occasional combining or splitting of clusters, or may allow points to be unassigned if they are *outliers* (points too far from any of the current clusters).

Algorithms for clustering can also be distinguished by:

(a) Whether the algorithm assumes a Euclidean space, or whether the algorithm works for an arbitrary distance measure. We shall see that a key distinction is that in a Euclidean space it is possible to summarize a collection of points by their *centroid* – the average of the points. In a non-Euclidean space, there is no notion of a centroid, and we are forced to develop another way to summarize clusters.

(b) Whether the algorithm assumes that the data is small enough to fit in main memory, or whether data must reside in secondary memory, primarily. Algorithms for large amounts of data often must take shortcuts, since it is infeasible to look at all pairs of points, for example. It is also necessary to summarize clusters in main memory, since we cannot hold all the points of all the clusters in main memory at the same time.

7.1.3   The Curse of Dimensionality

High-dimensional Euclidean spaces have a number of unintuitive properties that are sometimes referred to as the "curse of dimensionality." Non-Euclidean spaces usually share these anomalies as well. One manifestation of the "curse" is that in high dimensions, almost all pairs of points are equally far away from one another.

Another manifestation is that almost any two vectors are almost orthogonal. We shall explore each of these in turn.

The Distribution of Distances in a High-Dimensional Space

Let us consider a d-dimensional Euclidean space. Suppose we choose n random points in the unit cube, i.e., points $[x_1, x_2, \ldots, x_d]$, where each x_i is in the range 0 to 1. If $d = 1$, we are placing random points on a line of length 1. We expect that some pairs of points will be very close, e.g., consecutive points on the line. We also expect that some points will be very far away – those at or near opposite ends of the line. The average distance between a pair of points is $1/3$.[1]

Suppose that d is very large. The Euclidean distance between two random points $[x_1, x_2, \ldots, x_d]$ and $[y_1, y_2, \ldots, y_d]$ is

$$\sqrt{\sum_{i=1}^{d}(x_i - y_i)^2}$$

Here, each x_i and y_i is a random variable chosen uniformly in the range 0 to 1. Since d is large, we can expect that for some i, $|x_i - y_i|$ will be close to 1. That puts a lower bound of 1 on the distance between almost any two random points. In fact, a more careful argument can put a stronger lower bound on the distance between all but a vanishingly small fraction of the pairs of points. However, the maximum distance between two points is $\sqrt{d}$, and one can argue that all but a vanishingly small fraction of the pairs do not have a distance close to this upper limit. In fact, almost all points will have a distance close to the average distance.

If there are essentially no pairs of points that are close, it is hard to build clusters at all. There is little justification for grouping one pair of points and not another. Of course, the data may not be random, and there may be useful clusters, even in very high-dimensional spaces. However, the argument about random data suggests that it will be hard to find these clusters among so many pairs that are all at approximately the same distance.

Angles Between Vectors

Suppose again that we have three random points A, B, and C in a d-dimensional space, where d is large. Here, we do not assume points are in the unit cube; they can be anywhere in the space. What is angle ABC? We may assume that A is the point $[x_1, x_2, \ldots, x_d]$ and C is the point $[y_1, y_2, \ldots, y_d]$, while B is the origin. Recall from Section 3.5.4 that the cosine of the angle ABC is the dot product of A and C divided by the product of the lengths of the vectors A and C. That is, the cosine is

$$\frac{\sum_{i=0}^{d} x_i y_i}{\sqrt{\sum_{i=1}^{d} x_i^2}\sqrt{\sum_{i=1}^{d} y_i^2}}$$

---

[1] You can prove this fact by evaluating a double integral, but we shall not do the math here, as it is not central to the discussion.

As d grows, the denominator grows linearly in d, but the numerator is a sum of random values, which are as likely to be positive as negative. Thus, the expected value of the numerator is 0, and as d grows, its standard deviation grows only as $\sqrt{d}$. Thus, for large d, the cosine of the angle between any two vectors is almost certain to be close to 0, which means the angle is close to 90 degrees.

An important consequence of random vectors being orthogonal is that if we have three random points A, B, and C, and we know the distance from A to B is d_1, while the distance from B to C is d_2, we can assume the distance from A to C is approximately $\sqrt{d_1^2 + d_2^2}$. That rule does not hold, even approximately, if the number of dimensions is small. As an extreme case, if $d = 1$, then the distance from A to C would necessarily be $d_1 + d_2$ if A and C were on opposite sides of B, or $|d_1 - d_2|$ if they were on the same side.

7.1.4   Exercises for Section 7.1

! EXERCISE 7.1.1   Prove that if you choose two points uniformly and independently on a line of length 1, then the expected distance between the points is $1/3$.

!! EXERCISE 7.1.2   If you choose two points uniformly in the unit square, what is their expected Eclidean distance?

! EXERCISE 7.1.3   Suppose we have a d-dimensional Euclidean space. Consider vectors whose components are only $+1$ or -1 in each dimension. Note that each vector has length $\sqrt{d}$, so the product of their lengths (denominator in the formula for the cosine of the angle between them) is d. If we chose each component independently, and a component is as likely to be $+1$ as -1, what is the distribution of the value of the numerator of the formula (i.e., the sum of the products of the corresponding components from each vector)? What can you say about the expected value of the cosine of the angle between the vectors, as d grows large?

7.2   Hierarchical Clustering

We begin by considering hierarchical clustering in a Euclidean space. This algorithm can only be used for relatively small datasets, but even so, there are some efficiencies we can make by careful implementation. When the space is non-Euclidean, there are additional problems associated with hierarchical clustering. We therefore consider "clustroids" and the way we can represent a cluster when there is no centroid or average point in a cluster.

7.2.1   Hierarchical Clustering in a Euclidean Space

Any hierarchical clustering algorithm works as follows. We begin with every point in its own cluster. As time goes on, larger clusters will be constructed by combining two smaller clusters, and we have to decide in advance:

(1) How will clusters be represented?
(2) How will we choose which two clusters to merge?
(3) When will we stop combining clusters?

Once we have answers to these questions, the algorithm can be described succinctly as:

```
WHILE it is not time to stop DO
    pick the best two clusters to merge;
    combine those two clusters into one cluster;
END;
```

To begin, we shall assume the space is Euclidean. That allows us to represent a cluster by its centroid or average of the points in the cluster. Note that in a cluster of one point, that point is the centroid, so we can initialize the clusters straightforwardly. We can then use the merging rule that the distance between any two clusters is the Euclidean distance between their centroids, and we should pick the two clusters at the shortest distance. Other ways to define intercluster distance are possible, and we can also pick the best pair of clusters on a basis other than their distance. We shall discuss some options in Section 7.2.3.

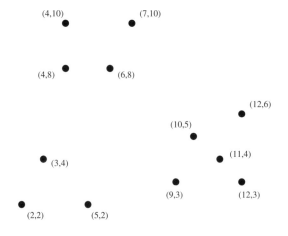

Figure 7.2 Twelve points to be clustered hierarchically

EXAMPLE 7.2   Let us see how the basic hierarchical clustering would work on the data of Fig. 7.2. These points live in a 2-dimensional Euclidean space, and each point is named by its (x, y) coordinates. Initially, each point is in a cluster by itself and is the centroid of that cluster. Among all the pairs of points, there are two pairs that are closest: (10,5) and (11,4) or (11,4) and (12,3). Each is at distance $\sqrt{2}$. Let us break ties arbitrarily and decide to combine (11,4) with (12,3). The result is shown in Fig. 7.3, including the centroid of the new cluster, which is at (11.5, 3.5).

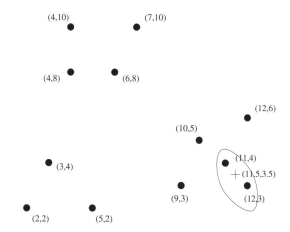

Figure 7.3 Combining the first two points into a cluster

You might think that (10,5) gets combined with the new cluster next, since it is so close to (11,4). But our distance rule requires us to compare only cluster centroids, and the distance from (10,5) to the centroid of the new cluster is $1.5\sqrt{2}$, which is slightly greater than 2. Thus, now the two closest clusters are those of the points (4,8) and (4,10). We combine them into one cluster with centroid (4,9).

At this point, the two closest centroids are (10,5) and (11.5, 3.5), so we combine these two clusters. The result is a cluster of three points (10,5), (11,4), and (12,3). The centroid of this cluster is (11,4), which happens to be one of the points of the cluster, but that situation is coincidental. The state of the clusters is shown in Fig. 7.4.

Now, there are several pairs of centroids that are at distance $\sqrt{5}$, and these are the closest centroids. We show in Fig. 7.5 the result of picking three of these:

(1) (6,8) is combined with the cluster of two elements having centroid (4,9).
(2) (2,2) is combined with (3,4).
(3) (9,3) is combined with the cluster of three elements having centroid (11,4).

We can proceed to combine clusters further. We shall discuss alternative stopping rules next.

There are several approaches we might use to stopping the clustering process.

(1) We could be told, or have a belief, about how many clusters there are in the data. For example, if we are told that the data about dogs is taken from

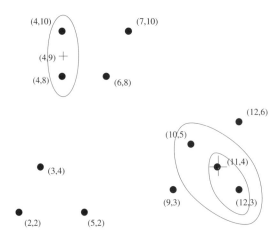

Figure 7.4 Clustering after two additional steps

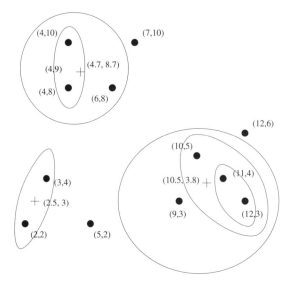

Figure 7.5 Three more steps of the hierarchical clustering

Chihuahuas, Dachshunds, and Beagles, then we know to stop when there are three clusters left.

(2) We could stop combining when at some point the best combination of existing clusters produces a cluster that is inadequate. We shall discuss various tests for the adequacy of a cluster in Section 7.2.3, but for an example, we could insist that any cluster have an average distance between the centroid and its points no greater than some limit. This approach is only sensible if we have a reason to believe that no cluster extends over too much of the space.

(3) We could continue clustering until there is only one cluster. However, it is

meaningless to return a single cluster consisting of all the points. Rather, we return the tree representing the way in which all the points were combined. This form of answer makes good sense in some applications, such as one in which the points are genomes of different species, and the distance measure reflects the difference in the genome.[2] Then, the tree represents the evolution of these species, that is, the likely order in which two species branched from a common ancestor.

EXAMPLE 7.3   If we complete the clustering of the data of Fig. 7.2, the tree describing how clusters were grouped is the tree shown in Fig. 7.6.

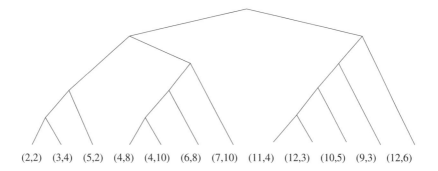

(2,2)   (3,4)   (5,2)   (4,8)   (4,10)   (6,8)   (7,10)   (11,4)   (12,3)   (10,5)   (9,3)   (12,6)

Figure 7.6 Tree showing the complete grouping of the points of Fig. 7.2

7.2.2   Efficiency of Hierarchical Clustering

The basic algorithm for hierarchical clustering is not very efficient. At each step, we must compute the distances between each pair of clusters, in order to find the best merger. The initial step takes $O(n^2)$ time, but subsequent steps take time proportional to $(n-1)^2, (n-2)^2, \ldots$. The sum of squares up to n is $O(n^3)$, so this algorithm is cubic. Thus, it cannot be run except for fairly small numbers of points.

However, there is a somewhat more efficient implementation of which we should be aware.

(1) We start, as we must, by computing the distances between all pairs of points, and this step is $O(n^2)$.
(2) Form the pairs and their distances into a priority queue, so we can always find the smallest distance in one step. This operation is also $O(n^2)$.
(3) When we decide to merge two clusters C and D, we remove all entries in the priority queue involving one of these two clusters; that requires work $O(n \log n)$ since there are at most $2n$ deletions to be performed, and priority-queue deletion can be performed in $O(\log n)$ time.

---

[2] This space would not be Euclidean, of course, but the principles regarding hierarchical clustering carry over, with some modifications, to non-Euclidean clustering.

(4) We then compute all the distances between the new cluster and the remaining clusters. This work is also $O(n \log n)$, as there are at most n entries to be inserted into the priority queue, and insertion into a priority queue can also be done in $O(\log n)$ time.

Since the last two steps are executed at most n times, and the first two steps are executed only once, the overall running time of this algorithm is $O(n^2 \log n)$. That is better than $O(n^3)$, but it still puts a strong limit on how large n can be before it becomes infeasible to use this clustering approach.

7.2.3 Alternative Rules for Controlling Hierarchical Clustering

We have seen one rule for picking the best clusters to merge: find the pair with the smallest distance between their centroids. Some other options are:

(1) Take the distance between two clusters to be the minimum of the distances between any two points, one chosen from each cluster. For example, in Fig. 7.3 we would next chose to cluster the point (10,5) with the cluster of two points, since (10,5) has distance $\sqrt{2}$, and no other pair of unclustered points is that close. Note that in Example 7.2, we did make this combination eventually, but not until we had combined another pair of points. In general, it is possible that this rule will result in an entirely different clustering from that obtained using the distance-of-centroids rule.
(2) Take the distance between two clusters to be the average distance of all pairs of points, one from each cluster.
(3) The *radius* of a cluster is the maximum distance between all the points and the centroid. Combine the two clusters whose resulting cluster has the lowest radius. A slight modification is to combine the clusters whose result has the lowest average distance between a point and the centroid. Another modification is to use the sum of the squares of the distances between the points and the centroid. In some algorithms, we shall find these variant definitions of "radius" referred to as "the radius."
(4) The *diameter* of a cluster is the maximum distance between any two points of the cluster. Note that the radius and diameter of a cluster are not related directly, as they are in a circle, but there is a tendency for them to be proportional. We may choose to merge those clusters whose resulting cluster has the smallest diameter. Variants of this rule, analogous to the rule for radius, are possible.

EXAMPLE 7.4   Let us consider the cluster consisting of the five points at the right of Fig. 7.2. The centroid of these five points is (10.8, 4.2). There is a tie for the two furthest points from the centroid: (9,3) and (12,6), both at distance $\sqrt{4.68} = 2.16$. Thus, the radius is 2.16. For the diameter, we find the two points in the cluster having the greatest distance. These are again (9,3) and (12,6).

Their distance is $\sqrt{18} = 4.24$, so that is the diameter. Notice that the diameter is not exactly twice the radius, although it is close in this case. The reason is that the centroid is not on the line between (9,3) and (12,6).

We also have options in determining when to stop the merging process. We already mentioned "stop when we have k clusters" for some predetermined k. Here are some other options.

(1) Stop if the diameter of the cluster that results from the best merger exceeds a threshold. We can also base this rule on the radius, or on any of the variants of the radius mentioned above.
(2) Stop if the *density* of the cluster that results from the best merger is below some threshold. The density can be defined in many different ways. Roughly, it should be the number of cluster points per unit volume of the cluster. That ratio can be estimated by the number of points divided by some power of the diameter or radius of the cluster. The correct power could be the number of dimensions of the space. Sometimes, 1 or 2 is chosen as the power, regardless of the number of dimensions.
(3) Stop when there is evidence that the next pair of clusters to be combined yields a bad cluster. For example, we could track the average diameter of all the current clusters. As long as we are combining points that belong in a cluster, this average will rise gradually. However, if we combine two clusters that really don't deserve to be combined, then the average diameter will take a sudden jump.

EXAMPLE 7.5   Let us reconsider Fig. 7.2. It has three natural clusters. We computed the diameter of the largest – the five points at the right – in Example 7.4; it is 4.24. The diameter of the 3-node cluster at the lower left is 3, the distance between (2,2) and (5,2). The diameter of the 4-node cluster at the upper left is $\sqrt{13} = 3.61$. The average diameter, 3.62, was reached starting from 0 after nine mergers, so the rise is evidently slow: about 0.4 per merger.

If we are forced to merge two of these natural clusters, the best we can do is merge the two at the left. The diameter of this cluster is $\sqrt{89} = 9.43$; that is the distance between the two points (2,2) and (7,10). Now, the average of the diameters is $(9.43 + 4.24)/2 = 6.84$. This average has jumped almost as much in one step as in all nine previous steps. That comparison indicates that the last merger was inadvisable, and we should roll it back and stop.

7.2.4   Hierarchical Clustering in Non-Euclidean Spaces

When the space is non-Euclidean, we need to use some distance measure that is computed from points, such as Jaccard, cosine, or edit distance. That is, we cannot base distances on "location" of points. The algorithm of Section 7.2.1 requires distances between points to be computed, but presumably we have a way to compute those distances. A problem arises when we need to represent a cluster, because we cannot replace a collection of points by their centroid.

EXAMPLE 7.6   The problem arises for any of the non-Euclidean distances we have discussed, but to be concrete, suppose we are using edit distance, and we decide to merge the strings `abcd` and `aecdb`. These have edit distance 3 and might well be merged. However, there is no string that represents their average, or that could be thought of as lying naturally between them. We could take one of the strings that we might pass through when transforming one string to the other by single insertions or deletions, such as `aebcd`, but there are many such options. Moreover, when clusters are formed from more than two strings, the notion of "on the path between" stops making sense.

Given that we cannot combine points in a cluster when the space is non-Euclidean, our only choice is to pick one of the points of the cluster itself to represent the cluster. Ideally, this point is close to all the points of the cluster, so it in some sense lies in the "center." We call the representative point the *clustroid*. We can select the clustroid in various ways, each designed to, in some sense, minimize the distances between the clustroid and the other points in the cluster. Common choices include selecting as the clustroid the point that minimizes:

(1) The sum of the distances to the other points in the cluster.
(2) The maximum distance to another point in the cluster.
(3) The sum of the squares of the distances to the other points in the cluster.

EXAMPLE 7.7   Suppose we are using edit distance, and a cluster consists of the four points `abcd`, `aecdb`, `abecb`, and `ecdab`. Their distances are found in the following table:

	ecdab	abecb	aecdb
abcd	5	3	3
aecdb	2	2	
abecb	4		

If we apply the three criteria for being the centroid to each of the four points of the cluster, we find:

Point	Sum	Max	Sum-Sq
abcd	11	5	43
aecdb	7	3	17
abecb	9	4	29
ecdab	11	5	45

We can see from these measurements that whichever of the three criteria we choose, `aecdb` will be selected as the clustroid. In general, different criteria could yield different clustroids.

The options for measuring the distance between clusters that were outlined in Section 7.2.3 can be applied in a non-Euclidean setting, provided we use the clustroid in place of the centroid. For example, we can merge the two clusters whose clustroids are closest. We could also use the average or minimum distance between all pairs of points from the clusters.

Other suggested criteria involved measuring the density of a cluster, based on the radius or diameter. Both these notions make sense in the non-Euclidean environment. The diameter is still the maximum distance between any two points in the cluster. The radius can be defined using the clustroid in place of the centroid. Moreover, it makes sense to use the same sort of evaluation for the radius as we used to select the clustroid in the first place. For example, if we take the clustroid to be the point with the smallest sum of squares of distances to the other nodes, then define the radius to be that sum of squares (or its square root).

Finally, Section 7.2.3 also discussed criteria for stopping the merging of clusters. None of these criteria made direct use of the centroid, except through the notion of radius, and we have already observed that "radius" makes good sense in non-Euclidean spaces. Thus, there is no substantial change in the options for stopping criteria when we move from Euclidean to non-Euclidean spaces.

7.2.5 Exercises for Section 7.2

EXERCISE 7.2.1 Perform a hierarchical clustering of the one-dimensional set of points 1, 4, 9, 16, 25, 36, 49, 64, 81, assuming clusters are represented by their centroid (average), and at each step the clusters with the closest centroids are merged.

EXERCISE 7.2.2 How would the clustering of Example 7.2 change if we used for the distance between two clusters:

(a) The minimum of the distances between any two points, one from each cluster.
(b) The average of the distances between pairs of points, one from each of the two clusters.

EXERCISE 7.2.3 Repeat the clustering of Example 7.2 if we choose to merge the two clusters whose resulting cluster has:

(a) The smallest radius.
(b) The smallest diameter.

EXERCISE 7.2.4 Compute the density of each of the three clusters in Fig. 7.2, if "density" is defined to be the number of points divided by

(a) The square of the radius.
(b) The diameter (not squared).

What are the densities, according to (a) and (b), of the clusters that result from the merger of any two of these three clusters. Does the difference in densities suggest the clusters should or should not be merged?

EXERCISE 7.2.5   We can select clustroids for clusters, even if the space is Euclidean. Consider the three natural clusters in Fig. 7.2, and compute the clustroids of each, assuming the criterion for selecting the clustroid is the point with the minimum sum of distances to the other point in the cluster.

! EXERCISE 7.2.6   Consider the space of strings with edit distance as the distance measure. Give an example of a set of strings such that if we choose the clustroid by minimizing the sum of the distances to the other points we get one point as the clustroid, but if we choose the clustroid by minimizing the maximum distance to the other points, another point becomes the clustroid.

7.3   K-means Algorithms

In this section we begin the study of point-assignment algorithms. The best known family of clustering algorithms of this type is called k-means. They assume a Euclidean space, and they also assume the number of clusters, k, is known in advance. It is, however, possible to deduce k by trial and error. After an introduction to the family of k-means algorithms, we shall focus on a particular algorithm, called BFR after its authors, that enables us to execute k-means on data that is too large to fit in main memory.

7.3.1   K-Means Basics

A k-means algorithm is outlined in Fig. 7.7. There are several ways to select the initial k points that represent the clusters, and we shall discuss them in Section 7.3.2. The heart of the algorithm is the for-loop, in which we consider each point other than the k selected points and assign it to the closest cluster, where "closest" means closest to the centroid of the cluster. Note that the centroid of a cluster can migrate as points are assigned to it. However, since only points near the cluster are likely to be assigned, the centroid tends not to move too much.

```
Initially choose k points that are likely to be in
    different clusters;
Make these points the centroids of their clusters;
FOR each remaining point p DO
    find the centroid to which p is closest;
    Add p to the cluster of that centroid;
    Adjust the centroid of that cluster to account for p;
END;
```

Figure 7.7 Outline of k-means algorithms

An optional step at the end is to fix the centroids of the clusters and to reassign each point, including the k initial points, to the k clusters. Usually, a point p will be assigned to the same cluster in which it was placed on the first pass. However, there are cases where the centroid of p's original cluster moved quite far from p after p was placed there, and p is assigned to a different cluster on the second pass. In fact, even some of the original k points could wind up being reassigned. As these examples are unusual, we shall not dwell on the subject.

7.3.2 Initializing Clusters for K-Means

We want to pick points that have a good chance of lying in different clusters. There are two approaches.

(1) Pick points that are as far away from one another as possible.
(2) Cluster a sample of the data, perhaps hierarchically, so there are k clusters. Pick a point from each cluster, perhaps that point closest to the centroid of the cluster.

The second approach requires little elaboration. For the first approach, there are variations. One good choice is:

```
Pick the first point at random;
WHILE there are fewer than k points DO
    Add the point whose minimum distance from the selected
        points is as large as possible;
END;
```

EXAMPLE 7.8   Let us consider the twelve points of Fig. 7.2, which we reproduce here as Fig. 7.8. In the worst case, our initial choice of a point is near the center, say (6,8). The furthest point from (6,8) is (12,3), so that point is chosen next.

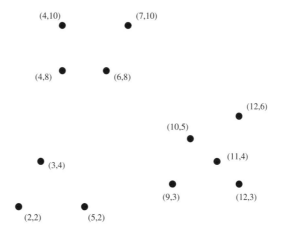

Figure 7.8 Repeat of Fig. 7.2

Among the remaining ten points, the one whose minimum distance to either (6,8) or (12,3) is a maximum is (2,2). That point has distance $\sqrt{52} = 7.21$ from (6,8) and distance $\sqrt{101} = 10.05$ to (12,3); thus its "score" is 7.21. You can check easily that any other point is less than distance 7.21 from at least one of (6,8) and (12.3). Our selection of three starting points is thus (6,8), (12,3), and (2,2). Notice that these three belong to different clusters.

Had we started with a different point, say (10,5), we would get a different set of three initial points. In this case, the starting points would be (10,5), (2,2), and (4,10). Again, these points belong to the three different clusters.

7.3.3   Picking the Right Value of k

We may not know the correct value of k to use in a k-means clustering. However, if we can measure the quality of the clustering for various values of k, we can usually guess what the right value of k is. Recall the discussion in Section 7.2.3, especially Example 7.5, where we observed that if we take a measure of appropriateness for clusters, such as average radius or diameter, that value will grow slowly, as long as the number of clusters we assume remains at or above the true number of clusters. However, as soon as we try to form fewer clusters than there really are, the measure will rise precipitously. The idea is expressed by the diagram of Fig. 7.9.

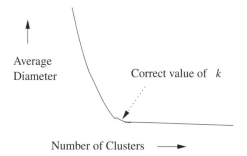

Figure 7.9 Average diameter or another measure of diffuseness rises quickly as soon as the number of clusters falls below the true number present in the data

If we have no idea what the correct value of k is, we can find a good value in a number of clustering operations that grows only logarithmically with the true number. Begin by running the k-means algorithm for $k = 1, 2, 4, 8, \ldots$. Eventually, you will find two values v and $2v$ between which there is very little decrease in the average diameter, or whatever measure of cluster cohesion you are using. We may conclude that the value of k that is justified by the data lies between $v/2$ and v. If you use a binary search (discussed below) in that range, you can find the best value for k in another $\log_2 v$ clustering operations, for a total of $2 \log_2 v$ clusterings. Since the true value of k is at least $v/2$, we have used a number of clusterings that is logarithmic in k.

Since the notion of "not much change" is imprecise, we cannot say exactly how much change is too much. However, the binary search can be conducted as follows, assuming the notion of "not much change" is made precise by some formula. We know that there is too much change between $v/2$ and v, or else we would not have gone on to run a clustering for $2v$ clusters. Suppose at some point we have narrowed the range of k to between x and y. Let $z = (x + y)/2$. Run a clustering with z as the target number of clusters. If there is not too much change between z and y, then the true value of k lies between x and z. So recursively narrow that range to find the correct value of k. On the other hand, if there is too much change between z and y, then use binary search in the range between z and y instead.

7.3.4   The Algorithm of Bradley, Fayyad, and Reina

This algorithm, which we shall refer to as *BFR* after its authors, is a variant of k-means that is designed to cluster data in a high-dimensional Euclidean space. It makes a very strong assumption about the shape of clusters: they must be normally distributed about a centroid. The mean and standard deviation for a cluster may differ for different dimensions, but the dimensions must be independent. For instance, in two dimensions a cluster may be cigar-shaped, but the cigar must not be rotated off of the axes. Figure 7.10 makes the point.

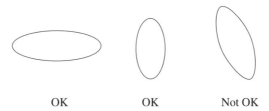

OK   OK   Not OK

Figure 7.10 The clusters in data for which the BFR algorithm may be used can have standard deviations that differ along different axes, but the axes of the cluster must align with the axes of the space

The BFR Algorithm begins by selecting k points, using one of the methods discussed in Section 7.3.2. Then, the points of the data file are read in chunks. These might be chunks from a distributed file system or a conventional file might be partitioned into chunks of the appropriate size. Each chunk must consist of few enough points that they can be processed in main memory. Also stored in main memory are summaries of the k clusters and some other data, so the entire memory is not available to store a chunk. The main-memory data other than the chunk from the input consists of three types of objects:

(1) *The Discard Set*: These are simple summaries of the clusters themselves. We shall address the form of cluster summarization shortly. Note that the cluster summaries are not "discarded"; they are in fact essential. However, the points

that the summary represents *are* discarded and have no representation in main memory other than through this summary.

(2) *The Compressed Set*: These are summaries, similar to the cluster summaries, but for sets of points that have been found close to one another, but not close to any cluster. The points represented by the compressed set are also discarded, in the sense that they do not appear explicitly in main memory. We call the represented sets of points *miniclusters*.

(3) *The Retained Set*: Certain points can neither be assigned to a cluster nor are they sufficiently close to any other points that we can represent them by a compressed set. These points are held in main memory exactly as they appear in the input file.

The picture in Fig. 7.11 suggests how the points processed so far are represented.

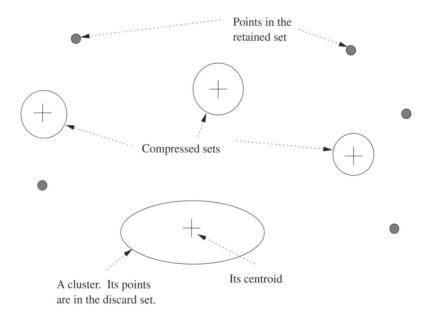

Points in the
retained set

Compressed sets

A cluster. Its points
are in the discard set.

Its centroid

Figure 7.11 Points in the discard, compressed, and retained sets

The discard and compressed sets are represented by $2d + 1$ values, if the data is d-dimensional. These numbers are:

(a) The number of points represented, N.

(b) The sum of the components of all the points in each dimension. This data is a vector SUM of length d, and the component in the ith dimension is SUM_i.

(c) The sum of the squares of the components of all the points in each dimension. This data is a vector SUMSQ of length d, and its component in the ith dimension is SUMSQ_i.

Our real goal is to represent a set of points by their count, their centroid and the standard deviation in each dimension. However, these $2d + 1$ values give us

---

> ## Benefits of the N, SUM, SUMSQ Representation
>
> There is a significant advantage to representing sets of points as it is done in the BFR Algorithm, rather than by storing N, the centroid, and the standard deviation in each dimension. Consider what we need to do when we add a new point to a cluster. N is increased by 1, of course. But we can also add the vector representing the location of the point to SUM to get the new SUM, and we can add the squares of the ith components of the vector to SUMSQ$_i$ to get the new SUMSQ$_i$. Had we used the centroid in place of SUM, then we could not adjust the centroid to account for the new point without doing some calculation involving N, and the recomputation of the standard deviations would be far more complex as well. Similarly, if we want to combine two sets, we just add corresponding values of N, SUM, and SUMSQ, while if we used the centroid and standard deviations as a representation, the calculation would be far more complex.

those statistics. N is the count. The centroid's coordinate in the ith dimension is the SUM$_i/N$, that is the sum in that dimension divided by the number of points. The variance in the ith dimension is SUMSQ$_i/N - (\text{SUM}_i/N)^2$. We can compute the standard deviation in each dimension, since it is the square root of the variance.

EXAMPLE 7.9   Suppose a cluster consists of the points $(5,1)$, $(6,-2)$, and $(7,0)$. Then $N = 3$, SUM $= [18,-1]$, and SUMSQ $= [110,5]$. The centroid is SUM$/N$, or $[6,-1/3]$. The variance in the first dimension is $110/3 - (18/3)^2 = 0.667$, so the standard deviation is $\sqrt{0.667} = 0.816$. In the second dimension, the variance is $5/3 - (-1/3)^2 = 1.56$, so the standard deviation is 1.25.

7.3.5   Processing Data in the BFR Algorithm

We shall now outline what happens when we process a chunk of points.

(1) First, all points that are sufficiently close to the centroid of a cluster are added to that cluster. As described in the box on benefits, it is simple to add the information about the point to the N, SUM, and SUMSQ that represent the cluster. We then discard the point. The question of what "sufficiently close" means will be addressed shortly.

(2) For the points that are not sufficiently close to any centroid, we cluster them, along with the points in the retained set. Any main-memory clustering algorithm can be used, such as the hierarchical methods discussed in Section 7.2. We must use some criterion for deciding when it is reasonable to combine two points into a cluster or two clusters into one. Section 7.2.3 covered the ways we might make this decision. Clusters of more than one point are summarized and added to the compressed set. Singleton clusters become the retained set of points.

(3) We now have miniclusters derived from our attempt to cluster new points and the old retained set, and we have the miniclusters from the old compressed set. Although none of these miniclusters can be merged with one of the k clusters, they might merge with one another. The criterion for merger may again be chosen according to the discussion in Section 7.2.3. Note that the form of representation for compressed sets (N, SUM, and SUMSQ) makes it easy to compute statistics such as the variance for the combination of two miniclusters that we consider merging.

(4) Points that are assigned to a cluster or a minicluster, i.e., those that are not in the retained set, are written out, with their assignment, to secondary memory.

Finally, if this is the last chunk of input data, we need to do something with the compressed and retained sets. We can treat them as outliers, and never cluster them at all. Or, we can assign each point in the retained set to the cluster of the nearest centroid. We can combine each minicluster with the cluster whose centroid is closest to the centroid of the minicluster.

An important decision that must be examined is how we decide whether a new point p is close enough to one of the k clusters that it makes sense to add p to the cluster. Two approaches have been suggested.

(a) Add p to a cluster if it not only has the centroid closest to p, but it is very unlikely that, after all the points have been processed, some other cluster centroid will be found to be nearer to p. This decision is a complex statistical calculation. It must assume that points are ordered randomly, and that we know how many points will be processed in the future. Its advantage is that if we find one centroid to be significantly closer to p than any other, we can add p to that cluster and be done with it, even if p is very far from all centroids.

(b) We can measure the probability that, if p belongs to a cluster, it would be found as far as it is from the centroid of that cluster. This calculation makes use of the fact that we believe each cluster to consist of normally distributed points with the axes of the distribution aligned with the axes of the space. It allows us to make the calculation through the *Mahalanobis distance* of the point, which we shall describe next.

The Mahalanobis distance is essentially the distance between a point and the centroid of a cluster, normalized by the standard deviation of the cluster in each dimension. Since the BFR Algorithm assumes the axes of the cluster align with the axes of the space, the computation of Mahalanobis distance is especially simple. Let $p = [p_1, p_2, \ldots, p_d]$ be a point and $c = [c_1, c_2, \ldots, c_d]$ the centroid of a cluster. Let σ_i be the standard deviation of points in the cluster in the ith dimension. Then the Mahalanobis distance between p and c is

$$\sqrt{\sum_{i=1}^{d} (\frac{p_i - c_i}{\sigma_i})^2}$$

That is, we normalize the difference between p and c in the ith dimension by dividing by the standard deviation of the cluster in that dimension. The rest of the formula combines the normalized distances in each dimension in the normal way for a Euclidean space.

To assign point p to a cluster, we compute the Mahalanobis distance between p and each of the cluster centroids. We choose that cluster whose centroid has the least Mahalanobis distance, and we add p to that cluster provided the Mahalanobis distance is less than a threshold. For instance, suppose we pick four as the threshold. If data is normally distributed, then the probability of a value as far as four standard deviations from the mean is less than one in a million. Thus, if the points in the cluster are really normally distributed, then the probability that we will fail to include a point that truly belongs is less than 10^{-6}. And such a point is likely to be assigned to that cluster eventually anyway, as long as it does not wind up closer to some other centroid as centroids migrate in response to points added to their cluster.

7.3.6 Exercises for Section 7.3

EXERCISE 7.3.1 For the points of Fig. 7.8, if we select three starting points using the method of Section 7.3.2, and the first point we choose is (3,4), which other points are selected.

!! EXERCISE 7.3.2 Prove that no matter what point we start with in Fig. 7.8, if we select three starting points by the method of Section 7.3.2 we obtain points in each of the three clusters. *Hint*: You could solve this exhaustively by begining with each of the twelve points in turn. However, a more generally applicable solution is to consider the diameters of the three clusters and also consider the *minimum intercluster distance*, that is, the minimum distance between two points chosen from two different clusters. Can you prove a general theorem based on these two parameters of a set of points?

! EXERCISE 7.3.3 Give an example of a dataset and a selection of k initial centroids such that when the points are reassigned to their nearest centroid at the end, at least one of the initial k points is reassigned to a different cluster.

EXERCISE 7.3.4 For the three clusters of Fig. 7.8:

(a) Compute the representation of the cluster as in the BFR Algorithm. That is, compute N, SUM, and SUMSQ.

(b) Compute the variance and standard deviation of each cluster in each of the two dimensions.

EXERCISE 7.3.5   Suppose a cluster of three-dimensional points has standard deviations of 2, 3, and 5, in the three dimensions, in that order. Compute the Mahalanobis distance between the origin $(0, 0, 0)$ and the point $(1, -3, 4)$.

7.4   The CURE Algorithm

We now turn to another large-scale-clustering algorithm in the point-assignment class. This algorithm, called *CURE* (Clustering Using REpresentatives), assumes a Euclidean space. However, it does not assume anything about the shape of clusters; they need not be normally distributed, and can even have strange bends, S-shapes, or even rings. Instead of representing clusters by their centroid, it uses a collection of representative points, as the name implies.

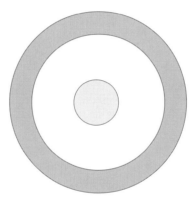

Figure 7.12 Two clusters, one surrounding the other

EXAMPLE 7.10   Figure 7.12 is an illustration of two clusters. The inner cluster is an ordinary circle, while the second is a ring around the circle. This arrangement is not completely pathological. A creature from another galaxy might look at our solar system and observe that the objects cluster into an inner circle (the planets) and an outer ring (the Kuyper belt), with little in between.

7.4.1   Initialization in CURE

We begin the CURE algorithm by:

(1) Take a small sample of the data and cluster it in main memory. In principle, any clustering method could be used, but as CURE is designed to handle oddly shaped clusters, it is often advisable to use a hierarchical method in which clusters are merged when they have a close pair of points. This issue is discussed in more detail in Example 7.11 below.

(2) Select a small set of points from each cluster to be *representative points*.

These points should be chosen to be as far from one another as possible, using the method described in Section 7.3.2.

(3) Move each of the representative points a fixed fraction of the distance between its location and the centroid of its cluster. Perhaps 20% is a good fraction to choose. Note that this step requires a Euclidean space, since otherwise, there might not be any notion of a line between two points.

EXAMPLE 7.11 We could use a hierarchical clustering algorithm on a sample of the data from Fig. 7.12. If we took as the distance between clusters the shortest distance between any pair of points, one from each cluster, then we would correctly find the two clusters. That is, pieces of the ring would stick together, and pieces of the inner circle would stick together, but pieces of ring would always be far away from the pieces of the circle. Note that if we used the rule that the distance between clusters was the distance between their centroids, then we might not get the intuitively correct result. The reason is that the centroids of both clusters are in the center of the diagram.

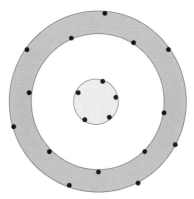

Figure 7.13 Select representative points from each cluster, as far from one another as possible

For the second step, we pick the representative points. If the sample from which the clusters are constructed is large enough, we can count on a cluster's sample points at greatest distance from one another lying on the boundary of the cluster. Figure 7.13 suggests what our initial selection of sample points might look like.

Finally, we move the representative points a fixed fraction of the distance from their true location toward the centroid of the cluster. Note that in Fig. 7.13 both clusters have their centroid in the same place: the center of the inner circle. Thus, the representative points from the circle move inside the cluster, as was intended. Points on the outer edge of the ring also move into their cluster, but points on the ring's inner edge move outside the cluster. The final locations of the representative points from Fig. 7.13 are suggested by Fig. 7.14.

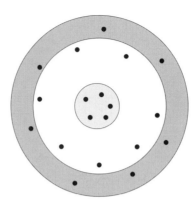

Figure 7.14 Moving the representative points 20% of the distance to the cluster's centroid

7.4.2   Completion of the CURE Algorithm

The next phase of CURE is to merge two clusters if they have a pair of representative points, one from each cluster, that are sufficiently close. The user may pick the distance that defines "close." This merging step can repeat, until there are no more sufficiently close clusters.

EXAMPLE 7.12   The situation of Fig. 7.14 serves as a useful illustration. There is some argument that the ring and circle should really be merged, because their centroids are the same. For instance, if the gap between the ring and circle were much smaller, it might well be argued that combining the points of the ring and circle into a single cluster reflected the true state of affairs. For instance, the rings of Saturn have narrow gaps between them, but it is reasonable to visualize the rings as a single object, rather than several concentric objects. In the case of Fig. 7.14 the choice of

(1) The fraction of the distance to the centroid that we move the representative points and
(2) The choice of how far apart representative points of two clusters need to be to avoid merger

together determine whether we regard Fig. 7.12 as one cluster or two.

The last step of CURE is point assignment. Each point p is brought from secondary storage and compared with the representative points. We assign p to the cluster of the representative point that is closest to p.

EXAMPLE 7.13   In our running example, points within the ring will surely be closer to one of the ring's representative points than to any representative point of the circle. Likewise, points within the circle will surely be closest to a representative point of the circle. An outlier – a point not within the ring or the circle – will be assigned to the ring if it is outside the ring. If the outlier is between the ring and the circle, it will be assigned to one or the other, somewhat favoring the ring because its representative points have been moved toward the circle.

7.4.3 Exercises for Section 7.4

EXERCISE 7.4.1 Consider two clusters that are a circle and a surrounding ring, as in the running example of this section. Suppose:

(a) The radius of the circle is c.
(b) The inner and outer circles forming the ring have radii i and o, respectively.
(c) All representative points for the two clusters are on the boundaries of the clusters.
(d) Representative points are moved 20% of the distance from their initial position toward the centroid of their cluster.
(e) Clusters are merged if, after repositioning, there are representative points from the two clusters at distance d or less.

In terms of d, c, i, and o, under what circumstances will the ring and circle be merged into a single cluster?

7.5 Clustering in Non-Euclidean Spaces

We shall next consider an algorithm that handles non-main-memory data, but does not require a Euclidean space. The algorithm, which we shall refer to as GRGPF for its authors (V. Ganti, R. Ramakrishnan, J. Gehrke, A. Powell, and J. French), takes ideas from both hierarchical and point-assignment approaches. Like CURE, it represents clusters by sample points in main memory. However, it also tries to organize the clusters hierarchically, in a tree, so a new point can be assigned to the appropriate cluster by passing it down the tree. Leaves of the tree hold summaries of some clusters, and interior nodes hold subsets of the information describing the clusters reachable through that node. An attempt is made to group clusters by their distance from one another, so the clusters at a leaf are close, and the clusters reachable from one interior node are relatively close as well.

7.5.1 Representing Clusters in the GRGPF Algorithm

As we assign points to clusters, the clusters can grow large. Most of the points in a cluster are stored on disk, and are not used in guiding the assignment of points, although they can be retrieved. The representation of a cluster in main memory consists of several *features*. Before listing these features, if p is any point in a cluster, let ROWSUM(p) be the sum of the squares of the distances from p to each of the other points in the cluster. Note that, although we are not in a

Euclidean space, there is some distance measure d that applies to points, or else
it is not possible to cluster points at all.

(1) N, the number of points in the cluster.
(2) The clustroid of the cluster, which is defined specifically to be the point
in the cluster that minimizes the sum of the squares of the distances to the
other points; that is, the clustroid is the point in the cluster with the smallest
ROWSUM.
(3) The rowsum of the clustroid of the cluster.
(4) For some chosen constant k, the k points of the cluster that are closest to the
clustroid, and their rowsums. These points are part of the representation in
case the addition of points to the cluster causes the clustroid to change. The
assumption is made that the new clustroid would be one of these k points
near the old clustroid.
(5) The k points of the cluster that are furthest from the clustroid and their
rowsums. These points are part of the representation so that we can consider
whether two clusters are close enough to merge. The assumption is made that
if two clusters are close, then a pair of points distant from their respective
clustroids would be close.

These features form the *representation* of a cluster.

7.5.2   Initializing the Cluster Tree

The clusters are organized into a tree, and the nodes of the tree may be very
large, perhaps disk blocks or pages, as would be the case for a B-tree or R-tree,
which the cluster-representing tree resembles. Each leaf of the tree holds as many
cluster representations as can fit. Note that a cluster representation has a size
that does not depend on the number of points in the cluster.

An interior node of the cluster tree holds a sample of the clustroids of the
clusters represented by each of its subtrees, along with pointers to the roots of
those subtrees. The samples are of fixed size, so the number of children that
an interior node may have is independent of its level. Notice that as we go up
the tree, the probability that a given cluster's clustroid is part of the sample
diminishes.

We initialize the cluster tree by taking a main-memory sample of the dataset
and clustering it hierarchically. The result of this clustering is a tree T, but T
is not exactly the tree used by the GRGPF Algorithm. Rather, we select from
T certain of its nodes that represent clusters of approximately some desired size
n. These are the initial clusters for the GRGPF Algorithm, and we place their
representations at the leaf of the cluster-representing tree. We then group clusters
with a common ancestor in T into interior nodes of the cluster-representing tree,
so in some sense, clusters descended from one interior node are close as possible.
In some cases, rebalancing of the cluster-representing tree will be necessary. This

process is similar to the reorganization of a B-tree, and we shall not examine this issue in detail.

7.5.3   Adding Points in the GRGPF Algorithm

We now read points from secondary storage and insert each one into the nearest cluster. We start at the root, and look at the samples of clustroids for each of the children of the root. Whichever child has the clustroid closest to the new point p is the node we examine next. When we reach any node in the tree, we look at the sample clustroids for its children and go next to the child with the clustroid closest to p. Note that some of the sample clustroids at a node may have been seen at a higher level, but each level provides more detail about the clusters lying below, so we see many new sample clustroids each time we go a level down the tree.

Finally, we reach a leaf. This leaf has the cluster features for each cluster represented by that leaf, and we pick the cluster whose clustroid is closest to p. We adjust the representation of this cluster to account for the new node p. In particular, we:

(1) Add 1 to N.
(2) Add the square of the distance between p and each of the nodes q mentioned in the representation to ROWSUM(q). These points q include the clustroid, the k nearest points, and the k furthest points.

We also estimate the rowsum of p, in case p needs to be part of the representation (e.g., it turns out to be one of the k points closest to the clustroid). Note we cannot compute ROWSUM(p) exactly, without going to disk and retrieving all the points of the cluster. The estimate we use is

$$\text{ROWSUM}(p) = \text{ROWSUM}(c) + N d^2(p, c)$$

where $d(p, c)$ is the distance between p and the clustroid c. Note that N and ROWSUM(c) in this formula are the values of these features before they were adjusted to account for the addition of p.

We might well wonder why this estimate works. In Section 7.1.3 we discussed the "curse of dimensionality," in particular the observation that in a high-dimensional Euclidean space, almost all angles are right angles. Of course the assumption of the GRGPF Algorithm is that the space might not be Euclidean, but typically a non-Euclidean space also suffers from the curse of dimensionality, in that it behaves in many ways like a high-dimensional Euclidean space. If we assume that the angle between p, c, and another point q in the cluster is a right angle, then the Pythagorean theorem tell us that

$$d^2(p, q) = d^2(p, c) + d^2(c, q)$$

If we sum over all q other than c, and then add $d^2(p, c)$ to ROWSUM(p) to account for the fact that the clustroid is one of the points in the cluster, we derive $\text{ROWSUM}(p) = \text{ROWSUM}(c) + Nd^2(p,c)$.

Now, we must see if the new point p is one of the k closest or furthest points from the clustroid, and if so, p and its rowsum become a cluster feature, replacing one of the other features – whichever is no longer one of the k closest or furthest. We also need to consider whether the rowsum for one of the k closest points q is now less than $\text{ROWSUM}(c)$. That situation could happen if p were closer to one of these points than to the current clustroid. If so, we swap the roles of c and q. Eventually, it is possible that the true clustroid will no longer be one of the original k closest points. We have no way of knowing, since we do not see the other points of the cluster in main memory. However, they are all stored on disk, and can be brought into main memory periodically for a recomputation of the cluster features.

7.5.4 Splitting and Merging Clusters

The GRGPF Algorithm assumes that there is a limit on the radius that a cluster may have. The particular definition used for the radius is $\sqrt{\text{ROWSUM}(c)/N}$, where c is the clustroid of the cluster and N the number of points in the cluster. That is, the radius is the square root of the average square of the distance from the clustroid of the points in the cluster. If a cluster's radius grows too large, it is split into two. The points of that cluster are brought into main memory, and divided into two clusters to minimize the rowsums. The cluster features for both clusters are computed.

As a result, the leaf of the split cluster now has one more cluster to represent. We should manage the cluster tree like a B-tree, so usually, there will be room in a leaf to add one more cluster. However, if not, then the leaf must be split into two leaves. To implement the split, we must add another pointer and more sample clustroids at the parent node. Again, there may be extra space, but if not, then this node too must be split, and we do so to minimize the squares of the distances between the sample clustroids assigned to different nodes. As in a B-tree, this splitting can ripple all the way up to the root, which can then be split if needed.

The worst thing that can happen is that the cluster-representing tree is now too large to fit in main memory. There is only one thing to do: we make it smaller by raising the limit on how large the radius of a cluster can be, and we consider merging pairs of clusters. It is normally sufficient to consider clusters that are "nearby," in the sense that their representatives are at the same leaf or at leaves with a common parent. However, in principle, we can consider merging any two clusters C_1 and C_2 into one cluster C.

To merge clusters, we assume that the clustroid of C will be one of the points that are as far as possible from the clustroid of C_1 or the clustroid of C_2. Suppose we want to compute the rowsum in C for the point p, which is one of the k points in C_1 that are as far as possible from the centroid of C_1. We use the curse-of-dimensionality argument that says all angles are approximately right angles, to justify the following formula.

$$\text{ROWSUM}_C(p) = \text{ROWSUM}_{C_1}(p) + N_{C_2}\big(d^2(p, c_1) + d^2(c_1, c_2)\big) + \text{ROWSUM}_{C_2}(c_2)$$

In the above, we subscript N and ROWSUM by the cluster to which that feature refers. We use c_1 and c_2 for the clustroids of C_1 and C_2, respectively.

In detail, we compute the sum of the squares of the distances from p to all the nodes in the combined cluster C by beginning with $\text{ROWSUM}_{C_1}(p)$ to get the terms for the points in the same cluster as p. For the N_{C_2} points q in C_2, we consider the path from p to the clustroid of C_1 and then to C_2, and finally to q. We assume there is a right angle between the legs from p to c_1 and c_1 to c_2, and another right angle between the shortest path from from p to c_2 and the leg from c_2 to q. We then use the Pythagorean theorem to justify computing the square of the length of the path to each q as the sum of the squares of the three legs.

We must then finish computing the features for the merged cluster. We need to consider all the points in the merged cluster for which we know the rowsum. These are, the centroids of the two clusters, the k points closest to the clustroids for each cluster, and the k points furthest from the clustroids for each cluster, with the exception of the point that was chosen as the new clustroid. We can compute the distances from the new clustroid for each of these $4k + 1$ points. We select the k with the smallest distances as the "close" points and the k with the largest distances as the "far" points. We can then compute the rowsums for the chosen points, using the same formulas above that we used to compute the rowsums for the candidate clustroids.

7.5.5   Exercises for Section 7.5

EXERCISE 7.5.1   Using the cluster representation of Section 7.5.1, represent the twelve points of Fig. 7.8 as a single cluster. Use parameter $k = 2$ as the number of close and distant points to be included in the representation. *Hint*: Since the distance is Euclidean, we can get the square of the distance between two points by taking the sum of the squares of the differences along the x- and y-axes.

EXERCISE 7.5.2   Compute the radius, in the sense used by the GRGPF Algorithm (square root of the average square of the distance from the clustroid) for the cluster that is the five points in the lower right of Fig. 7.8. Note that $(11,4)$ is the clustroid.

7.6   **Clustering for Streams and Parallelism**

In this section, we shall consider briefly how one might cluster a stream. The model we have in mind is one where there is a sliding window (recall Section 4.1.3) of N points, and we can ask for the centroids or clustroids of the best clusters formed from the last m of these points, for any $m \leq N$. We also study a similar approach to clustering a large, fixed set of points using map-reduce on a computing cluster (no pun intended). This section provides only a rough outline to suggest the possibilities, which depend on our assumptions about how clusters evolve in a stream.

7.6.1   The Stream-Computing Model

We assume that each stream element is a point in some space. The sliding window consists of the most recent N points. Our goal is to precluster subsets of the points in the stream, so that we may quickly answer queries of the form "what are the clusters of the last m points?" for any $m \leq N$. There are many variants of this query, depending on what we assume about what constitutes a cluster. For instance, we may use a k-means approach, where we are really asking that the last m points be partitioned into exactly k clusters. Or, we may allow the number of clusters to vary, but use one of the criteria in Section 7.2.3 or 7.2.4 to determine when to stop merging clusters into larger clusters.

We make no restriction regarding the space in which the points of the stream live. It may be a Euclidean space, in which case the answer to the query is the centroids of the selected clusters. The space may be non-Euclidean, in which case the answer is the clustroids of the selected clusters, where any of the definitions for "clustroid" may be used (see Section 7.2.4).

The problem is considerably easier if we assume that all stream elements are chosen with statistics that do not vary along the stream. Then, a sample of the stream is good enough to estimate the clusters, and we can in effect ignore the stream after a while. However, the stream model normally assumes that the statistics of the stream elements varies with time. For example, the centroids of the clusters may migrate slowly as time goes on, or clusters may expand, contract, divide, or merge.

7.6.2   A Stream-Clustering Algorithm

In this section, we shall present a greatly simplified version of an algorithm referred to as BDMO (for the authors, B. Babcock, M. Datar, R. Motwani, and L. O'Callaghan). The true version of the algorithm involves much more complex structures, which are designed to provide performance guarantees in the worst case.

The BDMO Algorithm builds on the methodology for counting ones in a stream that was described in Section 4.6. Here are the key similarities and differences:

- Like that algorithm, the points of the stream are partitioned into, and summarized by, buckets whose sizes are a power of two. Here, the *size* of a bucket is the number of points it represents, rather than the number of stream elements that are 1.

- As before, the sizes of buckets obey the restriction that there are one or two of each size, up to some limit. However, we do not assume that the sequence of allowable bucket sizes starts with 1. Rather, they are required only to form a sequence where each size is twice the previous size, e.g., $3, 6, 12, 24, \ldots$.
- Bucket sizes are again restrained to be nondecreasing as we go back in time. As in Section 4.6, we can conclude that there will be $O(\log N)$ buckets.
- The *contents* of a bucket consists of:
  (1) The size of the bucket.
  (2) The timestamp of the bucket, that is, the most recent point that contributes to the bucket. As in Section 4.6, timestamps can be recorded modulo N.
  (3) A collection of records that represent the clusters into which the points of that bucket have been partitioned. These records contain:
   (a) The number of points in the cluster.
   (b) The centroid or clustroid of the cluster.
   (c) Any other parameters necessary to enable us to merge clusters and maintain approximations to the full set of parameters for the merged cluster. We shall give some examples when we discuss the merger process in Section 7.6.4.

7.6.3 Initializing Buckets

Our smallest bucket size will be p, a power of 2. Thus, every p stream elements, we create a new bucket, with the most recent p points. The timestamp for this bucket is the timestamp of the most recent point in the bucket. We may leave each point in a cluster by itself, or we may perform a clustering of these points according to whatever clustering strategy we have chosen. For instance, if we choose a k-means algorithm, then (assuming $k < p$) we cluster the points into k clusters by some algorithm.

Whatever method we use to cluster initially, we assume it is possible to compute the centroids or clustroids for the clusters and count the points in each cluster. This information becomes part of the record for each cluster. We also compute whatever other parameters for the clusters will be needed in the merging process.

7.6.4 Merging Buckets

Following the strategy from Section 4.6, whenever we create a new bucket, we need to review the sequence of buckets. First, if some bucket has a timestamp that is more than N time units prior to the current time, then nothing of that bucket is in the window, and we may drop it from the list. Second, we may have created three buckets of size p, in which case we must merge the oldest two of the three. The merger may create two buckets of size $2p$, in which case we may have to merge buckets of increasing sizes, recursively, just as in Section 4.6.

To merge two consecutive buckets, we need to do several things:

(1) The size of the bucket is twice the sizes of the two buckets being merged.
(2) The timestamp for the merged bucket is the timestamp of the more recent of the two consecutive buckets.
(3) We must consider whether to merge clusters, and if so, we need to compute the parameters of the merged clusters. We shall elaborate on this part of the algorithm by considering several examples of criteria for merging and ways to estimate the needed parameters.

EXAMPLE 7.14   Perhaps the simplest case is where we are using a k-means approach in a Euclidean space. We represent clusters by the count of their points and their centroids. Each bucket has exactly k clusters, so we can pick $p = k$, or we can pick p larger than k and cluster the p points into k clusters when we create a bucket initially as in Section 7.6.3. We must find the best matching between the k clusters of the first bucket and the k clusters of the second. Here, "best" means the matching that minimizes the sum of the distances between the centroids of the matched clusters.

Note that we do not consider merging two clusters from the same bucket, because our assumption is that clusters do not evolve too much between consecutive buckets. Thus, we would expect to find in each of two adjacent buckets a representation of each of the k "true" clusters that exist in the stream.

When we decide to merge two clusters, one from each bucket, the number of points in the merged cluster is surely the sum of the numbers of points in the two clusters. The centroid of the merged cluster is the weighted average of the centroids of the two clusters, where the weighting is by the numbers of points in the clusters. That is, if the two clusters have n_1 and n_2 points, respectively, and have centroids $\mathbf{c}_1$ and $\mathbf{c}_2$ (the latter are d-dimensional vectors for some d), then the combined cluster has $n = n_1 + n_2$ points and has centroid

$$\mathbf{c} = \frac{n_1\mathbf{c}_1 + n_2\mathbf{c}_2}{n_1 + n_2}$$

EXAMPLE 7.15   The method of Example 7.14 suffices when the clusters are changing very slowly. Suppose we might expect the cluster centroids to migrate sufficiently quickly that when matching the centroids from two consecutive buckets, we might be faced with an ambiguous situation, where it is not clear which of two clusters best matches a given cluster from the other bucket. One way to protect against such a situation is to create more than k clusters in each bucket, even if we know that, when we query (see Section 7.6.5), we shall have to merge into exactly k clusters. For example, we might choose p to be much larger than k, and, when we merge, only merge clusters when the result is sufficiently coherent according to one of the criteria outlined in Section 7.2.3. Or, we could use a hierarchical strategy, and make the best merges, so as to maintain $p > k$ clusters in each bucket.

Suppose, to be specific, that we want to put a limit on the sum of the distances

between all the points of a cluster and its centroid. Then in addition to the count
of points and the centroid of a cluster, we can include an estimate of this sum
in the record for a cluster. When we initialize a bucket, we can compute the
sum exactly. But as we merge clusters, this parameter becomes an estimate only.
Suppose we merge two clusters, and want to compute the sum of distances for
the merged cluster. Use the notation for centroids and counts in Example 7.14,
and in addition, let s_1 and s_2 be the sums for the two clusters. Then we may
estimate the radius of the merged cluster to be

$$n_1|\mathbf{c}_1 - \mathbf{c}| + n_2|\mathbf{c}_2 - \mathbf{c}| + s_1 + s_2$$

That is, we estimate the distance between any point x and the new centroid $\mathbf{c}$ to
be the distance of that point to its old centroid (these distances sum to $s_1 + s_2$, the
last two terms in the above expression) plus the distance from the old centroid
to the new (these distances sum to the first two terms of the above expression).
Note that this estimate is an upper bound, by the triangle inequality.

An alternative is to replace the sum of distances by the sum of the squares of
the distances from the points to the centroid. If these sums for the two clusters
are t_1 and t_2, respectively, then we can produce an estimate for the same sum
in the new cluster as

$$n_1|\mathbf{c}_1 - \mathbf{c}|^2 + n_2|\mathbf{c}_2 - \mathbf{c}|^2 + t_1 + t_2$$

This estimate is close to correct if the space is high-dimensional, by the "curse
of dimensionality."

EXAMPLE 7.16   Our third example will assume a non-Euclidean space and no
constraint on the number of clusters. We shall borrow several of the techniques
from the GRGPF Algorithm of Section 7.5. Specifically, we represent clusters by
their clustroid and rowsum (sum of the squares of the distances from each node
of the cluster to its clustroid). We include in the record for a cluster information
about a set of points at maximum distance from the clustroid, including their
distances from the clustroid and their rowsums. Recall that their purpose is to
suggest a clustroid when this cluster is merged with another.

When we merge buckets, we may choose one of many ways to decide which
clusters to merge. For example, we may consider pairs of clusters in order of the
distance between their centroids. We may also choose to merge clusters when
we consider them, provided the sum of their rowsums is below a certain limit.
Alternatively, we may perform the merge if the sum of rowsums divided by the
number of points in the clusters is below a limit. Any of the other strategies
discussed for deciding when to merge clusters may be used as well, provided we
arrange to maintain the data (e.g., cluster diameter) necessary to make decisions.

We then must pick a new clustroid, from among the points most distant from
the clustroids of the two merged clusters. We can compute rowsums for each
of these candidate clustroids using the formulas given in Section 7.5.4. We also
follow the strategy given in that section to pick a subset of the distant points

from each cluster to be the set of distant points for the merged cluster, and to compute the new rowsum and distance-to-clustroid for each.

7.6.5   Answering Queries

Recall that we assume a query is a request for the clusters of the most recent m points in the stream, where $m \leq N$. Because of the strategy we have adopted of combining buckets as we go back in time, we may not be able to find a set of buckets that covers exactly the last m points. However, if we choose the smallest set of buckets that cover the last m points, we shall include in these buckets no more than the last $2m$ points. We shall produce, as answer to the query, the centroids or clustroids of all the points in the selected buckets. In order for the result to be a good approximation to the clusters for exactly the last m points, we must assume that the points between $2m$ and $m + 1$ will not have radically different statistics from the most recent m points. However, if the statistics vary too rapidly, recall from Section 4.6.6 that a more complex bucketing scheme can guarantee that we can find buckets to cover at most the last $m(1 + \epsilon)$ points, for any $\epsilon > 0$.

Having selected the desired buckets, we pool all their clusters. We then use some methodology for deciding which clusters to merge. Examples 7.14 and 7.16 are illustrations of two approaches to this merger. For instance, if we are required to produce exactly k clusters, then we can merge the clusters with the closest centroids until we are left with only k clusters, as in Example 7.14. Or we can make a decision whether or not to merge clusters in various ways, as we sampled in Example 7.16.

7.6.6   Clustering in a Parallel Environment

Now, let us briefly consider the use of parallelism available in a computing cluster.[3] We assume we are given a very large collection of points, and we wish to exploit parallelism to compute the centroids of their clusters. The simplest approach is to use a map-reduce strategy, but in most cases we are constrained to use a single Reduce task.

Begin by creating many Map tasks. Each task is assigned a subset of the points. The Map function's job is to cluster the points it is given. Its output is a set of key-value pairs with a fixed key 1, and a value that is the description of one cluster. This description can be any of the possibilities suggested in Section 7.6.2, such as the centroid, count, and diameter of the cluster.

Since all key-value pairs have the same key, there can be only one Reduce task. This task gets descriptions of the clusters produced by each of the Map tasks, and must merge them appropriately. We may use the discussion in Section 7.6.4 as representative of the various strategies we might use to produce the final clustering, which is the output of the Reduce task.

---

[3] Do not forget that the term "cluster" has two completely different meanings in this section.

7.6.7   Exercises for Section 7.6

EXERCISE 7.6.1   Execute the BDMO Algorithm with $p = 3$ on the following 1-dimensional, Euclidean data:

$$1, 45, 80, 24, 56, 71, 17, 40, 66, 32, 48, 96, 9, 41, 75, 11, 58, 93, 28, 39, 77$$

The clustering algorithms is k-means with $k = 3$. Only the centroid of a cluster, along with its count, is needed to represent a cluster.

EXERCISE 7.6.2   Using your clusters from Exercise 7.6.1, produce the best centroids in response to a query asking for a clustering of the last 10 points.

7.7   Summary of Chapter 7

✦ *Clustering*: Clusters are often a useful summary of data that is in the form of points in some space. To cluster points, we need a distance measure on that space. Ideally, points in the same cluster have small distances between them, while points in different clusters have large distances between them.

✦ *Clustering Algorithms*: Clustering algorithms generally have one of two forms. Hierarchical clustering algorithms begin with all points in a cluster of their own, and nearby clusters are merged iteratively. Point-assignment clustering algorithms consider points in turn and assign them to the cluster in which they best fit.

✦ *The Curse of Dimensionality*: Points in high-dimensional Euclidean spaces, as well as points in non-Euclidean spaces often behave unintuitively. Two unexpected properties of these spaces are that random points are almost always at about the same distance, and random vectors are almost always orthogonal.

✦ *Centroids and Clustroids*: In a Euclidean space, the members of a cluster can be averaged, and this average is called the centroid. In non-Euclidean spaces, there is no guarantee that points have an "average," so we are forced to use one of the members of the cluster as a representative or typical element of the cluster. That representative is called the clustroid.

✦ *Choosing the Clustroid*: There are many ways we can define a typical point of a cluster in a non-Euclidean space. For example, we could choose the point with the smallest sum of distances to the other points, the smallest sum of the squares of those distances, or the smallest maximum distance to any other point in the cluster.

✦ *Radius and Diameter*: Whether or not the space is Euclidean, we can define the radius of a cluster to be the maximum distance from the centroid or clustroid to any point in that cluster. We can define the diameter of the cluster to be the maximum distance between any two points in the cluster. Alternative definitions, especially of the radius, are also known, for example, average distance from the centroid to the other points.

✦ *Hierarchical Clustering*: This family of algorithms has many variations, which differ primarily in two areas. First, we may chose in various ways which two clusters to merge next. Second, we may decide when to stop the merge process in various ways.

✦ *Picking Clusters to Merge*: One strategy for deciding on the best pair of clusters to merge in a hierarchical clustering is to pick the clusters with the closest centroids or clustroids. Another approach is to pick the pair of clusters with the closest points, one from each cluster. A third approach is to use the average distance between points from the two clusters.

✦ *Stopping the Merger Process*: A hierarchical clustering can proceed until there are a fixed number of clusters left. Alternatively, we could merge until it is impossible to find a pair of clusters whose merger is sufficiently compact, e.g., the merged cluster has a radius or diameter below some threshold. Another approach involves merging as long as the resulting cluster has a sufficiently high "density," which can be defined in various ways, but is the number of points divided by some measure of the size of the cluster, e.g., the radius.

✦ *K-Means Algorithms*: This family of algorithms is of the point-assignment type and assumes a Euclidean space. It is assumed that there are exactly k clusters for some known k. After picking k initial cluster centroids, the points are considered one at a time and assigned to the closest centroid. The centroid of a cluster can migrate during point assignment, and an optional last step is to reassign all the points, while holding the centroids fixed at their final values obtained during the first pass.

✦ *Initializing K-Means Algorithms*: One way to find k initial centroids is to pick a random point, and then choose $k - 1$ additional points, each as far away as possible from the previously chosen points. An alternative is to start with a small sample of points and use a hierarchical clustering to merge them into k clusters.

✦ *Picking K in a K-Means Algorithm*: If the number of clusters is unknown, we can use a binary-search technique, trying a k-means clustering with different values of k. We search for the largest value of k for which a decrease below k clusters results in a radically higher average diameter of the clusters. This search can be carried out in a number of clustering operations that is logarithmic in the true value of k.

✦ *The BFR Algorithm*: This algorithm is a version of k-means designed to handle data that is too large to fit in main memory. It assumes clusters are normally distributed about the axes.

✦ *Representing Clusters in BFR*: Points are read from disk one chunk at a time. Clusters are represented in main memory by the count of the number of points, the vector sum of all the points, and the vector formed by summing the squares of the components of the points in each dimension. Other collection of points, too far from a cluster centroid to be included in a cluster, are represented as "miniclusters" in the same way as the k clusters, while still other points, which are not near any other point will be represented as themselves and called "retained" points.

✦ *Processing Points in BFR*: Most of the points in a main-memory load will be assigned to a nearby cluster and the parameters for that cluster will be adjusted to account for the new points. Unassigned points can be formed into new miniclusters, and these miniclusters can be merged with previously discovered miniclusters or retained points. After the last memory load, the miniclusters and retained points can be merged to their nearest cluster or kept as outliers.

✦ *The CURE Algorithm*: This algorithm is of the point-assignment type. It is designed for a Euclidean space, but clusters can have any shape. It handles data that is too large to fit in main memory.

✦ *Representing Clusters in CURE*: The algorithm begins by clustering a small sample of points. It then selects representative points for each cluster, by picking points in the cluster that are as far away from each other as possible. The goal is to find representative points on the fringes of the cluster. However, the representative points are then moved a fraction of the way toward the centroid of the cluster, so they lie somewhat in the interior of the cluster.

✦ *Processing Points in CURE*: After creating representative points for each cluster, the entire set of points can be read from disk and assigned to a cluster. We assign a given point to the cluster of the representative point that is closest to the given point.

✦ *The GRGPF Algorithm*: This algorithm is of the point-assignment type. It handles data that is too big to fit in main memory, and it does not assume a Euclidean space.

✦ *Representing Clusters in GRGPF*: A cluster is represented by the count of points in the cluster, the clustroid, a set of points nearest the clustroid and a set of points furthest from the clustroid. The nearby points allow us to change the clustroid if the cluster evolves, and the distant points allow for merging clusters efficiently in appropriate circumstances. For each of these points, we also record the rowsum, that is the square root of the sum of the squares of the distances from that point to all the other points of the cluster.

✦ *Tree Organization of Clusters in GRGPF*: Cluster representations are organized into a tree structure like a B-tree, where nodes of the tree are typically disk blocks and contain information about many clusters. The leaves hold the representation of as many clusters as possible, while interior nodes hold a sample of the clustroids of the clusters at their descendant leaves. We organize the tree so that the clusters whose representatives are in any subtree are as close as possible.

✦ *Processing Points in GRGPF*: After initializing clusters from a sample of points, we insert each point into the cluster with the nearest clustroid. Because of the tree structure, we can start at the root and choose to visit the child with the sample clustroid nearest to the given point. Following this rule down one path in the tree leads us to a leaf, where we insert the point into the cluster with the nearest clustroid on that leaf.

✦ *Clustering Streams*: A generalization of the DGIM Algorithm (for counting 1's in the sliding window of a stream) can be used to cluster points that are part of a slowly evolving stream. The BDMO Algorithm uses buckets similar to those of DGIM, with allowable bucket sizes forming a sequence where each size is twice the previous size.

✦ *Representation of Buckets in BDMO*: The size of a bucket is the number of points it represents. The bucket itself holds only a representation of the clusters of these points, not the points themselves. A cluster representation includes a count of the number of points, the centroid or clustroid, and other information that is needed for merging clusters according to some selected strategy.

✦ *Merging Buckets in BDMO*: When buckets must be merged, we find the best matching of clusters, one from each of the buckets, and merge them in pairs. If the stream evolves slowly, then we expect consecutive buckets to have almost the same cluster centroids, so this matching makes sense.

✦ *Answering Queries in DBMO*: A query is a length of a suffix of the sliding window. We take all the clusters in all the buckets that are at least partially within that suffix and merge them using some strategy. The resulting clusters are the answer to the query.

✦ *Clustering Using Map-Reduce*: We can divide the data into chunks and cluster each chunk in parallel, using a Map task. The clusters from each Map task can be further clustered in a single Reduce task.

7.8   References for Chapter 7

The ancestral study of clustering for large-scale data is the BIRCH Algorithm of [(6)]. The BFR Algorithm is from [(2)]. The CURE Algorithm is found in [(5)].

The paper on the GRGPF Algorithm is [(3)]. The necessary background regarding B-trees and R-trees can be found in [(4)]. The study of clustering on streams is taken from [(1)].

(1) B. Babcock, M. Datar, R. Motwani, and L. O'Callaghan, "Maintaining variance and k-medians over data stream windows," *Proc. ACM Symp. on Principles of Database Systems*, pp. 234–243, 2003.

(2) P.S. Bradley, U.M. Fayyad, and C. Reina, "Scaling clustering algorithms to large databases," *Proc. Knowledge Discovery and Data Mining*, pp. 9–15, 1998.

(3) V. Ganti, R. Ramakrishnan, J. Gehrke, A.L. Powell, and J.C. French:, "Clustering large datasets in arbitrary metric spaces," *Proc. Intl. Conf. on Data Engineering*, pp. 502–511, 1999.

(4) H. Garcia-Molina, J.D. Ullman, and J. Widom, *Database Systems: The Complete Book* Second Edition, Prentice-Hall, Upper Saddle River, NJ, 2009.

(5) S. Guha, R. Rastogi, and K. Shim, "CURE: An efficient clustering algorithm for large databases," *Proc. ACM SIGMOD Intl. Conf. on Management of Data*, pp. 73–84, 1998.

(6) T. Zhang, R. Ramakrishnan, and M. Livny, "BIRCH: an efficient data clustering method for very large databases," *Proc. ACM SIGMOD Intl. Conf. on Management of Data*, pp. 103–114, 1996.

8   Advertising on the Web

One of the big surprises of the 21st century has been the ability of all sorts of interesting Web applications to support themselves through advertising, rather than subscription. While radio and television have managed to use advertising as their primary revenue source, most media – newspapers and magazines, for example – have had to use a hybrid approach, combining revenue from advertising and subscriptions.

By far the most lucrative venue for on-line advertising has been search, and much of the effectiveness of search advertising comes from the "adwords" model of matching search queries to advertisements. We shall therefore devote much of this chapter to algorithms for optimizing the way this assignment is done. The algorithms used are of an unusual type; they are greedy and they are "on-line" in a particular technical sense to be discussed. We shall therefore digress to discuss these two algorithmic issues – greediness and on-line algorithms – in general, before tackling the adwords problem.

A second interesting on-line advertising problem involves selecting items to advertise at an on-line store. This problem involves "collaborative filtering," where we try to find customers with similar behavior in order to suggest they buy things that similar customers have bought. This subject will be treated in Section 9.3.

8.1   Issues in On-Line Advertising

In this section, we summarize the technical problems that are presented by the opportunities for on-line advertising. We begin by surveying the types of ads found on the Web.

8.1.1   Advertising Opportunities

The Web offers many ways for an advertiser to show their ads to potential customers. Here are the principal venues.

(1) Some sites, such as eBay, Craig's List or auto trading sites allow advertisers to post their ads directly, either for free, for a fee, or a commission.

(2) Display ads are placed on many Web sites. Advertisers pay for the display

at a fixed rate per *impression* (one display of the ad with the download of the page by some user). Normally, a second download of the page, even by the same user, will result in the display of a different ad and is a second impression.

(3) On-line stores such as Amazon show ads in many contexts. The ads are not paid for by the manufacturers of the product advertised, but are selected by the store to maximize the probability that the customer will be interested in the product. We consider this kind of advertising in Chapter 9.

(4) Search ads are placed among the results of a search query. Advertisers bid for the right to have their ad shown in response to certain queries, but they pay only if the ad is clicked on. The particular ads to be shown are selected by a complex process, to be discussed in this chapter, involving the search terms that the advertiser has bid for, the amount of their bid, the observed probability that the ad will be clicked on, and the total budget that the advertiser has offered for the service.

8.1.2 Direct Placement of Ads

When advertisers can place ads directly, such as a free ad on Craig's List or the "buy it now" feature at eBay, there are several problems that the site must deal with. Ads are displayed in response to query terms, e.g., "apartment Palo Alto." The Web site can use an inverted index of words, just as a search engine does (see Section 5.1.1) and return those ads that contain all the words in the query. Alternatively, one can ask the advertiser to specify parameters of the ad, which are stored in a database. For instance, an ad for a used car could specify the manufacturer, model, color, and year from pull-down menus, so only clearly understood terms can be used. Queryers can use the same menus of terms in their queries.

Ranking ads is a bit more problematic, since there is nothing like the links on the Web to tell us which ads are more "important." One strategy used is "most-recent first." That strategy, while equitable, is subject to abuse, where advertisers post small variations of their ads at frequent intervals. The technology for discovering ads that are too similar has already been covered, in Section 3.4.

An alternative approach is to try to measure the attractiveness of an ad. Each time it is displayed, record whether or not the queryer clicked on it. Presumably, attractive ads will be clicked on more frequently than those that are not. However, there are several factors that must be considered in evaluating ads:

(1) The position of the ad in a list has great influence on whether or not it is clicked. The first on the list has by far the highest probability, and the probability drops off exponentially as the position increases.

(2) The ad may have attractiveness that depends on the query terms. For example, an ad for a used convertible would be more attractive if the search query includes the term "convertible," even though it might be a valid response to

queries that look for that make of car, without specifying whether or not a convertible is wanted.

(3) All ads deserve the opportunity to be shown until their click probability can be approximated closely. If we start all ads out with a click probability of 0, we shall never show them and thus never learn whether or not they are attractive ads.

8.1.3   Issues for Display Ads

This form of advertising on the Web most resembles advertising in traditional media. An ad for a Chevrolet run in the pages of the *New York Times* is a display ad, and its effectiveness is limited. It may be seen by many people, but most of them are not interested in buying a car, just bought a car, don't drive, or have another good reason to ignore the ad. Yet the cost of printing the ad was still borne by the newspaper and hence by the advertiser. An impression of a similar ad on the Yahoo! home page is going to be relatively ineffective for essentially the same reason. The fee for placing such an ad is typically a fraction of a cent per impression.

The response of traditional media to this lack of focus was to create newspapers or magazines for special interests. If you are a manufacturer of golf clubs, running your ad in *Golf Digest* would give you an order-of-magnitude increase in the probability that the person seeing your ad would be interested in it. This phenomenon explains the existence of many specialized, low-circulation magazines. They are able to charge much more per impression for an ad than is a general-purpose outlet such as a daily newspaper. The same phenomenon appears on the Web. An ad for golf clubs on `sports.yahoo.com/golf` has much more value per impression than does the same ad on the Yahoo! home page or an ad for Chevrolets on the Yahoo! golf page.

However, the Web offers an opportunity to tailor display ads in a way that hardcopy media cannot: it is possible to use information about the user to determine which ad they should be shown, regardless of what page they are looking at. If it is known that Sally likes golf, then it makes sense to show her an ad for golf clubs, regardless of what page she is looking at. We could determine Sally's love for golf in various ways:

(1) She may belong to a golf-related group on Facebook.
(2) She may mention "golf" frequently in emails posted on her gmail account.
(3) She may spend a lot of time on the Yahoo! golf page.
(4) She may issue search queries with golf-related terms frequently.
(5) She may bookmark the Web sites of one or more golf courses.

Each of these methods, and many others like these, raise enormous privacy issues. It is not the purpose of this book to try to resolve those issues, which in practice probably have no solution that will satisfy all concerns. On the one hand, people like the free services that have recently become advertising-supported, and these services depend on advertising being much more effective than conventional ads. There is a general agreement that, if there must be ads, it is better to see things you might actually use than to have what pages you view cluttered with irrelevancies. On the other hand, there is great potential for misuse if the information leaves the realm of the machines that execute advertising algorithms and get into the hands of real people.

8.2   On-Line Algorithms

Before addressing the question of matching advertisements to search queries, we shall digress slightly by examining the general class to which such algorithms belong. This class is referred to as "on-line," and they generally involve an approach called "greedy." We also give, in the next section, a preliminary example of an on-line greedy algorithm for a simpler problem: maximal matching.

8.2.1   On-Line and Off-Line Algorithms

Typical algorithms work as follows. All the data needed by the algorithm is presented initially. The algorithm can access the data in any order. At the end, the algorithm produces its answer. Such an algorithm is called *off-line*.

However, there are times when we cannot see all the data before our algorithm must make some decisions. Chapter 4 covered stream mining, where we could store only a limited amount of the stream, and had to answer queries about the entire stream when called upon to do so. There is an extreme form of stream processing, where we must respond with an output after each stream element arrives. We thus must decide about each stream element knowing nothing at all of the future. Algorithms of this class are called *on-line* algorithms.[1]

As the case in point, selecting ads to show with search queries would be relatively simple if we could do it off-line. We would see a month's worth of search queries, and look at the bids advertisers made on search terms, as well as their advertising budgets for the month, and we could then assign ads to the queries in a way that maximized both the revenue to the search engine and the number of impressions that each advertiser got. The problem with off-line algorithms is that most queryers don't want to wait a month to get their search results.

Thus, we must use an on-line algorithm to assign ads to search queries. That is, when a search query arrives, we must select the ads to show with that query immediately. We can use information about the past, e.g., we do not have to show an ad if the advertiser's budget has already been spent, and we can examine the

---

[1] Unfortunately, we are faced with another case of dual meanings, like the coincidence involving the term "cluster" that we noted in Section 7.6.6, where we needed to interpret properly phrases such as "algorithms for computing clusters on computer clusters." Here, the term "on-line" refers to the nature of the algorithm, and should not be confused with "on-line" meaning "on the Internet" in phrases such as "on-line algorithms for on-line advertising."

click-through rate (fraction of the time the ad is clicked on when it is displayed) that an ad has obtained so far. However, we cannot use anything about future search queries. For instance, we cannot know whether there will be lots of queries arriving later and using search terms on which this advertiser has made higher bids.

EXAMPLE 8.1   Let us take a very simple example of why knowing the future could help. A manufacturer A of replica antique furniture has bid 10 cents on the search term "chesterfield".[2] A more conventional manufacturer B has bid 20 cents on both the terms "chesterfield" and "sofa." Both have monthly budgets of $100, and there are no other bidders on either of these terms. It is the beginning of the month, and a search query "chesterfield" has just arrived. We are allowed to display only one ad with the query.

The obvious thing to do is to display B's ad, because they bid more. However, suppose there will be lots of search queries this month for "sofa," but very few for "chesterfield." Then A will never spend its $100 budget, while B will spend its full budget even if we give the query to A. Specifically, if there will be at least 500 more queries for either "sofa" or "chesterfield," then there is no harm, and potentially a benefit, in giving the query to A. It will still be possible for B to spend its entire budget, while we are increasing the amount of A's budget that will be spent. Note that this argument makes sense both from the point of view of the search engine, which wants to maximize total revenue, and from the point of view of both A and B, who presumably want to get all the impressions that their budgets allow.

If we could know the future, then we would know how many more "sofa" queries and how many more "chesterfield" queries were going to arrive this month. If that number is below 500, then we want to give the query to B to maximize revenue, but if it is 500 or more, then we want to give it to A. Since we don't know the future, an on-line algorithm cannot always do as well as an off-line algorithm.

8.2.2   Greedy Algorithms

Many on-line algorithms are of the *greedy algorithm* type. These algorithms make their decision in response to each input element by maximizing some function of the input element and the past.

EXAMPLE 8.2   The obvious greedy algorithm for the situation described in Example 8.1 is to assign a query to the highest bidder who still has budget left. For the data of that example, what will happen is that the first 500 "sofa" or "chesterfield" queries will be assigned to B. At that time, B runs out of budget and is assigned no more queries. After that, the next 1000 "chesterfield" queries are assigned to A, and "sofa" queries get no ad and therefore earn the search engine no money.

---

[2] A chesterfield is a type of sofa. See, for example, `www.chesterfields.info`.

The worst thing that can happen is that 500 "chesterfield" queries arrive, followed by 500 "sofa" queries. An off-line algorithm could optimally assign the first 500 to A, earning $50, and the next 500 to B, earning $100, or a total of $150. However, the greedy algorithm will assign the first 500 to B, earning $100, and then has no ad for the next 500, earning nothing.

8.2.3 The Competitive Ratio

As we see from Example 8.2, an on-line algorithm need not give as good a result as the best off-line algorithm for the same problem. The most we can expect is that there will be some constant c less than 1, such that on any input, the result of a particular on-line algorithm is at least c times the result of the optimum off-line algorithm. The constant c, if it exists, is called the *competitive ratio* for the on-line algorithm.

EXAMPLE 8.3   The greedy algorithm, on the particular data of Example 8.2, gives a result that is $2/3$ as good as that of the optimum algorithm: $100 versus $150. That proves that the competitive ratio is no greater than $2/3$. But it could be less. The competitive ratio for an algorithm may depend on what kind of data is allowed to be input to the algorithm. Even if we restrict inputs to the situation described in Example 8.2, but with the bids allowed to vary, then we can show the greedy algorithm has a competitive ratio no greater than $1/2$. Just raise the bid by A to ϵ less than 20 cents. As ϵ approaches 0, the greedy algorithm still produces only $100, but the return from the optimum algorithm approaches $200. We can show that it is impossible to do worse than half the optimum in this simple case, so the competitive ratio is indeed $1/2$. However, we'll leave this sort of proof for later sections.

8.2.4 Exercises for Section 8.2

! EXERCISE 8.2.1   A popular example of the design of an on-line algorithm to minimize the competitive ratio is the *ski-buying problem*.[3] Suppose you can buy skis for $100, or you can rent skis for $10 per day. You decide to take up skiing, but you don't know if you will like it. You may try skiing for any number of days and then give it up. The merit of an algorithm is the cost per day of skis, and we must try to minimize this cost.

One on-line algorithm for making the rent/buy decision is "buy skis immediately." If you try skiing once, fall down and give it up, then this on-line algorithm costs you $100 per day, while the optimum off-line algorithm would have you rent skis for $10 for the one day you used them. Thus, the competitive ratio of the algorithm "buy skis immediately" is at most $1/10$th, and that is in fact the exact competitive ratio, since using the skis one day is the worst possible outcome for this algorithm. On the other hand, the on-line algorithm "always rent skis" has

---

[3] Thanks to Anna Karlin for this example.

an arbitrarily small competitive ratio. If you turn out to really like skiing and go regularly, then after n days, you will have paid $10n$ or $10/day, while the optimum off-line algorithm would have bought skis at once, and paid only $100, or $100/n$ per day.

Your question: design an on-line algorithm for the ski-buying problem that has the best possible competitive ratio. What is that competitive ratio? *Hint*: Since you could, at any time, have a fall and decide to give up skiing, the only thing the on-line algorithm can use in making its decision is how many times previously you have gone skiing.

8.3   The Matching Problem

We shall now take up a problem that is a simplified version of the problem of matching ads to search queries. This problem, called "maximal matching," is an abstract problem involving *bipartite graphs* (graphs with two sets of nodes – left and right – with all edges connecting a node in the left set to a node in the right set. Figure 8.1 is an example of a bipartite graph. Nodes 1, 2, 3, and 4 form the left set, while nodes a, b, c, and d form the right set.

8.3.1   Matches and Perfect Matches

Suppose we are given a bipartite graph. A *matching* is a subset of the edges such that no node is an end of two or more edges. A matching is said to be *perfect* if every node appears in the matching. Note that a matching can only be perfect if the left and right sets are of the same size. A matching that is as large as any other matching for the graph in question is said to be *maximal*.

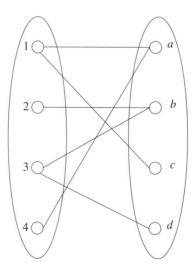

Figure 8.1 A bipartite graph

EXAMPLE 8.4   The set of edges $\{(1,a),\ (2,b),\ (3,d)\}$ is a matching for the bipartite graph of Fig. 8.1. Each member of the set is an edge of the bipartite graph, and no node appears more than once. The set of edges

$$\{(1,c),\ (2,b),\ (3,d),\ (4,a)\}$$

is a perfect matching, represented by heavy lines in Fig. 8.2. Every node appears exactly once. It is, in fact, the sole perfect matching for this graph, although some bipartite graphs have more than one perfect matching. The matching of Fig. 8.2 is also maximal, since every perfect matching is maximal.

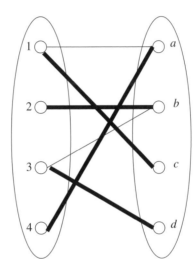

Figure 8.2 The only perfect matching for the graph of Fig. 8.1

8.3.2   The Greedy Algorithm for Maximal Matching

Off-line algorithms for finding a maximal matching have been studied for decades, and one can get very close to $O(n^2)$ for an n-node graph. On-line algorithms for the problem have also been studied, and it is this class of algorithms we shall consider here. In particular, the greedy algorithm for maximal matching works as follows. We consider the edges in whatever order they are given. When we consider (x, y), add this edge to the matching if neither x nor y are ends of any edge selected for the matching so far. Otherwise, skip (x, y).

EXAMPLE 8.5   Let us consider a greedy match for the graph of Fig. 8.1. Suppose we order the nodes lexicographically, that is, by order of their left node, breaking ties by the right node. Then we consider the edges in the order $(1, a)$, $(1, c)$, $(2, b)$, $(3, b)$, $(3, d)$, $(4, a)$. The first edge, $(1, a)$, surely becomes part of the matching. The second edge, $(1, c)$, cannot be chosen, because node 1 already appears in the matching. The third edge, $(2, b)$, is selected, because neither node 2 nor node b

appears in the matching so far. Edge $(3, b)$ is rejected for the match because b is already matched, but then $(3, d)$ is added to the match because neither 3 nor d has been matched so far. Finally, $(4, a)$ is rejected because a appears in the match. Thus, the matching produced by the greedy algorithm for this ordering of the edges is $\{(1, a), (2, b), (3, d)\}$. As we saw, this matching is not maximal.

EXAMPLE 8.6   A greedy match can be even worse than that of Example 8.5. On the graph of Fig. 8.1, any ordering that begins with the two edges $(1, a)$ and $(3, b)$, in either order, will match those two pairs but then will be unable to match nodes 2 or 4. Thus, the size of the resulting match is only 2.

8.3.3   Competitive Ratio for Greedy Matching

We can show a competitive ratio of $1/2$ for the greedy matching algorithm of Section 8.3.2. First, the ratio cannot be more than $1/2$. We already saw that for the graph of Fig. 8.1, there is a perfect matching of size 4. However, if the edges are presented in any of the orders discussed in Example 8.6, the size of the match is only 2, or half the optimum. Since the competitive ratio for an algorithm is the minimum over all possible inputs of the ratio of what that algorithm achieves to the optimum result, we see that $1/2$ is an upper bound on the competitive ratio.

Suppose M_o is a maximal matching, and M_g is the matching that the greedy algorithm produces. Let L be the set of left nodes that are matched in M_o but not in M_g. Let R be the set of right nodes that are connected by edges to any node in L. We claim that every node in R is matched in M_g. Suppose not; in particular, suppose node r in R is not matched in M_g. Then the greedy algorithm will eventually consider some edge (ℓ, r), where ℓ is in L. At that time, neither end of this edge is matched, because we have supposed that neither ℓ nor r is ever matched by the greedy algorithm. That observation contradicts the definition of how the greedy algorithm works; that is, the greedy algorithm would indeed match (ℓ, r). We conclude that every node in R is matched in M_g.

Now, we know several things about the sizes of sets and matchings.

(1) $|M_o| \leq |M_g| + |L|$, since among the nodes on the left, only nodes in L can be matched in M_o but not M_g.
(2) $|L| \leq |R|$, because in M_o, all the nodes in L were matched.
(3) $|R| \leq |M_g|$, because every node in R is matched in M_g.

Now, (2) and (3) give us $|L| \leq |M_g|$. That, together with (1), gives us $|M_o| \leq 2|M_g|$, or $|M_g| \geq \frac{1}{2}|M_o|$. The latter inequality says that the competitive ratio is at least $1/2$. Since we already observed that the competitive ratio is no more than $1/2$, we now conclude the ratio is exactly $1/2$.

8.3.4   Exercises for Section 8.3

EXERCISE 8.3.1   Define the graph G_n to have the $2n$ nodes

$$a_0, a_1, \ldots, a_{n-1}, b_0, b_1, \ldots, b_{n-1}$$

and the following edges. Each node a_i, for $i = 0, 1, \ldots, n-1$, is connected to the nodes b_j and b_k, where

$$j = 2i \mod n \text{ and } k = (2i+1) \mod n$$

For instance, the graph G_4 has the following edges: (a_0, b_0), (a_0, b_1), (a_1, b_2), (a_1, b_3), (a_2, b_0), (a_2, b_1), (a_3, b_2), and (a_3, b_3).

(a) Find a perfect matching for G_4.
(b) Find a perfect matching for G_5.
!! (c) Prove that for every n, G_n has a perfect matching.

! EXERCISE 8.3.2 How many perfect matchings do the graphs G_4 and G_5 of Exercise 8.3.1 have?

! EXERCISE 8.3.3 Whether or not the greedy algorithm gives us a perfect matching for the graph of Fig. 8.1 depends on the order in which we consider the edges. Of the 6! possible orders of the six edges, how many give us a perfect matching? Give a simple test for distinguishing those orders that do give the perfect matching from those that do not.

8.4   The Adwords Problem

We now consider the fundamental problem of search advertising, which we term the "adwords problem," because it was first encountered in the Google Adwords system. We then discuss a greedy algorithm called "Balance" that offers a good competitive ratio. We analyze this algorithm for a simplified case of the adwords problem.

8.4.1   History of Search Advertising

Around the year 2000, a company called Overture (later bought by Yahoo!) introduced a new kind of search. Advertisers bid on *keywords* (words in a search query), and when a user searched for that keyword, the links to all the advertisers who bid on that keyword are displayed in the order highest-bid-first. If the advertiser's link was clicked on, they paid what they had bid.

That sort of search was very useful for the case where the search queryer really was looking for advertisements, but it was rather useless for the queryer who was just looking for information. Recall our discussion in Section 5.1.1 about the point that unless a search engine can provide reliable responses to queries that are for general information, no one will want to use the search engine when they are looking to buy something.

Several years later, Google adapted the idea in a system called *Adwords*. By that time, the reliability of Google was well established, so people were willing to trust the ads they were shown. Google kept the list of responses based on

PageRank and other objective criteria separate from the list of ads, so the same system was useful for the queryer who just wanted information as well as the queryer looking to buy something.

The Adwords system went beyond the earlier system in several ways that made the selection of ads more complex.

(1) Google would show only a limited number of ads with each query. Thus, while Overture simply ordered all ads for a given keyword, Google had to decide which ads to show, as well as the order in which to show them.

(2) Users of the Adwords system specified a budget: the amount they were willing to pay for all clicks on their ads in a month. These constraints make the problem of assigning ads to search queries more complex, as we hinted at in Example 8.1.

(3) Google did not simply order ads by the amount of the bid, but by the amount they expected to receive for display of each ad. That is, the click-through rate was observed for each ad, based on the history of displays of that ad. The value of an ad was taken to be the product of the bid and the click-through rate.

8.4.2   Definition of the Adwords Problem

Of course, the decision regarding which ads to show must be made on-line. Thus, we are only going to consider on-line algorithms for solving the *adwords problem*, which is as follows.

- Given:
  (1) A set of bids by advertisers for search queries.
  (2) A click-through rate for each advertiser-query pair.
  (3) A budget for each advertiser. We shall assume budgets are for a month, although any unit of time could be used.
  (4) A limit on the number of ads to be displayed with each search query.
- Respond to each search query with a set of advertisers such that:
  (1) The size of the set is no larger than the limit on the number of ads per query.
  (2) Each advertiser has bid on the search query.
  (3) Each advertiser has enough budget left to pay for the ad if it is clicked upon.

The *revenue* of a selection of ads is the total value of the ads selected, where the *value* of an ad is the product of the bid and the click-through rate for the ad and query. The merit of an on-line algorithm is the total revenue obtained over a month (the time unit over which budgets are assumed to apply). We shall try to measure the competitive ratio for algorithms, that is, the minimum total revenue for that algorithm, on any sequence of search queries, divided by the revenue of the optimum off-line algorithm for the same sequence of search queries.

> ### Adwords Aspects not in Our Model
>
> There are several ways in which the real AdWords system differs from the simplified model of this section.
>
> *Matching Bids and Search Queries*: In our simplified model, advertisers bid on sets of words, and an advertiser's bid is eligible to be shown for search queries that have exactly the same set of words as the advertiser's bid. In reality, Google, Yahoo!, and Microsoft all offer advertisers a feature known as *broad matching*, where an ad is eligible to be shown for search queries that are inexact matches of the bid keywords. Examples include queries that include a subset or superset of keywords, and also queries that use words with very similar meanings to the words the advertiser bid on. For such broad matches, search engines charge the advertiser based on complicated formulas taking into account how closely related the search query is to the advertiser's bid. These formulas vary across search engines and are not made public.
>
> *Charging Advertisers for Clicks*: In our simplified model, when a user clicks on an advertiser's ad, the advertiser is charged the amount they bid. This policy is known as a *first-price auction*. In reality, search engines use a more complicated system known as a *second-price auction*, where each advertiser pays approximately the bid of the advertiser who placed immediately behind them in the auction. For example, the first-place advertiser for a search might pay the bid of the advertiser in second place, plus one cent. It has been shown that second-price auctions are less susceptible to being gamed by advertisers than first-price auctions and lead to higher revenues for the search engine.

8.4.3 The Greedy Approach to the Adwords Problem

Since only an on-line algorithm is suitable for the adwords problem, we should first examine the performance of the obvious greedy algorithm. We shall make a number of simplifications to the environment; our purpose is to show eventually that there is a better algorithm than the obvious greedy algorithm. The simplifications:

(a) There is one ad shown for each query.

(b) All advertisers have the same budget.

(c) All click-through rates are the same.

(d) All bids are either 0 or 1. Alternatively, we may assume that the value of each ad (product of bid and click-through rate) is the same.

The greedy algorithm picks, for each search query, any advertiser who has bid 1 for that query. The competitive ratio for this algorithm is $1/2$, as the following example shows.

EXAMPLE 8.7   Suppose there are two advertisers A and B, and only two possible queries, x and y. Advertiser A bids only on x, while B bids on both x and y. The budget for each advertiser is 2. Notice the similarity to the situation in

Example 8.1; the only differences are the fact that the bids by each advertiser are the same and the budgets are smaller here.

Let the sequence of queries be $xxyy$. The greedy algorithm is able to allocate the first two x's to B, whereupon there is no one with an unexpended budget to pay for the two y's. The revenue for the greedy algorithm in this case is thus 2. However, the optimum off-line algorithm will allocate the x's to A and the y's to B, achieving a revenue of 4. The competitive ratio for the greedy algorithm is thus no more than $1/2$. We can argue that on any sequence of queries the ratio of the revenues for the greedy and optimal algorithms is at least $1/2$, using essentially the same idea as in Section 8.3.3.

8.4.4   The Balance Algorithm

There is a simple improvement to the greedy algorithm that gives a competitive ratio of $3/4$ for the simple case of Section 8.4.3. This algorithm, called the *Balance Algorithm*, assigns a query to the advertiser who bids on the query and has the largest remaining budget. Ties may be broken arbitrarily.

EXAMPLE 8.8   Consider the same situation as in Example 8.7. The Balance Algorithm can assign the first query x to either A or B, because they both bid on x and their remaining budgets are the same. However, the second x must be assigned to the other of A and B, because they then have the larger remaining budget. The first y is assigned to B, since it has budget remaining and is the only bidder on y. The last y cannot be assigned, since B is out of budget, and A did not bid. Thus, the total revenue for the Balance Algorithm on this data is 3. In comparison, the total revenue for the optimum off-line algorithm is 4, since it can assign the x's to A and the y's to B. Our conclusion is that, for the simplified adwords problem of Section 8.4.3, the competitive ratio of the Balance Algorithm is no more than $3/4$. We shall see next that with only two advertisers, $3/4$ is exactly the competitive ratio, although as the number of advertisers grows, the competitive ratio lowers to 0.63 (actually $1 - 1/e$) but no lower.

8.4.5   A Lower Bound on Competitive Ratio for Balance

In this section we shall prove that in the simple case of the Balance Algorithm that we are considering, the competitive ratio is $3/4$. Given Example 8.8, we have only to prove that the total revenue obtained by the Balance Algorithm is at least $3/4$ of the revenue for the optimum off-line algorithm. Thus, consider a situation in which there are two advertisers, A_1 and A_2, each with a budget of B. We shall assume that each query is assigned to an advertiser by the optimum algorithm. If not, we can delete those queries without affecting the revenue of the optimum algorithm and possibly reducing the revenue of Balance. Thus, the lowest possible competitive ratio is achieved when the query sequence consists only of ads assigned by the optimum algorithm.

We shall also assume that both advertisers' budgets are consumed by the optimum algorithm. If not, we can reduce the budgets, and again argue that the revenue of the optimum algorithm is not reduced while that of Balance can only shrink. That change may force us to use different budgets for the two advertisers, but we shall continue to assume the budgets are both B. We leave as an exercise the extension of the proof to the case where the budgets of the two advertisers are different.

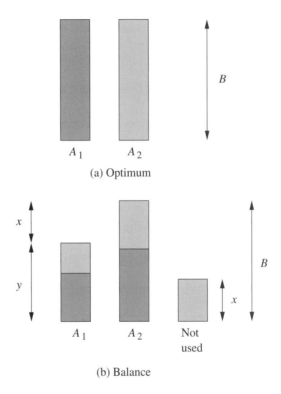

Figure 8.3 Illustration of the assignments of queries to advertisers in the optimum and Balance algorithms

Figure 8.3 suggests how the $2B$ queries are assigned to advertisers by the two algorithms. In (a) we see that B queries are assigned to each of A_1 and A_2 by the optimum algorithm. Now, consider how these same queries are assigned by Balance. First, observe that Balance must exhaust the budget of at least one of the advertisers, say A_2. If not, then there would be some query assigned to neither advertiser, even though both had budget. We know at least one of the advertisers bids on each query, because that query is assigned in the optimum algorithm. That situation contradicts how Balance is defined to operate; it always assigns a query if it can.

Thus, we see in Fig. 8.3(b) that A_2 is assigned B queries. These queries could have been assigned to either A_1 or A_2 by the optimum algorithm. We also see in Fig. 8.3(b) that we use y as the number of queries assigned to A_1 and x as

$B - y$. It is our goal to show $y \geq x$. That inequality will show the revenue of Balance is at least $3B/2$, or 3/4th the revenue of the optimum algorithm.

We note that x is also the number of unassigned queries for the Balance Algorithm, and that all the unassigned queries must have been assigned to A_2 by the optimum algorithm. The reason is that A_1 never runs out of budget, so any query assigned by the optimum algorithm to A_1 is surely bid on by A_1. Since A_1 always has budget during the running of the Balance Algorithm, that algorithm will surely assign this query, either to A_1 or to A_2.

There are two cases, depending on whether more of the queries that are assigned to A_1 by the optimum algorithm are assigned to A_1 or A_2 by Balance.

(1) Suppose at least half of these queries are assigned by Balance to A_1. Then $y \geq B/2$, so surely $y \geq x$.

(2) Suppose more than half of these queries are assigned by Balance to A_2. Consider the last of these queries q that is assigned to A_2 by the Balance Algorithm. At that time, A_2 must have had at least as great a budget available as A_1, or else Balance would have assigned query q to A_1, just as the optimum algorithm did. Since more than half of the B queries that the optimum algorithm assigns to A_1 are assigned to A_2 by Balance, we know that when q was assigned, the remaining budget of A_2 was less than $B/2$. Therefore, at that time, the remaining budget of A_1 was also less than $B/2$. Since budgets only decrease, we know that $x < B/2$. It follows that $y > x$, since $x + y = B$.

We conclude that $y \geq x$ in either case, so the competitive ratio of the Balance Algorithm is $3/4$.

8.4.6   The Balance Algorithm with Many Bidders

When there are many advertisers, the competitive ratio for the Balance Algorithm can be under $3/4$, but not too far below that fraction. The worst case for Balance is as follows.

(1) There are N advertisers, $A_1, A_2, \ldots, A_N$.
(2) Each advertiser has a budget $B = N!$.
(3) There are N queries $q_1, q_2, \ldots, q_N$.
(4) Advertiser A_i bids on queries $q_1, q_2, \ldots, q_i$ and no other queries.
(5) The query sequence consists of N rounds. The ith round consists of B occurrences of query q_i and nothing else.

The optimum off-line algorithm assigns the B queries q_i in the ith round to A_i for all i. Thus, all queries are assigned to a bidder, and the total revenue of the optimum algorithm is NB.

However, the Balance Algorithm assigns each of the queries in round 1 to the N advertisers equally, because all bid on q_1, and the Balance Algorithm prefers the bidder with the greatest remaining budget. Thus, each advertiser gets B/N of the queries q_1. Now consider the queries q_2 in round 2. All but A_1 bid on these queries, so they are divided equally among A_2 through A_N, with each of these $N-1$ bidders getting $B/(N-1)$ queries. The pattern, suggested by Fig. 8.4, repeats for each round $i = 3, 4, \ldots$, with A_i through A_N getting $B/(N-i)$ queries.

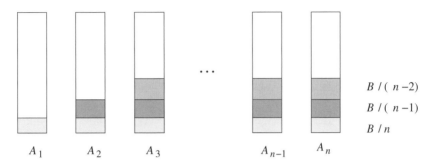

Figure 8.4 Apportioning queries to N advertisers in the worst case

However, eventually, the budgets of the higher-numbered advertisers will be exhausted. That will happen at the lowest round j such that

$$B\left(\frac{1}{N} + \frac{1}{N-1} + \cdots + \frac{1}{N-j+1}\right) \geq B$$

that is,

$$\frac{1}{N} + \frac{1}{N-1} + \cdots + \frac{1}{N-j+1} \geq 1$$

Euler showed that as k gets large, $\sum_{i=1}^{k} 1/i$ approaches $\log_e k$. Using this observation, we can approximate the above sum as $\log_e N - \log_e(N-j)$.

We are thus looking for the j such that $\log_e N - \log_e(N-j) = 1$, approximately. If we replace $\log_e N - \log_e(N-j)$ by the equivalent $\log_e\big(N/(N-j)\big)$ and exponentiate both sides of the equation $\log_e\big(N/(N-j)\big) = 1$, we get $N/(N-j) = e$. Solving this equation for j, we get

$$j = N\left(1 - \frac{1}{e}\right)$$

as the approximate value of j for which all advertisers are either out of budget or do not bid on any of the remaining queries. Thus, the approximate revenue obtained by the Balance Algorithm is $BN(1-\frac{1}{e})$, that is, the queries of the first j rounds. Therefore, the competitive ratio is $1 - \frac{1}{e}$, or approximately 0.63.

8.4.7 The Generalized Balance Algorithm

The Balance Algorithm works well when all bids are 0 or 1. However, in practice, bids can be arbitrary, and with arbitrary bids and budgets Balance fails to weight the sizes of the bids properly. The following example illustrates the point.

EXAMPLE 8.9   Suppose there are two advertisers A_1 and A_2, and one query q. The bids on q and budgets are:

Bidder	Bid	Budget
A_1	1	110
A_2	10	100

If there are 10 occurrences of q, the optimum off-line algorithm will assign them all to A_2 and gain revenue 100. However, because A_1's budget is larger, Balance will assign all ten queries to A_1 for a revenue of 10. In fact, one can extend this idea easily to show that for situations like this one, there is no competitive ratio higher than 0 that holds for the Balance Algorithm.

In order to make Balance work in more general situations, we need to make two modifications. First, we need to bias the choice of ad in favor of higher bids. Second, we need to be less absolute about the remaining budget. Rather, we consider the fraction of the budgets remaining, so we are biased toward using some of each advertiser's budget. The latter change will make the Balance Algorithm more "risk averse"; it will not leave too much of any advertiser's budget unused. It can be shown (see the chapter references) that the following generalization of the Balance Algorithm has a competitive ratio of $1 - 1/e = 0.63$.

• Suppose that a query q arrives, advertiser A_i has bid x_i for this query (note that x_i could be 0). Also, suppose that fraction f_i of the budget of A_i is currently unspent. Let $\Psi_i = x_i(1 - e^{f_i})$. Then assign q to the advertiser A_i such that Ψ_i is a maximum. Break ties arbitrarily.

EXAMPLE 8.10   Consider how the generalized Balance Algorithm would work on the data of Example 8.9. For the first occurrence of query q,

$$\Psi_1 = 1 \times (1 - e^{-1})$$

since A_1 has bid 1, and fraction 1 of A_1's budget remains. That is,

$$\Psi_1 = 1 - 1/e = 0.63$$

On the other hand, $\Psi_2 = 10 \times (1 - e^{-1}) = 6.3$. Thus, the first q is awarded to A_2.

The same thing happens for each of the q's. That is, Ψ_1 stays at 0.63, while Ψ_2 decreases. However, it never goes below 0.63. Even for the 10th q, when 90% of A_2's budget has already been used, $\Psi_2 = 10 \times (1 - e^{-1/10})$. Recall (Section 1.3.5) the Taylor expansion for $e^x = 1 + x + x^2/2! + x^3/3! + \cdots$. Thus,

$$e^{-1/10} = 1 - \frac{1}{10} + \frac{1}{200} - \frac{1}{6000} + \cdots$$

or approximately, $e^{-1/10} = 0.905$. Thus, $\Psi_2 = 10 \times 0.095 = 0.95$.

We leave unproved the assertion that the competitive ratio for this algorithm is $1 - 1/e$. We also leave unproved an additional surprising fact: no on-line algorithm for the adwords problem as described in this section can have a competitive ratio above $1 - 1/e$.

8.4.8 Final Observations About the Adwords Problem

The Balance Algorithm, as described, does not take into account the possibility that the click-through rate differs for different ads. It is simple to multiply the bid by the click-through rate when computing the Ψ_i's, and doing so will maximize the expected revenue. We can even incorporate information about the click-through rate for each ad on each query for which a nonzero amount has been bid. When faced with the problem of allocating a particular query q, we incorporate a factor that is the click-through rate for that ad on query q, when computing each of the Ψ's.

Another issue we must consider in practice is the historical frequency of queries. If, for example, we know that advertiser A_i has a budget sufficiently small that there are sure to be enough queries coming later in the month to satisfy A_i's demand, then there is no point in boosting Ψ_i if some of A_i's budget has already been expended. That is, maintain $\Psi_i = x_i(1 - e^{-1})$ as long as we can expect that there will be enough queries remaining in the month to give A_i its full budget of ads. This change can cause Balance to perform worse if the sequence of queries is governed by an adversary who can control the sequence of queries. Such an adversary can cause the queries A_i bid on suddenly to disappear. However, search engines get so many queries, and their generation is so random, that it is not necessary in practice to imagine significant deviation from the norm.

8.4.9 Exercises for Section 8.4

EXERCISE 8.4.1   Using the simplifying assumptions of Example 8.7, suppose that there are three advertisers, A, B, and C. There are three queries, x, y, and z. Each advertiser has a budget of 2. Advertiser A bids only on x; B bids on x and y, while C bids on x, y, and z. Note that on the query sequence $xxyyzz$, the optimum off-line algorithm would yield a revenue of 6, since all queries can be assigned.

! (a) Show that the greedy algorithm will assign at least 4 of these 6 queries.

!! (b) Find another sequence of queries such that the greedy algorithm can assign as few as half the queries that the optimum off-line algorithm assigns on that sequence.

!! EXERCISE 8.4.2   Extend the proof of Section 8.4.5 to the case where the two advertisers have unequal budgets.

! EXERCISE 8.4.3   Show how to modify Example 8.9 by changing the bids and/or budgets to make the competitive ratio come out as close to 0 as you like.

8.5   Adwords Implementation

While we should now have an idea of how ads are selected to go with the answer to a search query, we have not addressed the problem of finding the bids that have been made on a given query. As long as bids are for the exact set of words in a query, the solution is relatively easy. However, there are a number of extensions to the query/bid matching process that are not as simple. We shall explain the details in this section.

8.5.1   Matching Bids and Search Queries

As we have described the adwords problem, and as it normally appears in practice, advertisers bid on sets of words. If a search query occurs having exactly that set of words in some order, then the bid is said to match the query, and it becomes a candidate for selection. We can avoid having to deal with word order by storing all sets of words representing a bid in lexicographic (alphabetic) order. The list of words in sorted order forms the hash-key for the bid, and these bids may be stored in a hash table used as an index, as discussed in Section 1.3.2.

Search queries also have their words sorted prior to lookup. When we hash the sorted list, we find in the hash table all the bids for exactly that set of words. They can be retrieved quickly, since we have only to look at the contents of that bucket.

Moreover, there is a good chance that we can keep the entire hash table in main memory. If there are a million advertisers, each bidding on 100 queries, and the record of the bid requires 100 bytes, then we require ten gigabytes of main memory, which is well within the limits of what is feasible for a single machine. If more space is required, we can split the buckets of the hash table among as many machines as we need. Search queries can be hashed and sent to the appropriate machine.

In practice, search queries may be arriving far too rapidly for a single machine, or group of machines that collaborate on a single query at a time, to handle them all. In that case, the stream of queries is split into as many pieces as necessary, and each piece is handled by one group of machines. In fact, answering the search query, independent of ads, will require a group of machines working in parallel anyway, in order that the entire processing of a query can be done in main memory.

8.5.2   More Complex Matching Problems

However, the potential for matching bids to objects is not limited to the case where the objects are search queries and the match criterion is same-set-of-words. For example, Google also matches adwords bids to emails. There, the match criterion is not based on the equality of sets. Rather, a bid on a set of words S matches an email if all the words in S appear anywhere in the email.

This matching problem is much harder. We can still maintain a hash-table index for the bids, but the number of subsets of words in a hundred-word email is much too large to look up all the sets, or even all the small sets of (say) three or fewer words. There are a number of other potential applications of this sort of matching that, at the time of this writing, are not implemented but could be. They all involve *standing queries* – queries that users post to a site, expecting the site to notify them whenever something matching the query becomes available at the site. For example:

(1) Twitter allows one to follow all the "tweets" of a given person. However, it is feasible to allow users to specify a set of words, such as

> `ipod free music`

and see all the tweets where all these words appear, not necessarily in order, and not necessarily adjacent.

(2) On-line news sites often allow users to select from among certain keywords or phrases, e.g., "healthcare" or "Barack Obama," and receive alerts whenever a new news article contains that word or consecutive sequence of words. This problem is simpler than the email/adwords problem for several reasons. Matching single words or consecutive sequences of words, even in a long article, is not as time-consuming as matching small sets of words. Further, the sets of terms that one can search for is limited, so there aren't too many "bids." Even if many people want alerts about the same term, only one index entry, with the list of all those people associated, is required. However, a more advanced system could allow users to specify alerts for sets of words in a news article, just as the Adwords system allows anyone to bid on a set of words in an email.

8.5.3 A Matching Algorithm for Documents and Bids

We shall offer an algorithm that will match many "bids" against many "documents." As before, a *bid* is a (typically small) set of words. A document is a larger set of words, such as an email, tweet, or news article. We assume there may be hundreds of documents per second arriving, although if there are that many, the document stream may be split among many machines or groups of machines. We assume there are many bids, perhaps on the order of a hundred million or a billion. As always, we want to do as much in main memory as we can.

We shall, as before, represent a bid by its words listed in some order. There are two new elements in the representation. First, we shall include a *status* with each list of words. The status is an integer indicating how many of the first words on the list have been matched by the current document. When a bid is stored in the index, its status is always 0.

Second, while the order of words could be lexicographic, we can lower the amount of work by ordering words rarest-first. However, since the number of different words that can appear in emails is essentially unlimited, it is not feasible to order all words in this manner. As a compromise, we might identify the n most common words on the Web or in a sample of the stream of documents we are processing. Here, n might be a hundred thousand or a million. These n words are sorted by frequency, and they occupy the *end* of the list, with the most frequent words at the very end. All words not among the n most frequent can be assumed equally infrequent and ordered lexicographically. Then, the words of any document can be ordered. If a word does not appear on the list of n frequent words, place it at the front of the order, lexicographically. Those words in the document that do appear on the list of most frequent words appear after the infrequent words, in the reverse order of frequency (i.e., with the most frequent words of the documents ordered last).

EXAMPLE 8.11   Suppose our document is

    'Twas brillig, and the slithy toves

"The" is the most frequent word in English, and "and" is only slightly less frequent. Let us suppose that "twas" makes the list of frequent words, although its frequency is surely lower than that of "the" or "and." The other words do not make the list of frequent words.

Then the end of the list consists of "twas," "and," and "the," in that order, since that is the inverse order of frequency. The other three words are placed at the front of the list in lexicographic order. Thus,

    brillig slithy toves twas and the

is the sequence of words in the document, properly ordered.

The bids are stored in a hash-table, whose hash key is the first word of the bid, in the order explained above. The record for the bid will also include information about what to do when the bid is matched. The status is 0 and need not be stored explicitly. There is another hash table, whose job is to contain copies of those bids that have been partially matched. These bids have a status that is at least 1, but less than the number of words in the set. If the status is i, then the hash-key for this hash table is the $(i + 1)$st word. The arrangement of hash tables is suggested by Fig. 8.5. To process a document, do the following.

(1) Sort the words of the document in the order discussed above. Eliminate duplicate words.

(2) For each word w, in the sorted order:

    (i) Using w as the hash-key for the table of partially matched bids, find those bids having w as key.

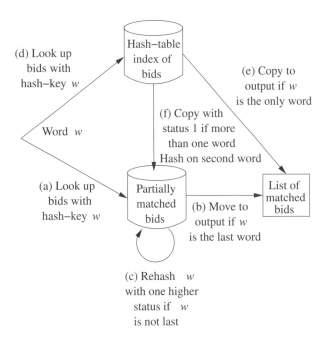

Figure 8.5 Managing large numbers of bids and large numbers of documents

(ii) For each such bid b, if w is the last word of b, move b to the table of matched bids.

(iii) If w is not the last word of b, add 1 to b's status, and rehash b using the word whose position is one more than the new status, as the hash-key.

(iv) Using w as the hash key for the table of all bids, find those bids for which w is their first word in the sorted order.

(v) For each such bid b, if there is only one word on its list, copy it to the table of matched bids.

(vi) If b consists of more than one word, add it, with status 1, to the table of partially matched bids, using the second word of b as the hash-key.

(3) Produce the list of matched bids as the output.

The benefit of the rarest-first order should now be visible. A bid is only copied to the second hash table if its rarest word appears in the document. In comparison, if lexicographic order was used, more bids would be copied to the second hash table. By minimizing the size of that table, we not only reduce the amount of work in steps 2(i)–2(iii), but we make it more likely that this entire table can be kept in main memory.

8.6   Summary of Chapter 8

✦ *Targeted Advertising*: The big advantage that Web-based advertising has over advertising in conventional media such as newspapers is that Web advertising can be selected according to the interests of each individual user. This advantage has enabled many Web services to be supported entirely by advertising revenue.

✦ *On- and Off-Line Algorithms*: Conventional algorithms that are allowed to see all their data before producing an answer are called off-line. An on-line algorithm is required to make a response to each element in a stream immediately, with knowledge of only the past, not the future elements in the stream.

✦ *Greedy Algorithms*: Many on-line algorithms are greedy, in the sense that they select their action at every step by minimizing some objective function.

✦ *Competitive Ratio*: We can measure the quality of an on-line algorithm by minimizing, over all possible inputs, the value of the result of the on-line algorithm compared with the value of the result of the best possible off-line algorithm.

✦ *Bipartite Matching*: This problem involves two sets of nodes and a set of edges between members of the two sets. The goal is to find a maximal matching – as large a set of edges as possible that includes no node more than once.

✦ *On-Line Solution to the Matching Problem*: One greedy algorithm for finding a match in a bipartite graph (or any graph, for that matter) is to order the edges in some way, and for each edge in turn, add it to the match if neither of its ends are yet part of an edge previously selected for the match. This algorithm can be proved to have a competitive ratio of $1/2$; that is, it never fails to match at least half as many nodes as the best off-line algorithm matches.

✦ *Search Ad Management*: A search engine receives bids from advertisers on certain search queries. Some ads are displayed with each search query, and the search engine is paid the amount of the bid only if the queryer clicks on the ad. Each advertiser can give a budget, the total amount they are willing to pay for clicks in a month.

✦ *The Adwords Problem*: The data for the adwords problem is a set of bids by advertisers on certain search queries, together with a total budget for each advertiser and information about the historical click-through rate for each ad for each query. Another part of the data is the stream of search queries received by the search engine. The objective is to select on-line a fixed-size set of ads in response to each query that will maximize the revenue to the search engine.

✦ *Simplified Adwords Problem*: To see some of the nuances of ad selection, we considered a simplified version in which all bids are either 0 or 1, only one ad is shown with each query, and all advertisers have the same budget. Under this model the obvious greedy algorithm of giving the ad placement to anyone who has bid on the query and has budget remaining can be shown to have a competitive ratio of $1/2$.

✦ *The Balance Algorithm*: This algorithm improves on the simple greedy algorithm. A query's ad is given to the advertiser who has bid on the query and has the largest remaining budget. Ties can be broken arbitrarily.

✦ *Competitive Ratio of the Balance Algorithm*: For the simplified adwords model, the competitive ratio of the Balance Algorithm is 3/4 for the case of two advertisers and $1 - 1/e$, or about 63% for any number of advertisers.

✦ *The Balance Algorithm for the Generalized Adwords Problem*: When bidders can make differing bids, have different budgets, and have different click-through rates for different queries, the Balance Algorithm awards an ad to the advertiser with the highest value of the function $\Psi = x(1 - e^{-f})$. Here, x is the product of the bid and the click-through rate for that advertiser and query, and f is the fraction of the advertiser's budget that remains unspent.

✦ *Implementing an Adwords Algorithm*: The simplest version of the implementation serves in situations where the bids are on exactly the set of words in the search query. We can represent a query by the list of its words, in sorted order. Bids are stored in a hash table or similar structure, with a hash key equal to the sorted list of words. A search query can then be matched against bids by a straightforward lookup in the table.

✦ *Matching Word Sets Against Documents*: A harder version of the adwords-implementation problem allows bids, which are still small sets of words as in a search query, to be matched against larger documents, such as emails or tweets. A bid set matches the document if all the words appear in the document, in any order and not necessarily adjacent.

✦ *Hash Storage of Word Sets*: A useful data structure stores the words of each bid set in the order rarest-first. Documents have their words sorted in the same order. Word sets are stored in a hash table with the first word, in the rarest-first order, as the key.

✦ *Processing Documents for Bid Matches*: We process the words of the document rarest-first. Word sets whose first word is the current word are copied to a temporary hash table, with the second word as the key. Sets already in the temporary hash table are examined to see if the word that is their key matches the current word, and, if so, they are rehashed using their next word. Sets whose last word is matched are copied to the output.

8.7   References for Chapter 8

[(1)] is an investigation of the way ad position influences the click-through rate.
   The Balance Algorithm was developed in [(2)] and its application to the adwords problem is from [(3)].

(1) N. Craswell, O. Zoeter, M. Taylor, and W. Ramsey, "An experimental comparison of click-position bias models," *Proc. Intl. Conf. on Web Search and Web Data Mining* pp. 87–94, 2008.

(2) B. Kalyanasundaram and K.R. Pruhs, "An optimal deterministic algorithm for b-matching," *Theoretical Computer Science* **233**:1–2, pp. 319–325, 2000.

(3) A Mehta, A. Saberi, U. Vazirani, and V. Vazirani, "Adwords and generalized on-line matching," *IEEE Symp. on Foundations of Computer Science*, pp. 264–273, 2005.

9 Recommendation Systems

There is an extensive class of Web applications that involve predicting user responses to options. Such a facility is called a *recommendation system*. We shall begin this chapter with a survey of the most important examples of these systems. However, to bring the problem into focus, two good examples of recommendation systems are:

(1) Offering news articles to on-line newspaper readers, based on a prediction of reader interests.

(2) Offering customers of an on-line retailer suggestions about what they might like to buy, based on their past history of purchases and/or product searches.

Recommendation systems use a number of different technologies. We can classify these systems into two broad groups.

- *Content-based systems* examine properties of the items recommended. For instance, if a Netflix user has watched many cowboy movies, then recommend a movie classified in the database as having the "cowboy" genre.

- *Collaborative filtering* systems recommend items based on similarity measures between users and/or items. The items recommended to a user are those preferred by similar users. This sort of recommendation system can use the groundwork laid in Chapter 3 on similarity search and Chapter 7 on clustering. However, these technologies by themselves are not sufficient, and there are some new algorithms that have proven effective for recommendation systems.

9.1 A Model for Recommendation Systems

In this section we introduce a model for recommendation systems, based on a utility matrix of preferences. We introduce the concept of a "long-tail," which explains the advantage of on-line vendors over conventional, brick-and-mortar vendors. We then briefly survey the sorts of applications in which recommendation systems have proved useful.

9.1.1   The Utility Matrix

In a recommendation-system application there are two classes of entities, which we shall refer to as *users* and *items*. Users have preferences for certain items, and these preferences must be teased out of the data. The data itself is represented as a *utility matrix*, giving for each user-item pair, a value that represents what is known about the degree of preference of that user for that item. Values come from an ordered set, e.g., integers 1–5 representing the number of stars that the user gave as a rating for that item. We assume that the matrix is sparse, meaning that most entries are "unknown." An unknown rating implies that we have no explicit information about the user's preference for the item.

EXAMPLE 9.1   In Fig. 9.1 we see an example utility matrix, representing users' ratings of movies on a 1–5 scale, with 5 the highest rating. Blanks represent the situation where the user has not rated the movie. The movie names are HP1, HP2, and HP3 for *Harry Potter* I, II, and III, TW for *Twilight*, and SW1, SW2, and SW3 for *Star Wars* episodes 1, 2, and 3. The users are represented by capital letters A through D.

	HP1	HP2	HP3	TW	SW1	SW2	SW3
A	4			5	1		
B	5	5	4				
C				2	4	5	
D		3					3

Figure 9.1 A utility matrix representing ratings of movies on a 1–5 scale

Notice that most user-movie pairs have blanks, meaning the user has not rated the movie. In practice, the matrix would be even sparser, with the typical user rating only a tiny fraction of all available movies.

The goal of a recommendation system is to predict the blanks in the utility matrix. For example, would user A like SW2? There is little evidence from the tiny matrix in Fig. 9.1. We might design our recommendation system to take into account properties of movies, such as their producer, director, stars, or even the similarity of their names. If so, we might then note the similarity between SW1 and SW2, and then conclude that since A did not like SW1, they were unlikely to enjoy SW2 either. Alternatively, with much more data, we might observe that the people who rated both SW1 and SW2 tended to give them similar ratings. Thus, we could conclude that A would also give SW2 a low rating, similar to A's rating of SW1.

We should also be aware of a slightly different goal that makes sense in many applications. It is not necessary to predict every blank entry in a utility matrix. Rather, it is only necessary to discover some entries in each row that are likely to be high. In most applications, the recommendation system does not offer users a ranking of all items, but rather suggests a few that the user should value highly. It may not even be necessary to find those items with the highest expected ratings, but only to find a large subset of those with the highest ratings.

9.1.2 The Long Tail

Before discussing the principal applications of recommendation systems, let us ponder the *long tail* phenomenon that makes recommendation systems necessary. Physical delivery systems are characterized by a scarcity of resources. Brick-and-mortar stores have limited shelf space, and can show the customer only a small fraction of all the choices that exist. On the other hand, on-line stores can make anything that exists available to the customer. Thus, a physical bookstore may have several thousand books on its shelves, but Amazon offers millions of books. A physical newspaper can print several dozen articles per day, while on-line news services offer thousands per day.

Recommendation in the physical world is fairly simple. First, it is not possible to tailor the store to each individual customer. Thus, the choice of what is made available is governed only by the aggregate numbers. Typically, a bookstore will display only the books that are most popular, and a newspaper will print only the articles it believes the most people will be interested in. In the first case, sales figures govern the choices, in the second case, editorial judgement serves.

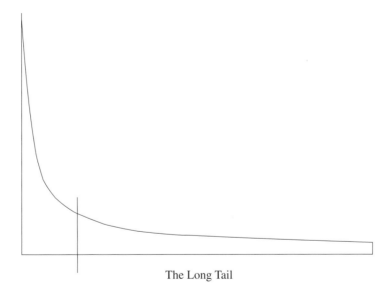

The Long Tail

Figure 9.2 The long tail: physical institutions can only provide what is popular, while on-line institutions can make everything available

The distinction between the physical and on-line worlds has been called the *long tail* phenomenon, and it is suggested in Fig. 9.2. The vertical axis represents *popularity* (the number of times an item is chosen). The items are ordered on the horizontal axis according to their popularity. Physical institutions provide only

---

> ### *Into Thin Air* and *Touching the Void*
>
> An extreme example of how the long tail, together with a well designed rec-ommendation system can influence events is the story told by Chris Anderson about a book called *Touching the Void*. This mountain-climbing book was not a big seller in its day, but many years after it was published, another book on the same topic, called *Into Thin Air* was published. Amazon's recommendation system noticed a few people who bought both books, and started recommending *Touching the Void* to people who bought, or were considering, *Into Thin Air*. Had there been no on-line bookseller, *Touching the Void* might never have been seen by potential buyers, but in the on-line world, *Touching the Void* eventually became very popular in its own right, in fact, more so than *Into Thin Air*.

the most popular items to the left of the vertical line, while the corresponding on-line institutions provide the entire range of items: the tail as well as the popular items.

The long-tail phenomenon forces on-line institutions to recommend items to individual users. It is not possible to present all available items to the user, the way physical institutions can, and it is not reasonable to expect users to have heard of all the many items they might like.

9.1.3   Applications of Recommendation Systems

We have mentioned several important applications of recommendation systems, but here we shall consolidate the list in a single place.

(1) *Product Recommendations*: Perhaps the most important use of recommen-dation systems is at on-line retailers. We have noted how Amazon or similar on-line vendors strive to present each returning user with some suggestions of products that they might like to buy. These suggestions are not random, but are based on the purchasing decisions made by similar customers or on other techniques we shall discuss in this chapter.

(2) *Movie Recommendations*: Netflix offers its customers recommendations of movies they might like. These recommendations are based on ratings pro-vided by users, much like the ratings suggested in the example utility matrix of Fig. 9.1. The importance of predicting ratings accurately is so high, that Netflix offered a prize of one million dollars for the first algorithm that could beat its own recommendation system by 10%.[1] The prize was finally won in 2009, by a team of researchers called "Bellkor's Pragmatic Chaos," after over three years of competition.

---

[1] To be exact, the algorithm had to have a root-mean-square error (RMSE) that was 10% less than the RMSE of the Netflix algorithm on a test set taken from actual ratings of Netflix users. To develop an algorithm, contestants were given a training set of data, also taken from actual Netflix data.

(3) *News Articles*: News services have attempted to identify articles of interest to readers, based on the articles that they have read in the past. The similarity might be based on the similarity of important words in the documents, or on the articles that are read by people with similar reading tastes. The same principles apply to recommending blogs from among the millions of blogs available, videos on YouTube, or other sites where content is provided regularly.

9.1.4 Populating the Utility Matrix

Without a utility matrix, it is almost impossible to recommend items. However, acquiring data from which to build a utility matrix is often difficult. There are two general approaches to discovering the value users place on items.

(1) We can ask users to rate items. Movie ratings are generally obtained this way, and some on-line stores try to obtain ratings from their purchasers. Sites providing content, such as some news sites or YouTube also ask users to rate items. This approach is limited in its effectiveness, since generally users are unwilling to provide responses, and the information from those who do may be biased by the very fact that it comes from people willing to provide ratings.

(2) We can make inferences from users' behavior. Most obviously, if a user buys a product at Amazon, watches a movie on YouTube, or reads a news article, then the user can be said to "like" this item. Note that this sort of rating system really has only one value: 1 means that the user likes the item. Often, we find a utility matrix with this kind of data shown with 0's rather than blanks where the user has not purchased or viewed the item. However, in this case 0 is not a lower rating than 1; it is no rating at all. More generally, one can infer interest from behavior other than purchasing. For example, if an Amazon customer views information about an item, we can infer that they are interested in the item, even if they don't buy it.

9.2 Content-Based Recommendations

As we mentioned at the beginning of the chapter, there are two basic architectures for a recommendation system:

(1) *Content-Based* systems focus on properties of items. Similarity of items is determined by measuring the similarity in their properties.

(2) *Collaborative-Filtering* systems focus on the relationship between users and items. Similarity of items is determined by the similarity of the ratings of those items by the users who have rated both items.

In this section, we focus on content-based recommendation systems. The next section will cover collaborative filtering.

9.2.1   Item Profiles

In a content-based system, we must construct for each item a *profile*, which is a record or collection of records representing important characteristics of that item. In simple cases, the profile consists of some characteristics of the item that are easily discovered. For example, consider the features of a movie that might be relevant to a recommendation system.

(1) The set of stars of the movie. Some viewers prefer movies with their favorite stars.
(2) The director. Some viewers have a preference for the work of certain directors.
(3) The year in which the movie was made. Some viewers prefer old movies; others watch only the latest releases.
(4) The *genre* or general type of movie. Some viewers like only comedies, others dramas or romances.

There are many other features of movies that could be used as well. Except for the last, genre, the information is readily available from descriptions of movies. Genre is a vaguer concept. However, movie reviews generally assign a genre from a set of commonly used terms. For example the *Internet Movie Database* (IMDB) assigns a genre or genres to every movie. We shall discuss mechanical construction of genres in Section 9.3.3.

Many other classes of items also allow us to obtain features from available data, even if that data must at some point be entered by hand. For instance, products often have descriptions written by the manufacturer, giving features relevant to that class of product (e.g., the screen size and cabinet color for a TV). Books have descriptions similar to those for movies, so we can obtain features such as author, year of publication, and genre. Music products such as CD's and MP3 downloads have available features such as artist, composer, and genre.

9.2.2   Discovering Features of Documents

There are other classes of item where it is not immediately apparent what the values of features should be. We shall consider two of them: document collections and images. Documents present special problems, but yields to a known technology. Images will be discussed in Section 9.2.3 as an important example where user-supplied features have some hope of success.

There are many kinds of documents for which a recommendation system can be useful. For example, there are many news articles published each day, and we cannot read all of them. A recommendation system can suggest articles on topics a user is interested in, but how can we distinguish among topics? Web pages are also a collection of documents. Can we suggest pages a user might want to see? Likewise, blogs could be recommended to interested users, if we could classify blogs by topics.

Unfortunately, these classes of documents do not tend to have readily available information giving features. A substitute that has been useful in practice is the identification of words that characterize the topic of a document. How we do the identification was outlined in Section 1.3.1. First, eliminate stop words – the several hundred most common words, which tend to say little about the topic of a document. For the remaining words, compute the TF.IDF score for each word in the document. The ones with the highest scores are the words that characterize the document.

We may then take as the features of a document the n words with the highest TF.IDF scores. It is possible to pick n to be the same for all documents, or to let n be a fixed percentage of the words in the document. We could also choose to make all words whose TF.IDF scores are above a given threshold to be a part of the feature set.

Now, documents are represented by sets of words. Intuitively, we expect these words to express the subjects or main ideas of the document. For example, in a news article, we would expect the words with the highest TF.IDF score to include the names of people discussed in the article, unusual properties of the event described, and the location of the event. To measure the similarity of two documents, there are several natural distance measures we can use:

(1) We could use the Jaccard distance between the sets of words (recall Section 3.5.3).
(2) We could use the cosine distance (recall Section 3.5.4) between the sets, treated as vectors.

To compute the cosine distance in option (2), think of the sets of high-TF.IDF words as a vector, with one component for each possible word. The vector has 1 if the word is in the set and 0 if not. Since between two documents there are only a finite number of words among their two sets, the infinite dimensionality of the vectors is unimportant. Almost all components are 0 in both, and 0's do not impact the value of the dot product. To be precise, the dot product is the size of the intersection of the two sets of words, and the lengths of the vectors are the square roots of the numbers of words in each set. That calculation lets us compute the cosine of the angle between the vectors as the dot product divided by the product of the vector lengths.

9.2.3   Obtaining Item Features From Tags

Let us consider a database of images as an example of a way that features have been obtained for items. The problem with images is that their data, typically an array of pixels, does not tell us anything useful about their features. We can calculate simple properties of pixels, such as the average amount of red in the picture, but few users are looking for red pictures or especially like red pictures.

There have been a number of attempts to obtain information about features of items by inviting users to *tag* the items by entering words or phrases that describe

---

Two Kinds of Document Similarity

Recall that in Section 3.4 we gave a method for finding documents that were "similar," using shingling, minhashing, and LSH. There, the notion of similarity was lexical – documents are similar if they contain large, identical sequences of characters. For recommendation systems, the notion of similarity is different. We are interested only in the occurrences of many important words in both documents, even if there is little lexical similarity between the documents. However, the methodology for finding similar documents remains almost the same. Once we have a distance measure, either Jaccard or cosine, we can use minhashing (for Jaccard) or random hyperplanes (for cosine distance; see Section 3.7.2) feeding data to an LSH algorithm to find the pairs of documents that are similar in the sense of sharing many common keywords.

Tags from Computer Games

An interesting direction for encouraging tagging is the "games" approach pioneered by Luis von Ahn. He enabled two players to collaborate on the tag for an image. In rounds, they would suggest a tag, and the tags would be exchanged. If they agreed, then they "won," and if not, they would play another round with the same image, trying to agree simultaneously on a tag. While an innovative direction to try, it is questionable whether sufficient public interest can be generated to produce enough free work to satisfy the needs for tagged data.

---

the item. Thus, one picture with a lot of red might be tagged "Tiananmen Square," while another is tagged "sunset at Malibu." The distinction is not something that could be discovered by existing image-analysis programs.

Almost any kind of data can have its features described by tags. One of the earliest attempts to tag massive amounts of data was the site del.icio.us, later bought by Yahoo!, which invited users to tag Web pages. The goal of this tagging was to make a new method of search available, where users entered a set of tags as their search query, and the system retrieved the Web pages that had been tagged that way. However, it is also possible to use the tags as a recommendation system. If it is observed that a user retrieves or bookmarks many pages with a certain set of tags, then we can recommend other pages with the same tags.

The problem with tagging as an approach to feature discovery is that the process only works if users are willing to take the trouble to create the tags, and there are enough tags that occasional erroneous ones will not bias the system too much.

9.2.4   Representing Item Profiles

Our ultimate goal for content-based recommendation is to create both an item profile consisting of feature-value pairs and a user profile summarizing the preferences of the user, based of their row of the utility matrix. In Section 9.2.2 we suggested how an item profile could be constructed. We imagined a vector of 0's and 1's, where a 1 represented the occurrence of a high-TF.IDF word in the document. Since features for documents were all words, it was easy to represent profiles this way.

We shall try to generalize this vector approach to all sorts of features. It is easy to do so for features that are sets of discrete values. For example, if one feature of movies is the set of stars, then imagine that there is a component for each star, with 1 if the star is in the movie, and 0 if not. Likewise, we can have a component for each possible director, and each possible genre. All these features can be represented using only 0's and 1's.

There is another class of feature that is not readily represented by boolean vectors: those features that are numerical. For instance, we might take the average rating for movies to be a feature,[2] and this average is a real number. It does not make sense to have one component for each of the possible average ratings, and doing so would cause us to lose the structure implicit in numbers. That is, two ratings that are close but not identical should be considered more similar than widely differing ratings. Likewise, numerical features of products, such as screen size or disk capacity for PC's, should be considered similar if their values do not differ greatly.

Numerical features should be represented by single components of vectors representing items. These components hold the exact value of that feature. There is no harm if some components of the vectors are boolean and others are real-valued or integer-valued. We can still compute the cosine distance between vectors, although if we do so, we should give some thought to the appropriate scaling of the nonboolean components, so that they neither dominate the calculation nor are they irrelevant.

EXAMPLE 9.2 Suppose the only features of movies are the set of stars and the average rating. Consider two movies with five stars each. Two of the stars are in both movies. Also, one movie has an average rating of 3 and the other an average of 4. The vectors look something like

$$0 \quad 1 \quad 1 \quad 0 \quad 1 \quad 1 \quad 0 \quad 1 \quad 3\alpha$$
$$1 \quad 1 \quad 0 \quad 1 \quad 0 \quad 1 \quad 1 \quad 0 \quad 4\alpha$$

However, there are in principle an infinite number of additional components, each with 0's for both vectors, representing all the possible stars that neither movie has. Since cosine distance of vectors is not affected by components in which both vectors have 0, we need not worry about the effect of stars that are not in either movie.

The last component shown represents the average rating. We have shown it as having an unknown scaling factor α. In terms of α, we can compute the cosine of the angle between the vectors. The dot product is $2 + 12\alpha^2$, and the lengths of

---

[2] The rating is not a very reliable feature, but it will serve as an example.

the vectors are $\sqrt{5 + 9\alpha^2}$ and $\sqrt{5 + 16\alpha^2}$. Thus, the cosine of the angle between the vectors is

$$\frac{2 + 12\alpha^2}{\sqrt{25 + 125\alpha^2 + 144\alpha^4}}$$

If we choose $\alpha = 1$, that is, we take the average ratings as they are, then the value of the above expression is 0.816. If we use $\alpha = 2$, that is, we double the ratings, then the cosine is 0.940. That is, the vectors appear much closer in direction than if we use $\alpha = 1$. Likewise, if we use $\alpha = 1/2$, then the cosine is 0.619, making the vectors look quite different. We cannot tell which value of α is "right," but we see that the choice of scaling factor for numerical features affects our decision about how similar items are.

9.2.5   User Profiles

We not only need to create vectors describing items; we need to create vectors with the same components that describe the user's preferences. We have the utility matrix representing the connection between users and items. Recall the nonblank matrix entries could be just 1's representing user purchases or a similar connection, or they could be arbitrary numbers representing a rating or degree of affection that the the user has for the item.

With this information, the best estimate we can make regarding which items the user likes is some aggregation of the profiles of those items. If the utility matrix has only 1's, then the natural aggregate is the average of the components of the vectors representing the item profiles for the items in which the utility matrix has 1 for that user.

EXAMPLE 9.3   Suppose items are movies, represented by boolean profiles with components corresponding to stars. Also, the utility matrix has a 1 if the user has seen the movie and is blank otherwise. If 20% of the movies that user U likes have Julia Roberts as one of the stars, then the user profile for U will have 0.2 in the component for Julia Roberts.

If the utility matrix is not boolean, e.g., ratings 1–5, then we can weight the vectors representing the profiles of items by the utility value. It makes sense to normalize the utilities by subtracting the average value for a user. That way, we get negative weights for items with a below-average rating, and positive weights for items with above-average ratings. That effect will prove useful when we discuss in Section 9.2.6 how to find items that a user should like.

EXAMPLE 9.4   Consider the same movie information as in Example 9.3, but now suppose the utility matrix has nonblank entries that are ratings in the 1–5 range. Suppose user U gives an average rating of 3. There are three movies with Julia Roberts as a star, and those movies got ratings of 3, 4, and 5. Then in the user profile of U, the component for Julia Roberts will have value that is the average of $3 - 3$, $4 - 3$, and $5 - 3$, that is, a value of 1.

On the other hand, user V gives an average rating of 4, and has also rated three movies starring Julia Roberts (it doesn't matter whether or not they are the same three movies U rated). User V gives these three movies ratings of 2, 3, and 5. The user profile for V has, in the component for Julia Roberts, the average of $2 - 4$, $3 - 4$, and $5 - 4$, that is, the value $-2/3$.

9.2.6 Recommending Items to Users Based on Content

With profile vectors for both users and items, we can estimate the degree to which a user would prefer an item by computing the cosine distance between the user's and item's vectors. As in Example 9.2, we may wish to scale various components whose values are not boolean. The random-hyperplane and locality-sensitive-hashing techniques can be used to place (just) item profiles in buckets. In that way, given a user to whom we want to recommend some items, we can apply the same two techniques – random hyperplanes and LSH – to determine in which buckets we must look for items that might have a small cosine distance from the user.

EXAMPLE 9.5 Consider first the data of Example 9.3. The user's profile will have components for stars proportional to the likelihood that the star will appear in a movie the user likes. Thus, the highest recommendations (lowest cosine distance) belong to the movies with lots of stars that appear in many of the movies the user likes. As long as stars are the only information we have about features of movies, that is probably the best we can do.[3]

Now, consider Example 9.4. There, we observed that the vector for a user will have positive numbers for stars that tend to appear in movies the user likes and negative numbers for stars that tend to appear in movies the user doesn't like. Consider a movie with many stars the user likes, and only a few or none that the user doesn't like. The cosine of the angle between the user's and movie's vectors will be a large positive fraction. That implies an angle close to 0, and therefore a small cosine distance between the vectors.

Next, consider a movie with about as many stars the user likes as doesn't like. In this situation, the cosine of the angle between the user and movie is around 0, and therefore the angle between the two vectors is around 90 degrees. Finally, consider a movie with mostly stars the user doesn't like. In that case, the cosine will be a large negative fraction, and the angle between the two vectors will be close to 180 degrees – the maximum possible cosine distance.

9.2.7 Classification Algorithms

A completely different approach to a recommendation system using item profiles and utility matrices is to treat the problem as one of machine learning. Regard

---

[3] Note that the fact all user-vector components will be small fractions does not affect the recommendation, since the cosine calculation involves dividing by the length of each vector. That is, user vectors will tend to be much shorter than movie vectors, but only the direction of vectors matters.

the given data as a training set, and for each user, build a classifier that predicts the rating of all items. There are a great number of different classifiers, and it is not our purpose to teach this subject here. However, you should be aware of the option of developing a classifier for recommendation, so we shall discuss one common classifier – decision trees – briefly.

A *decision tree* is a collection of nodes, arranged as a binary tree. The leaves render decisions; in our case, the decision would be "likes" or "doesn't like." Each interior node is a condition on the objects being classified; in our case the condition would be a predicate involving one or more features of an item.

To classify an item, we start at the root, and apply the predicate at the root to the item. If the predicate is true, go to the left child, and if it is false, go to the right child. Then repeat the same process at the node visited, until a leaf is reached. That leaf classifies the item as liked or not.

Construction of a decision tree requires selection of a predicate for each interior node. There are many ways of picking the best predicate, but they all try to arrange that one of the children gets all or most of the positive examples in the training set (i.e, the items that the given user likes, in our case) and the other child gets all or most of the negative examples (the items this user does not like).

Once we have selected a predicate for a node N, we divide the items into the two groups: those that satisfy the predicate and those that do not. For each group, we again find the predicate that best separates the positive and negative examples in that group. These predicates are assigned to the children of N. This process of dividing the examples and building children can proceed to any number of levels. We can stop, and create a leaf, if the group of items for a node is homogeneous; i.e., they are all positive or all negative examples.

However, we may wish to stop and create a leaf with the majority decision for a group, even if the group contains both positive and negative examples. The reason is that the statistical significance of a small group may not be high enough to rely on. For that reason a variant strategy is to create an *ensemble* of decision trees, each using different predicates, but allow the trees to be deeper than what the available data justifies. Such trees are called *overfitted*. To classify an item, apply all the trees in the ensemble, and let them vote on the outcome. We shall not consider this option here, but give a simple hypothetical example of a decision tree.

EXAMPLE 9.6 Suppose our items are news articles, and features are the high-TF.IDF words (*keywords*) in those documents. Further suppose there is a user U who likes articles about baseball, except articles about the New York Yankees. The row of the utility matrix for U has 1 if U has read the article and is blank if not. We shall take the 1's as "like" and the blanks as "doesn't like." Predicates will be boolean expressions of keywords.

Since U generally likes baseball, we might find that the best predicate for the root is "homerun" OR ("batter" AND "pitcher"). Items that satisfy the predicate will tend to be positive examples (articles with 1 in the row for U in the utility matrix), and items that fail to satisfy the predicate will tend to be negative examples (blanks in the utility-matrix row for U). Figure 9.3 shows the root as well as the rest of the decision tree.

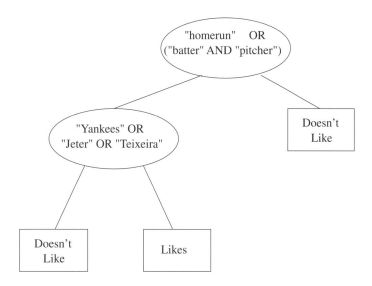

Figure 9.3 A decision tree

Suppose that the group of articles that do not satisfy the predicate includes sufficiently few positive examples that we can conclude all of these items are in the "don't-like" class. We may then put a leaf with decision "don't like" as the right child of the root. However, the articles that satisfy the predicate includes a number of articles that user U doesn't like; these are the articles that mention the Yankees. Thus, at the left child of the root, we build another predicate. We might find that the predicate "Yankees" OR "Jeter" OR "Teixeira" is the best possible indicator of an article about baseball and about the Yankees. Thus, we see in Fig. 9.3 the left child of the root, which applies this predicate. Both children of this node are leaves, since we may suppose that the items satisfying this predicate are predominantly negative and those not satisfying it are predominantly positive.

Unfortunately, classifiers of all types tend to take a long time to construct. For instance, if we wish to use decision trees, we need one tree per user. Constructing a tree not only requires that we look at all the item profiles, but we have to consider many different predicates, which could involve complex combinations of features. Thus, this approach tends to be used only for relatively small problem sizes.

9.2.8   Exercises for Section 9.2

EXERCISE 9.2.1   Three computers, A, B, and C, have the numerical features listed below:

Feature	A	B	C
Processor Speed	3.06	2.68	2.92
Disk Size	500	320	640
Main-Memory Size	6	4	6

We may imagine these values as defining a vector for each computer; for instance, A's vector is $[3.06, 500, 6]$. We can compute the cosine distance between any two of the vectors, but if we do not scale the components, then the disk size will dominate and make differences in the other components essentially invisible. Let us use 1 as the scale factor for processor speed, α for the disk size, and β for the main memory size.

(a) In terms of α and β, compute the cosines of the angles between the vectors for each pair of the three computers.
(b) What are the angles between the vectors if $\alpha = \beta = 1$?
(c) What are the angles between the vectors if $\alpha = 0.01$ and $\beta = 0.5$?
! (d) One fair way of selecting scale factors is to make each inversely proportional to the average value in its component. What would be the values of α and β, and what would be the angles between the vectors?

EXERCISE 9.2.2   An alternative way of scaling components of a vector is to begin by normalizing the vectors. That is, compute the average for each component and subtract it from that component's value in each of the vectors.

(a) Normalize the vectors for the three computers described in Exercise 9.2.1.
!! (b) This question does not require difficult calculation, but it requires some serious thought about what angles between vectors mean. When all components are nonnegative, as they are in the data of Exercise 9.2.1, no vectors can have an angle greater than 90 degrees. However, when we normalize vectors, we can (and must) get some negative components, so the angles can now be anything, that is, 0 to 180 degrees. Moreover, averages are now 0 in every component, so the suggestion in part (d) of Exercise 9.2.1 that we should scale in inverse proportion to the average makes no sense. Suggest a way of finding an appropriate scale for each component of normalized vectors. How would you interpret a large or small angle between normalized vectors? What would the angles be for the normalized vectors derived from the data in Exercise 9.2.1?

EXERCISE 9.2.3   A certain user has rated the three computers of Exercise 9.2.1 as follows: A: 4 stars, B: 2 stars, C: 5 stars.

(a) Normalize the ratings for this user.

(b) Compute a user profile for the user, with components for processor speed, disk size, and main memory size, based on the data of Exercise 9.2.1.

9.3   Collaborative Filtering

We shall now take up a significantly different approach to recommendation. Instead of using features of items to determine their similarity, we focus on the similarity of the user ratings for two items. That is, in place of the item-profile vector for an item, we use its column in the utility matrix. Further, instead of contriving a profile vector for users, we represent them by their rows in the utility matrix. Users are similar if their vectors are close according to some distance measure such as Jaccard or cosine distance. Recommendation for a user U is then made by looking at the users that are most similar to U in this sense, and recommending items that these users like. The process of identifying similar users and recommending what similar users like is called *collaborative filtering*.

9.3.1   Measuring Similarity

The first question we must deal with is how to measure similarity of users or items from their rows or columns in the utility matrix. We have reproduced Fig. 9.1 here as Fig. 9.4. This data is too small to draw any reliable conclusions, but its small size will make clear some of the pitfalls in picking a distance measure. Observe specifically the users A and C. They rated two movies in common, but they appear to have almost diametrically opposite opinions of these movies. We would expect that a good distance measure would make them rather far apart. Here are some alternative measures to consider.

	HP1	HP2	HP3	TW	SW1	SW2	SW3
A	4			5	1		
B	5	5	4				
C				2	4	5	
D		3					3

Figure 9.4 The utility matrix introduced in Fig. 9.1

Jaccard Distance
We could ignore values in the matrix and focus only on the sets of items rated. If the utility matrix only reflected purchases, this measure would be a good one to choose. However, when utilities are more detailed ratings, the Jaccard distance loses important information.

EXAMPLE 9.7 A and B have an intersection of size 1 and a union of size 5. Thus, their Jaccard similarity is 1/5, and their Jaccard distance is 4/5; i.e., they are very far apart. In comparison, A and C have a Jaccard similarity of $2/4$, so their Jaccard distance is the same, $1/2$. Thus, A appears closer to C than to B. Yet that conclusion seems intuitively wrong. A and C disagree on the two movies they both watched, while A and B seem both to have liked the one movie they watched in common.

Cosine Distance

We can treat blanks as a 0 value. This choice is questionable, since it has the effect of treating the lack of a rating as more similar to disliking the movie than liking it.

EXAMPLE 9.8   The cosine of the angle between A and B is

$$\frac{4 \times 5}{\sqrt{4^2 + 5^2 + 1^2}\sqrt{5^2 + 5^2 + 4^2}} = 0.386$$

The cosine of the angle between A and C is

$$\frac{5 \times 2 + 1 \times 4}{\sqrt{4^2 + 5^2 + 1^2}\sqrt{2^2 + 4^2 + 5^2}} = 0.322$$

This measure too tells us A is more similar to C than to B, a conclusion that defies our intuition.

Rounding the Data

We could try to eliminate the apparent similarity between movies a user rates highly and those with low scores by rounding the ratings. For instance, we could consider ratings of 3, 4, and 5 as a "1" and consider ratings 1 and 2 as unrated. The utility matrix would then look as in Fig. 9.5. Now, the Jaccard distance between A and B is $3/4$, while between A and C it is 1; i.e., C appears further from A than B does, which is intuitively correct. Applying cosine distance to Fig. 9.5 allows us to draw the same conclusion.

	HP1	HP2	HP3	TW	SW1	SW2	SW3
A	1			1			
B	1	1	1				
C					1	1	
D		1					1

Figure 9.5 Utilities of 3, 4, and 5 have been replaced by 1, while ratings of 1 and 2 are omitted

Normalizing Ratings

If we normalize ratings, by subtracting from each rating the average rating of that user, we turn low ratings into negative numbers and high ratings into positive numbers. If we then take the cosine distance, we find that users with opposite views of the movies they viewed in common will have vectors in almost opposite directions, and can be considered as far apart as possible. However, users with similar opinions about the movies rated in common will have a relatively small angle between them.

EXAMPLE 9.9   Figure 9.6 shows the matrix of Fig. 9.4 with all ratings normalized. An interesting effect is that D's ratings have effectively disappeared, because a 0 is the same as a blank when cosine distance is computed. Note that D gave only 3's and did not differentiate among movies, so it is quite possible that D's opinions are not worth taking seriously.

	HP1	HP2	HP3	TW	SW1	SW2	SW3
A	2/3			5/3	−7/3		
B	1/3	1/3	−2/3				
C				−5/3	1/3	4/3	
D		0					0

Figure 9.6 The utility matrix introduced in Fig. 9.1

Let us compute the cosine of the angle between A and B:

$$\frac{(2/3) \times (1/3)}{\sqrt{(2/3)^2 + (5/3)^2 + (-7/3)^2}\sqrt{(1/3)^2 + (1/3)^2 + (-2/3)^2}} = 0.092$$

The cosine of the angle between between A and C is

$$\frac{(5/3) \times (-5/3) + (-7/3) \times (1/3)}{\sqrt{(2/3)^2 + (5/3)^2 + (-7/3)^2}\sqrt{(-5/3)^2 + (1/3)^2 + (4/3)^2}} = -0.559$$

Notice that under this measure, A and C are much further apart than A and B, and neither pair is very close. Both these observations make intuitive sense, given that A and C disagree on the two movies they rated in common, while A and B give similar scores to the one movie they rated in common.

9.3.2   The Duality of Similarity

The utility matrix can be viewed as telling us about users or about items, or both. It is important to realize that any of the techniques we suggested in Section 9.3.1 for finding similar users can be used on columns of the utility matrix to find similar items. There are two ways in which the symmetry is broken in practice.

(1) We can use information about users to recommend items. That is, given a user, we can find some number of the most similar users, perhaps using the techniques of Chapter 3. We can base our recommendation on the decisions made by these similar users, e.g., recommend the items that the greatest number of them have purchased or rated highly. However, there is no symmetry. Even if we find pairs of similar items, we need to take an additional step in order to recommend items to users. This point is explored further at the end of this subsection.

(2) There is a difference in the typical behavior of users and items, as it pertains to similarity. Intuitively, items tend to be classifiable in simple terms. For example, music tends to belong to a single genre. It is impossible, e.g., for a piece of music to be both 60's rock and 1700's baroque. On the other hand, there are individuals who like both 60's rock and 1700's baroque, and who buy examples of both types of music. The consequence is that it is easier to discover items that are similar because they belong to the same genre, than it is to detect that two users are similar because they prefer one genre in common, while each also likes some genres that the other doesn't care for.

As we suggested in (1) above, one way of predicting the value of the utility-matrix entry for user U and item I is to find the n users (for some predetermined n) most similar to U and average their ratings for item I, counting only those among the n similar users who have rated I. It is generally better to normalize the matrix first. That is, for each of the n users subtract their average rating for items from their rating for i. Average the difference for those users who have rated I, and then add this average to the average rating that U gives for all items. This normalization adjusts the estimate in the case that U tends to give very high or very low ratings, or a large fraction of the similar users who rated I (of which there may be only a few) are users who tend to rate very high or very low.

Dually, we can use item similarity to estimate the entry for user U and item I. Find the m items most similar to I, for some m, and take the average rating, among the m items, of the ratings that U has given. As for user-user similarity, we consider only those items among the m that U has rated, and it is probably wise to normalize item ratings first.

Note that whichever approach to estimating entries in the utility matrix we use, it is not sufficient to find only one entry. In order to recommend items to a user U, we need to estimate every entry in the row of the utility matrix for U, or at least find all or most of the entries in that row that are blank but have a high estimated value. There is a tradeoff regarding whether we should work from similar users or similar items.

- If we find similar users, then we only have to do the process once for user U. From the set of similar users we can estimate all the blanks in the utility matrix for U. If we work from similar items, we have to compute similar items for almost all items, before we can estimate the row for U.

- On the other hand, item-item similarity often provides more reliable information, because of the phenomenon observed above, namely that it is easier to find items of the same genre than it is to find users that like only items of a single genre.

Whichever method we choose, we should precompute preferred items for each user, rather than waiting until we need to make a decision. Since the utility matrix evolves slowly, it is generally sufficient to compute it infrequently and assume that it remains fixed between recomputations.

9.3.3   Clustering Users and Items

It is hard to detect similarity among either items or users, because we have little information about user-item pairs in the sparse utility matrix. In the perspective of Section 9.3.2, even if two items belong to the same genre, there are likely to be very few users who bought or rated both. Likewise, even if two users both like a genre or genres, they may not have bought any items in common.

One way of dealing with this pitfall is to cluster items and/or users. Select any of the distance measures suggested in Section 9.3.1, or any other distance measure, and use it to perform a clustering of, say, items. Any of the methods suggested in Chapter 7 can be used. However, we shall see that there may be little reason to try to cluster into a small number of clusters immediately. Rather, a hierarchical approach, where we leave many clusters unmerged may suffice as a first step. For example, we might leave half as many clusters as there are items.

	HP	TW	SW
A	4	5	1
B	4.67		
C		2	4.5
D	3		3

Figure 9.7 Utility matrix for users and clusters of items

EXAMPLE 9.10   Figure 9.7 shows what happens to the utility matrix of Fig. 9.4 if we manage to cluster the three Harry-Potter movies into one cluster, denoted HP, and also cluster the three Star-Wars movies into one cluster SW.

Having clustered items to an extent, we can revise the utility matrix so the columns represent clusters of items, and the entry for user U and cluster C is the average rating that U gave to those members of cluster C that U did rate. Note that U may have rated none of the cluster members, in which case the entry for U and C is still blank.

We can use this revised utility matrix to cluster users, again using the distance measure we consider most appropriate. Use a clustering algorithm that again leaves many clusters, e.g., half as many clusters as there are users. Revise the utility matrix, so the rows correspond to clusters of users, just as the columns correspond to clusters of items. As for item-clusters, compute the entry for a user cluster by averaging the ratings of the users in the cluster.

Now, this process can be repeated several times if we like. That is, we can cluster the item clusters and again merge the columns of the utility matrix that belong to one cluster. We can then turn to the users again, and cluster the user clusters. The process can repeat until we have an intuitively reasonable number of clusters of each kind.

Once we have clustered the users and/or items to the desired extent and computed the cluster-cluster utility matrix, we can estimate entries in the original utility matrix as follows. Suppose we want to predict the entry for user U and item I:

(a) Find the clusters to which U and I belong, say clusters C and D, respectively.
(b) If the entry in the cluster-cluster utility matrix for C and D is something other than blank, use this value as the estimated value for the U–I entry in the original utility matrix.
(c) If the entry for C–D is blank, then use the method outlined in Section 9.3.2 to estimate that entry by considering clusters similar to C or D. Use the resulting estimate as the estimate for the U-I entry.

9.3.4   Exercises for Section 9.3

	a	b	c	d	e	f	g	h
A	4	5		5	1		3	2
B		3	4	3	1	2	1	
C	2		1	3		4	5	3

Figure 9.8 A utility matrix for exercises

EXERCISE 9.3.1   Figure 9.8 is a utility matrix, representing the ratings, on a 1–5 star scale, of eight items, a through h, by three users A, B, and C. Compute the following from the data of this matrix.

(a) Treating the utility matrix as boolean, compute the Jaccard distance between each pair of users.
(b) Repeat Part (a), but use the cosine distance.
(c) Treat ratings of 3, 4, and 5 as 1 and 1, 2, and blank as 0. Compute the Jaccard distance between each pair of users.
(d) Repeat Part (c), but use the cosine distance.
(e) Normalize the matrix by subtracting from each nonblank entry the average value for its user.
(f) Using the normalized matrix from Part (e), compute the cosine distance between each pair of users.

EXERCISE 9.3.2   In this exercise, we cluster items in the matrix of Fig. 9.8. Do the following steps.

(a) Cluster the eight items hierarchically into four clusters. The following method should be used to cluster. Replace all 3's, 4's, and 5's by 1 and replace 1's, 2's, and blanks by 0. use the Jaccard distance to measure the distance between the resulting column vectors. For clusters of more than one element, take the distance between clusters to be the minimum distance between pairs of elements, one from each cluster.

(b) Then, construct from the original matrix of Fig. 9.8 a new matrix whose rows correspond to users, as before, and whose columns correspond to clusters. Compute the entry for a user and cluster of items by averaging the nonblank entries for that user and all the items in the cluster.

(c) Compute the cosine distance between each pair of users, according to your matrix from Part (b).

9.4   Dimensionality Reduction

An entirely different approach to estimating the blank entries in the utility matrix is to conjecture that the utility matrix is actually the product of two long, thin matrices. This view makes sense if there are a relatively small set of features of items and users that determine the reaction of most users to most items. In this section, we sketch one approach to discovering two such matrices; the approach is called "UV-decomposition," and it is an instance of a more general theory called SVD (*singular-value decomposition*).

9.4.1   UV-Decomposition

Consider movies as a case in point. Most users respond to a small number of features; they like certain genres, they may have certain famous actors or actresses that they like, and perhaps there are a few directors with a significant following. If we start with the utility matrix M, with n rows and m columns (i.e., there are n users and m items), then we might be able to find a matrix U with n rows and d columns and a matrix V with d rows and m columns, such that UV closely approximates M in those entries where M is nonblank. If so, then we have established that there are d dimensions that allow us to characterize both users and items closely. We can then use the entry in the product UV to estimate the corresponding blank entry in utility matrix M. This process is called *UV-decomposition* of M.

$$\begin{bmatrix} 5 & 2 & 4 & 4 & 3 \\ 3 & 1 & 2 & 4 & 1 \\ 2 & & 3 & 1 & 4 \\ 2 & 5 & 4 & 3 & 5 \\ 4 & 4 & 5 & 4 & \end{bmatrix} = \begin{bmatrix} u_{11} & u_{12} \\ u_{21} & u_{22} \\ u_{31} & u_{32} \\ u_{41} & u_{42} \\ u_{51} & u_{52} \end{bmatrix} \times \begin{bmatrix} v_{11} & v_{12} & v_{13} & v_{14} & v_{15} \\ v_{21} & v_{22} & v_{23} & v_{24} & v_{25} \end{bmatrix}$$

Figure 9.9 UV-decomposition of matrix M

EXAMPLE 9.11   We shall use as a running example a 5-by-5 matrix M with all but two of its entries known. We wish to decompose M into a 5-by-2 and 2-by-5 matrix, U and V, respectively. The matrices M, U, and V are shown in Fig. 9.9 with the known entries of M indicated and the matrices U and V shown with their entries as variables to be determined. This example is essentially the smallest nontrivial case where there are more known entries than there are entries in U and V combined, and we therefore can expect that the best decomposition will not yield a product that agrees exactly in the nonblank entries of M.

9.4.2 Root-Mean-Square Error

While we can pick among several measures of how close the product UV is to M, the typical choice is the root-mean-square error (RMSE), where we

(1) Sum, over all nonblank entries in M the square of the difference between that entry and the corresponding entry in the product UV.
(2) Take the mean (average) of these squares by dividing by the number of terms in the sum (i.e., the number of nonblank entries in M).
(3) Take the square root of the mean.

Minimizing the sum of the squares is the same as minimizing the square root of the average square, so we generally omit the last two steps in our running example.

$$\begin{bmatrix} 1 & 1 \\ 1 & 1 \\ 1 & 1 \\ 1 & 1 \\ 1 & 1 \end{bmatrix} \times \begin{bmatrix} 1 & 1 & 1 & 1 & 1 \\ 1 & 1 & 1 & 1 & 1 \end{bmatrix} = \begin{bmatrix} 2 & 2 & 2 & 2 & 2 \\ 2 & 2 & 2 & 2 & 2 \\ 2 & 2 & 2 & 2 & 2 \\ 2 & 2 & 2 & 2 & 2 \\ 2 & 2 & 2 & 2 & 2 \end{bmatrix}$$

Figure 9.10 Matrices U and V with all entries 1

EXAMPLE 9.12 Suppose we guess that U and V should each have entries that are all 1's, as shown in Fig. 9.10. This is a poor guess, since the product, consisting of all 2's, has entries that are much below the average of the entries in M. Nonetheless, we can compute the RMSE for this U and V; in fact the regularity in the entries makes the calculation especially easy to follow. Consider the first rows of M and UV. We subtract 2 (each entry in UV) from the entries in the first row of M, to get $3, 0, 2, 2, 1$. We square and sum these to get 18. In the second row, we do the same to get $1, -1, 0, 2, -1$, square and sum to get 7. In the third row, the second column is blank, so that entry is ignored when computing the RMSE. The differences are $0, 1, -1, 2$ and the sum of squares is 6. For the fourth row, the differences are $0, 3, 2, 1, 3$ and the sum of squares is 23. The fifth row has a blank entry in the last column, so the differences are $2, 2, 3, 2$ and the sum of squares is 21. When we sum the sums from each of the five rows, we get $18 + 7 + 6 + 23 + 21 = 75$. Generally, we shall stop at this point, but if we want to compute the true RMSE, we divide by 23 (the number of nonblank entries in M) and take the square root. In this case $\sqrt{75/23} = 1.806$ is the RMSE.

9.4.3 Incremental Computation of a UV-Decomposition

Finding the UV-decomposition with the least RMSE involves starting with some arbitrarily chosen U and V, and repeatedly adjusting U and V to make the RMSE smaller. We shall consider only adjustments to a single element of U or V, although in principle, one could make more complex adjustments. Whatever adjustments we allow, in a typical example there will be many *local minima* – matrices U and V such that no allowable adjustment reduces the RMSE. Unfortunately, only one of these local minima will be the *global minimum* – the matrices U and V that produce the least possible RMSE. To increase our chances of finding the global minimum, we need to pick many different starting points, that is, different choices of the initial matrices U and V. However, there is never a guarantee that our best local minimum will be the global minimum.

We shall start with the U and V of Fig. 9.10, where all entries are 1, and do a few adjustments to some of the entries, finding the values of those entries that give the largest possible improvement to the RMSE. From these examples, the general calculation should become obvious, but we shall follow the examples by the formula for minimizing the RMSE by changing a single entry. In what follows, we shall refer to entries of U and V by their variable names u_{11}, and so on, as given in Fig. 9.9.

EXAMPLE 9.13 Suppose we start with U and V as in Fig. 9.10, and we decide to alter u_{11} to reduce the RMSE as much as possible. Let the value of u_{11} be x. Then the new U and V can be expressed as in Fig. 9.11.

$$
\begin{bmatrix} x & 1 \\ 1 & 1 \\ 1 & 1 \\ 1 & 1 \\ 1 & 1 \end{bmatrix} \times \begin{bmatrix} 1 & 1 & 1 & 1 & 1 \\ 1 & 1 & 1 & 1 & 1 \end{bmatrix} = \begin{bmatrix} x+1 & x+1 & x+1 & x+1 & x+1 \\ 2 & 2 & 2 & 2 & 2 \\ 2 & 2 & 2 & 2 & 2 \\ 2 & 2 & 2 & 2 & 2 \\ 2 & 2 & 2 & 2 & 2 \end{bmatrix}
$$

Figure 9.11 Making u_{11} a variable

Notice that the only entries of the product that have changed are those in the first row. Thus, when we compare UV with M, the only change to the RMSE comes from the first row. The contribution to the sum of squares from the first row is

$$\left(5 - (x+1)\right)^2 + \left(2 - (x+1)\right)^2 + \left(4 - (x+1)\right)^2 + \left(4 - (x+1)\right)^2 + \left(3 - (x+1)\right)^2$$

This sum simplifies to

$$(4-x)^2 + (1-x)^2 + (3-x)^2 + (3-x)^2 + (2-x)^2$$

We want the value of x that minimizes the sum, so we take the derivative and set that equal to 0, as:

$$-2 \times \big((4-x) + (1-x) + (3-x) + (3-x) + (2-x)\big) = 0$$

or $-2 \times (13 - 5x) = 0$, from which it follows that $x = 2.6$.

$$
\begin{bmatrix}
2.6 & 1 \\
1 & 1 \\
1 & 1 \\
1 & 1 \\
1 & 1
\end{bmatrix}
\times
\begin{bmatrix}
1 & 1 & 1 & 1 & 1 \\
1 & 1 & 1 & 1 & 1
\end{bmatrix}
=
\begin{bmatrix}
3.6 & 3.6 & 3.6 & 3.6 & 3.6 \\
2 & 2 & 2 & 2 & 2 \\
2 & 2 & 2 & 2 & 2 \\
2 & 2 & 2 & 2 & 2 \\
2 & 2 & 2 & 2 & 2
\end{bmatrix}
$$

Figure 9.12 The best value for u_{11} is found to be 2.6

Figure 9.12 shows U and V after u_{11} has been set to 2.6. Note that the sum of the squares of the errors in the first row has been reduced from 18 to 5.2, so the total RMSE (ignoring average and square root) has been reduced from 75 to 62.2.

$$
\begin{bmatrix}
2.6 & 1 \\
1 & 1 \\
1 & 1 \\
1 & 1 \\
1 & 1
\end{bmatrix}
\times
\begin{bmatrix}
y & 1 & 1 & 1 & 1 \\
1 & 1 & 1 & 1 & 1
\end{bmatrix}
=
\begin{bmatrix}
2.6y+1 & 3.6 & 3.6 & 3.6 & 3.6 \\
y+1 & 2 & 2 & 2 & 2 \\
y+1 & 2 & 2 & 2 & 2 \\
y+1 & 2 & 2 & 2 & 2 \\
y+1 & 2 & 2 & 2 & 2
\end{bmatrix}
$$

Figure 9.13 v_{11} becomes a variable y

Suppose our next entry to vary is v_{11}. Let the value of this entry be y, as suggested in Fig. 9.13. Only the first column of the product is affected by y, so we need only to compute the sum of the squares of the differences between the entries in the first columns of M and UV. This sum is

$$\big(5 - (2.6y+1)\big)^2 + \big(3 - (y+1)\big)^2 + \big(2 - (y+1)\big)^2 + \big(2 - (y+1)\big)^2 + \big(4 - (y+1)\big)^2$$

This expression simplifies to

$$(4 - 2.6y)^2 + (2 - y)^2 + (1 - y)^2 + (1 - y)^2 + (3 - y)^2$$

As before, we find the minimum value of this expression by differentiating and equating to 0, as:

$$-2 \times \big(2.6(4 - 2.6y) + (2 - y) + (1 - y) + (1 - y) + (3 - y)\big) = 0$$

The solution for y is $y = 17.4/10.76 = 1.617$. The improved estimates of U and V are shown in Fig. 9.14.

We shall do one more change, to illustrate what happens when entries of M are blank. We shall vary u_{31}, calling it z temporarily. The new U and V are shown in Fig. 9.15. The value of z affects only the entries in the third row.

$$\begin{bmatrix} 2.6 & 1 \\ 1 & 1 \\ 1 & 1 \\ 1 & 1 \\ 1 & 1 \end{bmatrix} \times \begin{bmatrix} 1.617 & 1 & 1 & 1 & 1 \\ 1 & & 1 & 1 & 1 & 1 \end{bmatrix} = \begin{bmatrix} 5.204 & 3.6 & 3.6 & 3.6 & 3.6 \\ 2.617 & 2 & 2 & 2 & 2 \\ 2.617 & 2 & 2 & 2 & 2 \\ 2.617 & 2 & 2 & 2 & 2 \\ 2.617 & 2 & 2 & 2 & 2 \end{bmatrix}$$

Figure 9.14 Replace y by 1.617

$$\begin{bmatrix} 2.6 & 1 \\ 1 & 1 \\ z & 1 \\ 1 & 1 \\ 1 & 1 \end{bmatrix} \times \begin{bmatrix} 1.617 & 1 & 1 & 1 & 1 \\ 1 & & 1 & 1 & 1 & 1 \end{bmatrix} = \begin{bmatrix} 5.204 & 3.6 & 3.6 & 3.6 & 3.6 \\ 2.617 & 2 & 2 & 2 & 2 \\ 1.617z+1 & z+1 & z+1 & z+1 & z+1 \\ 2.617 & 2 & 2 & 2 & 2 \\ 2.617 & 2 & 2 & 2 & 2 \end{bmatrix}$$

Figure 9.15 u_{31} becomes a variable z

We can express the sum of the squares of the errors as

$$\big(2 - (1.617z+1)\big)^2 + \big(3 - (z+1)\big)^2 + \big(1 - (z+1)\big)^2 + \big(4 - (z+1)\big)^2$$

Note that there is no contribution from the element in the second column of the third row, since this element is blank in M. The expression simplifies to

$$(1 - 1.617z)^2 + (2 - z)^2 + (-z)^2 + (3 - z)^2$$

The usual process of setting the derivative to 0 gives us

$$-2 \times \big(1.617(1 - 1.617z) + (2 - z) + (-z) + (3 - z)\big) = 0$$

whose solution is $z = 6.617/5.615 = 1.178$. The next estimate of the decomposition UV is shown in Fig. 9.16.

$$\begin{bmatrix} 2.6 & 1 \\ 1 & 1 \\ 1.178 & 1 \\ 1 & 1 \\ 1 & 1 \end{bmatrix} \times \begin{bmatrix} 1.617 & 1 & 1 & 1 & 1 \\ 1 & & 1 & 1 & 1 & 1 \end{bmatrix} = \begin{bmatrix} 5.204 & 3.6 & 3.6 & 3.6 & 3.6 \\ 2.617 & 2 & 2 & 2 & 2 \\ 2.905 & 2.178 & 2.178 & 2.178 & 2.178 \\ 2.617 & 2 & 2 & 2 & 2 \\ 2.617 & 2 & 2 & 2 & 2 \end{bmatrix}$$

Figure 9.16 Replace z by 1.178

9.4.4   Optimizing an Arbitrary Element

Having seen some examples of picking the optimum value for a single element in the matrix U or V, let us now develop the general formula. As before, assume that M is an n-by-m utility matrix with some entries blank, while U and V are matrices of dimensions n-by-d and d-by-m, for some d. We shall use m_{ij}, u_{ij}, and v_{ij} for the entries in row i and column j of M, U, and V, respectively. Also, let $P = UV$, and use p_{ij} for the element in row i and column j of the product matrix P.

Suppose we want to vary u_{rs} and find the value of this element that minimizes the RMSE between M and UV. Note that u_{rs} affects only the elements in row r of the product $P = UV$. Thus, we need only concern ourselves with the elements

$$p_{rj} = \sum_{k=1}^{d} u_{rk}v_{kj} = \sum_{k \neq s} u_{rk}v_{kj} + xv_{sj}$$

for all values of j such that m_{rj} is nonblank. In the expression above, we have replaced u_{rs}, the element we wish to vary, by a variable x, and we use the convention

• $\sum_{k \neq s}$ is shorthand for the sum for $k = 1, 2, \ldots, d$, except for $k = s$.

If m_{rj} is a nonblank entry of the matrix M, then the contribution of this element to the sum of the squares of the errors is

$$(m_{rj} - p_{rj})^2 = \left(m_{rj} - \sum_{k \neq s} u_{rk}v_{kj} - xv_{sj} \right)^2$$

We shall use another convention:

• $\sum_{j}$ is shorthand for the sum over all j such that m_{rj} is nonblank.

Then we can write the sum of the squares of the errors that are affected by the value of $x = u_{rs}$ as

$$\sum_{j} \left(m_{rj} - \sum_{k \neq s} u_{rk}v_{kj} - xv_{sj} \right)^2$$

Take the derivative of the above with respect to x, and set it equal to 0, in order to find the value of x that minimizes the RMSE. That is,

$$\sum_{j} -2v_{sj} \left(m_{rj} - \sum_{k \neq s} u_{rk}v_{kj} - xv_{sj} \right) = 0$$

As in the previous examples, the common factor -2 can be dropped. We solve the above equation for x, and get

$$x = \frac{\sum_{j} v_{sj} \left(m_{rj} - \sum_{k \neq s} u_{rk}v_{kj} \right)}{\sum_{j} v_{sj}^2}$$

There is an analogous formula for the optimum value of an element of V. If we want to vary $v_{rs} = y$, then the value of y that minimizes the RMSE is

$$y = \frac{\sum_{i} u_{ir} \left(m_{is} - \sum_{k \neq r} u_{ik}v_{ks} \right)}{\sum_{i} u_{ir}^2}$$

Here, $\sum_{i}$ is shorthand for the sum over all i such that m_{is} is nonblank, and $\sum_{k \neq r}$ is the sum over all values of k between 1 and d, except for $k = r$.

9.4.5 Building a Complete UV-Decomposition Algorithm

Now, we have the tools to search for the global optimum decomposition of a utility matrix M. There are four areas where we shall discuss the options.

(1) Preprocessing of the matrix M.
(2) Initializing U and V.
(3) Ordering the optimization of the elements of U and V.
(4) Ending the attempt at optimization.

Preprocessing

Because the differences in the quality of items and the rating scales of users are such important factors in determining the missing elements of the matrix M, it is often useful to remove these influences before doing anything else. The idea was introduced in Section 9.3.1. We can subtract from each nonblank element m_{ij} the average rating of user i. Then, the resulting matrix can be modified by subtracting the average rating (in the modified matrix) of item j. It is also possible to first subtract the average rating of item j and then subtract the average rating of user i in the modified matrix. The results one obtains from doing things in these two different orders need not be the same, but will tend to be close. A third option is to normalize by subtracting from m_{ij} the average of the average rating of user i and item j, that is, subtracting one half the sum of the user average and the item average.

If we choose to normalize M, then when we make predictions, we need to undo the normalization. That is, if whatever prediction method we use results in estimate e for an element m_{ij} of the normalized matrix, then the value we predict for m_{ij} in the true utility matrix is e plus whatever amount was subtracted from row i and from column j during the normalization process.

Initialization

As we mentioned, it is essential that there be some randomness in the way we seek an optimum solution, because the existence of many local minima justifies our running many different optimizations in the hope of reaching the global minimum on at least one run. We can vary the initial values of U and V, or we can vary the way we seek the optimum (to be discussed next), or both.

A simple starting point for U and V is to give each element the same value, and a good choice for this value is that which gives the elements of the product UV the average of the nonblank elements of M. Note that if we have normalized M, then this value will necessarily be 0. If we have chosen d as the lengths of the short sides of U and V, and a is the average nonblank element of M, then the elements of U and V should be $\sqrt{a/d}$.

If we want many starting points for U and V, then we can perturb the value $\sqrt{a/d}$ randomly and independently for each of the elements. There are many options for how we do the perturbation. We have a choice regarding the distribution of the difference. For example we could add to each element a normally distributed value with mean 0 and some chosen standard deviation. Or we could add a value uniformly chosen from the range $-c$ to $+c$ for some c.

Performing the Optimization

In order to reach a local minimum from a given starting value of U and V, we need to pick an order in which we visit the elements of U and V. The simplest thing to do is pick an order, e.g., row-by-row, for the elements of U and V, and visit them in round-robin fashion. Note that just because we optimized an element once does not mean we cannot find a better value for that element after other elements have been adjusted. Thus, we need to visit elements repeatedly, until we have reason to believe that no further improvements are possible.

Alternatively, we can follow many different optimization paths from a single starting value by randomly picking the element to optimize. To make sure that every element is considered in each round, we could instead choose a permutation of the elements and follow that order for every round.

Converging to a Minimum

Ideally, at some point the RMSE becomes 0, and we know we cannot do better. In practice, since there are normally many more nonblank elements in M than there are elements in U and V together, we have no right to expect that we can reduce the RMSE to 0. Thus, we have to detect when there is little benefit to be had in revisiting elements of U and/or V. We can track the amount of improvement in the RMSE obtained in one round of the optimization, and stop when that improvement falls below a threshold. A small variation is to observe the improvements resulting from the optimization of individual elements, and stop when the maximum improvement during a round is below a threshold.

Avoiding Overfitting

One problem that often arises when performing a UV-decomposition is that we arrive at one of the many local minima that conform well to the given data, but picks up values in the data that don't reflect well the underlying process that gives rise to the data. That is, although the RMSE may be small on the given data, it doesn't do well predicting future data. There are several things that can be done to cope with this problem, which is called *overfitting* by statisticians.

(1) Avoid favoring the first components to be optimized by only moving the value of a component a fraction of the way, say half way, from its current value toward its optimized value.
(2) Stop revisiting elements of U and V well before the process has converged.
(3) Take several different UV decompositions, and when predicting a new entry in the matrix M, take the average of the results of using each decomposition.

9.4.6   Exercises for Section 9.4

EXERCISE 9.4.1   Starting with the decomposition of Fig. 9.10, we may choose any of the 20 entries in U or V to optimize first. Perform this first optimization step assuming we choose: (a) u_{32} (b) v_{41}.

EXERCISE 9.4.2   If we wish to start out, as in Fig. 9.10, with all U and V entries set to the same value, what value minimizes the RMSE for the matrix M of our running example?

EXERCISE 9.4.3   Starting with the U and V matrices in Fig. 9.16, do the following in order:

(a) Reconsider the value of u_{11}. Find its new best value, given the changes that have been made so far.
(b) Then choose the best value for u_{52}.
(c) Then choose the best value for v_{22}.

EXERCISE 9.4.4   Derive the formula for y (the optimum value of element v_{rs} given at the end of Section 9.4.4.

EXERCISE 9.4.5   Normalize the matrix M of our running example by:

(a) First subtracting from each element the average of its row, and then subtracting from each element the average of its (modified) column.
(b) First subtracting from each element the average of its column, and then subtracting from each element the average of its (modified) row.

Are there any differences in the results of (a) and (b)?

9.5   The NetFlix Challenge

A significant boost to research into recommendation systems was given when NetFlix offered a prize of $1,000,000 to the first person or team to beat their own recommendation algorithm, called CineMatch, by 10%. After over three years of work, the prize was awarded in September, 2009.

The NetFlix challenge consisted of a published dataset, giving the ratings by approximately half a million users on (typically small subsets of) approximately 17,000 movies. This data was selected from a larger dataset, and proposed algorithms were tested on their ability to predict the ratings in a secret remainder of the larger dataset. The information for each (user, movie) pair in the published dataset included a rating (1–5 stars) and the date on which the rating was made.

The RMSE was used to measure the performance of algorithms. CineMatch has an RMSE of approximately 0.95; i.e., the typical rating would be off by almost one full star. To win the prize, it was necessary that your algorithm have an RMSE that was at most 90% of the RMSE of CineMatch.

The bibliographic notes for this chapter include references to descriptions of the winning algorithms. Here, we mention some interesting and perhaps unintuitive facts about the challenge.

- CineMatch was not a very good algorithm. In fact, it was discovered early that the obvious algorithm of predicting, for the rating by user u on movie m, the average of:

(1) The average rating given by u on all rated movies and

(2) The average of the ratings for movie m by all users who rated that movie.

was only 3% worse than CineMatch.

- The UV-decomposition algorithm described in Section 9.4 was found by three students (Michael Harris, Jeffrey Wang, and David Kamm) to give a 7% improvement over CineMatch, when coupled with normalization and a few other tricks.

- The winning entry was actually a combination of several different algorithms that had been developed independently. A second team, which submitted an entry that would have won, had it been submitted a few minutes earlier, also was a blend of independent algorithms. This strategy – combining different algorithms – has been used before in a number of hard problems and is something worth remembering.

- Several attempts have been made to use the data contained in IMDB, the Internet movie database, to match the names of movies from the NetFlix challenge with their names in IMDB, and thus extract useful information not contained in the NetFlix data itself. IMDB has information about actors and directors, and classifies movies into one or more of 28 genres. It was found that genre and other information was not useful. One possible reason is the machine-learning algorithms were able to discover the relevant information anyway, and a second is that the entity resolution problem of matching movie names as given in NetFlix and IMDB data is not that easy to solve exactly.

- Time of rating turned out to be useful. It appears there are movies that are more likely to be appreciated by people who rate it immediately after viewing than by those who wait a while and then rate it. "Patch Adams" was given as an example of such a movie. Conversely, there are other movies that were not liked by those who rated it immediately, but were better appreciated after a while; "Memento" was cited as an example. While one cannot tease out of the data information about how long was the delay between viewing and rating, it is generally safe to assume that most people see a movie shortly after it comes out. Thus, one can examine the ratings of any movie to see if its ratings have an upward or downward slope with time.

9.6   Summary of Chapter 9

- ✦ *Utility Matrices*: Recommendation systems deal with users and items. A utility matrix offers known information about the degree to which a user likes an item. Normally, most entries are unknown, and the essential problem of recommending items to users is predicting the values of the unknown entries based on the values of the known entries.

- ✦ *Two Classes of Recommendation Systems*: These systems attempt to predict a user's response to an item by discovering similar items and the response of the user to those. One class of recommendation system is content-based; it measures similarity by looking for common features of the items. A second class of recommendation system uses collaborative filtering; these measure similarity of users by their item preferences and/or measure similarity of items by the users who like them.

✦ *Item Profiles*: These consist of features of items. Different kinds of items have different features on which content-based similarity can be based. Features of documents are typically important or unusual words. Products have attributes such as screen size for a television. Media such as movies have a genre and details such as actor or performer. Tags can also be used as features if they can be acquired from interested users.

✦ *User Profiles*: A content-based collaborative filtering system can construct profiles for users by measuring the frequency with which features appear in the items the user likes. We can then estimate the degree to which a user will like an item by the closeness of the item's profile to the user's profile.

✦ *Classification of Items*: An alternative to constructing a user profile is to build a classifier for each user, e.g., a decision tree. The row of the utility matrix for that user becomes the training data, and the classifier must predict the response of the user to all items, whether or not the row had an entry for that item.

✦ *Similarity of Rows and Columns of the Utility Matrix*: Collaborative filtering algorithms must measure the similarity of rows and/or columns of the utility matrix. Jaccard distance is appropriate when the matrix consists only of 1's and blanks (for "not rated"). Cosine distance works for more general values in the utility matrix. It is often useful to normalize the utility matrix by subtracting the average value (either by row, by column, or both) before measuring the cosine distance.

✦ *Clustering Users and Items*: Since the utility matrix tends to be mostly blanks, distance measures such as Jaccard or cosine often have too little data with which to compare two rows or two columns. A preliminary step or steps, in which similarity is used to cluster users and/or items into small groups with strong similarity, can help provide more common components with which to compare rows or columns.

✦ *UV-Decomposition*: One way of predicting the blank values in a utility matrix is to find two long, thin matrices U and V, whose product is an approximation to the given utility matrix. Since the matrix product UV gives values for all user-item pairs, that value can be used to predict the value of a blank in the utility matrix. The intuitive reason this method makes sense is that often there are a relatively small number of issues (that number is the "thin" dimension of U and V) that determine whether or not a user likes an item.

✦ *Root-Mean-Square Error*: A good measure of how close the product UV is to the given utility matrix is the RMSE (root-mean-square error). The RMSE is computed by averaging the square of the differences between UV and the utility matrix, in those elements where the utility matrix is nonblank. The square root of this average is the RMSE.

✦ *Computing U and V*: One way of finding a good choice for U and V in a UV-decomposition is to start with arbitrary matrices U and V. Repeatedly adjust one of the elements of U or V to minimize the RMSE between the product UV and the given utility matrix. The process converges to a local optimum, although to have a good chance of obtaining a global optimum we must either repeat the process from many starting matrices, or search from the starting point in many different ways.

✦ *The NetFlix Challenge*: An important driver of research into recommendation systems was the NetFlix challenge. A prize of $1,000,000 was offered for a contestant who could produce an algorithm that was 10% better than NetFlix's own algorithm at predicting movie ratings by users. The prize was awarded in Sept., 2009.

9.7   References for Chapter 9

[(1)] is a survey of recommendation systems as of 2005. The argument regarding the importance of the long tail in on-line systems is from [(2)], which was expanded into a book [(3)].

[(8)] discusses the use of computer games to extract tags for items.

See [(5)] for a discussion of item-item similarity and how Amazon designed its collaborative-filtering algorithm for product recommendations.

There are three papers describing the three algorithms that, in combination, won the NetFlix challenge. They are [(4)], [(6)], and [(7)].

(1) G. Adomavicius and A. Tuzhilin, "Towards the next generation of recommender systems: a survey of the state-of-the-art and possible extensions," *IEEE Trans. on Data and Knowledge Engineering* **17**:6, pp. 734–749, 2005.

(2) C. Anderson,

    http://www.wired.com/wired/archive/12.10/tail.html

2004.

(3) C. Anderson, *The Long Tail: Why the Future of Business is Selling Less of More*, Hyperion Books, New York, 2006.

(4) Y. Koren, "The BellKor solution to the Netflix grand prize,"

    www.netflixprize.com/assets/GrandPrize2009_BPC_BellKor.pdf

2009.

(5) G. Linden, B. Smith, and J. York, "Amazon.com recommendations: item-to-item collaborative filtering," *Internet Computing* **7**:1, pp. 76–80, 2003.

(6) M. Piotte and M. Chabbert, "The Pragmatic Theory solution to the Netflix grand prize,"

    www.netflixprize.com/assets/
    GrandPrize2009_BPC_PragmaticTheory.pdf

2009.

(7) A. Toscher, M. Jahrer, and R. Bell, "The BigChaos solution to the Netflix grand prize,"

www.netflixprize.com/assets/GrandPrize2009_BPC_BigChaos.pdf

2009.

(8) L. von Ahn, "Games with a purpose," *IEEE Computer Magazine*, pp. 96–98, June 2006.

Index